GAYS AND LESBIANS IN THE DEMOCRATIC PROCESS

Power, Conflict, and Democracy: American Politics Into the
Twenty-first Century

ROBERT Y. SHAPIRO, EDITOR

This series focuses on how the will of the people and the public interest are promoted, encouraged, or thwarted. It aims to question not only the direction American politics will take as it enters the twenty-first century but also the direction American politics has already taken.

The series addresses the role of interest groups and social and political movements; openness in American politics; important developments in institutions such as the executive, legislative, and judicial branches at all levels of government as well as the bureaucracies thus created; the changing behavior of politicians and political parties; the role of public opinion; and the functioning of mass media. Because problems drive politics, the series also examines important policy issues in both domestic and foreign affairs.

The series welcomes all theoretical perspectives, methodologies, and types of evidence that answer important questions about trends in American politics.

Gays and Lesbians in the Democratic Process

PUBLIC POLICY, PUBLIC OPINION, AND POLITICAL REPRESENTATION

EDITED BY

Ellen D. B. Riggle and Barry L. Tadlock

COLUMBIA UNIVERSITY PRESS

NEW YORK

Columbia University Press
Publishers Since 1893
New York Chichester, West Sussex
Copyright © 1999 Columbia University Press

Library of Congress Cataloging-in-Publication Data

Gays and lesbians in the democratic process: public policy, public
opinion, and political representation / edited by Ellen D. B. Riggle
and Barry L, Tadlock.
    p.   cm. — (Power, conflict, and democracy)
Includes index.
ISBN 0-231-11584-9. — ISBN 0-231-11585-7 (pbk.)
1. Gay rights — United States.   2. Gay liberation movement — United
States.   3. Gays — United States — Political activity.   I. Riggle,
Ellen D. B.   II. Tadlock, Barry L.   III. Series.
HQ76.8.U5G39   1999
305.9'0664 — dc21   99-26256   CIP

Casebound editions of Columbia University Press books are printed on permanent and
durable acid-free paper.
Printed in the United States of America
c 10 9 8 7 6 5 4 3 2 1
p 10 9 8 7 6 5 4 3 2 1

To O. C. N., *Jr.*

CONTENTS

ACKNOWLEDGMENTS

This book contains twelve chapters of original research into the dynamics of American politics and its democratic processes. Many of these chapters began as papers presented at conferences; some were completed specifically for this book. All represent a growing body of literature that integrates past research on public policy, public opinion, and political representation with research on gays and lesbians in the current political environment. After reading original conference papers, attending lively presentations, and talking with several scholars we thought the time was right to bring together this unique set of work.

In doing so, this book demonstrates how the current literature has built on past theoretical advances in public policy, public opinion, and political representation. It provides us with interesting and timely findings that challenge past theories; these challenges result in stronger, more complete theories. This process of challenging theories and refining them is the essence of political science.

We would like to extend our thanks to many people for their help throughout this process. First, we would like to thank our editor at Columbia University Press, John Michel, who helped to guide this book through the process and whose encouragement was vital; Alexander Thorp; Susan Pensak; and Robert Shapiro, series editor. We would also like to express our gratitude to Mac Avery, Mike Gunter, Phyllis Hoovler, and Neal Woods, all of whom helped us enormously in different tasks associated with this long process. Janet Abel acted as the ever helpful, absolutely essential research assistant. The chapters of this book and the project as a whole benefited from the comments of Ron Hunt, Jennifer Segal, several anonymous re-viewers, and colleagues from the Lesbian, Gay, and Bisexual Caucus for Political Science.

As editors, we would like to thank the authors of the chapters that make up this book. Each contributed more than just a chapter. We have great respect for their work and their contributions to the discipline and could not have asked for a more responsive group of colleagues to engage with in this project.

Finally, we extend our professional and personal gratitude to Mitzi Johnson. She has many roles in our respective lives and her support has been essential and immeasurable.

GAYS AND LESBIANS IN THE DEMOCRATIC PROCESS

CHAPTER ONE

Gays and Lesbians in the Democratic Process: Past, Present, and Future

Ellen D. B. Riggle and Barry L. Tadlock

During the 1998 general election six openly gay and lesbian candidates ran for election to the U.S. House of Representatives; three won: incumbents Barney Frank (D-MA), Jim Kolbe (R-AZ), and newcomer Tammy Baldwin (D-WI). Scores of other openly gay men and women ran and won at the state and local levels, including Vermont state auditor Ed Flanagan (D), Karen Clark (D), re-elected to the Minnesota State House, and San Diego superior court judge Bonnie Dumanis (R). There are now over two hundred openly lesbian or gay public officials in the United States. Also in the 1998 general election, voters in Hawaii and Alaska made it possible for their legislatures to ban the recognition of same-gender marriages, joining numerous other states that have already recently passed such bans or are debating such legislation. At the same time, court cases are pending in Hawaii and Vermont in an effort to secure the right to same-gender marriage. The military's "Don't ask, don't tell" policy is the subject of federal litigation. State sodomy laws are the subject of ongoing state litigation and legislative battles. Local governments are debating and voting on ordinances to prohibit discrimination on the basis of sexual orientation. And pollsters are finding that more and more Americans support the right of equal opportunity for lesbians and gays. In short, the debate over issues involving the political rights of gay and lesbian citizens in the United States continues daily and in earnest.

Gays and lesbians (and, in recent times, many would add bisexuals and transgendered persons) have transitioned from outsiders to insiders in the political process, from the liberationists of the sixties and seventies to the lobbyists of the nineties.[1] As such, gays and lesbians are seeking to live with no more or less government interference, regulation, support, and protection, to be judged on the basis of merit and ability, to enjoy all the rights conferred and to assume all the responsibilities incurred by citizens of a democratic state. Through their attitudes and actions, citizens and government officials of a democracy help determine the extent to which the lives of lesbians and gays mirror those of the general public. As political scientists, we have the opportunity to "theorize" about rights and responsibilities as well as to study and map out the political context surrounding the democratic process. Past research can be used to understand current developments, and, in turn, the current application can be used to refine and develop new theories about how democratic processes work in general.

The authors in this collection examine the interaction of gays and lesbians with the democratic process. They put to the test the theoretical models of their specialties in public policy, public opinion, and political representation to explain relevant phenomena concerning gays and lesbians. Each chapter is a unique case study within American politics. And whether the authors find support for or contradictions to their hypotheses, the theoretical bases of these fields of study are expanded and strengthened.

We will begin with a broad overview of the democratic concepts of concern and the particular methodological approach used in this volume — empirical study. Then we will summarize the particular focus of each chapter. Finally, we will look at the contributions of these chapters to our understanding of public policy, public opinion, and political representation.

DISCUSSING DEMOCRACY

While each chapter of this volume makes a contribution to its specific *subject area* within political science and to the general study of lesbians and gays, the chapters also collectively comment on our understanding of democratic processes in the United States. We can make several conceptual distinctions when discussing democratic governments and our disciplinary study of them.

One distinction in discussing democracy is between the overall system and its component parts and processes. The chapters in this volume look at different parts of the process. Hopefully, taken together, they give a better picture of the whole. Part of the basis of democratic government in the United States is a system of checks and balances, based on the liberal democratic assumption that the rights of the minority are to be protected from the tyranny of the majority. The findings presented in this volume highlight participation by gays and lesbians in different components of the system and attest to greater and lesser degrees of "success" in gaining rights, protections, and representation.

A second distinction is between democratic processes and outcomes. Processes that are strictly majoritarian, and therefore quite democratic in nature, may yield outcomes that repress the rights of a minority and are repugnant to the spirit of democracy (or vice versa). As the past (and ongoing) civil rights struggles in the United States have shown, it is an important feature of democratic governments to arbitrate these conflicts. The chapters of this book implicitly underline this conflict and arbitration. The passage of nondiscrimination policies is a government effort to protect the rights of a minority. Yet these policies face opposition by organized groups. Each group uses different parts of the process to make its case.

A final conceptual distinction we will draw is the distinction of looking at democracy as a function of governmental institutions versus looking at the attributes of citizens. Theorists have suggested the necessary conditions of democracy to include many institutional attributes, such as citizen opportunity to influence governmental decisions (Lindsay 1967), rule in accord with the consent of the majority (Ely 1980), institutions that permit only competitively elected officeholders to make decisions (Schumpeter 1950), the presence of regular elections, universal suffrage, and civil liberties (Bowie and Simon 1977). Theorists also suggest many individual attributes necessary to democracy, such as the disposition to join groups (de Tocqueville 1835), a civic culture (Almond and Verba 1965), the capacity and will to join in deliberative processes to determine the common good (Tussman 1960), and a faith in human nature, intelligence, and experience (Dewey 1940).

The chapters of this book highlight both. The institutional features of how candidates are elected (district versus at-large elections) as well as how government institutions legally interact (e.g., Dillon's Rule versus Home Rule) illustrate how the features of government can determine the rights and responsibilities of the citizenry. On the other side is the exploration of the attitudes and actions of citizens and elites. For example, several chapters in this book find support for educational level as an indicator of political tolerance of gays and lesbians. On the other hand, support by citizens for the general principles of democracy does not necessarily translate into support for the rights of lesbians and gays. The ability of the gay community to initiate political actions reflects the capacity both of citizens to mobilize politically and of government institutions to respond.

GAYS AND LESBIANS IN THE POLITICAL WORLD

Over the past two (plus) decades writers have created a growing literature concerning gays and lesbians in the political world. Political pundits and practitioners have written their prescriptions (Bawer 1993; Vaid 1995) and their memoirs (Gunderson 1996; Mixner 1996). Journalists have chronicled conflicts (Bull and Gallagher 1996; Shilts 1993) and tragedies (Shilts 1987). Scholars have added some perspective by uncovering and reclaiming the political past and documenting the rise of a social and political movement in the lesbian and gay community (Blasius and Phelan 1997; Adam 1995; Marotta 1981; D'Emilio 1998). A number of normative theoretical studies have aided our understanding of participation, community, identity, and equality in the political process (Altman 1971, 1982; Phelan 1989; Blasius 1994; Hagland 1996).

Applied studies of public policies have contributed to our understanding of gays and lesbians in the political process. *Homosexuality: Research Implications for Public Policy* (Gonsiorek and Weinrich 1991) is a multidisciplinary look at how research can inform public policy decisions affecting gays and lesbians. *The Right to Privacy: Gays, Lesbians, and the Constitution* (Samar 1991) argues in favor of the right to privacy and against the Supreme Court's decision not to extend the right to consensual adult homosexual relations. *Legally Wed: Same-Sex Marriage and the Constitution* (Strasser 1997) analyzes the context of same-sex marriage and the Defense of Marriage Act. Strasser delineates an argument in favor of same-sex marriage based on the definition of marriage, the equal protection, due process, and full faith and credit clauses of the Constitution.

Two notable books by political scientists have dealt with the issue of gays and lesbians in the military: *Gay Rights, Military Wrongs* (Rimmerman 1996) and *Gays in the Military* (Wolinsky and Sherrill 1993). Wolinsky and Sherrill provide a collection of motions, memoranda, and affidavits, along with the judge's decision in the case of Joseph Steffan versus Richard Cheney, Secretary of Defense (1993). The affidavits include the testimony of Kenneth Sherrill, who develops a model of the relative political power of groups and then analyzes the disadvantages of gays and lesbians within the political arena. The contributors to Rimmerman detail the policy context, analysis, and implications of the military ban ("Don't ask, don't tell"). The book includes essays on race and gender as historical context, the positive consequences of the debate on public opinion, an analysis of the congressional response, the limitations of the court, an analysis of the first year's implementation of "Don't ask, don't tell," and the importance of coalition building to enhance the prospects for success in public policy change.

Legal case studies abound, though mostly in legal journals (and authored by legal scholars). The cases that have spawned the greatest commentary and study are *Bowers v Hardwick* (478 U.S. 186, 1986), in which the U.S. Supreme Court found no constitutional protection for acts of homosexual sodomy, leaving states to regulate, and *Romer v Evans* (116 S. Ct. 1620, 1996), in which the U.S. Supreme Court held that an amendment to the Colorado Constitution (Amendment 2), which prevented any government action designed to protect persons based on sexual orientation, violated the Fourteenth Amendment's equal protection clause. There is also a growing body of commentary on same-sex (or same-gender) marriage based on *Baerh v Lewin* (74 Haw. 530, 852 P2d 44, 1993). The Supreme Court of Hawaii ruled that restricting same-sex marriage violates the state's constitutional protection against discrimination based on sex (an appeal of the case is still pending at the time of this writing).

Political scientists have also contributed to the analysis of gay and lesbian issues in legal settings. Rebecca Mae Salokar (1997) makes an important contribution to the literature by creating a dynamic model of interest group activity by gay and lesbian rights organizations. This model includes the effects of litigation on both the state and federal levels of government. It accounts for the interactions of all three branches of government (executive, legislative, and judicial). Salokar explains how gay and lesbian rights litigation, which has affected political change in all three branches, is but one part of a strategy learned from previous civil rights movements. Rich Pacelle's (1996) work analyzing the impact of and response to judicial decisions concerning the military ban is consistent with Salokar's model. Pacelle outlines the effects of gays and lesbians' losses in the judiciary (traditionally the branch of government most receptive to appeals by minorities) on increasing political activity in electoral arenas. Daniel Pinello (1997) studies the successes and failures of gay rights cases at the appellate level in a broad range of areas. He uses an integrated model of judicial behavior to investigate the reasons for these outcomes. Pinello finds that a judge's age, religion, and minority group status affect her or his case votes (with younger, Jewish, and minority group judges more "sympathetic" to gay rights claims). The most important legal characteristic is whether the case involves a child custody dispute between a heterosexual and a homosexual parent, bringing into cases stereotypes about and prejudice toward homosexual parents.

The works cited above are relevant to the present studies through their unique contributions to the study of lesbians and gays in politics. They have contributed to our understanding of the events of the past and present. In-depth scholarly study of policy issues like gays and lesbians in the military leads us to ask more questions, such as who supports (or opposes) these issues and what is the impact of governmental institutions on policy processes and outcomes. In short, this literature illustrates the links between and importance of public policy, public opinion, and political representation. This volume builds upon previous work through the empirical study of these phenomena.

IDENTITY, SAMPLING, AND PUBLIC OPINION

Empirical (qualitative and quantitative) studies of gays and lesbians have encountered many roadblocks and have only recently begun to appear regularly in the literature. The most difficult part of research directly investigating gays and lesbians is identifying lesbians and gays. The gay and lesbian population is "invisible." Whether a researcher meets someone face to face, makes phone contact, or gives out anonymous confidential questionnaires, that researcher remains at the mercy of the participant to self-identify as lesbian or gay. (Gartner and Segura [1997] have written an insightful article using game theory logic that discusses the impact of this invisibility [as a repressed group] on decisions to self-identify and political mobilization.) This invisibility interacts with a second problem — what is the definition of *gay* or *lesbian*? Some researchers rely on questions about sexual behavior (this applies mostly to psychologists, social workers, and sociologists). Most political scientists have used self-identification as a marker of some sort of integration into the "gay/lesbian community." (The reader might wish to consult Blasius 1996 for a fuller theoretical exploration of gay/lesbian identity as relevant to politics.)

Beyond reliance on self-identification, sampling the gay and lesbian population is a problem; gays and lesbians live throughout all geographical regions. (See Sherrill 1996 for a discussion of this problem more generally.) There are few "geographical concentrations" of lesbians and gays, for example, the Castro in San Francisco or Northhampton, Massachusetts. Added to this is the problem of obtaining a reliable sample in national-level surveys. For instance, since there has not been an intentional effort made on the part of American National Election Studies nor other academic surveys to directly sample gays and lesbians (e.g., by oversampling in districts with a concentration of lesbian and gay voters), political scientists have no way of determining if gays and lesbians under- or overvote with respect to their percentage in the electorate. Also, the absence of "bisexual" from some forced-choice self-identification questions in academic surveys can depress the percentage of self-identifiers (Bailey 1998).

Samples of gays and lesbians have been drawn in a variety of ways, e.g., membership in various organizations, advertising, and internet posts. These samples are from self-selected groups, leaving generalizability in doubt. However, as more lesbians and gays self-identify on national and local surveys, more and more data will become available for analysis. For instance, the number of self-identifying lesbians, gays, and bisexuals in the 1996 Voter News Service exit polls was 5.0 percent, more than three times the number of self-identifying gay, lesbian, and bisexual voters in the 1994 VNS exit polls (see Bailey 1998 for a full discussion). (See Badgett 1997 for a discussion of bias in the sampling of gays and lesbians and its effects on conclusions that can be drawn.)

Beyond studying the attitudes and behaviors of lesbians and gays themselves, there are also problems in studying attitudes (and behaviors) toward gays and lesbians, or "homosexuals." Questions regarding the political rights of gays and lesbians have either not been asked at all or not asked consistently over time. As a group, gay men and lesbians are more likely to be seen as a part of the cultural landscape and not the political world. Despite decades-long (more accurately, centuries-long) participation in the political process, only recently have gays and lesbians been recognized as a group involved in, and not simply subjected to, the political process.

There is occasional public opinion data available concerning attitudes toward homosexuals dating from the 1960s (see Yang 1997, also summarized below). With the invisibility of gays and lesbians, and because lesbians and gays were considered at best "mentally ill" and/or "morally wrong," the political rights of lesbians and gays were simply not discussed. This meant that researchers were unlikely to (a) see this as a legitimate line of inquiry or (b) ask questions in surveys for fear of "offending" participants. Thus, the data are limited. While there is a vast literature on social desirability in answering survey questions, there is little to suggest that people do not feel free to express their opposition on gay issues. Some observers have considered antigay bias to be the last socially acceptable bias.

Only relatively recently have gays and lesbians come to be seen as a legitimate political group. Gays and lesbians have been helped along in this battle for recognition (in part and oddly enough) by their "perfect enemy"—the religious right. Journalists Chris Bull and John Gallagher (1996) chronicle this ongoing battle and how it has helped to define the political agenda of the lesbian and gay community and the United States. High-profile battles over legal protections against discrimination, the politicization of gays through AIDS, and the increasing voluntary visibility of gays and lesbians has resulted in increasing amounts of data available. Although researchers are still reluctant to ask about sexual identity/orientation, they seem more willing to ask questions about attitudes toward lesbians and gays. For example, the American National Election Study has included a thermometer rating for gays and lesbians since 1984 and has also included questions about the lesbians-and-gays-in-the-military debate, job protections for gays, and same-gender marriage in the last two presidential election–year studies. Researchers are starting to take advantage of data from such sources as well as collecting original data sets.

PAVING THE WAY

Taking advantage of developments in policy debate and implementation, and increasing data availability, a growing literature of empirical studies concerning the political behavior of gays and lesbians as well as attitudes toward gays and lesbians is taking shape in political science. We would like to summarize a major portion of this research (to date) to set the stage for the chapters that follow, providing an anchor for discussion.

Early empirical study of attitudes toward lesbians and gays used public opinion polling data to comment on political tolerance of lesbians and gays. McClosky and Brill's (1983) study of tolerance of a plethora of groups included questions about attitudes toward gays and lesbians. Summarizing the results of several surveys (from 1977–80), McClosky and Brill find that although respondents indicated they believed homosexuality to be morally wrong, they supported a "right to privacy" for consenting adults to engage in homosexual relations. At that time, however, most of the mass public (and in many cases also most of the community elites surveyed) did not support civil liberties for homosexuals. Yang's recent summary of a collection of public opinion polls from twenty-one sources from September 1965 to 1996 (including those from the time frame of McClosky and Brill's study) reveals that on a social level there has been little movement toward "acceptance" of gays and lesbians. However, for general civil rights, such as nondiscrimination in jobs (in general) and housing, there is a trend of growing support over time (Yang presents an analysis updated through 1997 in a report for the National Gay and Lesbian Task Force, 1998; see also Wilson 1994; Kite and Whitley 1996).

Numerous studies of political tolerance have included gays and lesbians as a target group and focused on "who" is (in)tolerant and the psychological basis for this (e.g., Sullivan, Piereson, and Marcus 1982, using the "least-liked group" approach). In 1985 Gibson and Tedin (1988) conducted a survey of Houston residents following an election referendum repealing a gay rights ordinance to explore the "etiology of intolerance" toward homosexuals. They found that perception of threat from homosexuals and support for social conservatism (the New Right) was associated with greater intolerance; support for democratic norms coincided with increased levels of tolerance. Gibson and Tedin link the former variables to low education levels and psychological inflexibility. Political tolerance of homosexuals can be distinguished from tolerance of other political groups. Cognitive-based intolerance related to the actions of a group (such as the Ku Klux Klan) differs from affective-based intolerance based on dislike of a group per se (i.e., homosexuals; Riggle and Ellis 1994). Further, lesbians and gays who fit gay stereotypes are tolerated less than those who do not fit the stereotype and are subject to group-targeted intolerance.

Empirical studies of voting behavior have provided insight into the impact of the political behavior of gays, lesbians, and bisexuals on the electoral process. Mark Hertzog's *The Lavender Vote* (1996) is the first book-length examination of voting behavior by gays and lesbians. Hertzog examines data from 1990 and 1992 general election exit polls. He finds that lesbian and gay voters are more liberal and Democratic than nongay voters. Hertzog also finds evidence for his hypothesis that lesbian and gay voters will "distinctively" support a pro-gay candidate, no matter party or ideology.

Robert Bailey has investigated the voting patterns of gays, lesbians, and bisexuals in presidential, urban, and congressional elections (1997, 1998). He also concludes that gay and lesbian voters are more liberal and Democratic but suggests that it was not until the 1992 election that a "gay vote" emerged. In 1992, for the first time, there appeared a statistically significant difference in the vote choice between individuals identifying as gay or lesbian and those identifying as heterosexual. This translated not only into support for Clinton in the presidential race but also for a Democratic Congress. Bailey also contends that, prior to 1992, the gay rights movement had already achieved a power base in larger urban areas, including the legitimation of gay/lesbian sexual identity and the request for political resources.

This power base and the adoption (or rejection) and implementation of public policies affecting gays and lesbians has been the subject of a number of studies. A four-city case study by Donald Rosenthal (1996) documents the response of municipal politicians and policies to the gay and lesbian community. Rosenthal looked at political mobilization versus regime responsiveness in four cities in New York state. The political opportunities available for participation mediated the mobilization of the gay and lesbian community to pursue political goals within the prevailing regime in the city. The case studies show that cities with a more open political culture valued and incorporated the gay and lesbian community (e.g., Rochester); cities with a more closed political culture left the gay and lesbian community marginalized and excluded (e.g., Albany). Mobilization of support from both lesbian and gay and nongay voters, however, can help to open opportunities even in a closed regime by eroding the base of support for that regime and promoting electoral competition. Elaine Sharp (1996) has similarly studied local government response as part of a "taxonomy of local government roles in controversies over culture-war issues" (753). The author classifies local government response to the proposal of gay rights legislation as evasive in one case (New York City, 1979), "unintentional and entrepreneurial instigation" in another (San Francisco, 1960s), and straightforward responsiveness in the third (Wichita, Kansas, 1977). Although both Rosenthal and Sharp use case studies, this has not been the only methodological approach used to study policy making. Haeberle (1996) expanded the scope of inquiry concerning public policy adoption to examine the question of why over half the nation's cities with populations more than 250,000 have enacted nondiscrimination policies based on sexual orientation. He finds that the demographic determinants include the density of the population (not merely size), the (estimated) size of the gay and lesbian population, and the percentage of college-educated residents.

Button, Rienzo, and Wald (1997) use a combination of methodological approaches. The authors combine a case study of five cities with a survey of public officials from cities with and without antidiscrimination policies to assess models of policy adoption. The focus of the study is on public policy battles over antidiscrimination legislation and legal protections. They find that (a) the debate over gay rights is rooted in identity politics, (b) models of urbanism/social diversity, political opportunity structures, resource mobilization, and communal protest can be used to explain why some cities adopt gay rights policies, and (c) public officials believe that the adoption of policies does help reduce discrimination, especially in employment.

A study by Riccucci and Gossett (1996) contradicts the last conclusion of Button, Rienzo, and Wald (see also Badgett 1997). Riccucci and Gossett studied the implementation and enforcement of antidiscrimination ordinances and policies, with a focus on hiring/firing and employee benefits. They gathered data from fifteen states and sixty-five cities/counties concerning grievances filed by lesbian and gay employees under nondiscrimination policies (although almost two-thirds of the respondent cities and one-third of the states reported no grievances filed). The data included the number of grievances filed and the disposition of the cases (although the texts of the grievances or dispositions were unavailable). The authors found that very few grievances were successful, with most being found to have "no probable cause." In addition, the presence of a policy did not easily translate into equal employee benefits, often known as domestic partner benefits.

As the movement has matured, segments of the gay and lesbian community have acted as an interest group within conflicts over public policy. Haider-Markel and Meier (1996) found that the pursuit of lesbian and gay rights resembles interest group politics when the issue is not salient, with a narrow scope of conflict contained in the legislative arena and among sympathetic elites. However, when opposition groups can make the issue more salient by expanding the scope of the conflict into the electoral arena to include an "audience of general citizens," the public policy debate more closely resemble morality politics, i.e., a culture war. Haider-Markel (1997) has also looked at the survival and potential for growth of gay and lesbian interest groups. The author applies population ecology theory and finds support for the hypothesis that "interest groups in competition for space (numbers) will share space by positioning the issue over into separate issue niches" (910). This has allowed several lesbian and gay interest groups to grow by representing different aspects of the collective interest (e.g., the Gay and Lesbian Victory Fund focuses on electoral campaigns while Lambda Legal Defense and Education Fund focuses on court cases).

The research summarized above has "broken ground" in the study of gays and lesbians and provided a strong foundation for the research presented in this book. Taken as a whole, it has established that gays and lesbians are an influential political group acting in the democratic process. The chapters in this collection both extend this research and expand the scope of inquiry.

THE CHAPTERS

The chapters of this volume are rooted in a variety of research traditions: from public policy to public opinion, electoral campaigns to interest groups. In this section we will summarize each chapter; in the next section we will highlight findings that impact upon future research.

The next three chapters focus on a timely public policy issue: the addition of sexual orientation to local nondiscrimination policies. In chapter 2 Marieka Klawitter and Brian Hammer use a model of spatial and temporal diffusion to understand the passage, or spread, of nondiscrimination policies through states, counties, and cities. Evidence of the geographical diffusion of policy innovations, including some civil rights policies, leads the authors to apply this theory to the present topic. Their findings give mixed support for this theory and lead to an additional dynamic — antidiffusion (the mobilization of opposition groups) — as a salient feature of the diffusion of policy adoption.

To determine why some cities pass nondiscrimination policies, John Dorris focuses on socioeconomic and demographic factors in chapter 3. Past research has shown several factors to be important in determining political attitudes toward issues of public policy, especially where the issue involves bimodal public opinion. Nondiscrimination policies that include sexual orientation are highly contentious and often viewed as a dichotomous issue. The study of 201 cities with and without the policy finds support for educational level, the size of the city, and the ethnic and racial heterogeneity of the city as determinants. Political culture also plays a role.

While the aforementioned two chapters look at geographical and demographic factors, Charles Gossett (chapter 4) conducts a multiple case study of cities that have considered nondiscrimination policies, focusing on an institutional factor that de facto (and de jure) can limit the ability of cities to adopt these policies. Dillon's Rule refers to the power of the state over local governments. Under this rule local governments must get permission from the state to exercise power. Local governments have used Dillon's Rule to both justify and reject (or nullify) the addition of sexual orientation to local policies. As Gossett points out, this fundamental principle of law may sometimes determine the "ultimate success or failure" of adopting such policies.

Even given an obstacle like Dillon's Rule, elite and mass public attitudes can still have a significant impact on the outcome of public policy battles. Jean Schroedel, in chapter 5, discusses elite attitudes and Greg Lewis and Marc Rogers, in chapter 6, investigate mass public attitudes toward employment rights. Steven Haeberle, in chapter 7, extends the study of mass attitudes to changes in attitudes and their effect on presidential elections.

Schroedel surveys the attitudes of systematically sampled elected officials to determine how political and personal demographics relate to support for and opposition to employment rights for lesbians and gays. Past studies have shown the elite to be more tolerant than the mass public; however, strong opposition to gay rights among conservative political officials calls into question the generalizability of this finding. Schroedel's unique survey of state legislators, city and county elected officials, and (elected) school board members reveals that, similar to findings about nonelites, educational level, religion, gender, partisanship, and political ideology affect elite attitudes toward tolerance of gays and lesbians.

Lewis and Rogers use the results of seven public opinion surveys conducted between 1977 and 1993 to find the sources of opposition to and support for gay employment rights. While the American public is quick to support broad statements of rights, such as "homosexuals should have equal rights concerning job opportunities," they seem equally quick to object to "having a homosexual as your child's elementary school teacher." This lack of support for applications of the general principle is often used in public policy debates against the extension of civil rights protections to gays and lesbians. The results are optimistic, however, in finding that increased levels of education increase support for specific equal job opportunities for gays and lesbians.

Haeberle uses data from the 1992 and 1996 American National Election Studies to determine trends in support of lesbians and gays in the military and employment protections as well as how these attitudes affected voting in the presidential elections. Public debates over gays in the military, the Defense of Marriage Act, and the Employment Non-Discrimination Act stimulated citizens to think about public policy issues affecting lesbians and gays. And while gays and lesbians may have lost the battles over these policies, Haeberle shows that they may be winning the war of public opinion.

Chapters 8 through 12 address the issues of representation through the electoral process and interest groups. Based on their sexual orientation, gays and lesbians receive similar treatment in the political world, thus leading to a common interest among a diverse group of citizens.[2] Gay and lesbian interest groups and leaders have attempted to address these issues by finding "friendly" elected officials to champion their case. Nevertheless, as lesbians and gays become more visible and integrated into communities, the desire for direct representation in governmental bodies and for political self-determination (including the notion that "anyone can grow up to be President") has grown.

As noted in the beginning paragraph of this chapter, openly lesbian and gay candidates for public office are running in increasing numbers. Rebekah Herrick and Sue Thomas (chapter 8) experimentally test the effects of candidate sexual orientation on perceptions of candidate viability and issue interests. The respondents see lesbian and gay candidates as more interested in rights issues (though it is not a topic mentioned in the descriptions of the candidate) and as less likely to win an election. Stereotypes of gays and lesbians play an important role in these inferences, especially for religious conservatives.

In chapter 9 Ewa Golebiowska and Cynthia Thomsen manipulate whether a description of a candidate is consistent or inconsistent with stereotypic expectations and when the voter learns about the candidate's sexual orientation. Although stereotype consistency has mixed effects, timing is very important. Knowing early that the candidate is gay biases the lens through which a voter perceives information about a candidate; however, finding out later in the process does not significantly bias perceptions. This is consistent with psychological research on perceptual biases and may help to explain, at least in part, why congressional members who come out after years in office have been reelected by their constituents.

Gary Segura employs computational logic in chapter 10 to challenge the existing "wisdom" that district-based elections benefit minority constituencies more than at-large elections. Using a case study of San Francisco, Segura shows that district-based election systems help gays and lesbians and other minorities gain representation only in certain scenarios. District-based systems at worst will institutionalize and exacerbate underrepresentation of minority groups. At-large systems, on the other hand, may have distinct advantages for minority groups (under certain circumstances), including incentives for coalition building.

Donald Haider-Markel explores federal response to the gay and lesbian rights movement in chapter 11, using an ARIMA time series analysis to test theories of agenda setting and issue definition. The findings suggest that lesbian and gay interest groups and opposition groups drive congressional activity. Grassroots activity may aid in changing public opinion but does not affect agenda setting. This chapter points to the power of lobbying groups — and also to the power of the opposition. Over the years both sides have defined issues, which has led to both positive and negative outcomes for lesbians and gays.

We end this volume with a chapter that signaled the beginning and shows us how far we have come — and how far we have yet to go. In 1973 Kenneth Sherrill presented a paper at the Annual Meeting of the American Political Science Association entitled "Leaders in the Gay Activist Movement: The Problem of Finding the Followers." In chapter 12 Sherrill revisits this paper. The original, a survey of than 69 gay "leaders" and 206 gay "followers," showed no significant differences on issue stands. This finding contradicted studies of leaders and followers in the general public and has had important implications for the lesbian and gay rights movement and its political agenda. The author comments on the applicability of those findings to the journey of the gay, lesbian, and bisexual rights movement over the last twenty-five years and to research today.

CASE STUDIES OF AMERICAN POLITICS: IMPLICATIONS

There are several major contributions offered by the chapters of this volume. Each chapter delineates its own contribution to the relevant literature in public policy, public opinion, or political representation. We would like to draw together some of their findings.

First, several of the authors find that education, religion, and living in an urban environment influence attitudes toward gays and lesbians. Although other factors also showed effects, these three provided a recurrent theme for elites as well as the mass public. Higher levels of education contribute on a personal level to political support of lesbians and gays and on a broader level to the passage of gay rights protections. Although past studies of political tolerance have found mixed support for the significance of education (Stouffer 1955; Sullivan, Piereson, and Marcus 1982), the studies in this volume find education important for political support of gays and lesbians. The process of obtaining an education, especially college and postgraduate, may contribute to the likelihood of contact with lesbians and gays or at least contact with a diverse group of people (Bobo and Licari 1989). It may also enhance the ability of individuals to cognitively overcome negative stereotypes (often learned as children). Additionally, scholars have hypothesized that living in a large urban environment increases contact with a variety of people, thus promoting support. In an increasingly urbanized and educated country this may be a positive trend over time for gays and lesbians.

Religion also plays an important role in support and tolerance. A consistent finding, here and elsewhere, is that religious conservatives (conservative in an ideological and also fundamentalist sense) are a major force of opposition to social tolerance and political rights (see Wilcox and Jelen 1990). Religious conservatives have a value-based belief that homosexuality is morally wrong. They apply this belief not only to attitudes about gays and lesbians but also to issue/policy debates. The intensity of this belief has led religious conservatives to form opposition groups, either as single-issue entities or as part of a larger political agenda. These groups are formidable foes for lesbian, gay, bisexual, and transgendered interest groups.

A second contribution of the book concerns the use of social group stereotypes about gays and lesbians in political decision making. Stereotypes are often used as the basis of opposition to policy issues. For example, using the stereotype of lesbians and gays as sexual predators, opposition groups fight basic rights protections for lesbians and gays. Stereotypes (negative) also affect perceptions of individual gays and lesbians (e.g., candidates for public office). Two positive trends concerning the use of stereotypes come out of this research. One, there are trends of growing support for gays and lesbians. This could be because stereotypes are less negative (perhaps linked to increasing education and urbanization) or less accessible. Two, stereotypes are not always used. Golebiowska and Thomsen's research shows that stereotypes have no effect on evaluations of gay and lesbian candidates who come out late in a race. This could help to explain why elected officials who come out while already in office, such as current and former Congress members Frank, Studds, Kolbe, and Gunderson, have been reelected. There are an increasing number of openly lesbian and gay candidates running; some undoubtedly lose votes due to stereotypes (negative), while others win by focusing attention on issues or running in supportive locales.

A third contribution of this collection lies in its tests of themes in American politics and democratic theory. All the volume's chapters use gays and lesbians and/or the social movement as the basis of investigation; each chapter adds evidence to tests of such themes that use other groups as the basis of investigation. For example, Haider-Markel provides further evidence that Schaatschneider's theory about expanding the scope of conflict still has relevance today. Similarly, Schroedel provides important evidence as to the function of social learning vis-à-vis the inculcation of values. Finally, the importance of institutional factors and their effect on public policies is demonstrated in an entirely new arena through the work of Gossett.

Finally, lesbians and gays are at the crossroads of being a cultural/social group and a political group. In essence, the gay, lesbian, bisexual and transgendered community has been transformed into both a social movement and a collection of interest groups. This development offers little surprise since the same path has been followed by other groups, including but not limited to women and African Americans. The prolonged public conflict between the social movements and religious institutions and the institutionalization of these forces as interest groups have influenced the political landscape from local school boards to presidential elections. Indeed, this protracted antagonism suggests that studies of social movements and policy change must account for all manifestations on both sides of an issue.

THE FUTURE

The research presented in this volume represents a significant advance in investigations into American politics and the democratic process. Yet, as with all intriguing research, many questions remain to suggest future work. One of the immediately apparent questions concerns the attitudes of lesbians, gays, bisexuals, and transgendered persons. Much of the research in this book represents attitudes *about* gays and lesbians. Because of the sampling issues discussed earlier in this chapter, few studies have attempted to sample the lesbian and gay community. This is a hole that future research will be left to fill. For example, knowing the issue stands and priorities of gays and lesbians will help to answer questions about representation by public officials and interest groups.

Although the research here and elsewhere can compare findings about gays and lesbians to research findings concerning African Americans and women as well as other minorities and political groups, future research should also explore the effects of multiple cultural identities. Just as identity politics has played a significant role in the political priorities and actions of women of color, so sexual identity interacts with cultural identity for many gays and lesbians. For example, the political issue attitudes of African American gays may reflect their unique experiences within the social and political landscape.

The implementation and effectiveness of public policies affecting lesbians and gays is both a practical and theoretical question. Americans support the rights of gays and lesbians to employment opportunities free of discrimination while simultaneously not "morally approving" of gays and lesbians. This dissonance in attitudes may not only fuel opposition to policies in the adoption stage but also impede effectiveness among implementing populations. Or, as has been hoped for when adopting nondiscrimination policies on the basis of race or ethnicity, policy adoption may lead public opinion to more tolerance and acceptance of gays and lesbians in political and social life.

Finally, the research presented in this volume is conducted using data from political phenomena in the United States. Yet many important political developments are taking place in countries worldwide. For instance, the South African Constitution now includes "sexual orientation" within its nondiscrimination provisions, countries such as Denmark and Iceland permit registered partnerships, providing most of the rights of marriage to same-gender couples, and Ireland has dropped its sodomy law and enacted job protections for gays and lesbians (also see Bamforth 1997 and Rayside 1998 for a comparison of gay and lesbian rights in Britain, Canada and the United States). A comparative approach to the study of these phenomena will provide information about what is unique in the case of each country and what is generalizable over nations. The structural and cultural features of each nation act as a natural experiment for researchers to learn more about political processes.

Gays, lesbians, bisexuals, and transgendered persons have had to create social support systems. With that social support has come a cultural identity and structure — in part of necessity and in part as a collective process of self-actualization. And with changes in the demographic landscape of the United States, lesbians and gays have reached the critical mass necessary to step into the political arena and oppose repressive policies/legislation as well as to champion policies to protect rights. This has marked the legitimation of lesbians and gays as a political group and ignited political conflict.

A major lesson of the movement for equal rights for women is that the "personal is political." Gays and lesbians have been persecuted by society and the government for their status (sexual orientation). Given this active discrimination, the politicization of gays and lesbians was and is inevitable. Concurrently, the increased saliency of issues related to sexual orientation has meant increased significance of attitudes about lesbians and gays. In a democracy, where government is responsible for maintaining order, distributing resources, and enhancing citizens' quality of life, the politics of public policy, public opinion, and political representation become the arena for conflict and resolution.

NOTES

1. Results reported in this book pertain to self-identified, perceived, and closeted gays and lesbians (or, *homosexuals*). Some results pertain more generally to *sexual orientation*, which includes bisexuals and heterosexuals. Fewer results, however, would pertain specifically to issues of gender identity as experienced by transgendered persons (except as they may relate to sexual identity issues). This helps illustrate the extent to which defining a community based on sexual orientation proves difficult. Members of the general public, activists within gay rights organizations, lesbians and gays in general, and scholars who study issues pertaining to sexual orientation all may mean slightly different things even when using similar terminology.

2. Factors modify this similar treatment, such as gender and race/ethnicity, in a societal context. And as research in this volume and elsewhere shows, there are distinctions made in the treatment of lesbians and gay men by individuals. However, public policy makes few such distinctions.

REFERENCES

Adam, Barry D. 1995. *The Rise of a Gay and Lesbian Movement*, rev. ed. New York: Simon and Schuster Macmillan.

Almond, Gabriel A. and Sidney Verba. 1965. *The Civic Culture: Political Attitudes and Culture in Five Nations*. Boston: Little, Brown.

Altman, Dennis. 1971. *Homosexual: Oppression and Liberation*. New York: Outerbridge and Dientsfrey.

—— 1982. *The Homosexualization of America: The Americanization of the Homosexual.* New York: St. Martin's.

Badgett, M. V. 1997. "Vulnerability in the Workplace: Evidence of Anti-Gay Discrimination." *Angles: The Policy Jounal of the Institute for Gay and Lesbian Strategic Studies* 22:1–4.

Bailey, Robert W. 1997. "The Sexual Identity Vote in House District Races: A First Look." Paper presented at the Annual Meeting of the American Political Science Association.

—— 1998. "Out and Voting: The Gay, Lesbian, and Bisexual Vote in Congressional House Elections, 1990–1996." Washington, DC: National Gay and Lesbian Task Force.

Bamforth, Nicholas. 1997. *Sexuality, Morals, and Justice: A Theory of Lesbian and Gay Rights Law*. London: Casell.

Bawer, Bruce. 1993. *A Place at the Table*. New York: Simon and Schuster.

Blasius, Mark. 1994. *Gay and Lesbian Politics: Sexuality and the Emergence of a New Ethic*. Philadelphia: Temple University Press.

—— 1996. *Gay and Lesbian Politics: Sexuality and the Emergence of a New Ethic*. Philadelphia: Temple University Press.

Blasius, Mark and Shane Phelan. 1997. *We Are Everywhere: A Historical Sourcebook of Gay and Lesbian Politics*. New York: Routledge.

Bobo, Lawrence and Frederick C. Licari. 1989. "Education and Political Tolerance: Testing the Effects of Cognitive Sophistication and Target Group Affect." *Public Opinion Quarterly* 53:285–308.

Bowie, Norman E. and Robert L. Simon. 1977. *The Individual and the Political Order*. Englewood Cliffs, NJ: Prentice-Hall.

Bull, Chris and John Gallagher. 1996. *Perfect Enemies: The Religious Right, the Gay Movement, and the Politics of the 1990s*. New York: Crown.

Button, James W., Barbara A. Rienzo, and Kenneth D. Wald. 1997. *Private Lives, Public Conflicts: Battles Over Gay Rights in American Communities*. Washington, DC: Congressional Quarterly Press.

D'Emilio, John. 1998. *Sexual Politics, Sexual Communities: The Making of a Homosexual Minority in the United States, 1940–1970*. 2d ed. Chicago: University of Chicago Press.

de Tocqueville, Alexis. [1835–1840] 1945. *Democracy in America*. Ed. Phillips Bradley, trans. Henry Reeve, and revised by Francis Bowen. New York: Knopf.

Dewey, John. [1940] 1972. *The Philosophy of the Common Man*. Excerpted in Carl Cohen, ed., *Communism, Fascism and Democracy*, p. 578. New York: Random House.

Ellison, Christopher G. and Marc A. Musick. 1993. "Southern Intolerance: A Fundamentalist Effect?" *Social Forces* 72:379–398.

Ely, John Hart. 1980. *Democracy and Distrust*. Cambridge: Harvard University Press.

Gartner, Scott S. and Gary Segura. 1997. "Appearances Can Be Deceptive: Self-Selection, Social Group and Political Mobilization." *Rationality and Society* 9:131–161.

Gibson, James and Kent L. Tedin. 1988. "The Etiology of Intolerance of Homosexual Politics." *Social Science Quarterly* 69:567–604.

Golebiowska, Ewa A. 1996. "The 'Pictures in Our Heads' and Individual-Targeted Tolerance." *Journal of Politics* 58:1010–1034.

Gonsiorek, John C. and James D. Weinrich, eds. 1991. *Homosexuality: Research Implications for Public Policy*. Newbury Park, CA: Sage.

Gunderson, Steven. 1996. *House and Home*. New York: Dutton.

Haeberle, Steven H. 1996. "Gay Men and Women at City Hall." *Social Science Quarterly*. 77:190–197.

Hagland, Paul Ee-Nam Park. 1996. "International Theory and LGBT Politics: Testing the Limits of a Human Rights-Based Strategy." *GLQ: A Journal of Lesbian and Gay Studies* 3:1–28.

Haider-Markel, Donald P. 1997. "Interest Group Survival: Shared Interests Versus Competition for Resources." *Journal of Politics* 59:903–912.

Haider-Markel, Donald P. and Kenneth J. Meier. 1996. "The Politics of Gay and Lesbian Rights: Expanding the Scope of Conflict." *Journal of Politics* 58:332–349.

Hertzog, Mark. 1996. *The Lavender Vote: Lesbians, Gay Men, and Bisexuals in American Electoral Politics.* New York: New York University Press.

Kite, Mary E. and Bernard Whitley. 1996. "Sex Differences in Attitudes Toward Homosexual Persons, Behaviors, and Civil Rights: A Meta-analysis." *Personality and Social Psychology Bulletin* 22:336–353.

Lewis, Gregory B. 1997. "Lifting the Ban in the Civil Service: Federal Policy Toward Gay and Lesbian Employees Since the Cold War." *Public Administration Review* 57:387–395.

Lindsay, Alexander Dunlop. 1967. *The Essentials of Democracy.* 2d ed. Oxford: Clarendon.

McClosky, Herbert and Alida Brill. 1983. *Dimensions of Tolerance: What Americans Believe about Civil Liberties.* New York: Russell Sage Foundation.

Marotta, Tony. 1981. *The Politics of Homosexuality.* Boston: Houghton Mifflin.

Mixner, David. 1996. *Stranger Among Friends.* New York: Bantam.

Pacelle, Richard. 1996. "Seeking Another Forum: The Courts and Lesbian and Gay Rights." In Craig A. Rimmerman, ed., *Gay Rights, Military Wrongs: Political Perspectives on Lesbians and Gays in the Military.* New York: Garland.

Phelan, Shane. 1989. *Identity Politics: Lesbian Feminism and the Limits of Community.* Philadelphia: Temple University Press.

Pinello, Daniel R. 1997. "Explaining Success and Failure of Lesbian and Gay Rights Claims in State Appellate Courts, 1982–1992." Unpublished paper.

Rayside, David. 1998. *On the Fringe: Gays and Lesbians in Politics.* Ithaca: Cornell University Press.

Riccucci, Norma M. and Charles W. Gossett. 1996. "Employment Discrimination in State and Local Government: The Lesbian and Gay Male Experience." *American Review of Public Administration* 26:175–200.

Riggle, Ellen D. and Alan L. Ellis. 1994. Political Tolerance of Homosexuals: The Role of Group Attitudes and Legal Principles." *Journal of Homosexuality* 26:135–148.

Rimmerman, Craig A., ed. 1996. *Gay Rights, Military Wrongs: Political Perspectives on Lesbians and Gays in the Military.* New York: Garland.

Rosenthal, Donald B. 1996. "Gay and Lesbian Political Mobilization and Regime Responsiveness in Four New York Cities." *Urban Affairs Review* 32:45–70.

Salokar, Rebecca Mae. 1997. "Beyond Gay Rights Litigation: Using a Systematic Strategy to Effect Political Change in the United States." *GLQ: A Journal of Gay and Lesbian Studies* 3:385–415.

Samar, Vincent J. 1991. *The Right to Privacy: Gays, Lesbians, and the Constitution.* Philadelphia: Temple University Press.

Schumpeter, Joseph. 1950. *Capitalism, Socialism, and Democracy*, 3d ed. New York: Harper.

Sharp, Elaine B. 1996. "Culture Wars and City Politics: Local Governments Role in Social Conflict." *Urban Affairs Quarterly* 31:773–758.

Sherrill, Kenneth. 1996. "The Political Power of Lesbians, Gays and Bisexuals." *PS: Political Science and Politics* 29:469–473.

Shilts, Randy. 1987. *And the Band Played On*. New York: St. Martin's.

—— 1993. *Conduct Unbecoming: Gays and Lesbians in the U.S. Military*. New York: St. Martin's.

Stouffer, Samuel. 1955. *Communism, Conformity, and Civil Liberties*. New York: Wiley.

Strasser, Mark. 1997. *Legally Wed: Same-Sex Marriage and the Constitution*. Ithaca: Cornell University Press.

Sullivan, John, James Piereson, and George Marcus. 1982. *Political Tolerance and American Democracy*. Chicago: University of Chicago Press.

Tussman, Joseph. 1960. *Obligation and the Body Politic*. Oxford: Oxford University Press.

Vaid, Urvashi. 1995. *Virtual Equality: The Mainstreaming of Gay and Lesbian Liberation*. New York: Doubleday.

Wilcox, Clyde and Ted G. Jelen. 1990. "Evangelicals and Political Tolerance." *American Politics Quarterly* 18:25–46.

Wilson, Thomas C. 1994. "Trends in Tolerance Toward Rightist and Leftist Groups, 1976–1988" *Public Opinion Quarterly* 58:539–556.

Wolinsky, Mark and Kenneth Sherrill, eds. 1993. *Gays and the Military*. Princeton: Princeton University Press.

Yang, Alan S. 1997. "The Polls—Trends: Attitudes Towards Homosexuality." *Public Opinion Quarterly* 61:477–507.

—— 1998. "From Wrongs to Rights: Public Opinion on Gay and Lesbian Americans Moves Toward Equality." Washington, DC: National Gay and Lesbian Task Force.

CHAPTER TWO

Spatial and Temporal Diffusion of Local Antidiscrimination Policies for Sexual Orientation

Marieka Klawitter and Brian Hammer

In 1972 East Lansing, Michigan adopted the first public policy banning discrimination on the basis of sexual orientation. Since then hundreds of cities and counties and a few states have followed suit. These laws and policies have banned discrimination in private employment, government employment, housing, public accommodations, education, and credit. Recent federal attention focused on these policies as the Supreme Court ruled that states could not selectively ban local governments from adopting sexual orientation protections (*Romer v Evans*, 1996) and the U.S. Senate turned down a federal antidiscrimination policy by one vote (Employment Nondiscrimination Act vote, 1996).

This chapter tells the story of the diffusion over time and space of local antidiscrimination policies for sexual orientation. Over time the rate of new adoptions could be influenced by previous adoptions or by changes in public opinion or political conditions. Neighboring jurisdictions may influence adoptions because policy makers or citizens learn about policies from nearby jurisdictions or because political interest group organizational efforts spill over into nearby areas. Alternatively, policies may be adopted in close jurisdictions because they are similar in economic or demographic characteristics. Adoptions by encompassing jurisdictions could dampen the demand for local policies. Previous research has investigated the effects of political and demographic determinants on the passage of these policies. No studies have yet investigated the geographic and temporal diffusion of the antidiscrimination laws.

To study these patterns we use information on the inclusion of sexual orientation in antidiscrimination policies covering private employment in states, counties, and cities from 1972 to 1995. In addition, the U.S. Census provides data on the economic and demographic characteristics of jurisdictions. We use discrete time hazard models to estimate the impacts of these factors and of spatial and temporal diffusion on local government adoption rates of antidiscrimination policies for private employment.

ANTIDISCRIMINATION POLICIES

Antidiscrimination policies for sexual orientation are modeled on similar policies based on race, sex, religion, and national origin. Often state and local legislative bodies have simply added sexual orientation to existing civil rights laws or policies; at other times they have created new policies with special exceptions. Antidiscrimination policies for private sector employment, the focus of this chapter, have prohibited employers from considering sexual orientation in decisions regarding hiring, pay, promotion, or firing. Before 1985 only two states and thirty local areas had adopted private employment protections for sexual orientation. By 1995 nine states and more than eighty cities or counties had passed these policies (Klawitter and Flatt 1998). Other employment policies cover only government employment; these have often been adopted by executive order rather than legislation. Coverage of government employment grew from four state and fifteen local policies in 1985 to twelve state and fifty-three local policies by 1995. This continued increase in the number of policies points to diffusion of the policies though not to specific patterns or explanations for that spread.

Although public opinion regarding gays and lesbians has improved markedly in the past twenty years, public support of nondiscrimination in employment is still conditional on the type of job and views about the nature of homosexuality (Moore 1993; Schmalz 1993). A recent poll found that about 80 percent of respondents supported equal job opportunities for homosexuals, but only 40 percent of respondents thought that antidiscrimination laws were necessary to ensure equal rights for homosexuals (Schmalz 1993). Changing attitudes have undoubtedly aided in passage of antidiscrimination policies; at the same time, the remaining diversity of opinions creates demand for the policies.

Researchers have found that adoptions of sexual orientation antidiscrimination policies are more likely in places with larger and more urban populations, more nonfamily households, and higher levels of education (Dorris, this volume; Haeberle 1996; Wald, Button, and Rienzo 1996) — all correlates of less hostile public opinion on homosexuality (Moore 1993). Dorris also finds that cities with more individualistic cultures or ethnic heterogeneity are more likely to adopt protections. In addition to these demographic correlates, studies have identified the influence of policy entrepreneurs, issue framing, interest group resources, and the salience of the issue (Button, Rienzo, and Wald 1997; Haider-Markel and Meier, in press). The quantitative studies of adoption of antidiscrimination policies have focused on characteristics of local areas (or voters) rather than the interrelations of actions across jurisdictions. None of these studies have systematically examined the geographic or temporal patterns of diffusion.

POLICY INNOVATION AND DIFFUSION

Jack Walker's 1969 article on the diffusion of innovative public policies posed the possibility that policy innovation and diffusion might follow systematic patterns. Walker hypothesized that particular states might serve as innovators in many types of policies and that policies would "diffuse" geographically outward from those innovators like spreading "inkblots" (1973:1187). Innovators could provide nearby states with information about policy options and implementation and might provoke emulation and competition. The case studies provided by Gossett (chapter 4, this volume) show support for this diffusion process in local antidiscrimination policies by highlighting the struggles of early adopters along with subsequent adoptions (or at least consideration) by other local governments in the same state.

Gray (1973) built on Walker's work by testing the temporal diffusion patterns of several types of state policies. She found that civil rights policies (but not all policies) evidenced stable "innovativeness" (the same states were usually early adopters) and strong association with wealth and party competition (the latter being contrary to Walker's findings). Gray showed that some, but not all, policies displayed an S-curve shape for the cumulative rate of adoptions over time — few adoptions by innovators early, many adoptions mid-cycle, and few adoptions late as the cycle tapered off. Gray also noted that some states might be "immune" to particular policies and that this would truncate the S-curve below full adoption by all states.

More recent research has extended both the theory and methodology of policy diffusion. Consistent with Gray's work, recent studies hypothesized different adoption patterns for policies covering "morality politics" and "distributive or economic politics." In contrast to economic policies, morality issues are more salient, require little technical knowledge, and provoke strong value-based opinions. The role for public opinion is larger in morality issues, and that could limit the influence of state innovation by political elites. Haider-Markel and Meier

(1996) found that support for gay rights policies was more likely if the scope of conflict and salience were limited. This allowed interest group resources to determine the policy outcomes within state legislatures rather than public opinion weighing in at the ballot box.

This points to a possible conflict with the earlier theories of diffusion, which hypothesized early adoptions as sources of information and emulation. Instead, as policies become more widespread, increased public salience could widen the scope of conflict and decrease the chances for further diffusion. The story of Portland, Maine in the chapter by Gossett (this volume) describes how passage of local policies in Portland and nearby Lewiston prompted opponents in both cities to broaden the conflict through the referendum process. Also consistent with the possible effects of salience is the finding of Wald, Button, and Rienzo (1996) that local ordinances for sexual orientation were less likely to be adopted in states that had adopted some kind of antidiscrimination policy. Although state policies could also discourage local action by providing statewide coverage of private employment and thereby dampening the demand for local policies.

Mooney and Lee (1995) examined diffusion and reinvention (changes in policies) for another morality policy: state abortion policies. They found that some of the standard political, demographic, and economic characteristics of states (e.g., urbanization, wealth, liberalism, and innovativeness) did not affect diffusion of abortion policies but that other abortion-specific characteristics did (e.g., religion and number of doctors). They found some evidence of regional patterns and a time trend in adoptions.[1] Their methodology builds on the work of Berry (1994) by using event history analysis of time series data for states. This methodology allows estimation of the probability of policy adoption in any given time period to depend on factors that vary over time, including adoptions in previous periods. Berry (1994) shows that this allows researchers to simultaneously allow for the influence of diffusion and internal demographic, political, or social characteristics on adoptions.

This discussion points to the ways we build upon earlier studies of the adoption of sexual orientation antidiscrimination policies and policy diffusion. Event history analysis allows us to model the effects of preceding actions by other jurisdictions and the effects of cumulative experience with similar policies. Adoptions in nearby jurisdictions could increase the chances of subsequent adoptions because of information and emulation. In contrast, adoptions might be dampened because of increased salience (spawning interest group activity) or decreased demand (in the case of encompassing jurisdictions). In addition, unlike most previous studies of innovation, our model accounts for a general time trend and the possibility of stable regional differences in the chances of adoption.

The time trend could reflect cumulative experience with similar policies or widespread changes in public opinion or interest group resources. Adoption rates could differ across regions because of stable political or cultural influences (Dorris, chapter 3, this volume). Along with these innovations, the model simultaneously assesses the impact of local demographic and economic factors on the chances of policy adoption.

DATA AND EMPIRICAL STRATEGY

Our analysis uses the 459 U.S. counties with populations over one hundred thousand in 1980. This criterion allowed us to examine the counties most likely to adopt antidiscrimination policies but maintain a manageable sample size for matching to census and policy information.[2] This study focuses on local government adoption of public policies prohibiting sexual orientation discrimination by private employers. As mentioned above, state and local governments have also legislated or (more often) issued executive orders banning sexual orientation discrimination in public employment. We focus on policies targeted at private employment because of their larger potential impact and more public and controversial adoption processes.

Our study uses a discrete multivariate logit to estimate an event history analysis. This method allows estimation of the probability of adoption of a policy as a function of county characteristics and the previous actions of other jurisdictions. The data set pools observations across counties and years by using a sample that includes one observation for each county in each year from 1972 until passage of the policy (if that occurs) or until 1995. Thus counties that never adopt private employment protections add twenty-four years to the sample; counties with adoptions add less with one observation for each year until the adoption. Prior to deletions for missing data, the sample includes 11,040 county-years.[3] The coefficients from the logit analyses show the effects of an explanatory factor on the log of the odds of passage in a year, conditional on the county not previously adopting the policy.

Our outcome variable indicates inclusion of sexual orientation in an antidiscrimination policy covering private employment passed by the county or by a city within the county. By including both county and city policies, we examine the availability of covered employment within geographic areas and avoid the issue of strategic choice between city and county adoptions by policy proponents.[4] Data for the outcome and for the measures of geographic spread are constructed from a list of antidiscrimination policies compiled from a number of private sources.[5] County-level census data for 1980 provided information on demographic and economic characteristics of the population. Data on church membership in counties came from a national census of churches (National Council of Churches 1982).

General time trends in adoptions are captured by a set of year indicators. These reflect trends from widespread changes in public opinion, elite opinion, national advocacy resources, or political events. The time trend could also reflect the effects of national interaction among policy makers that Virginia Gray (1973) hypothesized would result in an "S-shaped" curve in cumulative adoptions by states. We also use the measure of state policy innovation constructed by Walker (1969) to assess whether counties in innovative states are more likely to adopt policies.

Adoptions by other jurisdictions could provide information on the problem of discrimination and policy implementation, thereby creating spatial patterns of diffusion. As discussed above, nearby adoptions may have a greater impact because those jurisdictions may serve as standard-bearers (Walker 1969), associated advocacy resources may cross jurisdictional boundaries, or the public debates may create greater salience. We have modeled these spatial interactions in several ways. For each county-year we include a count of the number of local antidiscrimination policies covering private employment previously passed within its own state and, separately, within its region.[6] The emulation and resources hypotheses both suggest that previous adoptions within the state should increase the likelihood of passage, and adoptions within the region should have a positive but smaller impact. Alternatively, previous adoptions could increase the salience of the issue and the concentration of resources to fight adoptions, and these could make additional adoptions more difficult.

Our model includes an indicator of previous passage of a state-level private employment policy for sexual orientation. State policies could encourage local government adoptions by serving as a model or discourage them by providing coverage of local institutions.[7] The model also includes an indicator of previous adoption of a policy covering public employment or other type of sexual orientation discrimination within the county. Again, the effects of previous adoptions are ambiguous because they could serve as an indicator of the propensity to adopt or, in this case, as a consolation prize in a fight for private employment coverage. In summary, all kinds of previous adoptions could change the chances of adoption by increasing salience, concentrating interest group resources, or encouraging emulation by providing information or standards.

Regional indicators and local characteristics will capture static differences in adoption rates. Indicators for the eight census regions will estimate the size of stable regional propensities toward adoption (rather than the changes associated with the number of past adoptions). The county population and degree of urbanness capture social or economic influences, as do measures of the age and education distributions. Public opinion polls, especially important in morality political issues, show more positive attitudes toward homosexuality and antidiscrimination policies among younger, urban, and more highly educated people (Moore 1993; Dorris, this volume). To assess the effects of local economic well-being on adoptions, our model includes median personal income and the unemployment rate.[8] The county proportion of nonfamily households acts as another measure of diversity in household style that could be associated with public opinion. Opposition to gay rights is proxied by county-level information on the proportion of Catholics and conservative Protestants. An ideal model would include annual measures of the economic and demographic measures to assess the effects of changing characteristics. However, the data are not available, so the county characteristics show cross-sectional variation only.

RESULTS

Table 2.1 shows the results of logit analyses of the likelihood of adoption of sexual orientation antidiscrimination within the counties. Each of the multivariate models explains the pattern of adoptions significantly better than using the simple average adoption rate (p < .01).[9] In this section we discuss the temporal patterns, spatial diffusion, influence of county characteristics, and state innovation.

Temporal Pattern of Diffusion of Antidiscrimination Policies

Figure 2.1 shows the rates of cumulative and annual adoption of private employment antidiscrimination policies for our data. Adoptions have numbered between 0 and less than 10 per year until slightly higher rates in the 1990s. As we discussed above, a time trend could reflect the effects of changes in public opinion, issue salience, and advocacy infrastructure as well as a diffusion process driven by emulation. The coefficients on the year indicators in the multivariate model (not shown here) were not statistically significant, reinforcing the lack of a strong time trend in the adoption rate.[10]

Gray (1973) hypothesized that national interaction could create an S-shaped curve for the cumulative rate of state policy adoptions (a normal curve

TABLE 2.1.

Logit Estimates of the Effects of Policies, Regions, and County Characteristics on Adoption of Private Employment Protections

Variable	Model A Coefficient	S.E.	Model B Coefficient	S.E.	Model C Coefficient	S.E.	Model D Coefficient	S.E.
Local Policies within State	0.158**	0.062	0.251**	0.089	0.068	0.067	0.176*	0.106
Local Policies within Region	0.028	0.035	−0.260*	0.123	0.038	0.035	−0.219*	0.133
Prior Policy in County	−1.059	1.019	−2.002*	1.045	−1.054	1.019	−1.992*	1.045
Prior State Employment Policy	−0.979	0.688	−1.044	0.700	−0.823	0.646	−1.051	0.688
Regions:								
New England			0.914*	0.499			0.922*	0.506
East North Central			0.815	0.588			0.842	0.626
West North Central			−0.448	0.655			−0.069	0.878
South Atlantic			−1.328**	0.563			−0.972	0.849
East South Central			−8.887	17.604			−8.165	17.578
West South Central			−2.889**	1.118			−2.180	1.450
Mountain			−2.179*	1.041			−1.913*	1.145
Pacific			(reference category)					
County Characteristics (1980):								
Population (in 10,000s)			0.006**	0.001			0.006	0.001
Urbanness			3.599**	1.105			3.412**	1.122
Unemployment rate			−0.971	6.526			−1.601	7.131
Median Income (in 1000s)			0.033	0.087			0.040	0.093
Age distribution (proportion of Pop):								
under 20			−27.729**	10.166			−26.240**	10.916
20–34			3.324	9.722			4.936	10.355
35–49			−0.914	13.492			−2.492	14.071
50–64			−35.091*	19.468			−35.059*	20.622
65 and over			(reference category)					
Education (proportion of Pop):								
less than High School			−1.173	5.902			−0.270	6.240
High School only			−3.492	5.775			−2.972	6.141
some College			−14.320	9.616			−10.575	9.694
BA degree			−1.461	14.127			−2.247	14.808
beyond college			(reference category)					
Walker's Innovation Index			5.121**	1.613			3.650	3.603
Constant	−5.328**	0.188	−0.735	20.274	−7.879**	0.857	−3.979	20.721
N	10230		10230		10128		10128	
-2 log liklihood	812.500		618.700		790.500		606.100	

Notes: *indicates p < .102 ** indicates p < .05

Models B and D also include a set of year dummies not shown here.

Models C and D contain fewer cases because Walker did not define an index for Alaska and Hawaii.

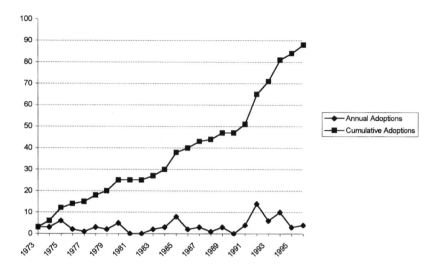

FIGURE 2.1. Adoptions of Private Employment Policies

for the adoption rate). Although some of the policies she examined did display this pattern, adoption of civil rights policies by states did not. The graph for our data does not show a completed S-shape because the rate of adoptions in the 1990s has been high relative to earlier periods. However, the rate could slow in future years if the remaining jurisdictions are, as Gray says, "immune" to the policy. Our multivariate model allows the adoption rate to vary in a nonlinear way by including a set of year indicators. Those indicators that allowed the effects of time to differ from the S-shape fit our data better than the linear time variable.[11] Thus the data suggest that the adoption patterns have not followed the S-curve but could approximate that pattern if future adoptions increase, then slow.

Spatial Diffusion of Policies

If interaction or comparison with nearby jurisdictions encourages adoption, then we would expect to see policies adopted in what Walker called "spreading ink-blots" (1973:1187). Figure 2.2 shows the diffusion of antidiscrimination policies over three time points: 1975, 1985, and 1995. Counties with city or county antidiscrimination policies in 1975 have the darkest shading, followed by those with policies in 1985 and 1995. Counties without policies are outlined but not colored. The map shows several clusters of policies in the Northeast and West.

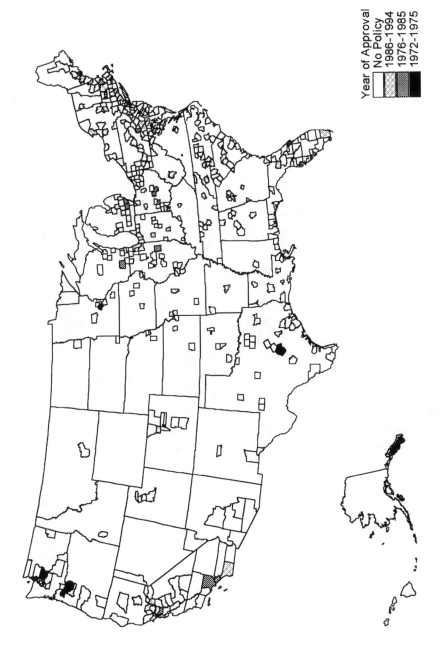

FIGURE 2.2. Distribution of Private Employment Protection Policies in Counties with Population Over 100,000 (1980 pop.), by Year of Approval

Some counties with policies in 1985 do have clusters of counties with 1995 policies in close proximity. However, the pattern is not overwhelming and, regardless, this graphic presentation does not differentiate between spatial patterns attributable to emulation and those due to static characteristics of nearby counties.

Our multivariate results in table 2.1 show some support for the spatial diffusion model for local adoptions. Before accounting for fixed regional and local characteristics (Model A), passage of private employment protection by other cities or counties within the state was associated with a greater probability of adoption ($p < .05$). Similarly, the number of adoptions by local governments within the region was positively associated with adoption, but this effect was small and not statistically significant ($p = .39$.) After accounting for other characteristics, Model B shows that the effect of local adoptions within the state remains positive and significant ($p < .05$), but additional regional adoptions are associated with lower adoption probabilities ($p < .10$) — completely offsetting the positive impact. As noted above, this negative effect could result from increased salience of the issue, making adoptions more difficult. It appears that similarities within the region accounted for the positive association of regional adoptions found in Model A.

Local governments that had previously adopted antidiscrimination policies for government employment or other activities (e.g., housing, education) were much less likely to adopt a private employment policy (Model B, $p < .10$). This suggests that the earlier adoptions of policies not targeting private employment are more likely to be consolation prizes rather than precursors or that these passages make the environment less hospitable to future policy adoptions.[12] The presence of state-level private employment protection also dampens the likelihood of a local adoption, though this effect is not statistically significant. Although some local areas do adopt subsequent to state implementation, these are often more symbolic than substantive victories given coverage of local private employers under state laws.

There are static regional differences in the chances of adoption (shown by coefficients on region indicators). Pacific (the reference region), New England, and East North Central cities and counties have been most likely to adopt. Local governments in the Mountain and Southern regions have been less likely to adopt sexual orientation protections. These regional differences could reflect cultural, political, and economic factors not captured within our model.[13] Indeed, polls have found the greatest public support for these antidiscrimination policies in the East and West, with much lower public support in the South (Moore 1993).

County Characteristics

Consistent with previous studies, we found that more populated and urban counties are more likely to adopt antidiscrimination policies. This could reflect cultural differences or political tolerance within areas. Also, more urban areas may attract larger numbers of gays and lesbians and therefore more advocacy resources devoted to passage. Neither of the economic variables, the unemployment rate and median income, appear to significantly affect adoption rates, though they have the expected signs reflecting fewer adoptions in places with lower economic well-being. This is consistent with the work by Mooney and Lee (1995) suggesting the morality issues are not influenced by economic considerations, though inconsistent with Gray's early finding that other civil rights laws were predicted by state wealth. County differences in age distribution did not significantly affect adoption rates. Adoption rates were lower in areas with more adults with education levels less than a bachelor's degree, though the pattern was not monotonic and most of the coefficients were not statistically significant. Although the education coefficients were large, all were imprecisely estimated, perhaps reflecting relatively little variation in these proportions. As expected, the proportion of nonfamily households was positively related to the likelihood of adoption, but the coefficient was statistically insignificant. Similarly, the proportions of Catholics and conservative Protestants were negatively related to adoptions but again statistically insignificant. The addition of time varying information on county characteristics would likely aid in more precise estimation of these influences by expanding the variation within the sample.

Walker's Innovation Index

Walker (1969) created an index of state innovativeness by compiling information on the timing of adoption of eighty-eight state policy issues before 1965. We used this index to assess whether antidiscrimination policies were adopted in counties within more innovative states. A logit model that included only the innovation index and the policy diffusion variables showed that the rate of adoptions was significantly higher within innovative states (Model C coefficient on Walker's index). However, after accounting for the demographic and economic characteristics of counties, the innovation index was no longer statistically significant (Model D). It appears that county and regional characteristics account for at least some of this general innovation.

A similar pattern was evident for a measure of public opinion about antidiscrimination policies for sexual orientation constructed by Gamble (1994).[14]

This measure of average state support for sexual orientation antidiscrimination policies was highly correlated with Walker's measure of innovativeness and, like that measure, was significantly related to adoption of the antidiscrimination policies only in models that did not control for county-level demographic characteristics. Thus antidiscrimination policies were adopted in places within more innovative states and those with higher levels of public support for gay rights. But those relationships were predicted to a large extent by the demographic characteristics of the counties.

The inclusion of sexual orientation in local antidiscrimination policies has grown steadily since 1972. The analysis presented here offers only mixed support for the application of patterns of spatial and temporal diffusion developed for state-level policies. However, it provides some additional support for the findings of cross-sectional studies of the effects of local characteristics on the adoption of antidiscrimination policies. Our findings speak to the adoption influences of political climate (policy information, salience, and interest group resources), perceived need for a policy, state law compatibility, and general public support for a policy.

Consistent with patterns of public opinion and earlier studies of adoptions, these adoptions have been more frequent in larger, more urban localities. Regional patterns also follow national poll data that shows less public support for gay rights in the South and Mountain regions. We found some patterns with education, religiosity, household type, and economic well-being, though imprecise estimation prevents definitive statements about association.

Private employment protections do not show the S-curve pattern of adoptions discussed by Gray (1973). Over time the rate of local adoption has increased slightly, with no real sign of exponential growth (for the middle of an S-shaped curve) or of dampening (for the top of an S-curve). This pattern could give credit to advocates who continue to achieve additional adoptions or to opponents who have prevented rapid diffusion of these policies. Perhaps the nature of morality politics precludes S-curve adoption patterns by increasing widespread salience of issues and expanding the scope of conflict (Haider-Markel and Meier 1996) to create what Gray termed "immunity."

The patterns of spatial diffusion are not inconsistent with the spreading inkblots hypothesized by Walker (1973), but a full multivariate treatment shows a more complex pattern. Local antidiscrimination adoptions within the state increase the chances of diffusion within the state, but regional adoptions may offset that effect. The differential effects of adoptions within the state could merely reflect proximity, but, alternatively, could be explained by the importance of state control of local actions as described by Gossett's article on Dillon's Rule (this volume). Adoptions within the same state serve as evidence of compatibility with state law, whereas adoptions within the region would only reflect influence through policy information, interest group resources, or salience.

We found that local adoption of nonemployment policies within a county and state-level employment policy adoptions both decrease the chances of adoption of county private employment protections. Clearly the need for a local policy diminishes with the adoption of a statewide policy; the negative effects of the local nonemployment adoption cannot be so easily explained. It is likely that the passage of a local policy that does not include employment is the outcome of a political system that would not support the passage of a more powerful policy including private protections. This explanation suggests that the nonemployment policy serves as a marker rather than a direct causal influence, though the process of adoption could also increase salience and drum up opposition.

Contrary to the work of Walker (1969) and Gray (1973), diffusion of local antidiscrimination policies seems better described by static characteristics and a mix of diffusion and "antidiffusion." The antidiffusion found here might be the result of increased salience of this morality issue or concentrations of interest group resources. Additional research could potentially map the temporal flows of policy information, interest group resources, and public salience to help explain their connections to adoptions.

In short, our work suggests that advocates would be most effective targeting urban local governments in Northern or Western states that have no statewide private employment protections but neighboring (in-state) local governments with sexual orientation protections. Cities or counties that have already considered employment protections or adopted other types of protections are not likely to be good candidates for private employment laws.

Adoptions of antidiscrimination policies for sexual orientation show no sign of slowing as we enter the twenty-first century. Perhaps only action at the federal level (the largest encompassing jurisdiction) could stem the tide of adoptions in the local policy arena. That pattern of upward diffusion from states to federal government would follow the pattern of civil rights policies for race and sex. Policy information, issue salience, and interest group resources generated by policy adoptions by state and local governments would most certainly play a role in that debate.

NOTES

1. Mooney and Lee (1995:616) did not differentiate between static regional differences and diffusion of policies within regions, perhaps because of the limitations of state-level observation. Their model did not include regional indicators but did include

a measure of average abortion policy permissiveness for the region. They included a linear time trend.

2. Button, Rienzo, and Wald (1997) show that the rate of adoptions is much higher for larger cities than for smaller cities.

3. Nine counties in Virginia could not be matched with data on church membership because of the structure of that data set. (Inclusion of these counties in a model without church information had little effect on the size or significance of other coefficients.) Also, counties in Alaska and Hawaii are missing in the models using Walker's index of innovation because he did not provide a measure for those states.

4. The choice of arena to push these policies would serve as an interesting research topic because they have been adopted by states, counties, and cities. Passage by an encompassing or internal jurisdiction may decrease the need for a local policy. Alternatively, a victory at one government level might spur action in other arena. Adoption at any level could also indicate the presence of support or interest group resources that could influence adoptions by other levels.

5. The list was compiled from information from the National Gay and Lesbian Task Force, Arthur Leonard, and Donald Haider-Markel.

6. The policy counts include adoptions in counties not included in our sample (by the size criterion) because these adoptions could affect the larger counties. We also tried models with similar counts of antidiscrimination policies covering situations other than private employment (e.g., government employment, education, credit, and housing). However, these variables were too highly correlated with the private employment measures to allow for estimation of separate coefficients so we excluded them from the models. The high correlations ($r > .70$) probably reflect the similar adoption processes and influences.

7. Gossett's work suggests another possible positive influence; adoption of a state-level policy could legislatively enable cities or counties to pass their own similar policies.

8. We also tried adding the county poverty rate, but this variable was very highly correlated with the median income ($r = -.78$).

9. The proportion of correct predictions of the outcome is over 99 percent for each model. However, this is not a good measure of model fit because adoptions are rare and the models predict no adoption for almost every period.

10. In an alternative model a simple linear year variable was statistically significant, showing some support for increased adoptions. However, the model with the year indicators fit the data better. The linear year model had -2 log likelihood of 667.2; for the year indicator model it was 618.7, which indicates a better fit.

11. A linear year variable within the logit model allows for the nonlinear S-shape because of the logit functional form.

12. Button, Rienzo, and Wald (1996:65–66) provide a counterexample to this with their description of the process in East Lansing, the first local government to include sexual orientation. It passed a private employment policy after first adopting a policy covering public employment.

13. Walker (1969) found support for diffusion of policies within regions, but he was not simultaneously accounting for demographic or economic characteristics of states.

14. Gamble (1994) used questions from the 1992 National Election Studies Post-Election Study to estimate the relationship of personal characteristics to responses to the question "Do you favor or oppose laws to protect homosexuals against job discrimination?." State-level measures of opposition were then calculated by using state representative samples from the National Election Studies Pooled Senate Election Studies and aggregating predicted opposition by using the regression coefficients. The mean level of the measure has been subtracted, leaving a measure with a mean of zero.

REFERENCES

Berry, Frances Stokes. 1994. "Sizing Up State Policy Innovation Research." *Policy Studies Journal* 22:442–456.

Button, James W., Barbara A. Rienzo, and Kenneth D. Wald. 1997. *Private Lives, Public Conflicts: Battles Over Gay Rights in American Communities*. Washington, DC: Congressional Quarterly.

Dorris, John B. 1999. "Antidiscrimination Laws in Local Government: A Public Policy Analysis of Municipal Lesbian and Gay Public Employment Protection." Chapter 3, this volume.

Gamble, Barbara S. 1994. "Anti-Gay Ballot Initiatives and the Christian Right." Unpublished paper.

—— 1997. "Putting Civil Rights to a Popular Vote." *American Journal of Political Science* 41:245–270.

Gossett, Charles W. 1999. "Dillon's Rule and Gay Rights: State Control Over Local Efforts to Protect the Rights of Lesbians and Gay Men." Chapter 4, this volume.

Gray, Virginia. 1973. "Innovation in the States: A Diffusion Study." *American Political Science Review* 67:1174–1185.

Haeberle, Steven. 1996. "Gay Men and Lesbians at City Hall." *Social Science Quarterly* 77:190–197.

Haider-Markel, Donald and Kenneth J. Meier. In press. "Legislative Victory, Electoral Uncertainty: Explaining Outcomes in the Battles Over Lesbian and Gay Rights." *Policy Studies Review*.

Haider-Markel, Donald P. and Kenneth J. Meier. 1996. "The Politics of Gay and Lesbian Rights: Expanding the Scope of the Conflict." *Journal of Politics* 58:332–350.

Klawitter, Marieka M. and Victor Flatt. 1998. "The Effects of State and Local Antidiscrimination Policies on Earnings for Gays and Lesbians." *Journal of Policy Analysis and Management* 17:658–686.

Mooney, Christopher Z. and Mei-Hsien Lee. 1995. "Legislating Morality in the American States: The Case of Pre-Roe Abortion Regulation Reform." *American Journal of Political Science* 39:599–627.

Moore, David W. 1993. "Public Polarized on Gay Issue." *Gallup Poll Monthly* (April) 331:30–34.

National Council of Churches. 1982. *Churches and Church Membership, U.S., 1980.* Electronic data file, Roper Center.

Romer v. Evans. 1996. 116 S. Ct. 1620.

Schmalz, Jeffrey. 1993. "Poll Finds Even Split on Homosexuality's Cause." *New York Times*, March 5.

Wald, Kenneth D., James W. Button, and Barbara A. Rienzo. 1996. "The Politics of Gay Rights in American Communities: Explaining Antidiscrimination Ordinances and Politics." *American Journal of Political Science* 40:1152–1178.

Walker, Jack L. 1969. "The Diffusion of Innovations Among the American States. *American Political Science Review* 63:880–899.

—— 1973. "Comment: Problems in Research on the Diffusion of Policy Innovations." *American Political Science Review* 67:1186–1191.

CHAPTER THREE

Antidiscrimination Laws in Local Government: A Public Policy Analysis of Municipal Lesbian and Gay Public Employment Protection

John B. Dorris

The struggle for equality in the United States continues today for many individuals. The civil rights movement for African Americans can be traced back through the antilynching efforts of Ida B. Wells and the voting rights efforts of Martin Luther King, Jr. The women's rights movement in the United States can be traced through the efforts of suffragists Lucy Stone and Susan B. Anthony. For the lesbigay community the struggle for equality under the law remains relatively young compared with the women's and African Americans' struggles.[1]

The messages of any minority group will either fail or succeed depending upon the political environment. A minority can cognitively discern an injustice, yet a remedy will not always be forthcoming. The policy makers with the ability to remedy an issue must be convinced that there is even an issue to address. And those with power (either executive, judicial, or legislative) must be positively oriented toward action.

With controversial issues policy makers can use their power of definition to keep a policy aimed at redressing these issues from coming into being. With policies that are incompatible with the morals or beliefs of the policy makers, a specific policy can be defined as nonessential and rarely appears on the agenda (Bachrach and Baratz 1962). This process of nondecision is what Crenson calls "un-politics" (Crenson 1971). Those with grievances are at a disadvantage if their issue is considered illegitimate. Consequently, their voice in the process may be muffled or even silenced (Bachrach and Baratz 1970).

The lesbigay community has had to face these same struggles, just as the women's and African Americans' civil rights movements did. And, with a similar strategy, the lesbigay community too has advanced a number of different messages at the federal, state, and local levels in hopes of redressing numerous perceived and actual cases of discrimination. At the local level the civil rights struggle revolves around issues that affect everyone's life directly: fair housing, access to credit, ability to participate in unions, and the ability to work. Variations within the populations of U.S. cities have caused different levels of advocacy success and receptiveness to opposing messages.

This chapter will specifically address the single issue of municipal public employment protection for lesbigay individuals. In most cities a public employee does not have protection against termination based on sexual orientation. However, there are currently 102 cities that do have such a policy. While there are currently efforts at the federal level to enact the Employment Non-Discrimination Act, the predominant arena for the struggle of public employment protection remains at the local level.

PUBLIC OPINION THEORY: UNIMODAL
VERSUS BIMODAL ISSUES

Public opinion theory is concerned with how an issue is discursively constructed among the adult population. Public opinion theory suggests that the nature of the discourse surrounding an issue will determine what policy positions will be viewed as legitimate by the participating population, with unimodal and bimodal issues creating different policy outcomes.

Unimodal issues are characterized by mild public disagreements. "Mainstream" public opinion is largely perceived to be in the center of the political spectrum. When the public is largely centrist, politicians often are required to be moderate when dealing with a particular unimodal issue (Strickland and Whicker 1986). Bimodal issues, however, feature wide disagreements within the public. These issues are characterized by two extreme positions that often cut across traditional party lines and reflect basic socioeconomic, religious, and class differences within the population (Downs 1957; Dawson 1973). When the public is divided, politicians often gravitate toward one of the extremes, and public debate becomes more irascible (Strickland and Whicker 1992).

There are several key features that delineate the differences between unimodal and bimodal opinions. The differences also point to distinctive variations in public policy pursuits and options. Unimodal issues have moderately intense, continuous issue positions, while bimodal public opinions have very intense, conflict-laden, dichotomous positions. Consequently, unimodal issues have numerous policy choices while bimodals have extreme and mutually exclusive options (Strickland and Whicker 1986). Unimodal issues are usually dealt with at the federal level, while bimodal issues are usually fought at each of the federal, state, and local levels. Whereas unimodal issues often have umbrella-type interest groups that support a number of issues, bimodal issues are often fought by interest groups that exist solely to fight for that single issue. The room for compromise seems nonexistent with a bimodal issue (Tatalovich and Daynes 1981; Monroe 1975). (See Strickland and Whicker 1986 for further discussion of unimodal and bimodal issues.)

Historically, lesbigay civil rights issues have often been framed within the U.S. political discourse as polar positions. The acceptance or rejection of lesbigay rights often hinges on adamant positions based on moral convictions, religious or secular in nature. Public opinion can be reasonably characterized as bimodal in character, therefore it is expected here that socioeconomic indicators will play a large explanatory role in understanding why certain cities have accorded public employment protection to lesbigay individuals.

SOCIOECONOMIC AND DEMOGRAPHIC CONTEXT

A number of researchers have successfully used socioeconomic and demographic variables as indicators and predictors of various political and social behaviors. Of particular interest are those studies that examine controversial public policy issues. These variables are expected to heavily influence the propensity to accept the messages for change that would lead to the adoption of a public employment protection ordinance.

Affluence

A number of studies examining public policy choices suggest that a higher level of affluence increases the propensity to a more liberal policy orientation. For example, affluence has been found to decrease the likelihood of states legislating restrictive abortion policies (Strickland and Whicker 1992).

The relationship between affluence and liberalism is not perfectly linked, however. Affluence may be associated with liberalism, but liberalism only in regard to social or moral issues; affluence may indicate conservatism on most economic issues and some social issues. Affluence as an indicator is inconclusive on those issues that have both a social and economic dimension (Himmelstein and McRae 1988). In general, however, many researchers still regard affluence as an adequate socioeconomic indicator for liberalism (Morgan and Hirlinger 1989).

Lesbigay civil rights are largely constructed as a moral issue. It is therefore expected that affluence will have the same effect in this study as it does with abortion policy. Thus it is hypothesized that more affluent cities as measured by per capita income are more likely to have an ordinance protecting lesbigay individuals in public employment.

Religion

The literature surrounding religion and its importance within the public sphere has undergone some recent reformulation. According to the theory of secularization, religion becomes less and less important as a nation modernizes (Grasmick, Morgan, and Kennedy 1992). Religion is expected to remain important in the private sphere, yet decline gradually even there. Religion would presumably be absent from the public political discourse in a secular society since it is not to be an important influencing agent in public policy.

An alternative school of thought, however, has suggested that the dichotomy between public and private is an artificial construct. Contemporary radical feminist theory has proposed that religion is a strong influencing agent in creating the status quo and then continually legitimizing it (MacKinnon 1989; Jaggar and Rothenberg 1993; Millet 1990; Snitow, Stansell, and Thompson 1983). Any understanding of public policy would require an understanding of the metaassumptions of the policy makers as well as the target population that is affected by specific policy outcomes. Religion is an integral part of many lives, and its tenets will undoubtedly affect what is perceived as the public sphere (Kelley, Evans, and Headey 1993; Melton 1989).

There are a number of additional studies that explore religion in politics. It has been hypothesized within this literature that religion can affect particular public policy outcomes by limiting what choices appear to be morally and politically legitimate (Sullivan 1973). A higher proportion of conservative religious adherents within the population would presumably increase the likelihood of conservative policy outcomes that either maintain or reestablish the perceived status quo.

Strickland and Whicker's 1992 research concerning abortion policy restrictions found a significant relationship between higher proportion of conservative religious believers within states and public policies aimed at decreasing a woman's access to an abortion. Since lesbigay public employment protection seems largely similar in its bimodal nature to the issue of abortion, it is expected the findings will be similar when using Strickland and Whicker's measurement of religion in this study.

At the core of the link between Protestant fundamentalism and conservatism is the tendency of fundamentalists to interpret the Bible literally (Bruce 1993;

Grasmick, Wilcox, and Bird 1990; Jelen 1989; Smith 1990). Hence it is hypothesized that cities with higher proportions of conservative religious believers are less likely to have an ordinance protecting lesbigay individuals in public employment.

Education

Several researchers have explored the relationship between educational attainment and political orientation (Davis 1987; Knocke 1979). It has largely been hypothesized that education has a liberalizing effect. Increasing education apparently creates an attitude that is more liberal, with qualifications. Education increases liberalism on some social issues, yet may not have any effect on economic issues (Davis 1987).

In a study of the 1980 GSS data and 1980 NES data, Himmelstein and McRae (1988) found that as education increased past the eighth grade there was an increased propensity to a liberal attitude on social and minority issues. Their tentative explanation was that during the K-8 years one is inculcated into allegiance to the status quo, while increasing education (especially past high school) may increase the critical skills of the individual.

Thus it is suspected that a city that had a higher proportion of the adult population with higher levels of education is more likely to have an ordinance protecting lesbigay individuals in public employment.

Ethnicity

The literature surrounding the issue of ethnicity suggests that African Americans and Hispanics may be more conservative on some social issues (Strickland and Whicker 1992). This perception is based on opinion polls, independent research, and cultural factors. Hispanics tend to be Roman Catholic, and Catholicism tends to be more conservative than other religions (Kelley, Evans, and Headey 1993). In addition, Hispanic culture is androcentric, which tends to be more conservative (Strickland and Whicker 1992). Finally, male Hispanic machismo supports traditional patriarchal values violated by homosexuality (Moraga and Anzaldúa 1983).

African Americans are also less likely to support lesbigay rights. According to findings by the National Opinion Research Center at the University of Chicago, between 1973 and 1989 African Americans have been anywhere from six to twelve percentage points more opposed to homosexual rights than whites from 1973 to 1989 (Singer and Deschamps 1994).

Thus it is hypothesized that a city with higher proportions of African Americans and/or Hispanics is less likely to have an ordinance protecting lesbigay individuals in public employment.

Population Size

The final demographic variable examined is the population of the city. The contemporary history of the lesbigay civil rights struggle is centered in the metropolitan areas. Dramatic population shifts that resulted from World War II further increased awareness of lesbigay issues since tens of thousands of lesbigay people came out of small-town isolation and into the larger cities and communities (D'Emilio 1983; Bérubé 1990). The coming together of people from all segments of the country through the armed forces further increased the creation of the lesbigay identity and helped create urban centers with a lesbigay presence.

Consequently, it seems reasonable to believe the larger cities will have larger lesbigay populations that can then petition the municipality for protection. This does not mean to suggest that gays and lesbians do not exist in smaller urban areas but rather that there are more in the larger cities, and numbers count. In Wald, Button, and Rienzo (1996) population size proved to be the single most important factor in predicting the presence of a local antidiscrimination policy. Thus it is hypothesized that larger cities are more likely to have a policy protecting lesbigay individuals in public employment.

Political Culture

Political culture today has come to be defined as the normative dimension of politics. Citing Clifford Geertz, Gabriel Almond, and Sidney Verba, among others, Kincaid suggests that political culture is "an enduring set of publicly shared and socially communicated beliefs, values, and traditions about politics which constitutes a general framework of plans, recipes, rules, and instructions for the conduct of political life, especially who gets what, when, and how" (Kincaid 1980:91).

Daniel J. Elazar (1986), in revisiting his Cities of the Prairie project, begins with the larger picture of American "national character" and then proceeds to delve into the subtleties and variations that exist at the local levels to better understand American political culture. Through a systematic examination of local cultures, it became possible to create a larger picture of American civil society using three dominant typologies: moralistic, individualistic, and traditionalistic (Elazar 1986).

The moralistic political culture developed from the Puritan, Yankee, and Scandinavian settlers in the northern areas. Elazar characterizes their attitude toward politics as being oriented toward "commonwealth" concerns and the desire for the "good society" (Elazar 1986). The moralistic municipality in Elazar's typology would be concerned with building the community and improving access to public and private resources. A commonwealth attitude encourages broad access to the increased services available to its members (Kincaid 1980).

The individualistic political culture is characteristic of the immigration wave consisting of the non-Puritan English, Continental, Eastern European, Irish, and Mediterranean people who settled in the middle states. Essentially, individualistic culture perceives government action as legitimate when encouraging access to the marketplace. This perspective views politics as managing the marketplace of competing private interests.

And the traditionalistic political culture, which is characteristic of the agrarian-based South, feels ambivalence toward the marketplace coupled with a paternalistic and elitist attitude toward the commonwealth (Elazar 1986). There is an emphasis on a structured social hierarchy rooted in familial, social, and political bonds (Kincaid 1980). Those at the top of the hierarchy are "naturally" expected to dominate politics. In the traditionalistic city, government can be active, but policy must be directed toward the maintenance of the existing social order (Elazar 1986).

The local political culture is more likely to have an effect when the municipality has more control over the policy (Kincaid 1980). The specific policy of lesbigay public employment protection is clearly one of those issues that the municipality grapples with on its own terms. While there are some state laws aimed at preventing discrimination within state government, there are at present no federal laws requiring a municipality to implement the policy.

It is hypothesized that the traditionalistic cities are the least likely to implement the lesbigay public employment protection policy because of their emphasis on the status quo. The individualistic political culture will be the most receptive to a message from the lesbigay population advocating change and to have the public employment protection policy. It is unclear where moralistic cities would stand.

With all of this in mind, it is clear that the variation of the population will largely determine which message is accorded greater credibility. A population that is more affluent, less aligned with conservative religions, and more highly educated seems the most likely to implement the policy. Populations with lower proportions of African Americans and Hispanics also seem more likely to implement the policy. A combination of socioeconomic and demographic differences as well as an individualistic political culture appears to be the most promising recipe for a lesbigay public employment protection ordinance.

METHOD AND DATA

There are currently 102 cities with an ordinance protecting lesbigay individuals in public employment. For coding purposes of the dichotomous dependent variable, those cities with the policy are 1 while those without are coded as 0. A complete list of the 102 cities included in this study can be found in appendix 3.A, and the complete listing of the sample of 100 cities without a policy is found in appendix 3.B.

The socioeconomic, demographic, and political culture independent variables were operationalized as follows. Recall the hypothesis that cities with the ordinance are expected to be more affluent than those without the policy. To measure *affluence* many researchers use per capita income (Morgan and Hirlinger 1989; Himmelstein and McRae 1988). Per capita income is calculated by dividing the total income of an area by the entire population of that area. The data for population and per capita income comes directly from the *County and City Data Book* (which publishes census data) for the cities with a population of twenty-five thousand and higher, and the smaller city data comes directly from the U.S. Census World Wide Web page.[2]

The next variable is *religion*. Recall it is expected that cities with lower proportions of conservative religious members are more likely to have an ordinance since their population would be more receptive to the messages for change. The measurement instrument to be used here is the same as used by Strickland and Whicker (1992) in their study of state abortion policy. They selected the more conservative religions within the United States and recorded the proportions of those religions within each state. They tallied the number of Catholic, American Baptist, Church of God, Southern Baptist, Assemblies of God, Latter Day Saints, and United Methodists members within the state. This total gave them a percentage of the entire population of the state that belonged to those denominations.

While their units of analysis are states, and the unit of analysis in this study is cities, the same instrument will be used since data for church membership by city is not readily available. While the measure is not as direct as one would prefer, it would still provide a general picture of the population within the state. There are, of course, limitations in using a state measurement to describe a city policy. It is possible that the conservative religious proportion of the population will be clumped in certain cities while other cities in the state may have considerably less. In larger states with many cities, such as California, this problem may be much greater than in smaller states such as Rhode Island.[3]

The next measurement instrument to be used indicates *educational attainment* of the city population. It is expected that cities with higher proportions of high levels of attainment are more likely to be receptive to the policy. The data comes from the *County and City Data Book* (1994) and the Bureau of the Census. Educational attainment represents the highest grade completed from a sample of people twenty-five years old and over from the 1990 decennial census.[4] All of the educational attainment data is available for cities with a population of 25,000 or higher, but the cities with a lower population do not have the percentages for bachelor's degree and higher. This creates another limitation for this study. Two additional measures are utilized to gauge the educational attainment within the cities: percentage with a high school diploma, or equivalent, and percentage of high school dropouts.

The final demographic variable selected for the study is *ethnicity*. And it is expected that lower percentages of African Americans and Hispanics within a city will result in a higher likelihood of cities accepting the messages of change. The data comes from the *County and City Data Book* (1994) and the Bureau of the Census.

The next measuring instrument to be used in this study is Elazar's nine-point scale (moralistic, moralistic individualistic, moralistic traditionalistic, individualistic moralistic, individualistic, individualistic traditionalistic, traditionalistic moralistic, traditionalistic individualistic, and traditionalistic), which measures a state's and city's *political culture*. The scale is firmly grounded in political theory, which gives the scale construct validity (Elazar 1986; Gibson 1992; Joslyn 1980; Kincaid 1980).

The data are not available for all cities. Ninety-four cities in the total data set do not have a coding. This creates another limitation for the study. Most of the metropolitan cities do have a measurement. Conclusions based on the city political culture data are limited to the larger metropolitan cities. State culture data are readily available, so state political culture will be used to complement the analysis.

Another measurement instrument used to complement Elazar's scale is the same as the instrument used in the Strickland and Whicker (1992) study of abortion policy restrictiveness. In their study they used an average of the Americans for Democratic Action (ADA) rankings of the two senators from the particular states. A high average would indicate a liberal political culture, and a mixed result would indicate a moderate political culture where ideology was not consequential. Data for the ADA rankings were collected from *Politics in America, 1996: The 104th Congress.*[5]

And, finally, the inclusions of dummy variables for the *South* and the *West* are included as additional complements to the political culture variables selected thus far. The West has traditionally been a leader in policy innovation (Walker 1968), and the South has been equally resistant to advances of civil rights. It is expected then that cities in the West are more likely to have the policy and cities in the South are less likely to have the policy.

RESULTS

The covariance between a number of the independent variables requires a multivariate model to enhance our understanding of why some cities appear more likely to have the policy of protection for lesbigay individuals. Since the dependent variable is dichotomous, logistic regression will be used to carry out the multivariate analysis. The coefficients for the logistic regression in table 3.1 include all independent variables.

The coefficient for "percentage white" indicates that the "more white" a city is the less chance of having the policy. Replacing the percentage of the white population with an index of Hispanic and African American percentages in the model results in a similar finding. Increased diversity appears to increase the likelihood of the city having a policy. Therefore we should accept a revised al-

TABLE 3.1
Logistic Regression Coefficients for the Relationships Between Independent Variables and the Policy of Protecting Lesbigay Individuals in Public Employment

Variable	b	Standard error
Population Size	.0054**	.0018
Affluence	.0002	.0001
Percentage White	−.0346*	.0169
Education	.1390***	.0340
ADA Rating	−.0121	.0115
Religion	0.0509	.0327
State Individualism	1.8059**	.7000
South Dummy	−.8385	.7489
West Dummy	−1.1579	.7002

$N = 157$; $*p < .05$, $**p < .01$, $***p < .001$; Percent predicted correctly: 82.80%.

ternative hypothesis, that ethnicity is indeed associated with a city having the policy. It is increased diversity rather than homogeneity that appears to increase the likelihood of a city having the public employment protection policy for lesbigay individuals.

Population, recoded as thousands for the model, has a significant relationship with the public employment policies. Larger cities can heighten awareness of different populations that have different concerns. At the same time, larger cities presumably have more lesbigay activists who can find strength and resources in a larger community. Small towns presumably have smaller lesbigay populations who may not have the pooled resources, such as time or money, to campaign effectively for change.

Higher levels of formal education seem very characteristic of those cities that have the policy protecting lesbigay individuals in public employment, consequently we should accept the alternative hypothesis, which states that the two variables are associated. Replacing the variable with one that measures the proportion of the population who do not have a high school diploma gives the same indication.

The Elazar political culture measure of state individualistic political culture does indicate a relationship. The enduring belief of individualism seems to provide a forum from which the lesbigay community can advance its civil rights struggle. Consequently, we can accept the alternative hypothesis that individualism increases the likelihood of a city having the policy of protection for lesbigay individuals.

The inclusion of the two dummy variables for the South and the West, however, failed to indicate a relationship. The multivariate model indicates that when controlling for all other variables the region of the United States does not predict whether a city will have a policy. This probably seems counter to one's "gut feeling," for who would suspect that the South is not less likely to have a city with the policy as other regions? Yet the data indicates that we should accept the null hypothesis, which states that the regions of the West and the South are independent of a city's likelihood of having the policy.

The remainder of the variables also failed to score as significant. Somewhat surprising is the variable of affluence. In early bivariate analysis it did score as significant. If the relationship depicted here is correct, then the issue of lesbigay public employment protection may no longer be a social issue but rather an economic one, or both. It appears we should accept the null hypothesis that affluence is not associated with the likelihood of a city having the policy of protection. The relationships of religion and ideology (as measured by the ADA rating) also fail to score as significant.[6]

INTERACTION PROBABILITIES

To better illustrate the interactions of the variables, one can create hypothetical city types using the logistic regression coefficients to predict the likelihood of such a city having the policy. Tables 3.2 and 3.3 offer two scenarios, the percentage likelihood for cities with or without an individualistic state political culture.[7]

Table 3.2 exhibits the percentage likelihood of cities having a policy without the Elazar individualistic component in the state political culture. Notice that as the city becomes larger, or as it becomes more formally educated, the likelihood increases. Equally interesting is the apparent improbability of a city with 50,000 people and with lower numbers of people holding a bachelor's degree or higher adopting an employment protection policy for gays and lesbians.

Table 3.3 exhibits the percentage likelihood of the cities with the Elazar individualistic political culture type. And here one sees the importance of political culture. In this table one sees a greater likelihood to have the policy of protecting lesbians and gays in public employment. A city with 250,000 people and with a fourth of the adult population having a bachelor's degree or higher reaches 92.5 percent likelihood, yet a similar type of city without the individualistic political culture component has a slightly better than 50 percent chance of having the policy.

It should be noted, however, that it appears political culture's effect is most pronounced at the lower and middle levels of the scale. The importance of political culture appears to be to make the adoption of a policy more likely once it becomes an issue that policy makers address. Its presence in larger cities or in cities with high levels of formally educated populations does not seem to carry a substantial impact.

TABLE 3.2.

Percentage Likelihood of a City without Individualistic Political Culture Having the Policy of Protection for Lesbians and Gays in Public Employment

Percent with Bachelors Degree and Higher	Population Size		
	50,000	250,000	500,000
15%	1.5%	38%	54%
25%	29%	57.5%	92.5%
35%	80%	94%	99%

TABLE 3.3.

Percentage Likelihood of a City with Individualistic Political Culture Having the Policy of Protection for Lesbians and Gays in Public Employment

Percent with Bachelors Degree and Higher	Population Size		
	50,000	250,000	500,000
15%	17%	46%	91%
25%	66%	92.5%	99.6%
35%	96.25%	99.7%	99.9%

DISCUSSION

The study has provided some revealing insights into the differences between the various cities with and without a policy protecting lesbigay people in public employment. The strongest relationship is clearly the level of educational attainment. Those cities with higher proportions of educated citizens are considerably more likely to have the policy.

It seems reasonable to conclude that increasing a person's education increases their knowledge of different points of view that may increase their tolerance of lesbigay rights. Also, going to college may increase the chances of meeting lesbigay people, which is in itself another step toward understanding.

The progress toward acceptance of difference seems connected to another association discovered in the study: the apparent importance of racial diversity within the population. After further thought the effects of higher heterogeneity may not be as surprising as previously believed. It seems reasonable to conclude that each race has within it a lesbigay population. And when the whole city population has substantial proportions of several races, there may be an increased visibility of different racial lesbigay populations. And by having a diverse lesbigay population, the rest of the nonlesbigay population may begin to question the stereotypes or the myths resulting in a reformulation of their opinions of gays and lesbians. Gays and lesbians may begin to appear just like the general population rather than as a distinct out-group.

Another reason why higher heterogeneity may increase the likelihood of implementing the policy of protection may be due to recognition of a unity of oppression (see Pharr 1988, for a discussion of this concept). African Americans especially have faced a great deal of discrimination within American society, and they may recognize a pattern of discrimination against gays and lesbians. All minority groups may recognize discrimination against gays and lesbians that creates an attitude on their part in favor of public employment protection.

Segura, in "Institutions Matter: Local Electoral Laws, Gay and Lesbian Representation, and Coalition Building Across Minority Communities" (chapter 10, this volume), points to this very possibility. He discusses the importance of the local electoral structure, which clearly affects the political power of specific ethnic or minority groups. The rich complexity of the issue provides a fertile ground for discussion of what this means for the lesbigay population inside and outside San Francisco.

The lack of a solid relationship between religion and the policy may be due to the instrument used. It did, however, show a pattern supporting the hypothesis that lower proportions of the conservative religious adherents increase the likelihood of having the policy. But definitive conclusions will need data from the actual cities.

The final socioeconomic variable examined, affluence, did show a tendency for more affluent cities to implement the policy when using a bivariate analysis. Yet the multivariate model indicates that its effect is minimal. It seems covariance between education and affluence is what drove the earlier bivariate relationship conclusions concerning affluence.

As for the political culture measurements, they are relatively mixed in their ability to describe the differences. The general weakness of some political culture variables in explaining the difference between the two city types is not that surprising. The Americans for Democratic Action rating proved largely insignificant, and herein lies the difficulty of using a liberal/conservative index. A population may be "liberal," yet waffle concerning lesbigay rights.[8]

These results seem in line with Haeberle's findings (chapter 7, this volume) concerning public opinion trends from 1992 to 1996 on such issues as gays in the military and the Employment Non-Discrimination Act. Haeberle found that for the issue of employment protection the polarization between the two parties is clearly still developing. Democrats were not more or less likely to support protection for the lesbigay community.

Obtaining some of the local variation in political culture was the purpose of using the Elazar typologies. And this variable did manage to give some insight into the differences between the cities. The state score allows for a general interpretation of all cities targeted in the study that includes the smaller nonmetropolitan cities. Since the lesbigay civil rights movement is relatively young, the observed relationship between political culture and policy may change in the future. But, for now, individualism seems a preferred forum for which lesbigay activists can advance their issues successfully.

The results of the project have squarely fit within the rubric of bimodal issue framing. As with the abortion controversy detailed in Strickland and Whicker (1986), lesbigay rights mobilizes opposing camps with different opinions as to what constitutes legitimate public policy. As predicted, we see the socioeconomic and demographic variables play pivotal roles in explaining why some cities rather than others have chosen to implement the policy of public employment protection for lesbigay individuals.

Klawitter and Hammer (chapter 2, this volume) also discuss this mobilization of opinion and action. Following the work of Walker (1969) and Gray (1973), they systematically examine the movement of success from one city to the next to determine if lesbigay policy innovation matches the policy innovation pattern first advanced by Walker. And, not surprisingly, their findings point to the mobilization of opposition. The "antidiffusion" of innovation in their study resembles clearly what Schattschneider (1975) discusses in his work *Semi-Sovereign People*. Put simply, when an interest group mobilizes with success, it brings about the mobilization of its counterinterest group. And this interaction of opposing public opinion can work to stop, slow down, or erase the public policy advances.

In a future revision of this study it would be interesting to incorporate the structures and institutions of city government. Variables such as mayor-council or council-manager form of government, weak mayor or strong mayor, at-large elections or district elections, and city council size may be important intervening elements that could help account for a city having an ordinance or not. Surveying the city clerks of the cities in this sample for the above-mentioned information could prove very useful in increasing the understanding of policy adoption.

Important to consider as well is the legal relationships between the local municipalities and state government. Gossett (chapter 4, this volume) examines the very complicated relationships that can prevent the passage or maintenance of lesbigay protection ordinances, regardless of the socioeconomic or demographic characteristics of the population. Challenging the ordinances in the courts can be very effective at repealing the changes. Yet the incorporation of home rule status as an independent variable can be very problematic, for, as Gossett reminds, there are fifty different relationships between state and local governments, and even more when one considers there can be different levels of incorporation.

Another variable that should be incorporated into the study would be a measure of the presence of a political lesbigay civil rights organization. Operationalization of this variable may be difficult, for any lesbigay organization seems political since its existence is a challenge to the status quo. Recall that the vast majority of cities do not have the policy. So the existence of an organization that operates on the assumption of legitimacy will in essence be political if it is relatively noticeable. Wald, Button, and Rienzo (1996) have done interesting work in this arena that warrants further elaboration.

It may also be prudent to include a variable that measures whether the city is a "college town." A look at the list of cities with a policy reveals that many are indeed places normally associated with universities (West Lafayette, Indiana, East Lansing, Michigan, Boulder, Colorado). Is the relationship a function of the increased education of the population, or is it the increased number of younger people? Or is it both?

An additional change for the study concerns the sample itself. It is possible the matching group of cities without a policy is not representative of the population. An improvement would be simply to take the whole universe of cities with a population of at least 100,000, or even 50,000. The conclusions based on such a sample would be more definitive than those advanced in this project.

In any event, the study has offered a number of useful and intriguing insights into the issue of lesbigay public employment protection. It is clearly a beginning in trying to understand the successes of the contemporary lesbigay civil rights movement. But as time progresses we may see the issue progress as well. I look forward to further discovering the patterns and interrelationships of their successes.

Appendix 3.A

Two lists of cities with an ordinance were found: one from the Queer Resources page on the World Wide Web and one from the National Gay and Lesbian Task Force and Policy Institute, with each complementing the other. Two additional cities were added from recent circulating news information.

Another decision had to be made at the time of the study concerning those cities in Colorado. The voters of Colorado voted 51 percent in favor of a vaguely worded initiative (Amendment 2) that repealed all local ordinances offering protection to lesbigay individuals. The decision was made to include the cities in Colorado in anticipation of the Supreme Court reversing Amendment 2, which it ultimately did.

On a similar note, Tampa is included in the study despite a citizen's initiative that overturned the city council's decision. The Florida Supreme Court has ruled that initiative unconstitutional. And Cincinnati is not included, since a United States Appeals Court ruled in favor of the citizen's initiative that overturned that city council's ordinance.

Finally, one exception was made to the "city only" rule: Honolulu. Hawaii does not have "cities only" census-designated places (CDP). While Honolulu was included in the population of cities with an ordinance, Alfred and Brighton, New York, Chapel Hill, North Carolina, Crested Butte and Telluride, Colorado, Yellow Springs and Oberlin, Ohio, and Amherst, Massachusetts were each excluded since they are villages or towns.

1.	Anchorage, AK	30.	Durham, NC
2.	Albany, NY	31.	East Lansing, MI
3.	Albuquerque, NM	32.	Evanston, IL
4.	Alexandria, VA	33.	Flint, MI
5.	Aspen, CO	34.	Gaithersburg, MD
6.	Atlanta, GA	35.	Honolulu, HI
7.	Austin, TX	36.	Houston, TX
8.	Baltimore, MD	37.	Iowa City, IA
9.	Berkeley, CA	38.	Ithaca, NY
10.	Bloomington, IN	39.	Kansas City, MO
11.	Boston, MA	40.	Key West, FL
12.	Boulder, CO	41.	Lafayette, IN
13.	Boynton Beach, FL	42.	Lancaster, PA
14.	Buffalo, NY	43.	Laguna Beach, CA
15.	Burlington, VT	44.	Long Beach, CA
16.	Cambridge, MA	45.	Los Angeles, CA
17.	Champaign, IL	46.	Madison, WI
18.	Charlottesville, VA	47.	Malden, MA
19.	Chicago, IL	48.	Marshall, MN
20.	Cleveland Heights, OH	49.	Miami Beach, FL
21.	Columbia, MO	50.	Milwaukee, WI
22.	Columbus, OH	51.	Minneapolis, MN
23.	Concord, CA	52.	Mountain View, CA
24.	Corvallis, OR	53.	New Haven, CT
25.	Cupertino, CA	54.	New Orleans, LA
26.	Davis, CA	55.	New York, NY
27.	Dayton, OH	56.	Oakland, CA
28.	Denver, CO	57.	Olympia, WA
29.	Detroit, MI	58.	Philadelphia, PA

59.	Phoenix, AZ	84.	Washington, DC
60.	Pittsburgh, PA	82.	Watertown, NY
61.	Portland, ME	83.	West Hollywood, CA
62.	Portland, OR	84.	West Palm Beach, CA
63.	Pullman, WA	85.	Worcester, MA
64.	Sacramento, CA	86.	York, PA
65.	St. Louis, MO	87.	Cathedral City, CA
66.	St. Paul, MN	88.	Hayward, CA
67.	San Diego, CA	89.	Riverside, CA
68.	San Francisco, CA	90.	Hartford, CT
69.	San Jose, CA	91.	West Lafayette, IN
70.	Santa Barbara, CA	92.	Ames, IA
71.	Santa Cruz, CA	93.	Rockville, MD
72.	Santa Monica, CA	94.	Ann Arbor, MI
73.	Seattle, WA	95.	Rochester, NY
74.	Stamford, CT	96.	Raleigh, NC
75.	Syracuse, NY	97.	Cleveland, OH
76.	Tampa, FL	98.	Youngstown, OH
77.	Troy, NY	99.	Harrisburg, PA
78.	Tucson, AZ	100.	Hollywood, FL
79.	Urbana, IL	101.	North Hampton, MA
80.	Virginia Beach, VA	102.	Dallas, TX

Appendix 3.B

To discover the differences between cities with and without a policy, a random sample of U.S. cities was taken. The population of cities to be considered are all cities with at least a population of 2,500 or more. Also, since more than 70 percent of the cities with an ordinance are metropolitan, it was decided the comparison group would correspond in this character.

Two sampling frames were obtained from the U.S. Census World Wide Web page. One sampling frame lists the 303 metropolitan statistical areas as of 1990. Those cities with an ordinance were crossed off the list of metropolitan statistical areas and the remaining cities were each marked to aid in the systematic random selection. The starting point was determined by consulting a table of random numbers and the remaining cities were selected with a K-interval of 5 (Frankfort-Nachmias and Nachmias 1992). A total of seventy-one cities was chosen from this sampling frame.

The remaining 30 percent of the sample was determined by using the list of "cities by place" from the census World Wide Web page as a sampling frame.

This list includes all cities greater than 2,500, which can include metropolitan cities, villages, towns, and census designated places (CDP). All of the cities on the census list of "places" were numbered, and cities with a policy were removed. The villages, towns, and census-designated places were also crossed out to ensure only cities would be included in the sample. Finally, the table of random numbers was used again to create a simple random sample.

1.	Albany, GA	34.	Hallandale, FL
2.	Auburn, WA	35.	Holland, MI
3.	Bangor, ME	36.	Hopkinsville, KY
4.	Banning, CA	37.	Houma, LA
5.	Bay City, MI	38.	Jackson, MI
6.	Bloomington, IL	39.	Janesville, WI
7.	Bridgeport, CT	40.	Johnston, PA
8.	Cape May, NJ	41.	Kenosha, WI
9.	Carson City, NV	42.	Kent, WA
10.	Centerville, OH	43.	Knoxville, TN
11.	Charleston, WV	44.	La Crosse, WI
12.	Cheyenne, WY	45.	Lansing, MI
13.	Clearwater, FL	46.	Lawton, OK
14.	Columbus, GA	47.	Lebanon, PA
15.	Coralville, IA	48.	Lincoln, NE
16.	Davenport, IA	49.	Longmont, CO
17.	Decatur, IL	50.	Louisville, KY
18.	Deerfield Beach, FL	51.	McAllen, TX
19.	Des Moines, IA	52.	Massillon, OH
20.	Dublin, CA	53.	Melbourne, FL
21.	Dublin, GA	54.	Miami, FL
22.	Dubuque, IA	55.	Montgomery, AL
23.	Easton, PA	56.	Moorehead, MN
24.	Elkhart, IN	57.	Natchez, MS
25.	Eugene, OR	58.	Newark, NJ
26.	Florence, AL	59.	Odessa, TX
27.	Fort Meyers, FL	60.	Ogden, UT
28.	Fort Walton Beach, FL	61.	Oil City, PA
29.	Gadsden, AL	62.	Osh Kosh, WI
30.	Georgetown, TX	63.	Oviedo, FL
31.	Glenns Falls, NY	64.	Owensboro, KY
32.	Goose Creek, SC	65.	Peoria, IL
33.	Gulfport, MS	66.	Port Arthur, TX

67.	Providence, RI	84.	St. Cloud, MN
68.	Pueblo, CO	85.	Stockton, CA
69.	Redding, CA	86.	Temecula, CA
70.	Richmond, IN	87.	Topeka, KS
71.	Richmond, VA	88.	Two Rivers, WI
72.	Rockford, IL	89.	Utica, NY
73.	Rocky River, OH	90.	Vacaville, CA
74.	San Antonio, TX	91.	Vancouver, WA
75.	Sanford, NC	92.	Vernon, TX
76.	Santa Rosa, CA	93.	Visalia, CA
77.	Sedalia, MO	94.	Warren, OH
78.	Sheboygan, WI	95.	Wasco, CA
79.	Sioux City, IA	96.	West Haven, CT
80.	South Ogden, UT	97.	Wheeling, WV
81.	Spartanburg, SC	98.	Wilkes-Barre, PA
82.	Springdale, AR	99.	Wilmington, DW
83.	Springfield, MO	100.	Winston-Salem, NC

NOTES

1. The term *lesbigay* is used as an inclusive noun to represent lesbians, bisexuals, and gays. The terms *queer* and *gay* are largely male identified, so a new term that conveys the sense of sexuality as a continuum seems appropriate.

2. All of the census data refers to the 1990 decennial census.

3. The data for church membership comes from *Churches and Church Membership in the United States* (Bradley and Green 1992) in 1990.

4. Those sampled were instructed to give the highest grade completed or highest degree received. Those people with degrees from foreign schools were coded as if they received the American equivalent, and honorary degrees were not reported (U.S. Bureau of the Census 1994).

5. After the 1994 elections a number of people were elected into the Senate who do not have an ADA rating. Therefore, data was not coded for the states of Tennessee, Michigan, and Missouri since the ADA has not rated one or both of their senators. This creates a total of 16 missing values from the total of 201.

6. These variables had weak associations in the preliminary analysis, but their effects have disappeared, suggesting that the measurement instruments here are too indirect to properly indicate the relationship. It is possible, of course, that even with precise data the relationships still will not hold. The likelihood of a city having a policy may be independent of liberalism and religiosity. Thus, it seems, we should reserve judgment on these hypotheses.

7. The variables of percentage white and per capita income are held constant at their

means in both tables when computing the likelihood percentages. The remaining variables are taken out of the model.

8. An index of liberalism/conservatism may be unable to capture the propensity to support lesbigay issues, especially if that index is based on roll call vote tallies.

REFERENCES

Bachrach, Peter and Morton Baratz. 1962. "The Two Faces of Power." *American Political Science Review* 56:947–952.

—— 1970. *Power and Poverty: Theory and Practice.* New York: Oxford University Press.

Bérubé, Allan. 1990. *Coming Out Under Fire.* New York: Plume.

Bradley, Martin and Norman M. Green, Jr. 1992. *Churches and Church Membership in the United States 1990 with Map: An Enumeration by Region, State, and County.* Washington, DC: Glenmary Research Center.

Brady, David W. and Kent L. Tedin. 1976. "Ladies in Pink: Religion and Political Ideology in the Anti-ERA Movement." *Social Science Quarterly* 56:545–559.

Bruce, Steve. 1993. "Identifying Conservative Protestantism." *Sociological Analysis* 44:65–70.

Crenson, Matthew A. 1971. *The Un-Politics of Air Pollution.* New York: Oxford University Press.

Davis, James A. 1987. "Achievement Variables and Class Cultures: Family, Schooling, Job, and Forty-Nine Dependent Variables in the Cumulative GSS." *American Sociological Review* 47:569–587.

Dawson, R. 1973. *Public Opinion in Contemporary Disarray.* New York: Harper and Row.

D'Emilio, John. 1983. *Sexual Politics, Sexual Communities: The Making of a Homosexual Minority in the United States, 1940–1970.* Chicago: University of Chicago Press.

Downs, A. 1957. *An Economic Theory of Democracy.* New York: Harper and Row.

Duncan, Philip D. and Christine C. Lawrence. 1995. *Politics in America, 1996: The 104th Congress.* Washington, DC: Congressional Quarterly Press.

Elazar, Daniel J. 1972. *American Federalism: A View from the States,* 2d ed. New York: Crowell.

—— 1986. *Cities of the Prairie Revisited.* Lincoln: University of Nebraska Press.

Frankfort-Nachmias, Chava and David Nachmias. 1992. *Research Methods in the Social Sciences,* 4th ed. New York: St. Martin's.

Gibson, James L. 1992. "Pluralism, Federalism, and the Protection of Civil Liberties." *Western Political Quarterly* 43:511–533.

Gosset, Charles W. 1999. "Dillon's Rule and Gay Rights: State Control over Local Efforts to Protect the Rights of Lesbians and Gay Men." Chapter 4, this volume.

Grasmick, Harold G., Carolyn S. Morgan, and Mary Baldwin Kennedy. 1992. "Support for Corporal Punishment in the Schools: A Comparison of the Effects of Socioeconomic Status and Religion." *Social Sciences Quarterly* 73:177–187.

Grasmick, Harold G., Linda Patterson Wilcox, and Sharon R. Bird. 1990. "Religion and the Patriarchal Family: The Effects of Religious Fundamentalism and Religiosity on Preference for Traditional Family Norms." *Sociological Inquiry* 60:352–369.

Gray, Virginia. 1973. "Innovation in the States: A Diffusion Study." *American Political Science Review* 67:1174–1185.

Hadden, Jeffrey K. 1987. "Toward Desacralizing Secularization Theory." *Social Forces* 65:587–611.

Haeberle, Steven H. "Gay and Lesbian Rights: Emerging Trends in Public Opinion and Voting Behavior." Chapter 7, this volume.

Hertel, Bradley R. and Michael Hughes. 1987. "Religious Affiliation, Attendance, and Support for Pro-Family Issues in the United States." *Social Forces* 65:858–882.

Himmelstein, Jerome L. and James A. McRae, Jr. 1988. "Social Issues and Socioeconomic Status." *Public Opinion Quarterly* 52:492–512.

Jaggar, Alison M. and Paula S. Rothenberg. 1993. *Feminist Frameworks: Alternative Theoretical Accounts of the Relations Between Women and Men*, 3d ed. New York: McGraw-Hill.

Jelen, Ted G. 1989. "Biblical Literalism and Inerrancy: Does the Difference Make a Difference?" *Sociological Analysis* 49:421–429.

Joslyn, Richard. 1980. "Manifestations of Elazar's Political Subcultures." *Publius* (Spring), 10:37–58.

Kelley, Jonathan, M. D. R. Evans, and Bruce Headey. 1993. "Moral Reasoning and Political Conflict: The Abortion Controversy." *British Journal of Sociology* 44:589–612.

Kincaid, John. 1980. "Political Culture and the Quality of Urban Life." *Publius* (Spring), 10:89–110.

Klawitter, Marieka and Brian Hammer. "Spatial and Temporal Diffusion of Local Antidiscrimination Policies for Sexual Orientation." Chapter 2, this volume.

Knocke, David. 1979. "Stratification and the Dimensions of American Political Orientations." *American Journal of Political Science* 23:772–791.

Luker, Kristen. 1984. *Abortion and the Politics of Motherhood*. Los Angeles: University of California Press.

MacKinnon, Catharine A. 1989. *Toward a Feminist Theory of the State*. Cambridge: Harvard University Press.

Melton, Gary B. 1989. "Public Policy and Private Prejudice: Psychology and Law on Gay Rights." *American Psychologist* 44:933–940.

Millet, Kate. 1990. *Sexual Politics*. New York: Simon and Schuster.

Monroe, Alan D. 1975. *Public Opinion in America*. New York: Dodd, Mead.

Moraga, Cherríe and Gloria Anzaldúa. 1983. *This Bridge Called My Back: Writings by Radical Women of Color*. New York: Kitchen Table/Women of Color.

Morgan, David R. and Michael W. Hirlinger. 1989. "Socioeconomic Dimensions of the American States: An Update." *Social Science Quarterly* 70:184–192.

Page, Ann L. and Donald A. Clelland. 1978. "The Kanawha County Textbook Controversy: A Study of the Politics of Life Style Concerns." *Social Forces* 57:265–281.

Pharr, Suzanne. 1988. *Homophobia: A Weapon of Sexism.* Little Rock, AR: Chardon.

Queer Resources Directory. 1996. Listing of Companies, Countries, States, and Cities with Gay Related Policies. Http://www.qrd.org/qrd/.

Schattschneider, Elmer E. 1975. *Semi-Sovereign People: A Realist's View of Democracy in America.* New York: Holt Rinehart and Winston.

Segura, Gary M. "Institutions Matter: Local Electoral Laws, Gay and Lesbian Representation, and Coalition Building Across Minority Communities." Chapter 10, this volume.

Singer, Bennett L. and David Deschamps. 1994. *Gay and Lesbian Stats.* New York: New Press.

Smith, Tom W. 1990. "Classifying Protestant Denominations." *Review of Religious Research* 31:225–245.

Snitow, Ann, Christine Stansell, and Sharon Thompson, eds. 1983. *Powers of Desire: The Politics of Sexuality.* New York: Monthly Review.

Strickland, R. A. and M. L. Whicker. 1986. "Banning Abortion: An Analysis of Senate Votes on a Bimodal Issue." *Women and Politics* 6:41–56.

—— 1992. "Political and Socioeconomic Indicators of State Restrictiveness Toward Abortion." *Policy Studies Journal* 20:4598–4617.

Sullivan, John L. 1973. "Political Correlates of Social, Economic, and Religious Diversity in the American States." *Journal of Politics* 35:70–84.

Tatalovich, Raymond and Byron W. Daynes. 1981. "From Abortion Reform to Abortion Repeal: The Trauma of Abortion Politics." *Commonweal* (November 21), 108:644–649.

U.S. Bureau of the Census. 1994. *County and City Data Book.* Washington, DC: U.S. Government Printing Office.

Wald, Kenneth D., James W. Button, and Barbara A. Rienzo. 1996. "The Politics of Gay Rights in American Communities: Explaining Antidiscrimination Ordinances and Policies." *American Journal of Political Science* 40:1152–1178.

Walker, Jack. 1969. "The Diffusion of Innovation Among the American States." *American Political Science Review* 63:880–899.

CHAPTER FOUR

Dillon's Rule and Gay Rights:
State Control Over Local Efforts to Protect the Rights of Lesbians and Gay Men

Charles W. Gossett

Local governments are the creations of their state governments (Zimmerman 1995; U.S. Advisory Commission on Intergovernmental Relations [hereafter, USACIR] 1993a, 1993b; McCarthy 1995). Any power a local government has to legislate or regulate residents derives from a grant of authority from the state government. This fundamental principle of law has been accepted for the last one hundred years with only minor periods of dissension. Even when states deign to provide some authority for independent action to local governments by granting them "home rule" status, such authority is always restricted by constitutional and/or statutory limitations on what local governments can and cannot do. And while most of the work that local governments do is of a routine nature and within well established parameters of authority, every now and then local governments see the need to take action on a matter that has not yet been addressed by either state law or by other local jurisdictions in the state. In taking steps in a new direction a local government always risks being challenged on its authority to act on that issue because the action is always subject to the superseding judgment of its "creator," the state government. Thus, innovation at the local government level always includes an element of political and legal risk. How local governments approach and deal with that risk and how states respond to local governments that take such risks will be the focus of this chapter. Specifically, the chapter will examine the experience of several cities in different states that were the first or were at least among the first cities to either propose and/or adopt laws prohibiting discrimination on the basis of sexual orientation.

In two recent articles Elaine Sharp (1996a, 1996b) has made the point that relatively little attention has been given to what she calls "culture war" politics at the level of local government. Passage of local gay rights laws provides one of the key examples of such political conflict, although Sharp notes the relative dearth of political science research on such topics, the notable exception being the work by Button, Rienzo, and Wald (1994, 1997). Haeberle (1996) and Haider-Markel and Meier (1996) have also done pioneering work in the area of municipal gay rights laws. In her work Sharp mentions in passing that state governments play a role in the process of policy innovation in city governments. Button, Rienzo, and Wald, Haeberle, and Haider-Markel and Meier focus principally on social, economic, and political factors associated with adoption of gay rights ordinances, giving little or no attention to the influence of state law on a city's actions or inactions in this area. The author hopes that this study will help to illustrate that the legal relationship between city and state governments is an important factor that needs to be considered when attempting to understand the differences between how local governments approach the issue of gay rights, the nature of the specific laws that they pass, and, in some instances, the ultimate success or failure in adopting such laws.

DILLON'S RULE AND HOME RULE

Recognizing the limited power of municipalities in the United States is sometimes difficult for citizens who tend to assume that policy decisions are best made closest to where they live. After all, the idea of federalism implies that there are shared powers and reserved powers between the different levels of government in this country. But federalism refers only to the relationship between the national and state governments; the relationship between the state government and its local governments is better understood as a unitary system. Municipalities have to be chartered as corporations by the state legislature before they are empowered to exercise legal authority of any kind. In 1868 John Dillon, chief justice of the Iowa Supreme Court, crystallized previous legal thinking about the relationship between cities and states into a pithy formula that has come to be known as "Dillon's Rule." The now classic statement reads:

> In determining the question now made, it must be taken for settled law, that a municipal corporation possesses and can exercise the following powers and no others: First, those granted in express words; second, those necessarily implied or necessarily incident to the powers expressly granted; third, those absolutely essential to the declared objects and purposes of the corporation — not simply convenient, but indispensable; fourth, any fair doubt as to the existence of a power is resolved by the courts against the

corporation — against the existence of the power. (*Merriam v Moody's Executor* 1868)

Although judges in some states tried to challenge this formulation claiming that cities had some inherent powers that could not be abridged by the state, such an approach failed to become the guiding principle for any state court system (US-ACIR 1993a:34). The U.S. Supreme Court, in a 1903 case, confirmed Dillon's Rule in a majority opinion (*Atkins v Kansas* 1903), effectively removing itself from disputes over the legal and political relationship between cities and states. If a local government wanted authority to pass an ordinance on a matter not specifically mentioned in its charter, it had to seek permission from the state legislature which, if agreeable, would amend the charter to allow the ordinance to be passed.

Beginning in the 1870s, however, some states began to permit cities to draft and modify their own charters with only limited involvement by the state legislature. Often called the "home rule" movement or the "devolution of powers" principle, the purpose was to reverse the underlying assumption of Dillon's Rule by asserting that local governments had broad powers to govern unless such powers were specifically limited by the state government. Even so, the state constitutional or statutory provisions that were required to create home rule in the first place made clear that the state government still had ultimate authority over local governments since it was capable of modifying the home rule authority itself, albeit the task would be somewhat more difficult if the home rule principle were embodied in the state constitution (Pagano 1990). Additionally, the laws establishing home rule almost always include some qualifying language indicating that local authority is by no means unlimited. Phrases similar to the following can be found in most state constitutions or laws:

> The governing authority of each municipal corporation shall have legislative power to adopt *clearly reasonable* ordinances, resolutions, or regulations relating to *its* property, affairs, and local government *for which no provision has been made by general law* and *which are not inconsistent with the Constitution or any charter provision applicable thereto.* (Georgia 1994; emphasis added)
>
> A municipality which adopts a charter may exercise all legislative powers and perform all functions not expressly denied by general law or charter. This grant of powers *shall not include* the power to enact private or civil laws governing civil relationships except as incident to the exercise of an independent municipal power. (New Mexico 1994; emphasis added)
>
> A home rule borough or city may exercise all legislative powers *not prohibited by law or charter.* (Alaska 1995; emphasis added)

In other words, even in states considered to have the most liberal home rule provisions, such as Alaska, there is a limitation imposed on local government authority that is set by the state. In states like Georgia home rule is circumscribed by a number of conditions including "reasonableness" and consistency with other state laws. Thus, even in home rule cities issues are likely to arise that will result in a difference of opinion as to whether or not the local government has the authority to act. Despite the long legal tradition and general acceptance of Dillon's Rule, local governments continuously test state limitations on their power by passing ordinances or adopting enforcement strategies that are not clearly authorized by local charters (Frug 1980; Briffault 1990a, 1990b). As with other differences of opinion between governmental levels or between citizens and their government, such differences must be resolved in either a political or judicial arena, or possibly both.

GAY RIGHTS AND LOCAL GOVERNMENT

The post–World War II era has seen a number of social movements aimed at ensuring the legal and political equality of classes of people who have not historically enjoyed the same treatment afforded to nondisabled Christian white heterosexual males by the judicial and policy-making institutions of American government. Federal laws have been adopted to provide legal remedies for discrimination on the basis of race, ethnicity, religion, color, sex, and disability. The United States Congress is considering, and has considered since 1974, legislation that would prohibit some forms of discrimination against lesbians, gay men, and bisexual persons, but has yet to pass such a law. Prior to the national government passing the Civil Rights Act of 1964, a number of states had passed nondiscrimination laws of their own (Lockard 1968). And both before and after states passed nondiscrimination laws municipalities within their boundaries passed similar laws on the local level. Thus, on many occasions, persons who feel that they have been discriminated against in employment, housing, or access to public accommodations on the basis of one of the classifications found in federal law may seek recourse at the local, state, or federal levels or, in some circumstances, at some combination of all three levels.

With respect to persons who wish to pursue complaints of discrimination on the basis of sexual orientation, there are fewer or no options, depending on where the alleged discrimination took place. As of 1998 ten states plus the District of Columbia had statutes that prohibited discrimination on the basis of sexual orientation and an additional seven had executive orders that applied to state government employees. Though counts differ, somewhere in the neighborhood of 150 city and county governments have also adopted sexual orientation nondiscrimination ordinances, although the nature, scope, and extent of enforcement of such ordinances vary widely (Riccucci and Gossett 1996; Wald, Button, and Rienzo 1995). The cities and counties that have passed such ordinances are found in about 60 percent of the states; in some of those states there are many local governments with such ordinances while in other states only one city has passed a sexual orientation nondiscrimination ordinance (see table 4.1). Because of this pattern, one question that arises concerns the social and economic factors that lead a particular city to be the first city in its state to try to adopt a gay rights law, though that is not the purpose of this study. Rather, this study looks at how the relationship between the city government and the state government affects a city's willingness, strategy, and success in becoming the first local jurisdiction to adopt legislation prohibiting discrimination on the basis of sexual orientation.

APPROACH TO THE STUDY

The specific question this study seeks to address is, "How does the principle that 'cities are creatures of the state' get put into effect when a city wishes to take action in an area of law where no clear precedent for authority to act has been established?" There are two possible ways of studying this question: 1) examine a variety of situations involving different types of laws in a single state or 2) examine a particular type of law in a variety of different states. This paper will adopt the latter approach and will examine local government ordinances proposed and/or adopted to prevent discrimination on the basis of sexual orientation.

In preparing this study various sources were used to identify the first city in a state to propose or adopt a local ordinance prohibiting discrimination on the basis of sexual orientation ("Constitutional Limits" 1993). The study focused principally on incorporated municipalities, although on occasion counties or consolidated governments of some sort were the pioneers in their particular states in this field of legislation. The focus was on "first cities" because of the likelihood that the question of municipal authority to act in this area would arise almost immediately following introduction or adoption of such protections. Identifying the first city to adopt a sexual orientation nondiscrimination provision was somewhat easier than identifying the first city to propose such a law, since there are a number of organizations and/or published works that have listed cities with such laws or cities where laws have been repealed (National Gay and Lesbian Task Force [hereafter, NGLTF] 1994; Keen 1993). An effort to

TABLE 4.1.

"First City" Proposals and Adoptions of Sexual Orientation Nondiscrimination
Ordinances and Resolutions

State (states with statewide laws)	First proposal— law failed to pass, was voided or repealed‡	Date	First law adopted and Still in effect‡	Date	Municipal jurisdictions currently with laws or executive orders as of 8/98
Alabama					
Alaska	Anchorage (repealed)	1/18/93 (5/93)			
Arizona			Tucson	2/77	2 cities
Arkansas	Fayetteville (repealed by referendum)	5/6/98 (11/3/98)			1 city
California 1992			San Francisco	1972	27 cities, 5 counties; whole state
Colorado	Boulder (failed)	(6/74)	Aspen	11/77	6 cities; 1 county
Connecticut 1991			Hartford	2/79	3 cities; whole state
Delaware					
Florida	Miami/Dade repealed by referendum)	1/18/77 (6/7/77)	Key West	1991	8 cities; 2 counties
Georgia			Atlanta	3/86	2 cities; 1 county
Hawaii 1991			Honolulu	2/88	1 city; whole state
Idaho			Troy	12/93	1 city
Illinois			Champaign	7/77	5 cities; 1 county
Indiana	Bloomington (voided)	1973 (7/26/77)	Bloomington	7/8/93	3 cities
Iowa			Iowa City	4/19/77	2 cities
Kansas	Wichita (repealed by referendum)	9/27/77 (5/9/78)	Lawrence	5/2/95	1 city
Kentucky*	Louisville (failed)	(3/28/95)			1 city
Louisiana			New Orleans	12/19/91	1 city

continued

TABLE 4.1.
(Continued)

State (states with statewide laws)	First proposal— law failed to pass, was voided or repealed‡	Date	First law adopted and Still in effect‡	Date	Municipal jurisdictions currently with laws or executive orders as of 8/98
Maine			Portland	5/11/92	3 cities
Maryland**	Baltimore (failed)	1980	Baltimore	6/88	3 cities; 3 counties
Massachusetts 1989			Amherst	5/76	8 cities; whole state
Michigan			East Lansing	3/7/72	9 cities
Minnesota 1993			Minneapolis	1974	4 cities; whole state
Mississippi					
Missouri			Columbia	7/20/92	3 cities
Montana					
Nebraska					
Nevada					
New Hampshire 1997	Portsmouth (failed)	(1993)			whole state
New Jersey 1992					whole state
New Mexico*					1 city
New York	New York City (failed)	(1/7/71)	Alfred	5/74	12 cities; 3 counties
North Carolina			Chapel Hill	9/75	6 cities
North Dakota					
Ohio			Yellow Springs	11/79	8 cities; 1 county
Oklahoma	Oklahoma City (failed)	(1/95)			
Oregon			Portland	12/74	4 cities; 1 county
Pennsylvania	Philadelphia (failed)	(12/75)	Philadelphia	8/82	7 cities; 1 county

continued

TABLE 4.1.

(Continued)

State (states with statewide laws)	First proposal—law failed to pass, was voided or repealed‡	Date	First law adopted and Still in effect‡	Date	Municipal jurisdictions currently with laws or executive orders as of 8/98
Rhode Island 1995					whole state
South Carolina*					1 city
South Dakota**					1 county
Tennessee					
Texas			Austin	8/75	3 cities; 1 county
Utah**	Salt Lake City (repealed by Council)	12/97 (1/98)			1 county
Vermont 1992			Burlington	6/85	1 city; whole state
Virginia			Alexandria	10/15/88	3 cities; 1 county
Washington			Seattle	9/73	6 cities; 2 counties
West Virginia			Morgantown	9/21/93	1 city
Wisconsin 1982			Madison	7/79	2 cities; 1 county; whole state
Wyoming					

‡Only municipalities where the first known effort in that state to introduce a nondiscrimination ordinance in a local legislative body failed to pass a vote of the local legislative body, was voided by a court or a higher legislative authority, or was repealed by a voter referendum or by a vote of the legislative body that passed it originally are included in the column labeled "First proposal-law failed to pass, was voided, or repealed." In several other states municipalities have passed and have repealed nondiscrimination ordinances locally, but they were not the first jurisdiction to pass a law. In the column labeled "First law adopted and still in effect," the first municipality to adopt an ordinance that has continued to the present is listed. States with shaded boxes are those with statewide nondiscrimination laws.

*Three states have cities that have administratively adopted nondiscrimination policies covering city employees—Kentucky (Henderson), New Mexico (Albuquerque-1994), and South Carolina (Columbia-1993), but there are no cities that have adopted such policies by the vote of elected officials.

**Two states have counties that adopted nondiscrimination ordinaces before any cities in the state did—Maryland (Howard County-1974) and Utah (Salt Lake County-1992); in South Dakota Minehaha County (1979) administratively adopted a nondiscrimination policy covering county employees.

check the accuracy of information about first cities was made by contacting organizations and individuals active in promoting equal rights for lesbians and gay
men in various states. The results of the research to date can be found in table 4.1.

When a first city was identified, efforts were made to locate persons who were
familiar with the events surrounding passage or consideration of the ordinance.
Preferred persons to be interviewed were council members who had voted on
the ordinance, city attorneys who had advised the council on the ordinance,
and/or activists who had been involved in advocating for the ordinance. Contacts with Internet discussion groups and use of World Wide Web sites proved
invaluable in finding many of the people who were subsequently interviewed.
Most interviews were by telephone, after the respondent had been sent a copy
of the interview guide that I was using so that he or she could recollect thoughts,
check any personal records, or talk to others who may have been involved. The
case studies described in the sections that follow are those in which successful
contacts were made and sufficient information was provided to answer the basic
research question.

Lexis searches were conducted to identify state court decisions and attorney
general opinions that addressed the issue of local authority to pass municipal civil rights ordinances providing protection against discrimination on the basis of
sexual orientation. These searches revealed that the question of local authority
was not always raised in the context of the first city to pass such ordinances, so
some of the discussion that follows will involve cities other than first cities.

THE STUDY

Interviews and secondary research material were collected on five cases for this
multiple case study. In two other cases, New York City, New York and Dade
County, Florida, those interviewed were of the opinion that the question of their
authority to pass an ordinance prohibiting discrimination on the basis of sexual
orientation was never an issue in the debate over the ordinance (Eldon Clingan,
former New York City Council member, personal communication, July 31,
1996; Ruth Shack, former Dade County commissioner, personal communication, August 15, 1996). In written material available there is no evidence to con-
tradict their recollections. In both cases the questions raised prior to passage, and
in Miami, prior to the referendum that ultimately repealed the ordinance, focused on questions of morality and individual rights. The state governments
seem to have played little role in the early debate. Thus detailed accounts of
these cities are not provided. For the remaining cities, presented in order of the

date on which they began to address this issue, more detailed accounts of the process are provided.

Bloomington, Indiana

In 1971 the state of Indiana passed a civil rights law that, among other things, empowered municipalities to adopt parallel legislation on a local basis, including the establishment of local human rights commissions that would be capable of enforcing their local ordinances in a manner similar to the way in which the Indiana Civil Rights Commission enforced the state law. Local laws were required to be consistent with the state law, but the law also permitted localities to prohibit discrimination against groups others than those named in the state law (i.e., race, religion, color, and national origin). In the next year the city of Bloomington adopted its own Human Rights ordinance that reflected only the categories covered by the state law (i.e., race, religion, color, sex, and national origin). An incident in which city inspectors denied a building permit to a gay person simply on the grounds of that person's homosexuality led the City Council to amend its local civil rights ordinance to cover discrimination based on sexual orientation (John Irvine, former Bloomington deputy mayor, personal communication, June 13, 1996; Charlotte Zietlow, former Bloomington Common Council member, personal communication, June 17, 1996). The revised ordinance would provide the same protections for persons discriminated against on the basis of sexual orientation as were available to persons discriminated against on the more traditional grounds of race, sex, religion, and ethnicity. Two of the seven council members were opposed to the change, basing their objections principally on moral arguments. There was some community support for their opposition, but little or no support for the inclusion of sexual orientation in the law came from the community (gay or straight) and defending the amendment was left up to the council members themselves. There was not much concern about whether or not the city had authority to adopt this ordinance because of the language in the civil rights act and because recent changes in Indiana municipal law were consciously made with the idea of moving away from Dillon's Rule toward home rule.

In 1973, before the sexual orientation provision was added, a female employee of Indiana University filed a complaint with the Bloomington Human Rights Commission claiming that she had been discriminated against on the basis of sex (*Indiana University v Ieva Hartwell and the Bloomington Human Rights Commission* 1977). The Commission found for Ms. Hartwell and ordered the university to provide her back pay, to involve employees in the creation of nondiscriminatory job descriptions, and to post signs about the right to take complaints to the state and local civil rights commissions. The trial court vacated the award of back pay but allowed the nonmonetary portions of the order to stand. Both sides appealed. The university claimed that it should not be subject to the Bloomington law because it was essentially a state agency not subject to local laws and that the award was arbitrary and capricious. Ms. Hartwell and the commission wanted the back pay award upheld. Surprisingly, since neither of the parties seemed to have raised this issue, the Court of Appeals decided to review the constitutionality of the provision in the state Civil Rights Act granting extensive discretionary authority in this area to local governments in the first place. In a case of "winning while losing," the Appeals Court found, in 1977, that the law did authorize local human rights commissions to award monetary damages. However, the court found the state law so broad as to qualify as one "which in effect reposes an absolute, unregulated, and undefined discretion in an administrative agency [and] bestows arbitrary powers and is an unlawful delegation of legislative powers." As a result, the court declared that "the opinion and order of the Human Rights Commission of Bloomington in this cause is null, void, and of no effect as there exists no legitimate statutory authority for the establishment of local commission agencies." This action nullified the sexual orientation addition to the local law. Before an appeal was made to the state supreme court the state legislature amended the law to provide for the creation of local human rights commissions, carefully limiting their authority and remedies to those provided to the state civil rights commission. The city of Bloomington quickly reestablished its local ordinance and commission but no longer covered sexual orientation.

In late 1992 and early 1993, following a well-publicized incident of alleged gay-bashing, the Bloomington Human Rights Commission held hearings on the problem of antigay prejudice in the city (Steve Sanders, vice chair, Bloomington Human Rights Commission, personal communication, June 13, 1996). Frustrated by the lack of authority to include coverage for sexual orientation discrimination among the categories that were protected by the local civil rights ordinance, the commissioners, commission staff, city attorney's office, and the City Council looked for some way to officially express their concern and yet avoid an unwinnable lawsuit. Upon the recommendation of the Human Rights Commission, the council, in July 1993, quickly and unanimously adopted several amendments to the existing law, which made clear that discrimination on the basis of sexual orientation was contrary to the public policy of the city and that the commission should educate people about the problem and how to reduce prejudice. At the same time, a new section was added to the enforcement provisions making clear that the city had no authority to exercise investigatory authority or provide remedies similar to those available to victims of race, religious, or sex discrimination and would have to rely on the voluntary cooperation of disputants in sexual orientation discrimination cases. No challenges to the city's authority to act in this manner have yet been made. The City of West Lafayette has adopted a similar ordinance and the City of Richmond has rejected such a law. The Fort Wayne Metropolitan Human Rights Commission sought a legal opinion from that city's Corporation Counsel about the city's authority to pass an "enforceable" ordinance prohibiting sexual orientation discrimination but was advised that attempting to enforce such an ordinance would violate the state's exclusive authority to regulate "civil actions between private persons" (McCauley 1994).

Wichita, Kansas

Lesbian and gay activists in Wichita began to formulate the idea of a city ordinance just prior to the municipal elections held in November 1976 (Glaze 1996). Two candidates for the City Commission who had expressed some support for adopting a nondiscrimination ordinance were elected, as were two candidates who had expressed disapproval. The fifth commissioner's position was not clear. In July 1977 activists presented the City Commission with a proposed amendment to the existing nondiscrimination ordinance adding the terms "sexual or affectional preference" and "marital status" to the list of protected categories. Three special public hearings were held in which lesbian and gay activists confronted religious conservatives, the latter group being energized by the recent successful repeal of a similar ordinance in Dade County, Florida. Recall of the commissioners who had spoken in favor of the ordinance was being sought by opponents of the law. Concerns about the city's authority to act in this manner resulted in a request for a formal opinion from the state attorney general. The attorney general synopsized his findings as follows:

> If the governing body of the City of Wichita determines that discrimination on the basis of either marital status or sexual or affectional preference, as defined in the proposed amendments, constitutes an arbitrary or artificial barrier to achievement of the city's declared policy of equal opportunity in employment, housing and access to public accommodations, it is within the police power of the city to prohibit discrimination on such grounds and neither of the proposed ordinances is contrary to state law or to any declared policy of the State of Kansas. (Kansas 1997a)

The last quoted portion of the attorney general's opinion was based on a specific analysis of whether or not Kansas' sodomy law, which only prohibited homosexual sodomy, would constitute a conflicting law sufficient to prevent adoption of the sexual preference portion of the nondiscrimination ordinance. The attorney general's point was that discrimination and sodomy were two separate issues since a policy of nondiscrimination in employment, housing, and public accommodation did not legalize conduct prohibited by the state, nor would it prevent enforcement of the sodomy laws. In an opinion sought by the Topeka elections commissioner, the attorney general made clear that commissioners could only be recalled for malfeasance or felony conviction and not on the basis of policy disagreements (Kansas 1997b). This may have given some courage to Wichita commissioners as they considered their votes on the gay rights ordinance.

The city attorney recommended that the commissioners redraft the ordinance as a freestanding law rather than as an amendment to the existing law. By this time, everyone was aware that should the ordinance be adopted a challenge from opponents seeking to overturn the provision was probable. Concern that the entire civil rights statute, not just the sexual preference clause, might be in jeopardy, probably led to even the supportive commissioners agreeing to this change. On September 27, 1976, the commissioners adopted the freestanding ordinance by a 3–2 vote. With the attorney general having stated that he could see no legal impediment to Wichita adopting such an ordinance if it chose to, opponents quickly developed and circulated petitions calling upon the commission to either rescind its vote or place the issue on a ballot for voters to decide. The commission did not rescind its vote, choosing instead to hold a referendum on May 9, 1978. In one of the worst defeats for a gay rights law ever, voters supported the repeal effort by a vote of 83 percent to 17 percent. Although other attempts to pass municipal gay rights ordinances were made in Kansas, none were successful until activists in Lawrence convinced their city commission to add an amendment to the existing city human rights ordinance in 1995 ("Lawrence Gets Human Rights Ordinance" 1995).

Atlanta, Georgia

On March 3, 1986, the City Council of Atlanta passed an ordinance prohibiting discrimination on the basis of sexual orientation in city employment and applied the nondiscrimination requirement to other government activities such as selecting artists for awards and making the holding of an alcoholic beverage or taxicab license dependent on not discriminating. There was no effort to make the nondiscrimination provisions applicable to the private sector (Larry Pelle-grini, lesbian and gay rights lobbyist, personal communication, August 12, 1996). Thirteen of the seventeen members of the City Council voted in favor of the or-dinance. Six months later two of the council members who had opposed the or-dinance introduced a measure to repeal it. As one element of their argument against the law the opponents raised the question as to whether or not the Atlanta nondiscrimination ordinance was in conflict with the Georgia sodomy statute that had just been upheld two months earlier by the U.S. Supreme Court in *Bowers v Hardwick* (Green 1986). A conflict would mean that the city ordinance would be invalid. Supporters of the law obtained an opinion from the city attor-ney that stated there was no conflict between the ordinance and the sodomy statutes (McCall 1986). The vote against the repeal effort was 12–4, with one member not voting. The law then went unchallenged for nearly a decade.

In 1993 Atlanta Council member Mary Davis introduced two bills, one to create a registry for domestic partners and a second to provide benefits for the domestic partners of city employees. The votes were held on June 21, 1993, and the bill establishing a registry passed by a 14–2 (1 abstention) vote while the bill providing benefits passed on a much closer 9–7 (1 abstention) vote, with costs being the primary expressed concern of the opposing council members. May-or Maynard Jackson signed the registry bill, but he vetoed the benefits bill, cit-ing concerns about costs and the city's legal authority to act. Several days of demonstrations by lesbian and gay Atlantans followed the veto, which the council failed to override. The question over the legal authority to pass such legislation centered around two constitutional provisions that seemed in con-flict in these circumstances — one provision permitted municipalities to es-tablish benefit programs for city employees while the other forbade local gov-ernments from passing law that affected "the private or civil law affecting civil relationships, except as is incident to the exercise of an independent govern-mental power" (Georgia 1995). Many supporters of the law felt as one com-mentator wrote:

> We are angry. The mayor says the partnership ordinance may have con-flicted with state law. That is by no means certain. The courageous thing to do would have been for the mayor to stand up and say that, yes, the city believes in this concept and the city will fight for it, in court if necessary." ("With Friends Like Maynard" 1993)

The mayor apparently had his concerns addressed because, less than a month later, a slightly modified version of the benefits bill was passed on a dramatic 7–7 (2 absences) vote, which required the council chair, who only votes in case of a tie, to cast the eighth vote in favor of the bill. The mayor lobbied for its passage and signed it.

Opponents of the bill quickly announced their intentions of invalidating the bill in any way they could. One prominent opponent, State Representative Billy McKinney (D-Atlanta) promised to introduce legislation to override any city or county domestic partnership benefits legislation. McKinney, along with others including the police chief and conservative activists, filed suit against not only the domestic partnership registry and benefits ordinances but against the original nondiscrimination ordinance as well. Representative McKinney did introduce a bill in the 1994 legislative session, but the legislature never brought it out of committee, preferring to let the courts make a ruling on the question first. The bête noire of the Georgia lesbian and gay community, State Attorney General Michael Bowers, weighed in on the debate in December 1993 when, in a formal opinion to the state commissioner of insurance, he advised the commissioner not to approve any proposed health insurance policies for domestic partners of Atlanta city employees because he believed that the domestic partnership laws exceeded the city's home rule authority and were in conflict with existing state laws (Georgia 1993). Without the insurance commissioner's approval of a domestic partnership health benefits policy, the city would be stymied in its efforts to offer such benefits, although the lawsuit had put the offering of benefits on hold anyway.

In June 1994 a Fulton County Superior Court judge ruled that the domestic partnership ordinances violated the state constitution and the state home rule act, but he dismissed the case against the nondiscrimination ordinance. Both sides appealed their loss to the state Supreme Court, which rendered its decision on March 14, 1995 (*City of Atlanta v McKinney* et al 1995). The decision addressed several key questions involved in a determination of a local government's authority to act. Advocates of both laws were pleased by the court's finding that the nondiscrimination ordinances were a legitimate exercise of the city's police powers and that no state laws preempted a city's right to prevent discrimination on the basis of sexual orientation in its own workforce as a dissenting opinion claimed. Additionally, the court found that cities had been explicitly granted the right to pass local nondiscrimination laws by the Georgia Fair Employment Practices Act of 1978. With respect to the creation of a domestic partnership registry, the Supreme Court overturned the lower court by finding that the city's establishment of a registry to identify certain people who would be allowed jail and hospital visitation privileges was merely an incidental mechanism enabling it to fulfill a specifically granted authority to "operate, maintain, regulate, [and] control" local jails and medical institutions. In a ruling that pleased opponents of the laws, the court found that the city could not provide health benefits for the domestic partners of city employees because it was "beyond the city's authority to define dependents inconsistent with state law." The Supreme Court noted that the state home rule act permitted cities to provide insurance benefits for its "employees, their dependents, and their survivors" but did not include a definition of "dependent." Other laws defined dependent to include spouses, children, and persons receiving more than half of their financial support from someone else. According to the court, domestic partners failed to meet any of the existing definitions of dependent and the ordinance's attempt to define domestic partners as "family" was clearly inconsistent with state laws establishing family relationships. Undeterred by this legal setback, supporters of the domestic partnership benefits ordinance have redrafted the law in an effort to define domestic partners as dependents in a way not inconsistent with state law, thus meeting the objections of the court's majority (Atlanta 1996).

In 1997, ruling on a suit brought against the revised domestic partnership ordinance, the Georgia Supreme Court ruled that the city was in compliance with existing state law (*City of Atlanta v Morgan* 1997). Conservative legislators then introduced bills in the 1998 legislative session to revise the state's definition of "dependents" to both invalidate Atlanta's law and prevent other cities from adopting such laws (Georgia 1998). Governments in the cities of Decatur, Tybee Island, and Lithia Springs and Fulton and DeKalb Counties have adopted nondiscrimination ordinances but have not yet addressed the issue of domestic partnership benefits.

Alexandria, Virginia

Virginia is often cited in discussions of local government authority as an exception to the general trend toward greater home rule for municipalities (USACIR 1993a). When presented with the opportunity to adopt a constitutional amendment that would reduce the need for local governments to seek special local legislation every time a city wanted to make a change in its powers, local government leaders successfully resisted the change. One consequence was that Dillon's Rule remained the guiding principle for understanding the limits of local government authority, although in fact Virginia local governments had been very successful in obtaining wide grants of specific authority to act in their charters.

Alexandria, a suburb of Washington, DC, began to address the question of including sexual orientation under its nondiscrimination ordinance in 1985 (Phillip G. Sunderland, Alexandria city attorney, personal communication,

March 18, 1996). In 1984 the Alexandria Human Rights Commission submitted a report to the mayor and council entitled "Report on Discrimination Based on Sexual Orientation in the City of Alexandria." Public hearings were held on the report and a recommendation to include sexual orientation in the city's human rights ordinance was made. In preparation for council consideration of such an ordinance, the acting city manager requested a legal opinion from the city attorney, who concluded "Under Dillon's Rule, I could find no express state authority for the city to use to enact a local ordinance that would prohibit discrimination based on sexual orientation" (Alexandria 1985). Subsequently, a member of the state legislative delegation from Alexandria requested an opinion from the state attorney general on the same point. Again, by citing Dillon's Rule specifically, the attorney general declaimed that the city had no authority to expand the categories of persons protected by the local human rights ordinance (Virginia 1985). Only slightly daunted, and following the election of a new attorney general, a new legal interpretation was sought, this time focusing on whether or not the city manager could administratively establish a nondiscrimination policy that included sexual orientation for city employees and city contractors. Again the response was negative (Virginia 1986). To add variety, the Alexandria Gay Community Association sought an independent legal opinion on the city's authority to pass a nondiscrimination ordinance, referring to Dillon's Rule as a "'fine point' of Virginia law." Not surprisingly, that opinion argued for a more expansive reading of the city's charter authority along the lines of a "devolution of power" theory of local government — if the law doesn't specifically say you can't, then you can (Smith 1986). In March 1986 the Alexandria Human Rights Commission issued another report on sexual orientation discrimination based on its earlier report and the public hearings that followed. They also indicated that they had read three legal opinions on the question of authority but felt they were not in a position to make a recommendation on which view was correct. Doubting its authority to act, no ordinance was adopted by the City Council.

In 1988 a proposal to add sexual orientation to the city's human rights ordinance was introduced to the council. The amendment would apply to all types of discrimination in both the private and public sectors. The city attorney's office, which was responsible for drafting the legislation at the request of the council member introducing it, transmitted it with a memorandum that reminded the council of the previous attorney general opinions. The letter also pointed out that state law had been amended to explicitly authorize local governments' ability to "enact an ordinance, not inconsistent with nor more stringent than any applicable state law, prohibiting discrimination" (Alexandria 1988a). Nevertheless, the council proceeded to adopt the ordinance following a debate that did not raise the issue of local authority to act in this manner (Alexandria 1988b). To date, the law is still in effect, but it has not been challenged in court, so whether or not application of Dillon's Rule will render it void remains to be seen. A similar law has been adopted in Arlington County while Charlottesville and Virginia Beach have adopted ordinances prohibiting sexual orientation discrimination in city employment.

Portland, Maine

In May 1991 the City Council of Portland, upon a motion from an openly lesbian council member, voted to revise the existing nondiscrimination policy covering city employees to include sexual orientation as a protected category (Barbara Wood, former Portland City Council member, personal communication, July 29, 1996). A year later another council member, at the urging of local activists and because of the persistent failure of the state legislature to pass a statewide law prohibiting sexual orientation discrimination, proposed a local human rights ordinance. The local law would cover all of the same classifications as the Maine Human Rights Act but would also prohibit discrimination on the basis of sexual orientation. The council chose not to create a local human rights commission to handle complaints, simply providing a law enforceable by private legal action. In preparing the ordinance the council was informally advised on two specific issues by the city attorney, who in turn had been in consultation with Boston representatives of the Gay and Lesbian Advocates and Defenders (GLAD). One issue concerned the ability of the council to create a cause of private action for discriminatory acts and the second had to do with whether or not Maine's home rule law permitted the council to legislate in the area at all. In both instances the city attorney advised the council that they could pass such an ordinance. The nine-member council voted 7–1, with one absence, to adopt the ordinance in May 1992.

Almost immediately, citizens opposing the ordinance began circulating petitions calling for a referendum in Portland to repeal the council's action. Sufficient signatures were gathered, and the referendum appeared on the November 1992 ballot. The ordinance was upheld when the voters, by a margin of approximately 57 percent–43 percent, turned back the repeal effort (Keen 1993). Following upon this success, opponents of local gay rights laws sought, via the statewide referendum process, to restrict the ability of local governments to pass ordinances prohibiting discrimination on the basis of sexual orientation. Unlike the Colorado constitutional initiative, the Maine referendum did not directly refer to sexual orientation. Rather, the opponents sought to specifically preempt the ability of local governments and the state government to create protected classes other than those listed in the referendum itself. The language of the referendum read:

"Be it enacted by the People of the State of Maine as follows:
5 M.R.S.A. Section 4552-A is enacted to read:
Section 4552-A. LIMITATION OF PROTECTED CLASS STATUS
    Notwithstanding any provision of this chapter or any other provision of law, protected classes or suspect classifications under state or local human rights laws, rules, regulations, ordinances, charter provisions or policies are limited to race, color, sex, physical or mental disability, religion, age, ancestry, national origin, familial status, and marital status. Any provision of State or local law, rule, regulation, ordinance, charter provision or policy inconsistent with this section is void and unenforceable.
    This section being necessary for the welfare of the State and the inhabitants of Maine, shall be liberally construed to accomplish its purpose and is not to be interpreted or applied as a limitation or restriction on authority as enumerated in the Maine Constitution."

In May 1995, following legislative consideration of the proposed referendum in accordance with the Maine constitution, the state legislature refused to adopt the referendum's language as state law, which meant that the issue would go before the voters. Five months later, after a long and hard-fought campaign, this referendum was defeated by a popular vote of 53 percent opposed to 47 percent in favor (Ford 1995). Portland's local ordinance had withstood a second political challenge. One of the arguments in the course of the campaign against the initiative stressed the importance of local autonomy in adopting ordinances favored by local citizens. To the extent that this argument was persuasive, it had the potential effect of undercutting support for a statewide law prohibiting sexual orientation discrimination. The argument protects the right of citizens in Portland to adopt such a law and the right of citizens in Lewiston to reject a similar law, as they did in 1993, all in the name of local autonomy.

In 1997, however, opponents of the 1995 referendum (i.e., advocates of local nondiscrimination ordinances) were successful in convincing Maine state legislators to pass a statewide law prohibiting discrimination on the basis of sexual orientation that applies not only to private sector employers but to local government entities as well, essentially ignoring the earlier argument about the need for local autonomy in making decisions in this sensitive area (Maine 1997). Opponents successfully petitioned the state to require a referendum with the potential of repealing the state law. While most of the arguments against the new state law were based on the moral beliefs of opponents and fears of burdening businesses, referendum supporters also pointed out that the new law's supporters seem to have abandoned their earlier alleged support for local autonomy (Harmon 1998). In February 1998 Maine voters repealed the state law prohibiting discrimination on the basis of sexual orientation. Thus local communities are now responsible for deciding whether or not to pass such ordinances.

While the Portland ordinance has established a firm base of political support, it has yet to be tested in court. Cases have been filed under the law and settled outside of court, but none have yet come to trial (Nacelewicz 1998). A recent review of the status of home rule authority in Maine, however, suggests that recent court decisions in the state would bode well for supporters of the ordinance (Taylor and Palmer 1996). Amendments to the home rule statute in 1987 made clear that the courts should liberally interpret the home rule act as granting authority to local governments to pass ordinances — even ordinances inconsistent with state laws — provided they did not actually frustrate a state purpose.

DISCUSSION

The case study information provided allows us to address several subordinate questions that arise in attempting to answer the principal research question, "How does the principle that 'cities are creatures of the state' get put into effect when a city wishes to take action in an area of law where no clear precedent for authority to act has been established?"

1. Does the city have specific constitutional, statutory, or judicial authority to take a certain action?

A "yes" answer to this question eliminates the need for any further investigation, since, almost by definition, cities taking such actions have the authority to act. A "no" answer does not necessarily mean that the local government cannot act, even in a state that operates with a strict interpretation of Dillon's Rule, but additional questions, described below, must then be addressed.

With respect to the issue of gay rights, city charter provisions or provisions in state civil rights laws that specifically authorize local governments to adopt local civil rights laws that may be more expansive than the state law have sometimes been written. This appears to be the case with New York City and Dade County, Florida. Challenges to these actions are unlikely to be successful *unless*, as in the case of Bloomington, Indiana, it can be established that the specific grant of authority to the local government was itself unconstitutional.

More commonly, however, there is no specific grant of authority that unquestionably covers a council seeking to legislate in a new area. In traditional Dillon's Rule jurisprudence, and even in basic analysis of home rule powers ("Municipal Civil Rights Legislation" 1968), a second question raised is:

2. Do any of the powers that are granted to the city reasonably imply that they have the authority to take a particular action?

With respect to gay rights ordinances, two general powers of municipal corporations are usually analyzed when trying to determine if a local government can reasonably imply that it is empowered to act in this area. The most commonly cited power is the "police power," which gives a city the responsibility to provide for the "protection, order, conduct, safety, health and well-being" of its citizens (McQuillan 1964; Hill 1964–1965). A second, closely related, general power that is sometimes cited is the "promotion of the public welfare" power. Nondiscrimination laws are frequently seen as legitimate exercises of the police power's grant of authority to regulate behavior that may be harmful to some citizens or as a way of promoting the public's welfare. In either case, however, someone must assume the role of arbiter as to whether or not the action taken is "reasonable." As seen in the cases described, there are a number of candidates who may be willing to perform this role.

a) The council has the initial responsibility to decide whether or not its proposed action is permissible under existing laws governing the power of local governments. Many council members feel perfectly competent to make this assessment of their power independently or as a group. This may, in reality, be a nonquestion for many council members, in that it never occurs to them to even consider whether or not they have the authority to act in a particular area. Even if the question does occur, council members may not be too concerned about the possibility of having insufficient authority to act. Such confidence may stem from an assumption that it is the state's responsibility to specifically prohibit the city from acting (even if the statutes or state constitution do not require the state to be so specific) or from experience in taking actions in the past that were either upheld or went unchallenged in the past. This approach seems to have characterized members of the Portland and Atlanta city councils.

b) The council may choose to seek advice from others on whether or not it has the necessary authority. Most commonly, that advice is sought from either the city attorney or the state attorney general. If such advice suggests that the council does have authority to act, as the attorney general of Kansas did in the case of Wichita, responsibility falls back to the council to make a decision on the merits of the issue. If the advice suggests that the council does not have the authority to act, the council may choose to claim the high ground of wanting to act but being prohibited from acting by state law. A council may also choose to ignore such advice altogether, as Alexandria did, and act anyway, or it may choose to modify legislative language and substance in order to create a situation where its ability to act is not so clearly proscribed, as did Bloomington in the 1993 version of its ordinance.

c) Individuals or groups opposed to the action taken by the council may challenge the council's authority to act through a legal suit. This action then places state court judges in the role of determining whether or not the action is consistent with the authority granted to local governments under that state's laws. Because this approach relies on third-party initiation, a law may be on the books and enforced for any number of years before a judicial decision is made on whether or not the action exceeded the powers of the municipality's governing body. This type of challenge occurred in Atlanta and had mixed results in that the authority to pass a limited nondiscrimination ordinance was upheld but the action to provide domestic partnership benefits to city employees was ruled *ultra vires* (i.e., beyond the city's authority).

If it is determined that the action taken by a council did not exceed the explicit or generally implied authority of local governments, there may yet be a third question that would be considered by judicial decision makers, namely:

3. Has the state acted in any way to preempt the authority of local governments to take action in a particular field, either explicitly or implicitly?

The issue of preemption refers to whether or not the state has attempted to regulate a particular field of activity in such a way that supplementary or complementary legislation at the local level should not be allowed. In some instances state laws are explicit in either permitting or denying local governments the authority to pass legislation in a particular area. For example, local governments are not usually permitted to make criminal laws that would apply only in their own jurisdiction. On the other hand, a number of state civil rights laws specifically authorize local governments to establish local civil rights ordinances, although the allowable scope of such ordinances may not be clear. The question of preemption usually arises when attorneys are asked to advise councils on a proposed action or when someone has filed suit against an ordinance claiming that local authority has been exceeded. Once a case reaches the courts, it becomes a judge's responsibility to determine whether or not the local ordinance has been preempted by state law.

With respect to gay rights laws, the preemption question arises when the state has passed a statewide civil rights law of some sort. In the absence of any specific statement of authority granting local governments the right to pass similar legislation, the question arises as to whether the state law is a comprehensive regulatory system precluding local action or one establishing a legal framework that can be copied, complemented, or expanded upon by local ordinances. The Indiana Civil Rights Act of 1971 clearly authorized cities to pass more expansive civil rights laws than the state, although the act was ultimately ruled unconstitutional and replaced by a new law that limited cities to essentially adopting carbon copy local versions of the state law.

If it is determined that the action taken by a council was not preempted by state law, there is still a fourth question that usually must be asked, namely:

4. Does the action taken by the council impermissibly conflict with any state laws?

The issue raised by this question is whether or not the proposed local action contradicts any of the public policies made at the state level in such a way as to undercut the general purpose of the state level policy. For example, local governments may not be allowed to pass laws that lower state-established standards of regulation, although they may be able to strengthen them. Nor may the local government be allowed to permit some activity that is specifically prohibited by the state. The question becomes a little more complex, often calling for legal advice or adjudication, when the local government policy and the state government policy are not addressing exactly the same issue.

With respect to gay rights laws, there are two particular ways in which the conflict question tends to be raised. One is when there is a statewide law governing civil rights and, while the preemption question may be resolved in the municipality's favor, the interpretation is that the local government cannot have a law that provides any greater or different protections than the state, whether in terms of categories protected, types of discrimination prohibited, procedures for resolving complaints, or penalties for violations of the ordinance. Virginia has done this by stating that local civil rights ordinances cannot be "more stringent" than the state law. The second way in which the conflict question comes up applies to states that still have sodomy laws on the books. Specifically, the question is whether or not there is a conflict between guaranteeing protection against discrimination for a class of people who are, in the public's mind at least, defined by the fact that they violate a state law. This was of specific concern to some of the Wichita commissioners and some Atlanta council members.

Dillon's Rule, the principle that local governments are created by the state government and have only those powers granted to them, whether granted in the form of an affirmative listing of specific powers or provided in a negative manner through a home rule law that identifies limitations on local authority, is still an important consideration when trying to understand innovation at the local level. In examining the experience of cities that attempted to pass laws prohibiting discrimination on the basis of sexual orientation, one can view a wide range of options available to the state for exercising control over local governments. The legal interpretation of the state's relationship with its municipalities can be a critical element in understanding the nature of the political debate over a "new" issue like gay rights, the choice of language and scope of legislation when formulating specific proposals, and, in some cases, the ability of the local government to adopt any law at all. In fact, in many instances, it may be a primary consideration before looking at the more traditional social, economic, and political factors political scientists traditionally turn to in efforts to explain policy variations across political jurisdictions, as Dorris does in chapter 3 of this volume. Those factors may be appropriate in studies of state policy innovation because legally all states have the same relationship to the federal government (Gray 1973; McCrone and Cnudde 1968; Nice 1994), but in local government comparisons attention must first be given to the legal context in which the local legislative body must act. Further, not only are there fifty different sets of laws governing the powers and activities of municipalities, but within each state there may be laws governing different classes of cities enabling some, but not others to take initiative in this matter (Washington 1981; USACIR 1993a).

Sharp (1996b) is correct in her call for more data with which to study local government activity in areas of culture war policy. But an important piece of data that needs to be collected, whether discussing culture war issues, economic development activities, or any other governmental activity that occurs at the local level, is how state law may limit or prohibit local action. Like other variables, this one is not constant over time or place. State laws change; city charters change; legal opinions change; court interpretations of existing laws change. All these changes mean that what served as an explanation for action or inaction at one time may no longer be applicable at another time. This is a formidable challenge for researchers, one that encourages team projects with researchers in several different locations and one that will lead to a better understanding of local level political obstacles and opportunities to being policy innovators. For activists who wish to secure greater legal protection from discrimination, the lesson from this study is that Dillon's Rule is not necessarily a permanent obstacle to the achievement of those ends but merely one of many with which they must reckon.

REFERENCES

Alaska. 1995. *The Constitution of the State of Alaska*, Article 10, Section 10.11.

Alexandria. 1985. Memorandum from Cyril D. Calley, Alexandria city attorney, to Vola Lawson, acting city manager, May 3.

—— 1988a. Memorandum from Philip G. Sunderand, Alexandria city attorney, and Nancy A. McBride, assistant city attorney, to mayor and members of the City Council, October 3.

—— 1988b. City Council of Alexandria, Ordinance No. 3328, October 15.

Atkins v Kansas. 1903. 191 U.S. 207, 220–1.

Atlanta. 1996. City Council Bill 96–0–1018, June 17.

Briffault, Richard. 1990a. "Our Localism: The Structure of Local Government Law." Part 1. *Columbia Law Review* (January 1990), 90:1–115.

Briffault, Richard. 1990b. "Our Localism: The Structure of Local Government Law." Part 2. *Columbia Law Review* (March 1990), 91:346–454.

Button, James W., Barbara A. Rienzo, and Kenneth D. Wald. 1994. "The Politics of Gay Rights in American Communities." Paper presented at the Annual Meeting of the American Political Science Association, New York City.

—— 1997. *Private Lives, Public Conflicts: Battles over Gay Rights in American Communities.* Washington, DC: Congressional Quarterly Press.

City of Atlanta v McKinney et al. 1995. 454 S.E.2d 517 (Ga. 1995), March 14. Available: 1995 Ga. LEXIS 151.

City of Atlanta v Morgan. 1997. 492 S.E.2d 193 (Ga. 1997), November 3. Available: 1997 Ga. LEXIS 708.

"Constitutional Limits on Anti-Gay-Rights Initiatives." *Harvard Law Review* (June 1993), 106:1905–1925.

Dorris, John. 1999. "Antidiscrimination Laws in Local Government: A Public Policy Analysis of Municipal Lesbian and Gay Public Employment Protection." Chapter 3, this volume.

Ford, Royal. 1995. "Bid to End Gay Rights Protection Defeated Amid Voter Signup Flap." *Boston Globe*, November 8.

Frug, Gerald E. 1980. "The City as a Legal Concept." *Harvard Law Review* 93:1057–1154.

Georgia. 1993. Attorney General Opinion 93–26, December 10.

—— 1994. *Official Code of Georgia Annotated*, Section 36–35–3(a).

—— 1995. *Constitution of the State of Georgia*, Article IX: Counties and Municipal Corporations, rev. ed.

—— 1998. General Assembly, Senate, SB 435–98.

Glaze, Douglas. 1996. "1978: A History of the Wichita Gay Rights Ordinance." Unpublished master's thesis, Washburn University, Topeka, Kansas.

Gray, Virginia. 1973. "Innovation in the States." *American Political Science Review* 67:1174–1185.

Green, Connie. 1986. "Two on Council Seek Repeal of Gay Law." *Atlanta Constitution*, September 5, p. A19.

Haeberle, Steven H. 1996. "Gay Men and Lesbians at City Hall." *Social Science Quarterly* 77:190–197.

Haider-Markel, Donald P. and Kenneth J. Meier. 1996. "The Politics of Gay and Lesbian Rights: Expanding the Scope of Conflict." *Journal of Politics* 58:332–349.

Harmon, M. D. 1998. "Campaign Against 'People's Veto' Turns Down and Dirty." *Portland Press Herald*, January 12.

Hill, Donald R. 1964–1965. "Power of a Municipal Corporation to Enact a Civil Rights Ordinance." *Washburn Law Journal* 4:128–144.

Indiana University v Ieva Hartwell and the Bloomington Human Rights Commission. 1977. 174 Ind. App. 325.

Kansas. 1977a. Attorney General Opinion No. 77–247, August 4.

—— 1997b. Attorney General Opinion No. 77–252, August 5.

Keen, Lisa. 1993. "Right-Wing Racks Up the Victories." *Washington [DC]*, November 12, p. 24.

"Lawrence Gets Human Rights Ordinance." 1995. *Lawrence News-Telegraph*, May 12–25, n.p.

Lockard, Duane. 1968. *Toward Equal Opportunity: A Study of State and Local Antidiscrimination Laws*. New York: Macmillan.

McCall, Nathan. 1986. "Council Refuses to Repeal Law Protecting Gays." *Atlanta Constitution*, p. A12.

McCarthy, Joseph F., Jr. 1995. *Local Government Law in a Nutshell*, 4th ed. St. Paul, MN: West.

McCauley, J. Timothy, Fort Wayne corporation counsel. 1994. Letter to Daniel J. Holocher, executive director, Fort Wayne Metropolitan Human Relations Commission, March 25.

McCrone, Donald J. and Charles F. Cnudde. 1968. "On Measuring Public Policy." In Robert E. Crew, Jr., ed., *State Politics*, pp. 523–530. Belmont, CA: Wadsworth.

McQuillan, John P. 1964. "Municipal Fair Employment Ordinances as a Valid Exercise of the Police Power." *Notre Dame Law Review*, pp. 607–613.

Maine. 1997. *Maine Statutes* 5§4552.

Merriam v Moody's Executor. 1868. 25 Iowa 164, 170.

"Municipal Civil Rights Legislation — Is the Power Conferred by the Grant of Home Rule?" 1968. *Minnesota Law Review* 53:342–357.

Nacelewicz, Tess. 1998. "Same Debate, Larger Scale for Gay Rights." *Portland (ME) Press Herald*, February 7.

National Gay and Lesbian Task Force. 1994. *Lesbian, Gay, and Bisexual Civil Rights in the U.S.* New York: National Gay and Lesbian Task Force.

New Mexico. 1994. *New Mexico Constitution*, Article X, Section 6.D.

Nice, David C. 1994. *Policy Innovation in State Government*. Ames: Iowa State University Press.

Pagano, Michael. 1990. "State-Local Relations in the 1990s." *Annals of the American Academy of Political and Social Science* 509:101.

Riccucci, Norma M. and Charles W. Gossett. 1996. "Employment Discrimination in State and Local Government: The Lesbian and Gay Male Experience." *American Review of Public Administration* 26:175–200.

Sharp, Elaine B. 1996a. "Culture Wars and City Politics: Local Government's Role in Social Conflict." *Urban Affairs Review* 31:738–758.

—— 1996b. "Culture Wars and the Study of Urban Politics." *Urban News: Newsletter of the Urban Politics Section/APSA* 10:1–10.

Smith, Jonathon M., Esq., 1986. Letter to James Clark, spokesman, Alexandria Gay Community Association, February 18.

Taylor, G. Thomas and Kenneth T. Palmer. 1996. "Home Rule and State Government in Maine." Paper presented at the annual conference of the American Society for Public Administration, Atlanta, GA, July.

U.S. Advisory Commission on Intergovernmental Relations (USACIR). 1993a. *Local Government Autonomy: Needs for State Constitutional, Statutory, and Judicial Clarification.* Washington, DC: ACIR.

U.S. Advisory Commission on Intergovernmental Relations (USACIR). 1993b. *State Laws Governing Local Government Structure and Administration.* Washington, DC: ACIR.

Virginia. 1985. Letter from Attorney General William G. Broaddus to State Senator Wiley F. Mitchell, September 18. Available: 1985 Va. AG LEXIS 157.

—— 1986. *1985–1986 Opinions of the Attorney General of Virginia,* No. 119, June 6. Available: 1986 Va. AG LEXIS 119.

Wald, Kenneth D., James W. Button, and Barbara A. Rienzo. 1995. "Where Local Laws Prohibit Discrimination Based on Sexual Orientation." *PM: Public Management* 77:9–14.

Washington [State]. 1981. Opinion of the Attorney General No. 14, October 5. Available: 1981 Wash. AG LEXIS 11.

"With Friends Like Maynard, Who Needs Enemies." 1993. *Southern Voice* [Atlanta], July 8, p. 8.

Zimmerman, Joseph F. 1995. *State-Local Relations: A Partnership Approach,* 2d ed. Westport, CT: Praeger.

CHAPTER FIVE

Elite Attitudes Toward Homosexuals

Jean Reith Schroedel

Gays and lesbians should get help. Don't tell me about genes and someone is born that way NOT CONVINCING. If that's true then they could be taken care of like someone born with a heart murmur or other medical problem.

— COUNTY COMMISSIONER AND POLITICAL INDEPENDENT

We should try to teach our children what is right. There should be a mother and a father figure. Not that it's wrong if you're gay but we are losing our American family life and values.

— REPUBLICAN SCHOOL BOARD MEMBER AND SELF-DESCRIBED HOUSEWIFE

American society has undergone enormous social changes over the past several decades, which makes it crucial to update the research examining elite levels of tolerance toward homosexuals. Forty years ago, when the first studies of political tolerance were being performed, engaging in a consensual homosexual act was a felony in all fifty states. Since then half the states have repealed, or the courts have declared unconstitutional, the criminal statutes dealing with consensual acts of oral or anal intercourse by same sex couples and at least 126 cities and counties have enacted gay rights laws or policies (Button, Rienzo, and Wald 1997).[1]

Although one might consider these acts to be prima facie evidence of increasing tolerance toward homosexuals, efforts to expand gay rights have triggered a sharp backlash. For example, Klawitter and Hammer (chapter 2, this volume) found evidence that antigay interest groups and religiously based opposition to gay rights can halt or slow the diffusion of local antidiscrimination ordinances. The 1992 passage of a statewide referendum banning civil rights protection for lesbians and gay men in Colorado is the most obvious example of the success of antigay rights activists in reversing the trend toward greater political and social acceptance for homosexuals. According to Herman (1997:138), the passage of Amendment 2 in Colorado was the result of nearly two decades of antigay organizing by the Christian right and it is being replicated throughout the country.[2] The increasingly important role of conservative Christians in the political arena and the growth of the New Right may have resulted in the creation of a segment of the political elite extremely opposed to the extension of civil liberties to homosexuals.[3] For these reasons it is unclear whether the overall trend is toward greater or lesser levels of elite political tolerance vis-à-vis gay men and lesbians.

In this project I will focus on two basic questions: 1) whether the demographic and social factors identified by early political tolerance researchers can be used to predict attitudes of political elites toward homosexuals; and 2) to what extent elite beliefs about the applicability of general democratic principles to homosexuals are affected by the context within which the actions occur.

HOMOSEXUALITY AND POLITICAL TOLERANCE

Although the public visibility of lesbians and gay men has increased dramatically over the past several decades, prejudicial attitudes continue to be widespread. Public opinion surveys designed to measure the degree of political tolerance accorded unpopular groups, such as Klan members, neo-Nazis, Communists, and homosexuals, typically measure respondents' general support for democratic principles and then examine their willingness to extend those principles to different disliked groups. These studies have consistently shown that gay men and lesbians are among the least liked groups in American society. Over the past fifteen years General Social Survey responses to a question on whether homosexual relations were always wrong, almost always wrong, sometimes wrong, or not wrong have remained stable with 70–75 percent indicating that it was always or almost always wrong (Rand National Defense Research Institute [hereafter, Rand] 1993).[4] Responses to National Election Studies (NES) provide another indication of the level of public antipathy. Sherrill (1993) in his examination of NES data found that no other group generated as many negative feelings as did homosexuals. For example, in 1988 35 percent of respondents gave gay men and lesbians a score of zero (the most negative score available on the NES scale). The total percentage of respondents holding negative feelings toward homosexuals was far greater than that of any other social grouping (Sherrill 1993:97–98).

Despite the prevalence of negative attitudes toward gay men and lesbians, these feelings are not equally prevalent in all sectors of the populace. A range of demographic and social factors (e.g., education, political ideology, party affiliation, religion, and biological sex) are related to respondents' attitudes toward homosexuals. In the past scholars (Gibson and Tedin 1988; Herek 1991) have found a strong positive correlation between political tolerance toward homosexuals and years of formal education. Political ideology and partisan affiliation also are correlated with attitudes toward homosexuals. Conservatives, as well as Republicans, typically exhibit lower levels of tolerance than do liberals and Democrats (Rand 1993; Button, Rienzo, and Wald 1997). Gibson and Tedin (1988) found that individuals who self-identified with the New Right movement felt far more threatened by homosexuality than did other citizens.[5] Although none of the mainstream Christian sects are supportive of homosexuality, fundamentalist Protestants are generally far more opposed to homosexuality than are other Protestants and Catholics (Nice 1988; Britton 1990; Haider-Markel and Meier 1996; Wald, Button, and Rienzo 1996; Button, Rienzo, and Wald 1997). Conversely, very high levels of political tolerance are typically found among Jews (Rand 1993). Women also tend to have more favorable attitudes toward gay men and lesbians than do men (Kite 1984; Herek 1984, 1988, 1993).

The relationship between social and demographic factors and levels of political tolerance within the general populace is explored in the chapters by Haeberle (chapter 7) and Lewis and Rogers (chapter 6) in this volume. Haeberle's analysis of public support for the passage of federal legislation prohibiting employment discrimination against gays and lesbians and for ending discrimination toward openly gay individuals in the military showed that gender, education levels, political ideology, party identification, and religious affiliation continue to be potent predictors of attitudes toward extending full political rights to lesbians and gay men. Lewis and Rogers use public opinion data from 1977–1993 to analyze changes in the level of support for the hiring of lesbians and gay men in a range of specific occupational categories. They also found these social and demographic factors could be used to predict attitudes about equal employment rights for homosexuals.

Other researchers (Nunn, Crockett, and Williams 1978; Chanley 1994; Riggle and Ellis 1994) have posited that the degree of political tolerance accorded a particular group is affected by three additional factors: 1) support for the general democratic principle involved; 2) the target population to whom the principle is being applied; and 3) the contextual situation. Riggle and Ellis (1994), in their comparison of student attitudes toward homosexuals, members of the Ku Klux Klan, and neo-Nazis, focused on the first and second of these factors. They found that for groups like the Ku Klux Klan and neo-Nazis the respondent's level of support for the general principle was the sole determinant of the applicability in each situation but for lesbians and gay men attitudes toward homosexuals, as well as support for the general principle, influenced its applicability.

The emphasis in this research is on the final component, the situational context, because it is possible that attitudes toward gay men and lesbians also vary enormously according to the specific situation within which a general democratic principle is being applied. For example, I would expect there to be higher levels of support for equal employment rights when gays are being considered for jobs as salesclerks than when they are seeking employment as primary school teachers.

THE ROLE OF ELITES IN FOSTERING POLITICAL TOLERANCE

In his pioneering work, *Communism, Conformity, and Civil Liberties*, Stouffer found significantly higher levels of political tolerance among elites than among the general public. Stouffer (1955) attributes greater political tolerance among community leaders to their understanding of the threat to democratic rights of denying civil liberties to despised groups. Based on this finding, Stouffer argues that elites play a critical role in educating the public about the importance of respecting the civil liberties of all in order to preserve a democratic form of government. Although McClosky (1964) found much higher levels of political tolerance among the elite sample, other researchers (Jackman 1972; Nunn, Crockett, and Williams 1978) found that much of the difference between elites and the general public disappears when controls for additional factors, most notably education levels, are included in the research design.

However, McClosky and Brill (1983), in their analysis of public opinion data and elite surveys, present evidence indicating that the gap between levels of political tolerance expressed by elite and public samples cannot simply be attributed to differences in education. Although education was usually associated with increased political tolerance, McClosky and Brill found this was not true for conservatives, who had absorbed an alternative set of values that are not always hospitable to civil liberties (1983:422).

As Gibson and Bingham (1985:17) note, there are conditions under which elite-directed repression occurs. The conditions occur regularly and, because elites have superior resources, motivations, and access to political power, the consequences for the maintenance of democracy are great. In subsequent research Gibson (1988) demonstrated that government repression of Communists during the McCarthy era was the result of intolerant attitudes among elites rather than among the mass public. Although both the mass public and elites held intolerant attitudes in the 1950s, the latter considered the issue of Communism to be far more politically salient. Elites, responding to the perceived threat posed by Communists within society, were responsible for the development of repressive policies designed to curtail the civil liberties of individuals suspected of Communist Party affiliations.[6]

As previously noted, the degree of social and political acceptance accorded lesbians and gay men appears to have increased dramatically over the past quarter of a century. It is, however, unclear whether the repeal of criminal sodomy statutes and the enactment of gay rights laws in many localities can be attributed to greater mass and elite tolerance toward this sector of the populace, given that public opinion polls continue to show that homosexuals are among the least liked groups in the country. Moreover, these advances have triggered a powerful backlash. Because political elites play a crucial role in formulating public policies (both policies that extend and those which restrict civil liberties), it is crucial to determine the current degree of political tolerance among elites toward homosexuals. This research project is designed to answer these questions by focusing on the impact of demographic and social factors on elite tolerance toward gay men and lesbians and the degree to which elite support for the applicability of democratic principles to homosexuals is context specific.

DATA COLLECTION AND METHODOLOGY

In order to answer these questions I conducted a national survey of state and local elected officials. Unlike previous research, which examined attitudes toward many different groups, this project focused solely on attitudes toward gay men and lesbians, which meant that far more detailed information about elite levels of political tolerance toward homosexuals in a variety of different contexts could be obtained. The survey instrument included background questions designed to elicit information about the social, political, and demographic characteristics of respondents as well as questions designed to assess general levels of political tolerance toward homosexuals and questions about the applicability of these democratic principles to a range of specific situations involving gay men and lesbians.

The survey was mailed to six hundred elected officials serving in state legislatures, county and municipal offices, and on local school boards.[7] Because financial and time constraints made it impractical to survey officeholders from all fifty states, I chose the following twelve states: Arizona, California, Florida, Georgia, Indiana, Iowa, Maryland, Michigan, New Hampshire, New Jersey, Oregon, and Virginia. These states were chosen because they encompass the broadest possible range of diversity in terms of geographic regions, political culture, legality of sodomy, presence or absence of openly gay elected officials, and whether the New Right had recently attempted to enact antigay ordinances.

Although it was quite easy to compile a list of state legislators in each of the twelve states, it was more difficult to identify all city and county elected officials and school board members. The National League of Cities, the National Association of Counties, and various government officials helped in this effort. Because there is no master list of school board members from throughout the country, we contacted the state school board organizations in the twelve states. Some of these organizations had membership lists for the local boards in their states. In the remaining states each local school district was contacted separately to obtain lists of their members.

To obtain a sample comprised of 200 state legislators, 200 city and county elected officials, and 200 school board members, I used systematic sampling techniques to identify survey recipients in each category of political office.[8] Because some of the people had died or were no longer in office, the actual sample turned out to be 582 rather than 600. The initial surveys were mailed in the late fall of 1994. Follow-up mailings and telephone calls continued into the spring of 1995. Useable responses were received from 220, or 38 percent of the elected officials.

There are two possible sources of potential bias in the group that chose to respond to the survey. First, some survey recipients refused to participate because they believed it was being done to further the homosexual agenda. Some even wrote that they were offended by receiving smut in the mail (i.e., the survey) and included comments about the purported sexual orientation of the researchers. For example, a Republican school board member wrote, "This survey seems to be slanted and pro-homosexual (bias oriented). This seems to have been prepared by a homosexual or a pro-homo." A political independent serving as county commissioner in a large urban area wrote, "I will not give my name for you to use against me. This is probably coming from the gay rights movement. Claremont Graduate School is made up of gay rights movement staff and students." One person even sent an obscene drawing depicting the researcher engaged in a sexual act. Second, despite trying to get roughly equal proportions of the three categories of officeholders, responses were received from 83 school board members, 78 county and municipal officeholders, and only 59 state legislators. Quite a few of the latter group wrote or called to say that they were fed up with being asked to fill out surveys and would no longer do so.

Although it is risky to speculate about the impact of possible sample bias, there are reasons to believe that the average nonrespondent to this survey is less tolerant than the average respondent. The language used by the first category of nonrespondents was very hostile, in some cases bordering on paranoid. To some degree this may be counteracted by the second group of nonrespondents, state legislators. Although it is difficult to make predictions with any certainty about the attitudes of nonresponding state legislators toward gay men and lesbians, the mere fact that they serve in state legislatures rather than local communities increases the likelihood of their being more broadly exposed to democratic norms and principles.[9]

The remainder of the chapter is devoted to an analysis of the responses of the elected officials. Because this is the first in-depth study of the attitudes of elected officials toward homosexuality, a fair amount of attention is paid to basic patterns of responses, primarily derived from cross tabulations. More sophisticated statistical techniques, including logit, regression analysis, and ANOVA, are used to explain the overall impact of demographic and social factors on the levels of political tolerance that these elected officials believe should be accorded gay men and lesbians within different social contexts.

Because previous researchers have found gender, party identification, educational levels, ideology, and religious affiliation to be related to political tolerance, this study will focus on their relationship to elite attitudes. The political ideology variable was measured by a five-point ordered scale ranging from very conservative to very liberal, with the former coded as 0 and the latter as 4. Gender is dichotomous, with male coded as 0 and female as 1. Education attainment was measured by a four-point ordered scale with 0 = high school degree or less, 1 = some college, 2 = college degree, and 3 = graduate/professional degree. Political party affiliation was coded as 0 = Republican, 1 = independent, and 2 = Democrat. Religious affiliation was also measured by a four-point ordered scale, based on the social conservatism of the denominations, with Protestants coded as 0, Catholics as 1, Jews as 2, and those without religious affiliation as 3.

OVERALL LEVELS OF POLITICAL TOLERANCE

The survey included three broad categories of questions assessing levels of political tolerance: 1) a question designed to probe respondents' attitudes toward homosexual relationships; 2) questions that broadly address whether these general democratic principles should apply to gay men and lesbians; and 3) narrower questions dealing with the applicability of those principles to specific situations involving homosexuals. In presenting the results for each question, a summary of the overall character of responses will be presented first. When methodologically appropriate that will be followed by a discussion of statistical models designed to show the causal relationships between different variables.

On all the questions the elite sample's responses were more accepting of gays and lesbians than were those given in public opinion polls using the same language. On some questions the elite sample was far more tolerant than the general public. The elite group was nearly twice as tolerant as the general public on questions about the morality of homosexual relationships. This is consistent with previous research showing that elites tend to be more socially and politically tolerant than the general public.

When asked, Do you personally think that homosexual relationships between consenting adults are morally wrong or not a moral issue? just over 40 percent answered "morally wrong," while just under half said it was not a moral issue. Because responses to the survey question about the morality of homosexual relationships required a "yes" or "no" response, it was possible to create a logit model incorporating the demographic and social factors previously identified as important predictors of attitudes toward homosexuality.[10] The dependent variable is whether respondents answered "yes" or "no" to the question about the morality of homosexual relationships. The independent variables are the respondent's gender, level of educational attainment, party identification, political ideology, and religious affiliation. In this particular model only the latter two independent variables were significant.

Although the R-square measure used in regression cannot be used to evaluate the overall performance of models with dichotomous dependent variables, early goodness-of-fit measures (e.g., Cox and Snell's and Nagelkerke's pseudo R-squares) developed for use in logit analysis turned out to be unreliable; they also do not provide natural interpretations of how well the overall model performs.[11] The percentage of correctly predicted responses is often used as an alternative, but it has its own problems. While intuitively appealing and easily understood, the percentage correctly predicted is misleading because it does not compare the model's performance to the null hypothesis (i.e., chance). This model correctly predicted nearly three-quarters of the responses to the morality question. To determine whether this was substantially better than results achieved due to chance, two additional statistical measures, Lambda-p and Goodman and Kruskal's Tau-c, were calculated. Although the statistical assumptions are somewhat different, Lambda-p and Kruskal's Tau-c measure the model's proportional reduction in error over the null hypothesis.[12] Both showed that the model performed far better than would be randomly expected by chance. The Lambda-p statistic showed a proportional reduction of error of .52 and the Goodman and Kruskal's Tau-c statistic was .66. See table 5.1 for a summary of the results.

The survey included two broad questions designed to measure whether respondents believed that democratic principles should apply to homosexuals.

TABLE 5.1.

Logit Models of Elite Beliefs About Homosexuality and Democratic Rights

Variables	Morality	Legalization	Civil Rights
Education	.188	.483*	.036
	(.182)	(.191)	(.179)
Ideology	1.202***	.727**	.971***
	(.275)	(.282)	(.248)
Party	.044	.181	.196
	(.203)	(.230)	(.203)
Religion	.672*	.480*	.461*
	(.212)	(.219)	(.171)
Gender	−.077	−.142	.119
	(.418)	(.479)	(.398)
Intercept	−2.802	−2.012	−2.378
N Size	184	156	183
Correct Pred	75%	74%	73%
Lambda-p	.52	.39	.23
G/K Tau-c	.66	.57	.62

Note: Table entries are logit coefficients with standardized errors in parentheses. *** indicates $p = .001$, ** indicates $p = .01$, and * indicates $p = .05$.

The most general of these questions asked, Do you think homosexual relations between consenting adults should or should not be legal? Slightly more than half (51.2 percent) indicated that homosexual relations should be legal, with just over one in four indicating they should not be legal. A logit model using the five demographic and social variables was used to predict favorable and unfavorable responses to the question. Educational attainment, political ideology, and religious affiliation were significant. Again, the model correctly predicted nearly three-quarters of the responses. More important, it resulted in a proportional reduction of error of 39 percent according to Lambda-p and a Goodman and Kruskal's Tau-c of .57, both of which indicate a substantial improvement over the null hypothesis. The results are summarized in table 5.1.

On the second general democratic principles question, Do you think that laws which protect the civil rights of racial or religious minorities should be used to protect the rights of homosexuals? respondents were almost equally divided: 44.8 percent supported and 44.3 percent opposed their use. A logit model, using the same set of predictor variables, was able to correctly predict nearly 73 percent of responses. Respondents' political ideology and religious affiliation accounted for most of the model's predictive ability. Although the Lambda-p proportional reduction in error was lower than in the previous models (only .23), the Goodman and Kruskal's Tau-c score was .62. See table 5.1 for a summary of results.

THE IMPACT OF CONTEXT ON SUPPORT FOR APPLYING DEMOCRATIC PRINCIPLES TO HOMOSEXUALS

In order to measure the support for the applicability of democratic norms to homosexuals in different contexts, a series of questions designed to measure support for equal employment rights for homosexuals, both as a general principle and when applied to different occupations, were included in the survey. The first question was designed to identify the degree of support for the general principle, In general, do you think that homosexuals should or should not have equal rights in terms of job opportunities? A substantial majority (80.5 percent) supported equal employment rights and only 11.2 percent were opposed. However, when applied to different occupational categories the responses were markedly different. The degree of support dropped in five of the seven cases where respondents were asked to consider specific categories of employment (Do you think homosexuals should or should not be hired for each of the following occupations?) Favorable responses ranged from: 92.7 percent for salespersons to 62 percent for the armed forces.[13] These results are summarized in figure 5.1.

In order to understand the reasons for the differential responses, I created logit models for each of the seven occupational categories. The dependent variable

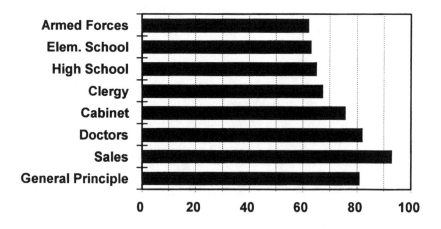

FIGURE 5.1. Equal Employment for Gays

TABLE 5.2.

Logit Models of Elite Beliefs About Equal Employment for Homosexuals

Variables	General Principle	Sales	Doctors	Cabinet	Clergy	High School	Elem School	Armed Forces
Education	.203	.566	.940***	.381	.267	.238	.272	.162
	(.238)	(.319)	(.245)	(.209)	(.187)	(.191)	(.192)	(.190)
Ideology	.693*	.978*	.512	.481	.656*	.765**	.642	.750**
	(.338)	(.498)	(.332)	(.316)	(.262)	(.268)	(.261)	(.262)
Party	.291	.257	.299	.725**	.208	.497*	.614*	.488*
	(.283)	(.390)	(.272)	(.264)	(.214)	(.218)	(.216)	(.214)
Religion	.272	.914	.384	.680*	.529*	.463*	.463*	.448*
	(.283)	(.714)	(.310)	(.314)	(.224)	(.214)	(.207)	(.204)
Gender	.251	−.374	.303	.622	.481	.153	.003	.777
	(.621)	(.795)	(.601)	(.566)	(.453)	(.449)	(.439)	(.454)
Intercept	.064	−.275	−1.475	−1.467	−1.533	−1.915	−1.999	−2.051
N Size	181	160	159	159	165	165	164	167
Correct Pred	88%	94%	85%	81%	75%	78%	75%	73%
Lambda-p	.77	.87	.67	.57	.43	.42	.38	.35
G/K Tau-c		.59	.68	.65	.60	.69	.65	.60

Note: Table entries are logit coefficients with standardized errors in parentheses. *** indicates $p = .001$, ** indicates $p = .01$ and * indicates $p = .05$. It was impossible to calculated the Goodman and Kruskal's Tau-c because of a 0 in the numerator during the final step for the General Principle Model.

in each model is whether respondents believed that homosexuals should or should not be hired for the particular job. The same group of demographic and social factors are used as predictors in the models. Although the mix of statistically significant variables was different in each of the models, all found a strong relationship between social and demographic factors and the level of support for equal employment for homosexuals. Somewhat surprisingly, the gender variable was not a significant predictor in any of the models. In contrast, the ideology variable reached significance in five of the seven occupational categories. Although the models varied in the percentage of responses correctly placed, all placed an extremely high percentage (73 percent to 94 percent). The lambda-p scores were impressive, ranging from .35 to .87, and the Goodman and Kruskal's Tau-c scores were equally strong, ranging from a low of .59 to a high of .69. On the basis of these results it is clear that these social and demographic factors explain a large amount of the variance in elite attitudes about whether the general principle of supporting equal employment rights should be applied to gay men and lesbians in different occupational categories. The results are summarized in table 5.2.

Because respondents' attitudes toward employment rights for homosexuals in the different occupations are interrelated, I developed an additive scale designed to measure overall levels of support for extending employment rights to lesbians and gay men. The scale was created by awarding points for each occupation that a respondent believed homosexuals should be allowed to perform. Because respondents had scores that ranged from 0 to 7 rather than being limited to a dichotomous (0,1) choice, it was possible to perform a regression analysis with the additive scores as the dependent variable and the social and demographic variables as predictors. As can be seen in table 5.3, the regression model explains just over a quarter of the variance. Although all the coefficients had the expected signs, only the political ideology, religion, and party identification variables had significant coefficients.

THE RELATIONSHIP OF EDUCATION, IDEOLOGY, AND PARTY TO POLITICAL TOLERANCE

Although scholars disagree over the extent to which higher levels of elite political tolerance can be explained by educational attainment as measured by years

TABLE 5.3.
Regression Analysis of Elite Support for Extending Employment Rights Homosexuals

Variables	Coeffients	t Scores	Significance
Education	.241	1.370	.173
	(.176)		
Ideology	.625**	2.891	.004
	(.216)		
Party	.500*	2.451	.015
	(.204)		
Religion	.386*	2.164	.032
	(.178)		
Gender	.283	.739	.461
	(.383)		
Intercept	2.648	5.534	.000
R-Square .28			
Adjusted R-Square .25			

Note: The table entries are regression coefficients with standardized errors in parentheses. *** indicates significance = .001, ** indicates significance = .01; and * indicates significance = .05.

of formal schooling or whether social learning outside the classroom has an independent effect, no one disputes the importance of formal education in fostering political tolerance. However, McClosky and Brill (1983) found some evidence of the existence of a subset of highly educated conservative elites who are willing to accept some infringements on civil liberties in order to preserve social order. This section examines whether previous researchers are correct in positing a strong positive relationship between educational attainment and political tolerance. It also examines whether political ideology (particularly conservatism) has an independent effect on levels of political tolerance. Because the principal difference between the two major political parties is their degree of liberalism versus conservatism, I also consider the relationship between party identification and political tolerance in this section.

On every political tolerance survey question there was a direct positive correlation between increased formal education and levels of political tolerance. A general linear model (or ANOVA) reveals that education is an important factor in the morality question.[14] As education levels increased, the percentage of respondents considering homosexual relationships to be morally wrong declined (e.g., 60.9 percent high school education, 53.4 percent of those with some college, 39.1 percent of those with college degrees, and 32.9 percent of those with postgraduate education). These results also hold up for questions concerning the legalization of homosexual relationships and the use of civil rights laws to protect the rights of homosexuals. In the latter two questions, however, there is a sharp split between those with high school degrees or some college and those with college or professional degrees. For example, on the legalization question the favorable percentages of those with high school education and some college were 30.4 percent and 31.0 percent, respectively, as opposed to 58.3 percent and 62.5 percent for respondents with college and postgraduate degrees. Only on the question about extending civil rights laws to homosexuals did ANOVA show that the differences among the sample means were not statistically significant at the .05 level. The ANOVA results are summarized in table 5.4.

Likewise, support of equal employment opportunities for homosexuals, both as a general principle and in specific applications, increased as education levels increased. In the case of the general principle there was a sharp split in support between those with high school degrees (59.1 percent) and those with some or more college (with 80 percent or higher levels of support). When support for the general principle was compared to that accorded the various occupational categories, support for equal employment opportunities drops off most dramatically and consistently for those with a high school education; support also drops off for respondents with some college, but not as dramatically. Support among those with college degrees and postgraduate degrees drops off for four of the seven oc-

TABLE 5.4.

Relationship Between Educational Attainment and Elite Levels of Political Tolerance Toward Homosexuals

Models	Source	Summary of ANOVA Models				
		Sum of Squares	df	Mean Square	F	Significance
Morality	Between groups	2.619	3	.873	3.637	.014
	Within groups	44.407	185	.240		
	Total	47.026	188			
Legalization	Between groups	3.958	3	1.319	6.450	.001
	Within groups	31.703	155	.205		
	Total	35.660	158			
Civil Rights	Between groups	1.015	3	.338	1.354	.258
	Within groups	45.733	183	.250		
	Total	46.749	186			
Employment	Between groups	.567	3	.189	1.764	.156
	Within groups	19.604	183	.107		
	Total	20.171	186			
Sales	Between groups	.802	3	.267	4.142	.007
	Within groups	10.320	160	.064		
	Total	11.122	163			
Doctors	Between groups	4.926	3	1.642	13.415	.001
	Within groups	19.586	160	.122		
	Total	24.512	163			
Cabinet	Between groups	2.481	3	.827	4.747	.003
	Within groups	27.703	159	.174		
	Total	30.184	162			
Clergy	Between groups	3.144	3	1.048	5.055	.002
	Within groups	34.409	166	.207		
	Total	37.553	169			
High School	Between groups	2.646	3	.882	4.048	.008
	Within groups	36.177	166	.218		
	Total	38.824	169			
Elem School	Between groups	3.271	3	1.090	4.964	.003
	Within groups	36.243	165	.220		
	Total	39.515	168			
Armed Forces	Between groups	1.809	3	.603	2.617	.053
	Within groups	38.483	167	.230		
	Total	40.292	170			

cupational categories, but not as much as for those with lower education levels. The only job for which support was higher than general support at all levels of education was salesperson. The ANOVA results provide additional corroboration that educational levels are related to support for equal employment opportunities for lesbians and gay men. Although differences in the mean support for the general question did not reach the .05 cutoff level, they were highly significant with respect to six of the seven occupational categories. Perhaps the principle of equal employment rights has been so deeply inculcated within society that it is extremely difficult even for highly intolerant individuals to register opposition to it as a general social norm. The ANOVA results are presented in table 5.4.

A clear relationship was found between political ideology and political tolerance toward homosexuals. On all the questions political conservatism was inversely related to political tolerance for homosexuals. For example, the percentages indicating that homosexual relationships among consenting adults were "morally wrong" are as follows: 86.7 percent of the very conservative group, 55.2 percent of the conservative group, 39.5 percent of moderates, 13.3 percent of liberals, and 0 percent of the very liberal group. This pattern of having a big drop off between the very conservative and conservative groups was not replicated on the other questions. Instead, on the questions about the legalization of homosexual relationships and the extension of civil rights protections to lesbians and gay men there was a much bigger gap between self-identified conservatives and moderates than between the very conservative and conservative groups. For example, on the civil rights question only 13.3 percent and 18.8 percent, respectively, of individuals who placed themselves in the very conservative and conservative categories supported applying these laws to homosexuals, but clear majorities of self-described moderates, liberals, and very liberal individuals favored it: 54.5 percent, 71.0 percent, and 90.0 percent, respectively.

Only 21.4 percent of the most conservative group favored legalization of homosexual relationships, as opposed to 33.3 percent of conservatives, 54.8 percent of moderates, 80.0 percent of liberals, and 81.8 percent of the very liberal group. Individuals who self-identified as very conservative or conservative had even lower levels of support for using civil rights laws to protect the rights of homosexuals, 13.3 percent and 18.8 percent, respectively. In contrast, clear majorities of those whose ideological orientations were moderate, liberal, or very liberal favored the use of civil rights laws to protect the rights of gay men and lesbians: 54.5 percent, 71.0 percent, and 90.0 percent, respectively.

ANOVA models were used to assess the strength of the relationship between political conservatism and political tolerance for homosexuals. In every case the differences in means was highly significant ($p < .001$), providing very strong support for the proposition that political conservatism is inversely related to tolerance toward homosexuals. The ANOVA models are presented in table 5.5.

Despite the previously mentioned high overall levels of support for the principle of equal employment rights for homosexuals, only a minority of those who classified their political ideology as very conservative felt this principle should apply to gay men and lesbians. Only 40.0 percent of the very conservative group as opposed to 70.5 percent of conservatives, 87.2 percent of moderates, 93.1 percent of liberals, and 90.9 percent of the very liberal group supported equal employment rights for lesbians and gay men. For each of the seven occupational categories the percentages indicating that gay men and lesbians should be allowed to work in the job was positively correlated to increasing degrees of political liberalism. For example, only 20 percent of the very conservative group believed that gay men and lesbians should be allowed as members of the clergy, but that figure increased to 55.8 percent for conservatives, 69.0 percent for moderates, 88.0 percent for liberals, and 100 percent for very liberal respondents. The ANOVA models again provide corroboration for this finding. See table 5.5 for the results of the general linear models.

These results give credence to McClosky and Brill's argument that some on the far right exhibit less concern for specific civil liberties than for the values and institutions associated with law and order and tradition, social stability, national security, and conventionality (McClosky and Brill 1983:422). Although one must be hesitant about generalizing based on a relatively small sample (n = 15), I did find some evidence for the development of a highly educated group of extremely conservative individuals who were willing to trade civil liberties for unpopular groups against the goals of preserving social order. Nearly half (47.1 percent) of respondents classifying themselves as very conservative had college degrees or advanced graduate degrees.

There also were stark differences between the levels of political tolerance espoused by Democrats, Republicans, and political independents. On the general question about the morality of homosexual relationships, Democrats and Republicans gave very different responses. Although a majority (53.6 percent) of Republicans labeled homosexual relationships among consenting adults as "morally wrong," only 30.2 percent of Democrats agreed. The response of political independents was nearly identical to that of Republicans; 53.3 percent classified homosexual relationships as "morally wrong." However, on other questions the pattern was somewhat different, with Democrats exhibiting the greatest degree of political tolerance, independents in an intermediate position (albeit somewhat closer to the Republican position than the Democratic one), and Republicans markedly less tolerant occurring again on the question that involved

TABLE 5.5.

Relationship Between Political Ideology and Elite Levels of Political Tolerance
Toward Homosexuals

| Models | Source | Summary of ANOVA Models | | | | |
		Sum of Squares	df	Mean Square	F	Significance
Morality	Between groups	11.218	4	2.804	2.804	.001
	Within groups	35.591	183	.194		
	Total	46.809	187			
Legalization	Between groups	5.619	4	1.405	7.182	.001
	Within groups	29.926	153	.196		
	Total	35.544	157			
Civil Rights	Between groups	10.304	4	2.576	12.864	.001
	Within groups	36.445	182	.200		
	Total	46.749	186			
Employment	Between groups	1.715	4	.429	4.207	.003
	Within groups	18.441	181	.102		
	Total	20.156	185			
Sales	Between groups	.544	4	.136	2.033	.092
	Within groups	10.572	158	.067		
	Total	11.117	162			
Doctors	Between groups	1.556	4	.389	2.682	.034
	Within groups	22.922	158	.145		
	Total	24.479	162			
Cabinet	Between groups	3.844	4	.961	5.741	.001
	Within groups	26.280	157	.167		
	Total	30.123	161			
Clergy	Between groups	5.194	4	1.298	6.603	.001
	Within groups	32.250	164	.197		
	Total	37.444	168			
High School	Between groups	7.076	4	1.769	9.174	.001
	Within groups	31.622	164	.193		
	Total	38.698	168			
Elem School	Between groups	6.659	4	1.665	8.294	.001
	Within groups	32.716	163	.201		
	Total	39.375	167			
Armed Forces	Between groups	7.817	4	1.954	9.973	.001
	Within groups	32.331	165	.196		
	Total	40.147	169			

the legalization of homosexual relationships. Again, the ANOVA models strongly support the descriptive statistics that there is a significant partisan difference in the degree of political tolerance accorded homosexuals. These results are summarized in table 5.6.

Although substantial majorities of Democrats, Republicans, and independents favor the general principle of equal employment opportunity for homosexuals, this is one area where the responses of independents resemble those of Democrats rather than Republicans. Almost 90 percent (89.4 percent) of Democrats and 86.7 percent of independents agree with the statement that homosexuals should have equal rights in terms of job opportunities, but only 69.6 percent of Republicans do. On questions about whether homosexuals should be hired to perform specific types of jobs, independents staked out a middle position, albeit usually closer to Democrats. With the exception of the question about serving in the armed forces, the positions of political independents were closer to that of Democrats than Republicans. In some cases there was virtually no difference between Democrats and independents. Again, the ANOVA models provide corroboration of these findings. See table 5.6 for a summary of the ANOVA models using the questions about hiring homosexuals for specific types of employment.

THE RELATIONSHIP OF RELIGION AND GENDER TO POLITICAL TOLERANCE

Both the descriptive statistics and ANOVA models based on the results of the elite surveys confirm earlier studies showing that religious affiliation is closely tied to attitudes toward homosexuality. In general, Protestant survey respondents were somewhat less tolerant of homosexuality than were Catholics, but Jews were far more accepting. On the general question about the morality of homosexual relationships, 51.3 percent of Protestants, 40.4 percent of Catholics, and only 9.1 percent of Jews considered the relationships to be "morally wrong."[15]

This pattern was replicated on the questions about whether homosexual relationships should be legalized and whether civil rights laws should be used to protect the rights of homosexuals. More than 40 percent (42.5 percent) of Protestants, 44.2 percent of Catholics, and 100 percent of Jews came out in favor of legalization. On the question about extending civil rights protection to gay men and lesbians, the differences between Protestants and Catholics were more pronounced, with 34.5 percent of Protestants as opposed to 48.1 percent of Catholics

TABLE 5.6.

Relationship Between Party Identity and Elite Levels of Political Tolerance
Toward Homosexuals

Models	Source	Summary of ANOVA Models				
		Sum of Squares	df	Mean Square	F	Significance
Morality	Between groups	3.611	2	1.806	7.767	.001
	Within groups	42.545	183	.232		
	Total	46.156	185			
Legalization	Between groups	3.398	2	1.699	8.193	.001
	Within groups	32.146	155	.207		
	Total	35.544	157			
Civil Rights	Between groups	4.750	2	2.375	10.431	.010
	Within groups	40.987	180	.228		
	Total	45.738	182			
Employment	Between groups	.689	2	.345	3.465	.033
	Within groups	17.901	180	.099		
	Total	18.590	182			
Sales	Between groups	.360	2	.180	2.895	.058
	Within groups	9.893	159	.062		
	Total	10.253	161			
Doctors	Between groups	1.464	2	.732	5.337	.006
	Within groups	21.667	158	.137		
	Total	23.130	160			
Cabinet	Between groups	5.048	2	2.524	16.627	.001
	Within groups	23.983	158	.152		
	Total	29.031	160			
Clergy	Between groups	2.967	2	1.483	7.324	.001
	Within groups	33.213	164	.203		
	Total	36.180	166			
High School	Between groups	6.224	2	3.112	16.134	.001
	Within groups	31.632	164	.193		
	Total	37.856	166			
Elem School	Between groups	7.368	2	3.684	19.236	.001
	Within groups	31.217	163	.192		
	Total	38.584	165			
Armed Forces	Between groups	6.691	2	3.346	16.920	.001
	Within groups	32.824	166	.198		
	Total	39.515	168			

supporting the action. Over 80 percent (81.8 percent) of Jews favored applying civil rights laws to homosexuals.

Not surprisingly, the ANOVA models provided strong support for the argument that religious affiliation is a significant determinant of whether respondents believe that democratic principles and protections should apply to gay men and lesbians. On all these questions the likelihood that the sample means came from the same population was .001 or less. These results are summarized in table 5.7.

High levels of support for the general principle of equal employment opportunity were found in all three groups, but, again, the Protestants (75.7 percent) were the lowest, followed by Catholics, (84.0 percent) and then by Jews (100 percent). Sharp differences, however, appeared when the respondents were asked to apply this principle to the hiring of homosexuals for specific types of work. Although most respondents were willing to have homosexuals employed as salespersons, some Protestants (11.4 percent) and Catholics (5.3 percent) did not believe they should even be hired for these positions. For every occupational category Jews were the most willing to accord homosexuals equal rights in terms of employment opportunity. In fact, the only category where Jewish respondents did not universally support the employment of homosexuals was the armed forces. Protestants in every case were the least tolerant. In several cases Protestants were almost equally divided between allowing homosexuals to be hired and opposing their employment.

In general, the ANOVA models support the contention that religious affiliation affects respondents' willingness to support the rights of homosexuals to perform a range of occupations. Probably because the overwhelming majority of all respondents support the hiring of gay men and lesbians as salesclerks, there was no statistically significant difference between the sample means (i.e., could not disprove the hypothesis that they came from the same general population.) For all the other categories of employment the chances of the means coming from the same population was unlikely. These results are presented in table 5.7.

This research provided limited support for earlier findings showing women to be more tolerant of homosexuals than men. Although the responses of women on all questions were more favorable toward homosexuals than those given by men, the differences on several of the questions were relatively modest. For example, on the general question of whether homosexual relationships are morally wrong, 44.4 percent of men as opposed to 33.9 percent of women believed they were. The gender gap was even narrower on the question about legalization of homosexual relationships, where 50 percent of male respondents and 55.2 percent of female respondents favored legalization. The difference was

TABLE 5.7.
Relationship Between Religion and Elite Levels of Political Tolerance
Toward Homosexuals

| Models | Source | Summary of ANOVA Models | | | | |
		Sum of Squares	df	Mean Square	F	Significance
Morality	Between groups	6.111	4	1.528	6.870	.001
	Within groups	40.698	183	.222		
	Total	46.809	187			
Legalization	Between groups	4.022	4	1.006	4.881	.001
	Within groups	31.522	153	.206		
	Total	35.544	157			
Civil Rights	Between groups	4.900	4	1.225	5.328	.001
	Within groups	41.848	182	.230		
	Total	46.749	186			
Employment	Between groups	.690	4	.173	1.605	.175
	Within groups	19.466	181	.108		
	Total	20.156	185			
Sales	Between groups	.345	4	.086	1.267	.285
	Within groups	10.771	158	.068		
	Total	11.117	162			
Doctors	Between groups	1.417	4	.354	2.427	.050
	Within groups	23.062	158	.146		
	Total	24.479	162			
Cabinet	Between groups	2.426	4	.607	3.438	.010
	Within groups	27.697	157	.176		
	Total	30.123	161			
Clergy	Between groups	3.544	4	.886	4.286	.003
	Within groups	33.900	164	.207		
	Total	37.444	168			
High School	Between groups	4.999	4	1.250	6.082	.001
	Within groups	33.699	164	.205		
	Total	38.698	168			
Elem School	Between groups	5.205	4	1.301	6.207	.001
	Within groups	34.170	163	.210		
	Total	39.375	167			
Armed Forces	Between groups	3.644	4	.911	4.118	.003
	Within groups	36.503	165	.221		
	Total	40.147	169			

more pronounced on the question about extending civil rights protection to gay men and lesbians, which generated a gender gaps of sixteen points. The ANOVA models generated very similar results. The ANOVA model examining the relationship between sex and the legalization of homosexual relationships did not find a statistically significant difference between the means of the samples. Nor did the model analyzing the morality of homosexual relationships. Only the ANOVA model analyzing responses to the civil rights question found significant differences between sample means. See table 5.8.

The analysis of gender impact on equal employment rights for lesbians and gay men is quite similar. Women were somewhat more likely than men to support the general principle of equal employment opportunity applying to homosexuals, but the gender gap was relatively narrow (i.e., 8.5 points). Although both groups had virtually identical responses (93 percent versus 93.9 percent marking "Yes") to the question of whether homosexuals should be hired as salespersons, there were differences on the other questions about the suitability of homosexuals for specific jobs. The largest difference was on the question about the military, where only 55 percent of males and 80 percent of females thought that homosexuals should be able to serve and the smallest (5.5 points) was on whether homosexuals should be allowed as doctors. The ANOVA models were completely consistent with results of the descriptive analysis; these are summarized in table 5.8.

DISCUSSION OF FINDINGS

This research shows that the demographic and social characteristics previously identified as related to the public's level of political tolerance toward homosexuals are related to attitudes among the political elites in this sample. But the strength of those relationships varied, depending upon the particular demographic/social factor and the question being analyzed. Across nearly the entire range of questions there was less of a relationship between sex than was found with the other four demographic and social variables.

Education was associated with increased levels of political tolerance. By far the lowest levels of political tolerance occurred among respondents whose education did not extend beyond high school. Although each incremental increase in educational attainment was associated with an increase in political tolerance vis-à-vis homosexuals, the increase was not equally large on all questions. Also the largest increases occurred at different points in the educational process.

As expected, there was a positive relationship between liberalism and politi-

TABLE 5.8.

Relationship Between Gender and Elite Levels of Political Tolerance
Toward Homosexuals

| | | Summary of ANOVA Models | | | | |
Models	Source	Sum of Squares	df	Mean Square	F	Significance
Morality	Between groups	.807	1	.807	3.264	.072
	Within groups	46.220	187	.247		
	Total	47.026	188			
Legalization	Between groups	.272	1	.272	1.208	.273
	Within groups	35.388	157	.225		
	Total	35.660	158			
Civil Rights	Between groups	1.040	1	1.040	4.207	.042
	Within groups	45.709	185	.247		
	Total	46.749	186			
Employment	Between groups	.197	1	.197	1.823	.179
	Within groups	19.974	185	.108		
	Total	20.171	186			
Sales	Between groups	.010	1	.001	.145	.145
	Within groups	11.112	162	.069		
	Total	11.122	163			
Doctors	Between groups	.133	1	.133	.881	.349
	Within groups	24.380	162	.150		
	Total	24.512	163			
Cabinet	Between groups	.986	1	.986	5.438	.021
	Within groups	29.198	161	.181		
	Total	30.184	162			
Clergy	Between groups	1.041	1	1.041	4.789	.030
	Within groups	36.512	168	.217		
	Total	37.553	169			
High School	Between groups	.700	1	.700	3.086	.081
	Within groups	38.123	168	.227		
	Total	38.824	169			
Elem School	Between groups	.452	1	.452	1.932	.166
	Within groups	39.063	167	.234		
	Total	39.515	168			
Armed Forces	Between groups	2.292	1	2.292	10.195	.002
	Within groups	38.00	169	.225		
	Total	40.292	170			

cal tolerance toward homosexuals. The relationship held up across the entire range of questions, which indicates that measures of political ideology at least as they relate to gay rights can be characterized as a single continuum, with conservatism at one end and liberalism at the other. Probably the most interesting finding was that on some questions there is a big difference between those who consider themselves to be very conservative and those who classify themselves simply as conservative, while on other questions the largest gap is between conservatives and moderates. In contrast, on all questions there were only minimal differences between the responses of those who label themselves very liberal and those self-identifying as liberal.

Not surprisingly, there were distinct differences between Democrats and Republicans, with the former recording significantly higher levels of support for homosexual rights than the latter. The most interesting finding with regard to party identification involved those who consider themselves to be independents. On questions involving equal employment, aside from the one about serving in the armed forces, the responses of political independents were nearly indistinguishable from those given by Democrats. But on questions about the morality of homosexual relationships, the legalization of those relationships, and the use of civil rights laws to protect the rights of lesbians and gay men, the responses of independents were closer to those of Republican identifiers.

As expected, attitudes toward homosexuality were related to religious identification. Although Protestants were less tolerant on every dimension than were Catholics, the biggest difference was between these two groups and Jewish identifiers, who were far more tolerant than the others. On many questions there were differences of forty points or more between the responses of Protestants and those of Jews. Although these findings might lead one to conclude that intolerance toward homosexuality is more strongly rooted in Christianity than in Judaism, that interpretation could be spurious. It fails to consider the high levels of education, political liberalism, and adherence to the Democratic Party found among Jews.

There was also evidence of a gender gap, albeit a somewhat limited one. On most questions women were ten to fifteen percentage points more tolerant than men, but the difference between male and female respondents to the question about homosexuals serving in the armed forces was twenty-five points. Gender was not a significant predictor in any of the logit models, nor in the regression model. The ANOVA models also revealed that gender differences were not nearly as strongly related to attitudes toward homosexuality than were the other social and demographic variables as predictors.

Probably the most important finding of this research is that elite political tolerance toward homosexuals varies, both according to the democratic principle being invoked and the specific context within which the principle is being applied. For example, there was very strong support for the principle of equal employment opportunity for homosexuals across all social and demographic groups, but far lower support for the legalization of homosexual relationships, which can be viewed as basically a privacy issue. Moreover, high levels of support for a general democratic principle do not necessarily translate into support for its application in different contexts. Many respondents who favored equal employment opportunity in the abstract did not favor its application in some situations (e.g., homosexuals in the military, as elementary school teachers, etc.).

Although any conclusions about why some democratic principles garner far higher levels of support than others and which contextual factors lead to a rejection of a general principle would have to be considered speculative at this time, I do have some thoughts about areas that future researchers might want to examine. Most scholars believe that social learning plays an important role in inculcating democratic norms within society. The civil rights struggle of African Americans over the past forty years has forced the American people as a whole to undergo an enormous amount of social learning about the importance of extending basic democratic rights to all citizens. Many suspect that levels of support for those democratic principles that figured prominently in the civil rights struggle are far higher than for ones that were not of primary importance. That could explain why this study consistently found much higher levels of support for the principle of equal employment opportunity than for the legalization of homosexual relationships.

Social learning could also play an important role in explaining why support for principles varies according to the specific context. Much of the opposition to gays and lesbians serving in the armed forces could be related to congressional testimony and media accounts about how soldiers and sailors would be uncomfortable taking showers with homosexuals. After all, if the fear is simply that a homosexual might see you naked, one might expect there to be high levels of opposition to homosexuals being hired as doctors, but that was not the case. In a similar vein, fears about homosexuals preying on children have figured prominently in campaigns against gay rights over the past quarter of a century and could explain the opposition to their being hired as elementary school teachers.

Finally, it is worth remembering that elites are key disseminators of cultural values and norms within a society. If, as this research suggests, there is an enormous difference between the level of respect that very conservative elites have for democratic principles and that espoused by conservative, moderate, liberal, and very liberal elites, then there are reasons for concern. Despite the general evidence that political tolerance increases with levels of education, this research points toward a different pattern when it comes to the most conservative sector of elected officials. I would encourage researchers to explore more fully the role of political elites in purveying values (both democratic and authoritarian) to the broader society.

NOTES

The author would like to express appreciation to the Fletcher Jones Foundation and the G. E. Bradshaw Foundation for their financial support. I would also like to thank Bruce Snyder, Daniel Jordan, Pamela Fiber, Erik Root, and Gordon Babst for their research assistance. I also am very appreciative of the suggestions made by the editors and the outside reviewers. These comments resulted in substantial changes and improvements in the chapter.

The epigraphs to this chapter are handwritten statements by a couple of the elected officials who responded to our survey of attitudes toward homosexuality. They are typical of the many additional comments scribbled on the sides and margins of surveys that were sent back to us.

1. In 1961 Illinois became the first state to decriminalize oral or anal sexual acts. Eight years later Connecticut became the second state to do so. In the 1970s an additional twenty states also decriminalized these acts. In 1983 and 1993 Wisconsin and Nevada followed suit. Kentucky's supreme court found their criminal sodomy statute unconstitutional.

2. For a history of the Christian right's involvement in creating an antigay backlash throughout the country, see Herman (1997).

3. Although libertarians typically exhibit high levels of political tolerance toward lesbians and gay men, adherents to the other two main conservative intellectual traditions strongly condemn homosexuality. Conservatives whose views are primarily influenced by Straussianism and natural law theory believe that homosexuality is a perversion that undermines civilization. See for example, Jaffa (1990). The other strand of conservative thinking derives its positions on gay political rights from traditional Christian prohibitions on homosexuality. See Howe (1998) for a recent example of fundamentalist Christian writing on the issue.

4. One needs to exercise extreme caution in interpreting the public opinion data on attitudes toward homosexuality. Responses to general questions, such as those asked by the General Social Survey, have fluctuated very little, but responses to more narrowly worded questions have shifted considerably. For example, a Gallup poll found that when people were asked if homosexuality was an "unacceptable lifestyle" only 57 percent concurred, and 44 percent believed that homosexual acts between consenting adults should be illegal (Hugick 1992).

5. According to Marcus, Sullivan, Theiss-Morse, and Wood (1995), the reasons why some people perceive actions as threatening while others do not perceive the same actions as threatening has long been an unanswered question within the political tolerance literature. In grappling with this question the authors found that subjects are

more likely to perceive actions as threatening when they are told to rely on their emotional responses rather than on intellectual deliberations. Negative emotions, such as fear and hostility, were particularly likely to trigger intolerant responses.

6. See also Gibson's (1989) research on politically repressive policies during the Vietnam War era.

7. It is important to recognize that the operational definition of elites in this project is narrower than that used by previous researchers, who included community influentials (i.e., clergy, press, lawyers, judges, and university officials) as well as elected officials in their sample of elites. See, for example, the discussion by McClosky and Brill (1983) on pages 25–29.

8. A systematic sample is very similar to a random sample but is easier to execute. A random starting point is chosen and then every nth unit is selected for inclusion in the sample. The nth unit is obtained by dividing the population size by the desired sample size (Williamson, Karp, and Dalphin 1977:114–115).

9. Although it would be desirable to systematically compare the social and demographic characteristics of survey respondents with those of nonrespondents, that is not possible. Party identification is generally one of the easier characteristics to ascertain, but that is not true for local elected officials. All school board races are nonpartisan, as are a significant proportion of other electoral contests at the local level. An examination of the presumed gender of nonrespondents, based on their first names, showed that male survey recipients were less likely than female survey recipients to respond. Those from the South were also less likely to respond. Since males and Southerners typically are less tolerant of homosexuality, their overrepresentation in the nonresponding group would tend to indicate that the sample is biased and more favorable toward gays and lesbians than the entire class of state and local elected officials from which it is drawn.

10. Logit analysis, which uses the logarithm of the odds that a particular outcome will occur, is superior to ordinary least squares regression when the probabilities of the dependent variable fall within the (0,1) interval (Kennedy 1979:36; Bohrnstedt and Knoke 1994:332–337).

11. For a summary of the econometric literature on early goodness-of-fit measures for qualitative response models, see Ameniya (1981) and Greene (1983:651–653.)

12. Goodman and Kruskal's Tau-c is a better measure of the goodness-of-fit when the responses are skewed.

13. Lewis and Rogers, in chapter 6, this volume, present the results of public opinion polls measuring support for equal job opportunities for homosexuals in five of the seven occupational categories (salespersons, armed forces, doctors, clergy, and elementary school teachers) that are included in this project. For each occupational category the elite survey respondents were more supportive of allowing the employment of homosexuals. The differences in support range from five points on the serving in the military question to twenty-nine points on the question about whether homosexuals should be allowed to be physicians.

14. Analysis of variance is a statistical test used to determine whether there are significant

differences between sample means, which is used to estimate the likelihood of significant differences within the corresponding populations. See Bohrnstedt and Knoke (1994:121–137) for a good introduction to the procedure.

15. One weakness of the survey instrument is that it did not ask respondents to list their denominational affiliation. This failure may mask very significant differences within the Protestant category, which encompasses socially liberal denominations, such as Episcopalians, as well as very conservative ones, such as Southern Baptists. The survey instrument included an "other" category, which asked respondents to specify religious affiliation.

REFERENCES

Ameniya, Takeshi. 1981. "Qualitative Response Models: A Survey." *Journal of Economic Literature* 19:1483–1536.

Bohrnstedt, George W. and David Knoke. 1994. *Statistics for Social Data Analysis*, 3d ed. Itasca, IL: Peacock.

Britton, Dana M. 1990. "Homophobia and Homosociality: An Analysis of Boundary Maintenance." *Sociological Quarterly* 31:423–439.

Button, James W., Barbara A. Rienzo, and Kenneth D. Wald. 1997. *Private Lives, Public Conflicts: Battles Over Gay Rights in American Communities*. Washington, DC: Congressional Quarterly Press.

Chanley, Virginia. 1994. "Commitment to Political Tolerance: Situational and Activity-Based Differences." *Political Behavior* 16:343–363.

Gibson, James L. 1988. "Political Intolerance and Political Repression During the McCarthy Red Scare." *American Political Science Review* 82:512–529.

—— 1989. "The Policy Consequences of Political Intolerance: Political Repression During the Vietnam War Era." *Journal of Politics* 51:13–35.

Gibson, James L. and Richard D. Bingham. 1985. *Civil Liberties and Nazis: The Skokie Free-Speech Controversy*. New York: Praeger.

Gibson, James L. and Kent L. Tedin. 1988. "Etiology of Intolerance of Homosexual Politics." *Social Science Quarterly* 69:587–604.

Greene, William H. 1983. *Econometric Analysis*, 2d ed. New York: MacMillan.

Haider-Markel, Donald P. and Kenneth J. Meier. 1996. "The Politics of Gay and Lesbian Rights: Expanding the Scope of the Conflict." *Journal of Politics* 58:332–349.

Herek, Gregory M. 1984. "Beyond Homophobia: A Social Psychological Perspective on Attitudes Toward Lesbians and Gay Men." *Journal of Homosexuality* 10:1–21.

—— 1988. "Heterosexuals' Attitudes Toward Lesbians and Gay Men: Correlates and Gender Differences." *Journal of Sex Research* 25:451–477.

—— 1991. "Stigma, Prejudice, and Violence Against Lesbians and Gay Men." In John C. Gonsiorek and James D. Weinrich, eds., *Homosexuality: Research Implications for Public Policy*. Newbury Park, CA: Sage.

—— 1993. "On Prejudice Toward Gay People and Gays as Security Risks." In Marc

Wolinsky and Kenneth Sherrill, eds., *Gays and the Military.* Princeton: Princeton University Press.

Herman, Didi. 1997. *The Antigay Agenda: Orthodox Vision and the Christian Right.* Chicago: University of Chicago Press.

Howe, Richard G. 1998. *Homosexuality in America: Exposing the Myths.* Charlotte, NC: Issachar Institute.

Hugick, Larry. 1992. "Public Opinion Divided on Gay Rights." *Gallup Poll Monthly* (June), 321:2–6.

Jackman, Robert W. 1972. "Political Elites, Mass Publics, and Support for Democratic Principles." *Journal of Politics* 34:753–773.

Jaffa, Harry V. 1990. *Homosexuality and the Natural Law.* Claremont, CA: Claremont Institute.

Kennedy, Peter. 1979. *A Guide to Econometrics.* Cambridge: MIT Press.

Kite, M. E. 1984. "Sex Differences in Attitudes Toward Homosexuals: A Meta-Analytic Review." *Journal of Homosexuality* 10:69–81.

McClosky, Herbert. 1964. "Consensus and Ideology in American Politics." *American Political Science Review* 58:361–382.

McClosky, Herbert and Alida Brill. 1983. *Dimensions of Tolerance: What Americans Believe About Civil Liberties.* New York: Russell Sage Foundation.

Marcus, George E., John L. Sullivan, Elizabeth Theiss-Morse, and Sandra L. Wood. 1995. *With Malice Toward Some: How People Make Civil Liberties Judgments.* New York: Cambridge University Press.

Nice, David C. 1988. "State Deregulation of Intimate Behavior." *Social Science Quarterly* 69:203–211.

Nunn, Clyde A., Harry J. Crockett, Jr., and J. Allen Williams, Jr. 1978. *Tolerance for Nonconformity: A National Survey of Changing Commitment to Civil Liberties.* San Francisco: Jossey-Bass.

Rand National Defense Research Institute. 1993. *Sexual Orientation and U.S. Military Personnel Policy: Options and Assessment.* Santa Monica: Rand.

Riggle, Ellen D. and Alan L. Ellis. 1994. "Political Tolerance of Homosexuals: The Role of Group Attitudes and Legal Principles." *Journal of Homosexuality* 26:135–147.

Sherrill, Kenneth. 1993. "On Gay People as a Politically Powerless Group." In Marc Wolinsky and Kenneth Sherrill, eds., *Gays and the Military.* Princeton: Princeton University Press.

Stouffer, Samuel. 1955. *Communism, Conformity, and Civil Liberties.* New York: Doubleday.

Wald, Kenneth D., James W. Button, and Barbara A. Rienzo. 1996. "The Politics of Gay Rights in American Communities: Explaining Antidiscrimination Ordinances and Policies." *American Journal of Political Science* 40:1152–1178.

Williamson, John B., David A. Karp, and John R. Dalphin. 1977. *The Research Craft.* Boston: Little, Brown.

CHAPTER SIX

Does the Public Support Equal Employment Rights for Gays and Lesbians?

Gregory B. Lewis and Marc A. Rogers

Although public opinion polls suggest that most Americans support equal employment rights for lesbians and gay men, the strength of their opposition to antigay discrimination is open to question. Few states outlaw employment discrimination on the basis of sexual orientation. Federal antidiscrimination legislation was defeated the only time it reached the floor of one house of Congress (the Senate in 1996). Public votes on gay rights ordinances have typically resulted in defeats for the gay community.

This chapter seeks an explanation for conflicting opinions about employment opportunity, hiring decisions, and antidiscrimination legislation. We begin by examining general trends in public opinion. Most Americans believe that antigay discrimination is fairly prevalent and that homosexuals should "have equal rights in terms of job opportunities." Yet many have grave doubts about hiring gays into specific occupations (e.g., elementary school teachers) and about the wisdom or necessity of passing laws to outlaw discrimination. We look for the sources of opposition to gay rights legislation both in the types of questions that generate little support and in the characteristics of people who oppose hiring homosexuals in at least some occupations. Using seven surveys conducted by Gallup and CBS, we assess both demographic and attitudinal sources of support for gay employment rights.

AMERICANS' BELIEFS ABOUT GAY EMPLOYMENT DISCRIMINATION

Gays have clearly faced discrimination in the past. During the cold war, when fear of Communism led to official concerns about security risks, the federal government explicitly prohibited the military, federal civilian agencies, and federal contractors from hiring homosexuals. The U.S. Senate (1954) held hearings on how to prevent "Employment of Homosexuals and Other Sex Perverts in Government," and in a 1953 executive order President Eisenhower declared "sexual perversion" to constitute a security risk. Many state and local governments also outlawed the employment of homosexuals in government jobs, and licensing agencies for a wide variety of professions (in particular, teaching, law, and medicine) made homosexuality sufficient grounds for revoking one's license. Indeed, homosexuals were officially prohibited from working in over 20 percent of all jobs in the U.S. economy by the mid-1950s (Brown 1958; Bérubé 1990). These prohibitions continued even as anticommunism waned, with the justification shifting from security risks to immorality. Public opinion supported these exclusions: in the 1960s Americans rated homosexuals as more harmful to the country than any other group named, except Communists and atheists (cited in Aguero, Bloch, and Byrne 1984:95).

Today, outside the military, few government prohibitions on the employment of gay men and lesbians remain, largely due to court decisions in the late 1960s and early 1970s (Lewis 1997). Merely lifting an official prohibition on employment does not guarantee fair treatment, of course, and gay people continue to perceive discrimination in the workplace. In a variety of surveys, one-quarter or more of lesbians and gay men report that they have lost jobs or promotions due to discrimination; many more fear the repercussions if their sexual orientations became known (Badgett 1997:1).[1] Despite a stereotype of homosexuals as a well-educated and well-paid elite, average earnings of gay men are actually somewhat lower than those of straight men (Badgett 1997:3).[2] Statistical analyses indicate that gay men earn, on average, one-quarter less than comparably educated and experienced heterosexual men (Badgett 1995; Klawitter and Flatt 1998; their comparisons of lesbians and heterosexual women yield inconclusive results).

Most Americans agree that homosexuals face discrimination.[3] A 1984 Roper survey found that 35 percent of respondents believed that "there is a great deal of discrimination against . . . homosexuals" and an additional 26 percent believe there is "a fair amount." In a 1992 Marttila and Kiley survey, conducted for the Anti-Defamation League of B'nai B'rith, 21 percent felt that homosexuals "face a tremendous amount of discrimination," and an additional 52 percent said that they face "a lot."

Public belief that gay people deserve civil liberties has grown consistently and substantially in recent decades (Davis 1992; Wilson 1994; Yang 1997), even in the face of the AIDS epidemic (Sniderman, Brody, and Tetlock 1991). Acceptance of homosexuality is evolving more slowly. (See Yang [1997] for a good display of trends in public opinion on gay issues.) From 1973 through 1991 the General Social Survey found that about 70 percent of Americans believed that "sexual relations between two adults of the same sex" are "always wrong." (That percentage appeared to fall as low as 67 percent in the mid-1970s but rose to about 75 percent in the mid-1980s, quite possibly in response to the AIDS epidemic.) Strikingly, that percentage fell to 63 percent in 1993 and has continued dropping, to 56 percent in 1996. In fifteen surveys conducted since 1977 the percentage saying that "homosexual relations between consenting adults . . . should not be legal" has fluctuated fairly widely, but it was consistently about 55 percent between 1986 and 1988 and has consistently been about 45 percent since 1992 (Yang 1997:487).

Much, but not all, of that disapproval reflects a belief that homosexuality is immoral. Several surveys between 1978 and 1996 consistently found about 55 percent saying that homosexual relations between consenting adults are "morally wrong," with no trend away from moral disapproval (see Yang 1997: 485–486). Thus, recent declines in the percentage finding homosexual relations "always wrong" probably reflect the diminishing importance of other reasons for disapproving of homosexuals (e.g., concerns about sexual promiscuity, mental illness, or gender nonconformity, personal distaste at the thought of two men or women having sex).

Polling firms have asked three sorts of questions about employment rights for gays: whether respondents support the general principle of equal employment opportunity, how they feel about hiring homosexuals in particular occupations, and whether they would support laws to outlaw discrimination. The percentage saying that "homosexuals should . . . have equal rights in terms of job opportunities" has been high since the mid-1970s (56 percent in 1977) and has been rising steadily and substantially since, to 83 percent in 1996. These high percentages probably overstate public opposition to employment discrimination against gays, as the words *equal rights* make the socially desirable response obvious and the word *opportunities* does not force respondents to deal directly with the desirability of hiring or working with homosexuals. Questions that raise those issues yield less favorable responses. In a 1987 Roper poll 25 percent would "strongly object to working around" homosexuals and an additional 27 percent would "prefer not to"; only 45 percent "wouldn't mind" (Tiemeyer 1993:443). Only about half the respondents in two 1985 *Los Angeles Times* surveys were "in favor of hiring an employee regardless of whether he or she is a homosexual or a lesbian."

Questions about the desirability of hiring gays for specific occupations may also heighten concerns about the immorality or wrongness of homosexuality. Gallup has repeatedly asked whether "homosexuals should or should not be hired" in five specific occupations (see table 6.1). People appear comfortable

TABLE 6.1.
Support for Employment Rights for Gays

	Gallup 1977	Gallup 1982	Gallup 1985	Gallup 1987	Gallup 1989	Gallup 1992	CBS 1993
In general, do you think homosexuals should have equal rights in terms of job opportunities? (Yes)	56	59			71	74	78
Do you think homosexuals should or should not be hired for the following occupations:							
Salespersons	68	70	71	72	79	82	
The armed forces	51	52	55	55	60	57	
Doctors	44	50	52	49	56	53	
The clergy	36	38	41	42	44	43	
Elementary school teachers	27	32	36	33	42	41	
Average of five (job index)	45	48	51	50	56	55	
Would you object to having an airline pilot who is homosexual, or wouldn't that bother you? (Not bother)							86
Would you object to having an accountant who is homosexual, or wouldn't that bother you? (Not bother)							83
Would you object to having a doctor who is homosexual, or wouldn't that bother you? (Not bother)							48
Would you object to having a homosexual as your Representative in Congress, or wouldn't that bother you? (Not bother)							59
Suppose you had a child of elementary school age. Would you object to having a homosexual as your child's elementary school teacher, or wouldn't that bother you? (Not bother)							41

with gay salespeople but are much less inclined to hire homosexuals for the other four jobs than their support for the principle of equal opportunity would suggest. In 1992, for instance, when 74 percent supported equal rights, the percentage saying homosexuals *should* be hired was only 41 percent for elementary school teachers, 43 percent for the clergy, 53 percent for doctors, and 57 percent for the armed forces. In four years Gallup immediately followed the question on "equal rights in terms of job opportunities" with questions about the five occupations; only 37 percent of those who supported the principle of equal rights also favored hiring homosexuals for all five occupations — 30 percent of them preferred to see homosexuals in two or fewer of those jobs. Support for equal job opportunities does not necessarily mean that people want gays in all occupations.

Nonetheless, support for hiring homosexuals rose for all five occupations between 1977 and 1992. Surprisingly, support appeared to grow fastest in the most and least objectionable occupations: fourteen-percentage-point rises for both elementary school teachers and salespersons. A majority favored hiring homosexuals in the armed forces throughout this period, but support rose by only seven percentage points.[4] While the public clearly opposed gay elementary school teachers more than gay clergy in 1977, that difference had essentially disappeared by 1992. The average percentage across the five occupations grew fairly steadily, from 45 percent in 1977 to 55 percent in 1992, though this ten-point rise is substantially smaller than the eighteen-point rise in approval of the principle of equal rights in terms of job opportunities over the same period.

A 1993 survey conducted by CBS News and the *New York Times* also asked whether "homosexuals should . . . have equal rights in terms of job opportunities" and followed by asking whether they would object to having a homosexual as an airline pilot, doctor, accountant, representative in Congress, or elementary school teacher for their child. As in the Gallup surveys, a large majority (78 percent) supported the principle of equal rights, but only 39 percent of those supporters wouldn't be bothered by homosexuals in any of the five occupations, and 25 percent would object to gays in at least three.

Why do people object to homosexuals more in certain occupations? The intimacy and moral content of interactions with people in these occupations may be the key. Respondents expressed few doubts about the competence of gay professionals, such as pilots and accountants. Long-standing images of gays as sexually dangerous may not impinge on these arm's-length relationships but may cause people to object to gay doctors (to whom they expose their bodies), to gay elementary school teachers (especially men, about whom fears of child molestation appear high), and even to gay soldiers (as shown starkly in the "gays in the showers" aspect of the military debate). Many people also expect doctors, teachers, and clergy to provide moral guidance, a perhaps insuperable obstacle to accepting gays for those who believe homosexuality to be immoral.[5]

Support for hiring homosexuals in these "more difficult" occupations is probably a better measure of people's real opposition to discrimination than the broader equal rights question.[6] Public support for hiring homosexuals as elementary school teachers, for example, is especially weak, and gay rights opponents have emphasized fears about gay teachers in many referenda. The two major antigay rights referenda of the late 1970s (Anita Bryant's 1977 campaign in Dade County and the 1978 Briggs Initiative in California) focused on gay teachers. When the survey question shifts from the principle of equal rights to "extending [existing] civil rights laws to include homosexuals" or passing "special legislation to guarantee equal rights for gays" (see below), support drops to levels close to that for hiring gay elementary school teachers.

Questions asking whether people would support laws to outlaw discrimination vary widely in wording and favorable responses. Approval of such laws is probably growing, but the rate is not clear. The percentage favoring "laws to protect homosexuals against job discrimination" rose from 52 percent in 1983 to 60 percent in 1996. However, about 60 percent also said that "homosexuals should be guaranteed equal treatment under the law in jobs and housing" as early as 1977 and 1978, though separate polls from the same period found only half saying that "fair housing and fair employment laws should be extended to cover homosexuals." This latter discrepancy seems to fit a pattern of lower support for passing laws than for laws per se. In separate polls conducted in the 1990s a full 60 percent supported "laws to protect homosexuals against job discrimination," but only 44 percent to 48 percent agreed that "the laws which protect the civil rights of racial or religious minorities should be used to protect the rights of homosexuals," only 39 percent to 46 percent favored "extending . . . civil rights laws to include homosexuals," and only 26 percent to 43 percent believed that "homosexuals should get protection under civil rights laws in the way racial minorities and women have been protected." Questions that ask about extending civil rights laws may raise both doubts that gays are as "legitimate" a minority as blacks or women and fears that affirmative action will be extended to gays, in ways that a question about "laws to protect homosexuals against job discrimination" does not. Also in the 1990s only 26 percent to 43 percent felt that there should be "special legislation to guarantee equal rights for gays," but that question wording may have biased the percentages downward by echoing gay rights opponents' distinction between "special rights" and "equal rights." (See Yang 1997:496–499 for full details on these polls).

The most current and most positive survey results come from a 1997 Tarrance Group poll commissioned by the Human Rights Campaign (HRC), a gay rights organization. A long lead-in explains,

> There are currently no federal laws protecting gays and lesbians in the workplace. Only nine states now have laws protecting gays and lesbians from workplace discrimination, and a lesbian or gay man can be fired for being gay in the other 41 states. The Employment Non-Discrimination Act, which is currently being considered in Congress, would extend civil rights and prevent job discrimination against gays and lesbians. Would you favor or oppose this law?

Overall, 68 percent said they favored ENDA, with 43 percent strongly favoring it. In another HRC-sponsored poll the previous year 70 percent thought "gays and lesbians should be protected from discrimination in the workplace," but only 55 percent responded favorably (24 percent strongly) to the follow-up question: "There is a measure before Congress called the Employment Non-Discrimination Act, which would extend current civil rights protections in the workplace to cover gays and lesbians. Do you favor or oppose this bill?" Thus, apparent support for ENDA rose thirteen percentage points between 1996 and 1997, and strong support nearly doubled, but much of that increase was probably due to the lead-in to the 1997 question. Whether that lead-in provides a sound factual basis for making a policy decision or excessively biases the responses by highlighting the socially desirable response is arguable; in either case it differs so strongly from previous questions that it has little value for assessing trends.

None of the questions about laws receives anywhere near the level of support garnered by questions about the principle of equal employment rights for gays, and the discrepancy between 70 percent favoring workplace protections and 55 percent supporting ENDA (in the same poll) suggests that many people feel protections should come from something other than laws. Public support appears higher for laws tailored to prevent job discrimination than for broader "equal rights" or "civil rights" laws, which people may fear would be open to excessively broad interpretations by the courts (perhaps to recognize gay marriages or require affirmative action). When question wording has this much impact on responses, however, it suggests that opinions are not clearly formed and that voter support will depend on how the issue is framed in the political debate. Wald, Button, Rienzo (1996:1155) argue that the debate over almost any local ordinance becomes "a referendum on the principle of gay rights," whatever its provisions. Widespread disapproval of homosexuality on moral and other grounds may cause support for gay civil rights to shrink when public debate becomes intense. Though surveys suggested majority support for hiring homosexuals in the armed forces throughout the decade leading up to the gays in the military debate, for instance, public support dropped about ten points in the first six months of the debate. Public support may rise again in the aftermath of the debate (Haeberle, chapter 7, this volume), but too late to have much impact on legislation.

WHO SUPPORTS EMPLOYMENT RIGHTS FOR GAYS?

In the remainder of this chapter we analyze the factors affecting support for gay employment rights in six surveys conducted by Gallup and one performed by

CBS and the *New York Times* (the CBS poll).[7] We obtained all seven data sets from the Roper Center for Public Opinion Research at the University of Connecticut. Six Gallup polls between 1977 and 1992 asked whether homosexuals should be hired in five occupations (armed forces, clergy, doctors, elementary school teachers, and salespersons). We combined the data from these six surveys (a total of 7,296 cases) and created a scale of support for employing gays by giving respondents 20 points for each occupation they said homosexuals should be hired for. Coding the variable this way gives the scale values from 0 to 100, which represent the percentage of jobs for which they accept gays. The scale has an acceptable reliability (Cronbach's alpha = .84).

The 1993 CBS poll asked 1,154 respondents whether they would object to having homosexuals in a variety of jobs or if that wouldn't bother them. We constructed a second scale by scoring 33.3 points each if they said they wouldn't be bothered by having a gay doctor, elementary school teacher, or member of Congress. The scale again runs from 0 to 100 and represents the percentage of these occupations in which they will accept homosexuals. Reliability is again acceptably high (Cronbach's alpha = .80). The CBS poll also asks whether "it is necessary . . . to pass laws to make sure that homosexuals have equal rights." Though the proposed law covers more than workplace discrimination and confounds desirability with necessity, the 42 percent support is comparable to percentages favoring passing or extending civil rights laws to protect gays. This question allows a general test of the validity of both job indexes by seeing how well this one predicts support for gay rights legislation. We coded a "yes" answer as 100 and all other responses as 0 to put this question on the same scale as the two indexes.

Where should gay rights advocates look for allies and supporters? Support for gay civil rights should depend on people's attitudes toward both homosexuality and political tolerance. In our search for factors that influence support, we reviewed research done both by psychologists, who have focused on the former, and political scientists, who have concentrated on the latter.

Religion Given the importance of moral judgments in condemnation of homosexuality, religion has been found consistently to be a key factor in beliefs about homosexuality and support for gay rights (e.g., Nyberg and Alston 1976–1977; Levitt and Klassen 1974; Gentry 1987; Herek 1988; Ellison and Musick 1993; Herek and Capitanio 1995, 1996; Seltzer 1993). The best measure of religion is not clear. Denomination, frequency of church attendance, religiosity, and religious conservatism are all significant predictors. In both polls we use dummy variables to distinguish Jews, Catholics, Protestants, and those with no religion from other respondents. In the Gallup surveys dummy variables indicate whether the respondent has been "born again" and whether he or she attended church within the previous week.[8] In the CBS poll we use a four-point scale for how important religion is in the respondent's life (1 = not at all important, 4 = extremely important).

Education   Increased education appears to lead to greater acceptance of difference in others, more liberal sexual attitudes, greater interaction with lesbians and gay men, and heightened commitment to democratic values and civil liberties. Most studies find strong relationships between education and attitudes toward homosexuality (e.g., Nyberg and Alston 1976–1977; Irwin and Thompson 1977; Seltzer 1993; Herek and Glunt 1993; Herek and Capitanio 1996). Education is also a key variable in determining political tolerance (e.g., Gibson and Tedin 1988; Ellison and Musick 1993). The effect may be due more to learning than to schooling. Kurdek (1988) showed low academic performance to be strongly correlated to negative attitudes among college students, and Bobo and Licari (1989) found that education increased tolerance largely by enhancing cognitive sophistication (their measure was a vocabulary test score), which had a stronger direct effect than education. We measure education with three dummy variables distinguishing high school graduates, those with some college, and college graduates from those who did not complete high school.

Age   Political tolerance is negatively related to age. Davis (1992) finds this pattern to be due less to people becoming more socially conservative as they age than to succeeding cohorts being raised in increasingly socially liberal environments; he finds little continuing shift toward tolerance among people born since 1946, however. Older adults have more negative attitudes toward homosexuals (Levitt and Klassen 1974; Nyberg and Alston 1976–1977; Herek and Glunt 1993; Irwin and Thompson 1977). Given findings suggesting that the age effect is not linear (Davis 1992), we represent age through a set of dummy variables representing decade of birth. We expect to find the oldest respondents the least supportive but make no prediction about patterns among the youngest respondents.

Gender   In two meta-analyses of studies that examine gender differences Kite (1984) and Kite and Whitley (1996) demonstrate that men have more negative attitudes than women toward both homosexual behavior and homosexuals themselves. The gender differences increased over time and were widest in attitudes toward gay men. (Men and women had similar views about lesbians.) This is likely to widen the gender differences in our study, as Black and Stevenson (1983) found that when a question asked about "homosexuals" (as ours do), 75 percent of men and 41 percent of women thought only of gay men; almost all the rest thought of both men and women. Surprisingly, however, respondent gender tends *not* to be a significant factor in determining political tolerance, even when the topic is homosexuals (e.g., Ellison and Musick 1993). Indeed, Bobo and Licari (1989) find that women tend to be less supportive than men of civil liberties for unpopular groups generally.

Race Although civil rights leaders and the Black Congressional Caucus have been key allies of those struggling for gay rights, blacks appear to be no more tolerant of homosexuality or supportive of gay rights than are whites. Levitt and Klassen (1974) found that whites had significantly more negative attitudes than blacks, but Hudson and Ricketts (1980) found the opposite. Millham, San Miguel, and Kellogg (1976), Nyberg and Alston (1976–1977), and Herek and Capitanio (1995) found no significant race difference in attitudes toward homosexuals, and Ellison and Musick (1993) and Bobo and Licari (1989) found no significant impact of race on political tolerance.

Marital status Because condemnation of homosexuality is related to sexual conservatism and condemnation of premarital and extramarital sex (Nyberg and Alston 1976–1977; Irwin and Thompson 1977), the divorced and single, who tend to deviate from traditional social norms themselves, should have less negative attitudes toward homosexuals than the married and widowed. The evidence on this point, however, is quite mixed (Levitt and Klassen 1974; Herek and Capitanio 1995, 1996; Seltzer 1993).

Region Ellison and Musick (1993) cite four decades of research indicating that Southerners are less tolerant of unpopular groups than the rest of the country, and they find only a partial explanation in the greater religious conservatism of the region. Tiemeyer (1993) reports that Southerners are the most likely to say that homosexual relations are "always wrong" and that those in New England, followed by those on the Pacific Coast, are the least likely to agree. Levitt and Klassen (1974) reported that Midwesterners and Southerners held more negative attitudes, while Herek and Capitanio (1996) found increased contact with gays and lesbians and, therefore, more positive attitudes for those in Pacific Coast states. Button, Rienzo, and Wald (1997) found gay rights ordinances to be least common in the South and Midwest and most common in the West and Northeast.

City size A long tradition in sociology suggests that the size, density, and heterogeneity of large cities force social interactions with diverse people, which enhances tolerance; Abrahamson and Carter (1986), however, find only a small effect of urban life on tolerance, an effect that has been shrinking over time. Those who live in metropolitan areas do appear to have more positive attitudes toward homosexuals than do those in rural areas (Levitt and Klassen 1974; Irwin and Thompson 1977; and Herek and Capitanio 1996). City dwellers are also more likely to support gay civil rights (Bobo and Licari 1989; Ellison and Musick

1993). Button, Rienzo, and Wald (1997) also found that larger, more diverse communities are more likely to pass antidiscrimination legislation, though Haider-Markel and Meier (1996) found no significant relationship between the degree of urbanization in a state and the level of protection it provided to gays.

Political ideology   Conservatives have more negative attitudes toward homosexuals than liberals (Levitt and Klassen 1974; Herek and Glunt 1993; Seltzer 1993), though this may be primarily due to their social rather than their political conservatism. Conservatives also tend to be less politically tolerant of unpopular groups across the board (e.g., McClosky and Brill 1983), though Sullivan, Pierson, and Marcus (1982) argue that the research in this area is biased by focusing on unpopular left-wing rather than right-wing groups. Our data set requires us to substitute party identification for ideology in our analysis, but the 1992 presidential campaign made clear how strongly the parties' electoral strategies differed on the gay issue. The 1996 Senate vote on ENDA lined up largely on partisan lines, with the Democrats supporting nondiscrimination legislation and Republicans opposing it. If party elites reflect party masses, we should see the same pattern in these surveys.

Gay friends and family   Those who know gays have more positive attitudes toward gays and gay rights than those who don't (Millham, San Miguel, and Kellogg 1976; Aguero, Bloch, and Byrne 1984; Gentry 1987; Lance 1987; Herek 1988; Ellis and Vasseur 1993; Haddock, Zanna, and Esses 1993; Herek and Glunt 1993; Herek and Capitanio 1996). The causal direction is not completely clear, as gay people are more likely to come out to people they expect to be supportive, so that having positive attitudes may lead to having friends one knows are gay (Herek and Glunt 1993). On the other hand, Herek and Capitanio (1996) present evidence that knowing gay people changes one's attitude. The percentage of the public reporting at least one gay friend or acquaintance rose from 24 percent in 1983 to 56 percent in 1996, and 22 percent indicated at least one "close friend or family member" in 1993 (Yang 1997), which could be fueling public support for gay rights. Unfortunately, only the CBS poll asked whether respondents had a close friend or family member who was gay or lesbian.

Is it a choice?   People who believe that being gay is a choice are more likely than others to have negative attitudes toward gays and lesbians (Aguero, Bloch, and Byrne 1984; Ernulf, Innala, and Whitam 1989; Herek and Capitanio 1995). They are likely to think it is a bad or sinful choice that can be overcome with prayer or counseling; they are also more likely than others to worry that children who are exposed to homosexuals will choose (or be recruited into) homosexuality. Those who think homosexuality is biologically determined, on the other hand, typically interpret it as an immutable characteristic with little or no moral content. The effects of believing that homosexuality is largely determined by one's upbringing and early environment (e.g., having a domineering mother and a distant father) have been studied less. However, relative to believing homosexuality is a choice, this should lessen concern about recruitment of children (since sexual orientation is determined by an early age) and should attribute less moral taint (since homosexuals can overcome their orientation only with great struggle, if at all).

Unfortunately, an appropriate but problematic question is available in the Gallup data set for only three years: "Just your opinion, is homosexuality something a person is born with or is homosexuality due to other factors such as upbringing or environment?" Those who believe homosexuality is a choice will be lumped together with those who think it is determined in the early years after birth. Our dummy variable distinguishes those who say it is at least partially determined at birth from all others. The CBS question uses a better two-way split: "Do you think being homosexual is something people choose to be, or do you think it is something they cannot change?" Our dummy variable distinguishes those who say it is a choice from others.

Condemnation of homosexuality   Sullivan, Piereson, and Marcus (1982) argue that "political tolerance" is directed only at groups one dislikes. Political tolerance of gays, therefore, *has* grown, since support for gay civil liberties increased steadily for two decades while over two-thirds of the population believed that homosexual relations were "always wrong." Nonetheless, opinions of gays are related to attitudes toward gay rights (Wilson 1994). Controlling for attitudes toward homosexuality should make clearer which variables are affecting the political tolerance portion of the gay rights attitudes. The best question in the Gallup data set asks, "Do you think homosexual relations between consenting adults should or should not be legal?" Unfortunately, this question combines a moral judgment with a political tolerance decision. The CBS poll asked, "Do you think homosexual relations between adults are morally wrong, or that they are OK, or don't you care much either way?" Our dummy variable distinguishes those who feel them to be morally wrong from all others.

FINDINGS

Gallup, 1977–92

In our basic model we regressed the job index (which represents the percentage of five occupations that respondents felt homosexuals *should* be hired for) on the survey year, level of education, three measures of religion, decade of birth, sex, race, region of the country, and party identification (see table 6.2). These

TABLE 6.2.

Factors Influencing Support for Hiring Homosexuals Gallup surveys, 1977–92

	Basic Model	
	Coefficients	Standard Errors
Year	0.4***	.1
Education (reference = no high school diploma)		
High school graduate	4.1***	1.1
Some college	12.2***	1.4
College graduate	19.7***	1.4
Religion (reference =other)		
Protestant	3.7*	1.9
Catholic	7.7***	1.9
Jewish	14.8***	3.4
None	9.3***	2.3
Born again? (reference = no)		
Yes	−12.0***	1.7
Attend church this week? (reference = no)		
Yes	−9.7	1.0
When were you born (reference = after 1959)		
Before 1920	−15.8***	1.6
1920–29	−7.1***	1.6
1930–39	−3.4*	1.5
1940–49	−2.0	1.4
1950–59	1.3	1.3
Sex (reference = female)		
Male	−9.2	.8
Race (reference = other)		
Black	9.1**	2.8
White	2.3	2.5
Region (reference = New England)		
Pacific Coast	−5.2*	2.1
Middle Atlantic	−6.9***	2.0
West Central	−8.2***	2.2
East Central	−8.8***	2.0
Rocky Mountains	−10.0***	2.5
Southwest	−14.5***	2.2
Southeast	−14.7***	2.0
Party identification (reference = independent)		
Democrat	−1.9	1.0
Republican	−5.6***	1.1
Sample size	7272	
Adjusted R^2	.15	

continued

TABLE 6.2.
(Continued)

	Alternative Specifications[a]	
	Coefficients	Standard Errors
Marital status (reference = married)		
Divorced	6.5**	2.4
Single	2.7	1.7
Separated	.6	4.5
Widowed	−4.2	2.4
Sample size	3744	
Adjusted R^2	.15	
City size (reference = under 50,000)		
50,000+	5.6***	1.2
Sample size	5064	
Adjusted R^2	.15	
Homosexuals are born that way.		
Yes	12.3***	1.2
Sample size	4247	
Adjusted R^2	.18	
Homosexual relations should be legal.		
Yes	34.4***	.8
Sample size	7272	
Adjusted R^2	.33	

*** Significant at .0001 level
** Significant at .01 level
* Significant at .05 level
[a] All alternative specification include all variables from basic model.

variables were available for all six survey years. Nearly all the coefficients were statistically significant at the .001 level (not too surprising given a sample of near-ly 7,300 cases), but they collectively explained only about 15 percent of the variation in the dependent variable. To assess the impact of variables that were available only for selected years, we ran several "alternative specifications," which added each variable separately to the "basic model" in a data set including only the survey years in which the question was asked.

The coefficient on Year shows that the average score on the job index rose 0.4 percentage points per year, among people of the same educational level, religion, birth cohort, sex, race, region, and party identification. A simple bivariate regression with Year as the only independent variable (not shown) yielded a Year coefficient of 0.7, a time trend nearly twice as fast as the net trend in the basic model. That suggests that nearly half the rise in job index scores between 1977 and 1992 (0.3 out of 0.7) can be attributed to changes in the demographics of the population over time, predominantly rising educational levels and the replacement of older birth cohorts with more socially liberal younger ones. Most of the liberalizing trend (0.4 out of 0.7), however, appears to be due to individuals changing their minds: people tended to be more gay-supportive in 1992 than comparable people were fifteen years earlier.

Education, religion, and birth cohort were the three most important demographic variables in determining scores on the job index. Each explained about 5 percent of the variation in the dependent variable when it was the only independent variable in the model (not shown). Support for employing gay people rose substantially with education. On average, high school graduates, those with some college, and college graduates favored hiring homosexuals in 4 percent, 12 percent, and 20 percent, respectively, more of the five occupations than did comparable high school dropouts in the same year. Opposition was strongest among church-attending, born-again Protestants. Jews and the nonreligious tended to be the most supportive of gay employment rights, followed by Catholics, Protestants who had not been born again, and other non-Christians (the reference group). Respondents who said they had been born again were twelve points less supportive than those of the same religion who had not, and those who had attended church in the previous week were ten points less supportive than those who had not. Support for employing gays is higher among younger people. People born before 1940 favored hiring homosexuals in fewer occupations than did people born since then, with the effect being stronger the earlier the person was born. This liberalization plateaued, however, with the Baby Boomers — people born since 1960 tended to be no more gay-supportive than those born in the 1940s and 1950s.

Though previous studies of political tolerance of homosexuals (based primarily on the General Social Survey [GSS]) have found no substantial gender differences, women supported hiring homosexuals significantly more than men did, a gender difference of about nine percentage points after controlling for other demographic differences. (The difference was six percentage points before the controls.) Each of the three racial groupings had about the same mean score on the job index, but blacks tended to be more supportive than others of the same level of education, age, and religion living in the same region.[9]

Though gay rights has been an important wedge issue between the political parties in the 1990s, regional differences were much more substantial than partisan differences in the Gallup polls. Political independents and third-party members were two points more supportive than Democrats, who were only four points more supportive than Republicans. New Englanders, on the other hand, scored fifteen points higher than Southerners overall, even controlling for religion and education. Those on the Pacific Coast and in the Middle Atlantic states were less supportive than New Englanders but more supportive than those in the Midwest and Rocky Mountain states, who were more supportive than those in the South.

As expected, divorced people supported hiring gays more than comparable, currently married people did. On average, single people were significantly more gay-supportive than married people (not shown), but that is probably because singles are younger; the single-married difference largely disappeared with demographic controls in the model. Support for hiring gays was about twelve points higher in cities of at least fifty thousand than in smaller communities (not shown), helping to explain why the former are so much more likely to have gay rights ordinances. That was partly because large cities have populations that are demographically different, but city residents were six points more gay-supportive than similar people in less urban settings. City living may liberalize people's attitudes toward gay civil rights. (Cities may also attract social liberals.)

As expected, those who agreed, at least in part, that "homosexuality [is] something a person is born with" were significantly more supportive than others on employment issues. Finally, people who thought that homosexual relations between consenting adults should be legal were substantially more likely to support hiring gays, scoring thirty-four points higher on the job index than others who were equal on the demographic variables. Adding this variable to the basic model more than doubled the explained variation, raising it from 15 percent to 33 percent. Clearly—and unsurprisingly—attitudes toward homosexual sex affect attitudes toward gay employment rights.

CBS/New York Times, 1993

Analysis of the CBS survey confirmed most of the patterns found in the Gallup survey but provided some additional insights. In Model 1 (demographics only) education had a strong positive impact on the job index, with about the same strength as in the Gallup data (see table 6.3). Age again had a fairly strong non-linear impact: those born before 1930 were more negative than those born after, but there was limited variation among those born in the 1930s through the 1970s.

The more importance religion had in their lives (on a four-point scale), the more negative respondents were to hiring gays; this variable had the strongest impact of any in the data set.[10] Beyond that, religious denomination had no direct impact on the job index; however, those who identified themselves as fundamentalists were substantially more negative than others. Men were again sig-

TABLE 6.3.
Factors Influencing Support for Hiring Homosexxuals

	1993 CBS/New York Times Poll			
	Model 1		Model 2	
	Coefficient	Std. Err.	Coefficient	Std. Error
Education (reference = no high school diploma)				
High school graduate	11.6**	2.3	9.2**	3.4
Some college	20.4***	4.0	16.4***	3.6
College graduate	26.0***	4.0	17.4***	3.6
Religion (reference = other)				
Protestant	−4.9	5.0	−5.3	4.5
Catholic	−3.7	5.3	−4.6	4.8
Jewish	−2.6	9.3	−4.2	8.4
None	0.0	6.3	−.2	5.6
Fundamentalist?				
Yes	−13.0***	3.6	-5.6	4.5
Religion important in life				
(4-point scale)	−9.3***	1.3	−3.5**	1.2
When were you born (reference = after 1959)				
Before 1920	−12.5*	5.4	−16.8***	4.9
1920–29	−9.7*	4.3	−10.6**	3.9
1930–39	−1.8	4.0	−2.3	3.6
1940–49	−3.4	3.5	−3.0	3.1
1950–59	−.3	3.1	−1.8	2.8
Sex (reference = female)				
Male	−15.1***	2.3	−8.5***	2.1
Race (reference = other)				
Black	−3.9	5.0	−4.2	5.4
White	−4.3	4.5	−4.9	4.0
Region (reference = Northeast)				
West	−3.8	3.4	−3.5	3.1
Midwest	−10.0***	3.3	−5.5	3.0
South	−17.9***	3.2	−10.5***	2.9
Party Identification (reference = independent)				
Democrat	6.7*	2.7	4.3	2.4
Republican	−9.8**	3.3	−5.7*	2.5
Marital status (reference = married)				
Divorced/separated	9.3**	3.1	6.0*	2.8
Single	5.6	3.3	−1.1	3.0
Widowed	.8	4.5	−1.1	3.0
Is it a choice?				
Yes			−13.2***	2.3
Homosexual relations morally wrong?				
Yes			−26.1***	2.3
Have gay friend/family member?				
Yes			13.7***	2.4
Sample size	1151		1151	
Adjusted R2		.23		.38

nificantly less supportive than women, but there was little evidence of racial differences. In contrast to the Gallup patterns, Democrats were significantly more supportive than independents in this poll and substantially more supportive than Republicans (a difference of 17 points). Regional differences were clear but not as strong as in the Gallup data, probably because CBS used only four regions, which combined each of the most socially liberal regions (New England and Pacific Coast) with a somewhat less supportive region (Middle Atlantic and Rocky Mountains, respectively). The Northeast and West were still the most supportive, the South was the least supportive, and the Midwest was in between.

Model 2 adds three measures of knowledge of and attitudes toward gays. Even with the full set of control variables, those who believed that "homosexual relations between adults are morally wrong" were twenty-six points less supportive than those who did not, those who thought "being homosexual is something people choose to be" were thirteen points less supportive than those who did not, and those who had close friends or family members who were gay were fourteen points more supportive than those who did not. Since the demographic variables that affected people's attitudes toward gay employment rights also influenced their opinions about homosexuality and their acquaintance with gay people, adding these three variables to the regression model lowered the coefficients of almost all the independent variables. Oddly, the impact of being born before 1930 appeared to become stronger after controlling for these attitudinal variables.

Table 6.4 presents regression analyses for whether people believed "it is necessary . . . to pass laws to make sure that homosexuals have equal rights."[11] In the demographics-only Model 1 religion was still a key factor, with those who said that their religion was extremely important in their lives about fifteen percentage points less likely to support a gay rights laws than comparable people who said that it was not at all important in their lives (three points lower on the four-point scale). Age was still an important factor, though the division now was between those born before and after 1950. Men remained less supportive than women. Democrats were substantially more supportive of gay rights laws than Republicans (by twenty-three points). Southerners and Midwesterners were still substantially less supportive than Easterners and Westerners.

The striking difference was that education appeared to play no role in support for passing a gay rights law. The education coefficients were substantively trivial and statistically insignificant. Education was a key factor in determining whether respondents favored hiring homosexuals in a variety of occupations, but not for whether they felt it necessary to pass laws to ensure equal treatment. This finding flies in the face of most prior research in this area, which finds a

TABLE 6.4.

Necessary to Pass Law to Make Sure that Homosexuals Have Equal Rights?

| | 1993 CBS/New York Times Poll | | | |
| | Model 1 | | Model 2 | |
	Coefficient	Std. Err.	Coefficient	Std. Error
Education (reference = no high school diploma)				
High school graduate	−1.0	4.9	−7.0	4.6
Some college	−3.5	5.2	−13.3**	4.9
College graduate	.4	5.1	−13.4**	4.9
Religion (reference = other)				
Protestant	6.0	6.4	6.9	6.0
Catholic	7.5	6.8	7.3	6.4
Jewish	6.6	12.0	4.2	11.1
None	6.4	8.1	6.0	7.5
Fundamentalist?				
Yes	−3.9	4.6	4.9	4.3
Religion important in life				
(4-point scale)	−4.9**	1.7	−1.0	1.6
When were you born (reference = after 1959)				
Before 1920	−15.3*	6.9	−13.7*	6.5
1920–29	−16.4**	5.5	−15.1**	5.2
1930–39	−9.6	5.1	−9.9	4.8
1940–49	−14.3	4.5	−13.3***	4.2
1950–59	−5.1	3.9	−6.2	3.7
Sex (reference = female)				
Male	−6.6*	2.9	−2.1	2.8
Race (reference = other)				
Black	−2.9	7.7	−.8	7.2
White	−5.6	5.7	−4.2	5.3
Region (reference = Northeast)				
West	−1.4	4.4	.5	4.1
Midwest	−11.4**	4.3	−6.2	4.0
South	−13.2***	4.1	−3.4	3.9
Party Identification (reference = independent)				
Democrat	12.7***	3.4	9.5**	3.2
Republican	−10.5**	3.6	−5.1	3.3
Marital status (reference = married)				
Divorced/separated	6.3	4.0	1.6	3.7
Single	8.6*	4.2	4.0	4.0
Widowed	−2.9	5.7	−1.7	5.3
Is it a choice?				
Yes			−12.2***	3.1
Homosexual relations morally wrong?				
Yes			−7.1***	3.3

continued

TABLE 6.4.

(Continued)

| | 1993 CBS/New York Times Poll | | | |
| | Model 1 | | Model 2 | |
	Coefficient	Std. Err.	Coefficient	Std. Error
Have gay friend/family member?				
Yes			3.7***	3.2
Jobs index			3.7	3.2
Equal rights in job opportunities?				
Yes			9.8**	3.6
Sample size	1151		1151	
Adjusted R2	.10		.22	

strong positive relationship between education and support for civil liberties for gays. Haeberle (chapter 7, this volume), for instance, finds the standard pattern of more educated respondents being more likely to favor "laws to protect homosexuals against job discrimination." Haeberle's question does not ask about *passing* laws, however, and it may be worth investigating whether education weakens the desire to create new laws to protect gays, even among gay-supportive people.

Model 2 adds five measures of knowledge of and attitudes toward gays. The most important factor in support for passing gay rights laws was our job index, which had about three times the impact of one's opinion on whether gays should "have equal rights in terms of job opportunities." (This substantiates the validity of the job index.) The belief that homosexuality is a choice continued to decrease support for gay rights laws substantially, even with these other attitude measures in the model. The belief that homosexual relations are morally wrong also diminished support, but far less than it affected the job index. Whether one had a close gay friend or family member had no direct impact on support for gay rights laws.[12]

Adding attitudes toward gays to the equation more than doubled the explanatory power of the model and, naturally, decreased the coefficients on the demographic variables. Model 1 gives a more accurate picture of the effect of demographics on support for passing a gay rights law, but Model 2 coefficients allow us to see which variables create their impact by influencing other attitudes toward gays, which in turn affect support for a gay rights law. This is the pattern for religion, sex, and region, which have no direct effect on support for a gay rights law beyond their effects on other gay-related attitudes. Three demographic variables retained significant direct effects on support for passing a law, however, even among people with similar attitudes toward lesbians and gay men. Because education increased socially liberal attitudes toward gays, but not support for gay rights laws, those who had attended college favored passing laws strikingly less than did respondents with less education who had similar attitudes toward gays. Democrats favored gay rights laws substantially more than equally gay-supportive Republicans, presumably because Democrats are more likely to look for government solutions to social ills. Those born before 1950 were substantially less supportive of gay rights laws than those born later; indeed, the age coefficients were nearly identical before and after including the attitudinal variables. In separate analyses (not shown) age was not significantly related to believing homosexuality is immoral or to having a close gay friend or family member, and older people were actually *less* likely to believe that people choose to be homosexual.[13] The extra opposition of older voters to passing gay rights laws might arise from a predisposition against passing laws in general (as we have hypothesized for Republicans). Alternatively, questions about immorality and choice may not tap antigay attitudes as well for older respondents as for younger ones.

SUMMARY

Our findings were generally consistent with those of other researchers (e.g., Schroedel, Haeberle this volume). Women, the well-educated, the young, the less religious, Democrats, and urbanites tend to be more gay-supportive than men, the less-educated, older citizens, the more religious, Republicans, and those outside metropolitan areas. Regional differences were clear, with those in New England and on the Pacific Coast far more supportive than those in the South. Personal knowledge of gay people and a belief that homosexuality is inborn or unchangeable are important determinants of attitudes toward employment rights and discrimination laws. Those who disapprove of homosexuals and of homosexual sex were less gay-supportive on policy issues. In contrast to previous research on related questions, the better educated were *not* more supportive of antidiscrimination laws; indeed, they were less supportive than less educated respondents with similar attitudes toward gay people.

Americans embrace the principle of equal employment rights for homosexuals, an embrace that has grown steadily warmer over the past two decades. This support is undercut both by continuing disapproval of homosexuality and by qualms about hiring gays into particular occupations, especially those involving intimate contact (especially with children) or moral guidance (e.g., clergy). The belief that homosexual relations are always wrong has declined in the 1990s, however, and the qualms have weakened, with support for hiring homosexuals in a variety of occupations growing steadily over the past two decades.

Americans support the concept of equal rights more than they favor laws to enforce them, especially when they are asked to expand legal coverage rather than just to support existing laws. If the debate over gay employment protections can be framed as simply preventing employment discrimination, gay rights supporters should garner majority support, but opponents have frequently been able to reframe the issue around morality or to focus attention on the occupations where public distrust is greatest, especially elementary school teachers. Defusing fears of gay teachers will be a key issue in winning employment protections for gay and lesbian people in all occupations.

After two decades of stability the percentage saying that homosexual relations are "always wrong" dropped fifteen points between 1991 and 1996. If this trend continues, it should speed the adoption of gay rights laws. Individual lesbians and gay men should also find it easier to come out in the workplace. This daunting step, which intimidates most of us before we take it but few of us regret afterward (Woods and Lucas 1993), depends upon a reasonable expectation of acceptance or a belief that protections and options exist if the response is negative. Openness of some lesbian and gay workers should make it easier for others to come out and should increase acceptance of a gay presence among straights on the job, the key to a safe workplace whether antidiscrimination laws exist or not.

Does this mean that the moral fervor of the debate over gay rights will subside anytime soon? Unfortunately, the belief that homosexual relations are "morally wrong" (rather than just "always wrong") has not declined. Since the trend is clearly toward greater legal protection for the rights of gay people, yet this moral source of opposition seems not to have abated, resistance to further protections could grow even more shrill as a significant segment of the population perceives a possibly unstoppable moral threat. Religious conservatives are among the strongest opponents of gay rights laws, but opposition seems to rise with religiosity generally — those who attended church last week or who say that religion is very important in their lives are more likely to oppose hiring homosexuals than less religious members of their same denomination. Long-run trends toward secularization of American society bode well for the gay rights movement, but this stable level of belief in the immorality of homosexuality suggests a ceiling to acceptance of gay people, particularly in occupations with a large perceived moral component. Increasing evidence of a genetic basis for homosexuality has some hope of diminishing this judgment of immorality, as it weakens the justification for believing that sexual orientation (if not sexual behavior) is a choice. Convincing people that we are "born this way" appears to contribute to greater support for hiring gays and providing legal protections.

The hypothesis that gay rights protections are most likely where public opinion most supports them leads to an expectation that gay rights laws will emerge first in New England, followed by the Pacific Coast and Mid-Atlantic states, then in the Midwest and the Rocky Mountain states, and finally in the South. Indeed, all six New England states have passed gay rights laws (though Maine has since overturned its law by referendum). Of the other five states with laws, three are in the Pacific and Mid-Atlantic states (California, Hawaii, and New Jersey), and the final two are in the Midwest (Wisconsin and Minnesota). Washington, Oregon, New York, and Pennsylvania, and perhaps Maine again, would seem to be the next logical candidates. Local gay rights ordinances should continue to be concentrated in cities with populations over fifty thousand, but public opinion data give no particular reason for them to be less common in cities of fifty thousand to one hundred thousand than in cities over one million, though they still are. Wald, Button, Rienzo (1997) indicate an increasing trend toward ordinances in these moderate-sized cities.

Americans accept the principle of equal employment rights for gay people, and the trends are positive. They have had a harder time accepting gay people in certain occupations or in believing that it is desirable to pass laws to guarantee protections, but public opinion is moving in that direction. Government protections emerged in localities and then in states where the public was most likely to accept homosexuals or support civil rights for unpopular minorities. Those protections have often been quite limited, covering only public employees, for instance, and frequently excluding teachers. As public support for hiring homosexuals has grown, those protections have expanded. With rising educational levels, the natural replacement of older, less accepting cohorts by younger, more socially liberal ones, and long-run trends toward secularization—plus a clear upward trend in public support for gay rights independent of these other trends—we should see continuing passage of laws guaranteeing the employment rights of gay men and lesbians, even when the public recognizes that this will mean more openly gay teachers.

NOTES

The authors are grateful to American University for funding the purchase of the data used in this chapter and to the Roper Center for Public Opinion Research at the University of Connecticut for providing the data.

1. Badgett notes that none of these surveys uses representative samples, casting doubts on their generalizability.
2. Badgett points out that the myth is based largely on clearly biased marketing studies intended to emphasize the strength of the gay market. The Simmons Marketing Research Bureau and Overlooked Opinions report high household incomes for gay men in particular, based on surveys of readers of gay publications who tend to be much better educated and paid than the gay population generally. She notes that readers of *Ebony* and *Jet* earn 40 percent to 80 percent more than the black population generally.
3. Unless otherwise stated, all survey results were found through the Roper Center for Public Opinion Research at the University of Connecticut, which keeps the largest archive of public opinion surveys in the United States. We conducted a Lexis-Nexis search of the RPOLL files for all survey questions that included the words *homosexual, gay,* or *lesbian*. Most of the survey questions we discuss are also presented well in Yang (1997).
4. The 1992 figure preceded the serious public debate on gays in the military, but the polling data suggest that while opposition rose in early 1993, it receded in the following years (see Yang 1997:502–3; Haeberle, chapter 7, this volume).
5. See Rudolph (1990) for a similar argument. In an experimental setting Jackson and Sullivan (1989) found that undergraduates rated otherwise identical male applicants for a graduate program in elementary education as superior on femininity and creativity but inferior on moral character if their applications suggested that they were gay; they were more likely to reject the gay applicants for admission, presumably because of their moral judgment.
6. In a similar situation Smith (1981) found that 86 percent of respondents who said they would not approve of a policeman hitting a private citizen in any situation they could imagine then went on to approve of such hitting in at least one situation presented by the pollster. Smith concluded that opposing police violence was less difficult in the "universal" question than in two of the four situations presented, and he proposed using an index instead.
7. The six Gallup polls were conducted on June 14, 1977 (N = 1513), June 25–28, 1982 (N = 1531), November 11–18, 1985 (N = 1008), March 14–18, 1987 (N = 1015), October 12–15, 1989 (N = 1227), and June 4–8, 1992 (N = 1002). CBS News and *New York Times* conducted their survey on February 9–11, 1993 (N = 1154).
8. Unfortunately, Gallup never asked both questions in the same survey, so for each respondent we imputed a fractional value for the missing variable, based on the percentage of those in his or her religious denomination who answered "yes" in the years the question was asked.
9. White men were, on average, less religious and more educated than women and blacks. Those characteristics typically lead to more gay-supportive attitudes. Yet, overall, whites were no more supportive than blacks, and men were less supportive than women, despite those "advantages." When the multiple regression model compared

white men to women and minorities who were equally religious and educated, the male-female and white-black differences in support for gay rights widened.

10. Though other regression coefficients are larger, the importance of religion has the largest beta-weight. (It is a four-point scale while all other variables are dichotomous.)

11. Since this is a dichotomous dependent variable (coded 100 for a "yes" answer, 0 for all other answers), regression analysis is suboptimal but still appropriate, since the sample was almost evenly split over this question (Neter and Wasserman 1974).

12. In separate analyses having a gay friend or family member was an important predictor of attitudes on equal employment rights, the job index, whether homosexuality is a choice, and whether homosexual relations are morally wrong. Thus a close attachment to a gay person may have its full effect through its impact on these other attitudes.

13. These are the net effects, holding constant the demographic variables from Model 1. People born since 1960 were the most likely to believe that homosexuality is a choice.

REFERENCES

Abrahamson, Mark and Valerie J. Carter. 1986. "Tolerance, Urbanism, and Region." *American Sociological Review* 51:287–94.

Aguero, Joseph E., Laura Bloch, and Donn Byrne. 1984. "The Relationships Among Sexual Beliefs, Attitudes, Experience, and Homophobia." In John De Cecco, ed., *Homophobia: An Overview*. New York: Haworth.

Badgett, M. V. Lee. 1995. "The Wage Effects of Sexual Orientation Discrimination." *Industrial and Labor Relations Review* 48:726–39.

—— 1997. "Vulnerability in the Workplace: Evidence of Anti-Gay Discrimination." *Angles: The Policy Journal of the Institute for Gay and Lesbian Strategic Studies* 2:1–4.

Bérubé, Allan. 1990. *Coming Out Under Fire: The History of Gay Men and Women in World War II*. New York: Free Press.

Black, Kathryn N. and Michael R. Stevenson. 1983. "The Relationship of Self-Reported Sex-Role Characteristics and Attitudes Toward Homosexuality." In John De Cecco, ed., *Homophobia: An Overview*. New York: Haworth.

Bobo, Laurence and Frederick C. Licari. 1989. "Education and Political Tolerance: Testing the Effects of Cognitive Sophistication and Target Group Affect." *Public Opinion Quarterly* 53:285–308.

Brown, Ralph S., Jr. 1958. *Loyalty and Security: Employment Tests in the United States*. New Haven: Yale University Press.

Button, James W., Barbara A. Rienzo, and Kenneth D. Wald. 1997. *Private Lives, Public Conflicts: Battles Over Gay Rights in American Communities*. Washington, DC: Congressional Quarterly Press.

Davis, James A. 1992. "Changeable Weather in a Cooling Climate Atop the Liberal Plateau: Conversion an Replacement in Forty-two General Social Survey Items, 1972–1989." *Public Opinion Quarterly* 56:261–306.

Dunbar, John, Marvin Brown, and Donald M. Amoroso. 1973. "Some Correlates of Attitudes Toward Homosexuality." *Journal of Social Psychology* 89:271–279.

Ellis, Alan L. and R. Brent Vasseur. 1993. "Prior Interpersonal Contact with and Attitudes Towards Gays and Lesbians in an Interviewing Context." *Journal of Homosexuality* 25:31–45.

Ellison, Christopher G. and Marc A. Musick. 1993. "Southern Intolerance: A Fundamentalist Effect?" *Social Forces* 72:379–98.

Ernulf, Kurt E. and Sune M. Innala. 1987. "The Relationship Between Affective and Cognitive Components of Homophobic Reaction." *Archives of Sexual Behavior* 16:501–509.

Ernulf, Kurt E., Sune M. Innala, and Frederick L. Whitam. 1989. "Biological Explanation, Psychological Explanation, and Tolerance of Homosexuals: A Cross-National Analysis of Beliefs and Attitudes." *Psychological Reports* 65:1003–1010.

Gentry, Cynthia S. 1987. "Social Distance Regarding Male and Female Homosexuals." *Journal of Social Psychology* 127:199–208.

Gibson, James L. and Kent L. Tedin. 1988. "The Etiology of Intolerance of Homosexual Politics." *Social Science Quarterly* 69:587–604.

Haddock, Geoffrey, Mark P. Zanna, and Victoria M. Esses. 1993. "Assessing the Structure of Prejudicial Attitudes: The Case of Attitudes Toward Homosexuals." *Journal of Personality and Social Psychology* 65:1105–1118.

Haeberle, Steven H. 1999. "Gay and Lesbian Rights: Emerging Trends in Public Opinion and Voting Behavior." Chapter 7, this volume.

Haider-Markel, Donald P. and Kenneth J. Meier. 1996. "The Politics of Gay and Lesbian Rights": Expanding the Scope of the Conflict." *Journal of Politics* 58:332–349.

Herek, Gregory M. 1988. "Heterosexuals' Attitudes Toward Lesbians and Gay Men: Correlates and Gender Differences." *Journal of Sex Research* 25:457–477.

Herek, Gregory M. and Eric K. Glunt. 1993. "Interpersonal Contact and Heterosexuals' Attitudes Toward Gay Men: Results from a National Survey." *Journal of Sex Research* 30:239–244.

Herek, Gregory M. and John P. Capitanio. 1995. "Black Heterosexuals' Attitudes Toward Lesbians and Gay Men in the United States." *Journal of Sex Research* 32:95–105.

—— 1996. "'Some of My Best Friends': Intergroup Contact, Concealable Stigma, and Heterosexuals' Attitudes Toward Gay Men and Lesbians." *Personality and Social Psychology Bulletin* 22:412–424.

Hudson, Walter W. and Wendell A. Ricketts. 1980. "A Strategy for the Measurement of Homophobia." *Journal of Homosexuality* 5:357–372.

Irwin, Patrick and Norman L. Thompson. 1977. "Acceptance of the Rights of Homosexuals: A Social Profile." *Journal of Homosexuality* 3:107–121.

Jackson, Linda A. and Linda A. Sullivan. 1989. "Cognition and Affect in Evaluations of Stereotyped Group Members." *Journal of Social Psychology* 129:659–672.

Kite, Mary E. 1984. "Sex Differences in Attitudes Toward Homosexuals: A Meta-Analytic Review." In John De Cecco, ed., *Homophobia: An Overview.* New York: Haworth.

Kite, Mary E., and Bernard E. Whitley, Jr. 1996. "Sex Differences in Attitudes Toward Homosexual Persons, Behaviors, and Civil Rights: A Meta-Analysis." *Personality and Social Psychology Bulletin* 22:336–353.

Klawitter, Marieka M. and Victor Flatt. 1998. "The Effects of State and Local Antidiscrimination Policies for Sexual Orientation." *Journal of Policy Analysis and Management* 17(4).

Kurdek, Lawrence. 1988. "Correlates of Negative Attitudes Toward Homosexuals in Heterosexual College Students." *Sex Roles* 18:727–738.

Lance, Larry M. 1987. "The Effects of Interaction with Gay Persons on Attitudes Toward Homosexuality." *Human Relations* 40:329–336.

Levitt, Eugene E. and Albert D. Klassen. 1974. "Public Attitudes Toward Homosexuality. Part of the 1970 National Survey by the Institute for Sex Research." *Journal of Homosexuality* 1:29–43.

Lewis, Gregory B. 1997. "Lifting the Ban on Gays in the Civil Service: Federal Policy Toward Gay and Lesbian Employees Since the Cold War." *Public Administration Review* 57:387–395.

Millham, Jim, Christopher L. San Miguel, and Richard Kellogg. 1976. "A Factor Analytic Conceptualization of Attitudes Toward Male and Female Homosexuality." *Journal of Homosexuality* 2:3–10.

Neter, John and William Wasserman. 1974. *Applied Linear Statistical Models: Regression, Analysis of Variance, and Experimental Designs.* Homewood, IL: Irwin.

Nyberg, Kenneth L. and Jon P. Alston. 1976–1977. "Analysis of Public Attitudes Toward Homosexual Behavior." *Journal of Homosexuality* 2:99–107.

Pratte, Trish. 1993. "A Comparative Study of Attitudes Toward Homosexuality: 1986 and 1991." *Journal of Homosexuality* 26:77–83.

Rudolph, James. 1990. "Counselors' Attitudes Toward Homosexuality: Some Tentative Findings." *Psychological Reports* 66:1352–1354.

Schwanberg, Sandra L. 1993. "Attitudes Toward Gay Men and Lesbian Women: Instrumentation Issues." *Journal of Homosexuality* 26:99–136.

Seltzer, Richard. 1993. "AIDS, Homosexuality, Public Opinion, and Changing Correlates Over Time." *Journal of Homosexuality* 26:85–97.

Smith, Tom W. 1981. "Qualifications to Generalized Absolutes: 'Approval of Hitting' Questions on the General Social Survey." *Public Opinion Quarterly* 45:224–230.

Sniderman, Paul M., Richard A. Brody, and Philip E. Tetlock. 1991. *Reasoning and Choice: Explorations in Political Psychology.* New York: Cambridge University Press.

Sullivan, John L., James Piereson, and George E. Marcus. 1982. *Political Tolerance and American Democracy.* Chicago: University of Chicago Press.

Tiemeyer, Peter E. 1993. "Relevant Public Opinion." *Sexual Orientation and U.S. Military Personnel Policy: Options and Assessments,* pp. 191–208. Washington, DC: National Defense Research Institute.

U.S. Senate. 1950. Committee on Expenditures in the Executive Departments. Subcommittee on Investigations. *Employment of Homosexuals and Other Sex Perverts in*

Government. 81st Cong., 2d sess. Document No. 241, November 27. Washington, DC: U.S. Government Printing Office.

Wald, Kenneth D., James W. Button, and Barbara A. Rienzo. 1996. "The Politics of Gay Rights in American Communities: Explaining Antidiscrimination Ordinances and Policies." *American Journal of Political Science* 40:1152–1178.

—— 1997. *All Politics Is Local: Analyzing Local Gay Rights Legislation.* Washington, DC: National Gay and Lesbian Task Force.

Whitley, Bernard E., Jr. 1987. "The Relationship of Sex-Role Orientation to Heterosexuals' Attitudes Toward Homosexuals." *Sex Roles* 17:103–113.

—— 1990. "The Relationship of Heterosexuals' Attributions for the Causes of Homosexuality to Attitudes Toward Lesbians and Gay Men." *Personality and Social Psychology Bulletin* 16:369–377.

Wilson, Thomas C. 1994. "Trends in Tolerance Toward Rightist and Leftist Groups, 1976–1988: Effects of Attitude Change and Cohort Succession." *Public Opinion Quarterly* 58:539–556.

Woods, James D., and Jay H. Lucas. 1993. *The Corporate Closet: The Professional Lives of Gay Men in America.* New York: Free Press.

Yang, Alan S. 1997. "Attitudes Toward Homosexuality." *Public Opinion Quarterly* 61: 477–507.

Young, Michael and Jean Whertvine. 1982. "Attitudes of Heterosexual Students Toward Homosexual Behavior." *Psychological Reports* 51:673–674.

CHAPTER SEVEN

Gay and Lesbian Rights: Emerging Trends in Public Opinion and Voting Behavior

Steven H. Haeberle

In recent years issues concerning lesbians and gay men as well as discussion of the nature of sexual orientation have received increasing coverage in the national media. People who, in the past, had never given much consideration to these matters might likely have had their attention drawn to what for them are new issues or, at least, new ways of thinking about old prejudices. In particular, the issues raised during the 1992 and 1996 presidential campaigns and the political debates on the rights of gays and lesbians that occurred during the first Clinton administration, including gays in the military, openly gay and lesbian personnel appointments, the Employment Non-Discrimination Act, and the Defense of Marriage Act, provide an opportunity to examine what people think about these matters, whether opinion is changing, and whether their views on gay and lesbian rights are consistent with their voting behavior.

The status of gays and lesbians in American society has entered the discourse of national politics and will remain there well into the twenty-first century. In the years following World War II the homophile movement took root in the country's large urban centers (Bérubé 1990; D'Emilio 1983, 1992; and Marcus 1992), maturing into the gay liberation movement and bringing lesbians and gays into the pluralist politics of the urban U.S. (Adam 1987; Bailey 1999; Cooper 1994; DeLeon 1992; Haeberle 1996; Haider-Markel and Meier 1996; and Button, Rienzo, and Wald 1997). Big city governments began enacting bans on discrimination based on sexual orientation in the mid 1970s. By 1992 more than one hundred municipalities had antidiscrimination policies in place and eight states had prohibited discrimination in the work force. Additionally, many other city councils and state legislatures had raised and debated the issues surrounding the rights of lesbians and gay men. The success of the movement in urban politics also generated a community backlash whose most active backers were often fundamentalist, especially evangelical Christians (Button, Rienzo, and Wald 1997). These events provided many people in select states and urban areas a chance to think about the position, rights, and status of homosexuals in American society.

The presidential elections of the 1990s devoted more attention to the issues of concern to gays and lesbians and to courting the votes of lesbians and gay men than have any other previous election cycles in U.S. history. This newfound national interest in sexual orientation gave many citizens who had never really thought seriously about gays and lesbians the opportunity to contemplate their beliefs. The 1992 electorate, thus, contained persons who were widely varied in their experience with regard to gay and lesbian themes in politics. Among many residents of large urban centers the issues were well known. To others in the electorate the debates were quite new.

The 1992 election cycle brought gays and lesbians into the political discourse in three ways. First, beginning in the Democratic primaries, Bill Clinton, as a presidential candidate, actively sought out the support of lesbian and gay voters. His campaign organization included openly gay individuals in prominent positions. As long as their sexual orientation could be kept from becoming an issue in and of itself, their association with Clinton probably worked subtly to attract lesbian and gay voters without repelling antigay opponents in the electorate. Second, the Christian Coalition occupied a conspicuous place in the Republican Party. At the 1992 convention Patrick J. Buchanan welcomed delegates to the Republican National Convention by using his opening address to assure the crowd he stood against "the amoral idea that gay and lesbian couples should have the same standing in law as married men and women . . . in a nation that we still call God's country" (Berke 1992). The tone of the convention probably left a durable negative impression on many voters throughout the campaign (Abramson, Aldrich, and Rohde 1995). Third, and indirectly, incumbent president George Bush came under increasingly harsh criticism for his handling of policy on AIDS/HIV, and the failure of the Bush administration to take more aggressive action on AIDS/HIV research was becoming a campaign issue. Challenger Clinton accused Bush of "ignoring" AIDS. By October 1992 several members of the bipartisan National Commission on AIDS were openly critical of the Bush administration, including the vice chairperson Bush had appointed. Critics expressed disappointment that, while spending on AIDS had increased 50 percent under the Bush administration, spending on research had gone up by only 33 percent (Pear 1992). This too probably worked to Clinton's advantage by helping him draw the support of voters' discontent with the sluggish pace of federal AIDS/HIV policy implementation. In the end economic issues were probably the most important determinants of the election outcome (Abramson, Aldrich, and Rohde 1995; Pomper 1993; Quirk and Dalager 1993; Stokes and DiIulio 1993), but gays and lesbians had gained a place at the table of national political discourse.

During the first Clinton administration, 1993–1997, two issues of particular interest to lesbians and gays received significant political attention and press coverage. The first, "gays in the military," burst into the spotlight almost immediately after Clinton took office. During the campaign Clinton had made a casual promise to lift the ban on homosexuals serving in the armed forces if he were elected. On the heels of his inauguration the Joint Chiefs of Staff sought a meeting to force his hand on the issue. Some Democratic members of Congress openly backed the joint chiefs. After months of negotiations the administration announced its "Don't ask, don't tell" policy in 1993, delaying the public disclosure of its position until after the third national gay and lesbian march in Washington. Many lesbians and gays felt abandoned by the president, and Clinton had wasted much political capital on an issue of low priority to the administration. The three issues Clinton had hoped to pursue most vigorously in his first year in office were health care, NAFTA, and a budget package that would increase taxes on the highest income brackets (Burnham 1997). Clinton's encounter with gays in the military left lesbian and gay voters skeptical of the sincerity of his support and at the same time did little to endear him to those opposed to allowing homosexuals to serve in the armed forces.

After the 1994 midterm election, when Republicans gained control of both houses of Congress, Clinton purposefully recast his image. He tried as hard as he could to leave behind his liberal issue positions, such as ending the military's ban on homosexuals, and he adopted more conservative themes, many of which were copied from popular Republican rhetoric (McWilliams 1997). The second highly visible issue relevant to lesbians and gays was the 1996 Defense of Marriage Act (DOMA), which Clinton backed as part of his new conservative image in preparation for his reelection. The federal "defense" of marriage was sparked by an impending decision of the Supreme Court of Hawaii that would open the possibility of same-sex marriage in that state. The congressional Republican leadership took up the cause on what appeared to be an election-year valence issue for many voters. Clinton's decision to sign the bill, again, left many gays and lesbians doubtful of his commitment to equal rights. These two high-profile issues, gays in the military and DOMA, share two significant political qualities. Both were made into national issues by opponents of the rights of lesbians and gays and the Clinton administration was not the primary agent for bringing the questions to public attention.

During Clinton's first four years in office two other less highly visible matters also attracted the interest of the gay and lesbian community as well as other active policy watchers. First, as a presidential candidate in 1992, Clinton had promised to appoint gays and lesbians to public office. He followed through in 1993 by placing AIDS advocate Robert Hattoy on the White House staff as White House associate director of personnel (Berke 1993). Hattoy gained national prominence in 1992 when he delivered a speech at the Democratic National Convention. Clinton made two additional appointments that required Senate approval. The first was San Francisco politician Roberta Achtenberg, in the Department of Housing and Urban Development, as assistant secretary for fair housing and equal opportunity (Dewar 1993). The second was Bruce A. Lehman to be an assistant secretary of commerce in the department where he served as commissioner of patents and trademarks (Riordan 1993). These events were closely watched by lesbians and gays and likely mollified some of the community in the wake of the president's behavior on the military issue. Second, the Employment Non-Discrimination Act (ENDA) received more serious congressional scrutiny than it ever had in the past. ENDA would ban employment discrimination on the basis of sexual orientation. It would guarantee equal opportunity in the workforce for gays and lesbians in the same way the 1964 Civil Rights Act had for racial minorities but without the imposition of affirmative action requirements. Bills to end discrimination based on sexual orientation had been introduced in every Congress since 1974. The ENDA failed to pass the Senate on September 10, 1996, on a 49–50 vote. Ending employment discrimination had always been a goal of the Human Rights Campaign, which is the largest national gay and lesbian lobbying organization in the U.S. The ENDA was a matter of great concern both to the lesbian and gay political leadership as well as to the lesbian and gay community at large. It was well covered in the gay press. Clinton's endorsement of the proposed legislation occurred about the same time as the more visible scuffle over the DOMA. In all likelihood the ENDA could have had a much more profound effect on the lives of gay men and lesbians than will the DOMA. Clinton's position on ENDA may have offset some of the negative effects of his signing the DOMA in the gay community.

In short, the president sent a series of mixed messages to the public about his stands on the rights of homosexuals. He backed down under pressure from opponents on the policy of allowing gays in the military and he never supported DOMA. These were the most widely publicized gay- and lesbian-related issues of his first term. On the other hand, his executive appointments and symbolic support on ENDA assuaged many in the lesbian and gay community without attracting much attention from opponents of gay and lesbian rights.

LEARNING FROM POLITICS

Putting it all together — gays in the military, DOMA, executive appointments, and ENDA — the Clinton administration stimulated the public to think about gay and lesbian issues. Although some people had had well thought out positions on the issues for a long period of time, the national debates drew attention to the policy questions in an unprecedented way. Public opinion usually reacts and changes in response to events and new information (Page and Shapiro 1992). Furthermore, the presentation of new ideas tends to have the greatest effect on those who know least about the subject (Graber 1997). The years 1992 through 1996 provided the mass public with a significant amount of information on lesbians and gays, and to many this was unfamiliar territory. At least two effects on opinion in the mass public are likely to occur, as summarized in two hypotheses:

1. Public opinion on the rights of gays and lesbians should have changed significantly between 1992 and 1996 because of exposure to public debate.
2. Opinion should change most on the issues receiving the greatest coverage.

The hypotheses will be tested by looking at public opinion on two issues: military service and employment discrimination. Specifically, the analysis will rely on two items in the 1992 and 1996 American National Election Study. The questions are:

1. Do you think homosexuals should be allowed to serve in the United States Armed Forces or don't you think so?
2. Do you FAVOR or OPPOSE laws to protect homosexuals against job discrimination?

When people are asked to comment on the rights of a group of people, they evaluate two elements. The first is their attitude or disposition toward the group. Those with a negative view are less likely to endorse the right. The second is the potential consequences of the act to be sanctioned (Kuklinski et al. 1991; Riggle and Ellis 1994). When people hold a negative affect toward a group, they are more likely to weigh the impact of exercising the right, and they become less willing to sanction it (Kuklinski et al. 1991).

The survey items covering employment discrimination and military service differ with regard to the type of action they reference and the role of government. The military service item asks if the government itself should have an active policy of discrimination against homosexuals. Allowing gays and lesbians into the military could have effects on two sets of others, military personnel and the public at large. At first glance, the military policy question should appeal both to political liberals who generally endorse full rights for gays and lesbians and to libertarian conservatives, who value minimal government. If homosexuals are an unpreferred group to a respondent because of religious or social conservatism, the respondent is more likely to weigh the negative implications of allowing homosexuals in the military. That person is then likely to ponder the possibility of predatory gay men molesting the infantry or the lapse in security that may result from armed lesbians defending the borders. If the negative perceptions are sufficiently strong, the person will decline to sanction homosexuals in the service.

The employment question references a different level of government involvement. Here the government would become proactive, preventing private employers from practicing one form of discrimination. In spirit it is consistent with antidiscrimination policies regarding race, sex, religion, national origin, disability, and veteran status that have been a center piece of twentieth-century American liberalism. Opponents of the government ban may be motivated either by a belief in a conservative political principle that government regulation is to be avoided or by a prejudice against lesbians and gays. The way the employment item is worded leaves open the question of consequences flowing from exercise of the right. In other words, it contains no information on where homosexuals might be employed. Persons not negatively prejudiced against gays or lesbians should be expected to endorse the right without giving much consideration to the outcome. In contrast, those holding negative prejudices will be more likely to think about the repercussions. If their imaginations wander, they are less likely to contemplate the outcome as having homosexuals sort their mail than they are to envision homosexuals teaching kindergartners. Speculation on the implications of the right may lead the respondent to support discrimination.

Many previous studies of public opinion and homosexuality have examined popular attitudes toward gays and lesbians as a group. The group evaluation may affect endorsement of rights, but asking people whether they support civil rights for members of a marginalized group is fundamentally different from asking their evaluation of the group itself. To summarize briefly, antigay and antilesbian attitudes are strongly related to Christian fundamentalism (Haeberle 1991; Hartman 1996: Seltzer 1993; VanderStoep and Green 1988; Button, Rienzo, and

Wald 1997), to political conservatism (Gibson 1987; Gibson and Tedin 1988; Seltzer 1993), and to lower levels of educational attainment (Gibson 1987; Gibson and Tedin 1988; Haeberle 1996; Seltzer 1993). Women have fewer negative attitudes toward lesbians and gays than do men (D'Emilio 1992; Logan 1996). The research on differences between African Americans and whites has produced mixed results (for a good discussion of this research, see Lewis and Rogers, chapter 6, this volume). Some findings suggest younger persons are more tolerant than older persons (Gibson 1987). Last, to the extent that the passage of local ordinances to ban discrimination based on sexual orientation is indirect evidence of mass support for the rights of lesbians and gays, big city residents are more supportive than others (Haeberle 1996; Wald, Button, and Rienzo 1996). The connection between place of residence and attitudes toward homosexuals assumes, as do many gay and lesbian activists, that exposure to lesbians and gay men will build acceptance (Vaid 1995). The NES data are used to explore each of these linkages.

FINDINGS AND RESULTS

The first hypothesis posits that opinion changed in response to public debate between 1992 and 1996. Analysis of the data offers two sets of opinion comparisons. There are consistencies in patterns observed at both points in time and the magnitude of opinion response to the stimulus experienced during the first Clinton administration. Tables 7.1A and 7.1B show the percentages of persons in various political and social groups who favor a law banning job discrimination based on sexual orientation. Data on support for allowing homosexuals to serve in the military are in tables 7.2A and 7.2B. Overall, the data indicate that sizable majorities of the adult population sanction the rights of lesbians and gays to serve in the armed forces and to be protected from arbitrary employment discrimination.

Politically, the data indicate that rank-and-file partisans hold different opinions on policies to protect the civil rights of lesbians and gay men. All groups of Democrats, including strong partisans, weak partisans, and independents who lean toward the Democratic Party, maintain high levels of support both for a law to ban job discrimination and to allow gays and lesbians in the military. Republicans are more divided internally. A majority of weak Republicans favor both policies in the 1992 and 1996 surveys. However, among strong Republicans support for employment rights and military service rights falls to between 30 and 40 percent in both election-year analyses. The respondents who report that they lean toward the Democratic or Republican Parties tend to hold views on the gay

TABLE 7.1A.
Support of Employment Rights for Homosexuals by Political Party and Ideology

	Percent who favor a law to protect homosexuals from job discrimination	
	1992	1996
All	60.4 (2129)	63.8 (1438)*
Strong Democrats	71.4 (384)	78.5 (288)*
Weak Democrats	65.3 (363)	68.4 (285)
Independent-Leans Democratic	71.2 (309)	78.5 (191)
Independent	61.3 (235)	63.4 (112)
Independent-Leans Republican	51.1 (262)	48.7 (152)
Weak Republicans	55.2 (310)	58.9 (214)
Strong Republicans	36.4 (247)	37.4 (187)
Extremely Liberal	71.7 (46)	80.0 (20)
Liberal	86.1 (187)	87.5 (120)
Slightly Liberal	76.0 (217)	81.7 (153)
Moderate	62.5 (496)	67.1 (340)
Slightly Conservative	53.1 (322)	61.9 (223)*
Conservative	42.9 (273)	40.0 (245)
Extremely Conservative	38.8 (49)	25.7 (35)

Significance levels for 2-tailed t-tests: * p .05; ** p .01; *** p .001; and **** p .0001.
Source: 1992 and 1996 NES; the numbers in parentheses are the total N of persons who favor and oppose the statement.

and lesbian issues closer to the strong identifiers of their respective parties than to the weak partisans. The effect in this case is more noticeable for Democrats than Republicans. Consequently, degrees of partisanship do not vary ordinally with views on the rights of gays and lesbians. This pattern of party leaners being more partisan than the weak identifiers appears on many other issues (Keith et al. 1992). Pure independents tend to favor the antidiscrimination law and admission of gays and lesbians to the military, although not as strongly as Democrats. Finally, these survey results gathered from the mass public mirror the findings of Schroedel (chapter 5, this volume), who studied elite opinion by examining state and local elected officials. Both mass and elite Democratic identifiers strongly endorsed policies to protect the rights of homosexuals. The Republican elected officials were as divided in their opinions as were the Republicans in the mass samples. Difference of opinion on the rights of lesbians and gay men is both a matter for interparty dispute and Republican intraparty contention.

The differences in opinion across ideological categories were greater than the partisan differences. The respondents placed themselves on a seven-point

TABLE 7.1B.

Support of Employment Rights for Homosexuals by Social Characteristics

	Percent who favor a law to protect homosexuals from job discrimination	
	1992	1996
Males	54.2 (987)	59.0 (634)
Females	65.2 (1152)	67.7 (804)
Whites	58.8 (1784)	62.7 (1241)*
Blacks	68.8 (276)	72.4 (156)
High School or Less Education	55.6 (1023)	60.7 (623)
Some College	60.9 (501)	64.0 (400)*
College Graduates	68.5 (483)	68.4 (412)
R in Core City where MSA > 2,000,000	73.8 (240)	69.9 (163)
R in Suburb where MSA > 2,000,000	65.7 (495)	71.8 (323)
R in Core City where MSA < 2,000,000	65.6 (295)	65.7 (207)
R in Suburb where MSA < 2,000,000	56.5 (570)	81.0 (268)****
R not in Metropolitan Area	49.7 (539)	58.1 (377)*
18–29 Years of Age	62.2 (418)	69.7 (175)
30–44 Years of Age	61.7 (762)	63.4 (519)
45–64 Years of Age	58.1 (559)	64.2 (424)*
Over 65 Years of Age	57.8 (400)	59.6 (297)
Born again Christian	49.5 (652)	49.1 (466)
Charismatic/Spirit Filled Christian	60.6 (320)	68.6 (220)
Evangelical Christian	41.7 (228)	45.3 (223)
Fundamentalist Christian	50.3 (193)	52.1 (146)
Moderate to Liberal Christian	66.6 (661)	69.2 (519)

Significance levels for 2-tailed t-tests: * p .05; ** p .01; *** p .001; and **** p .0001.

Source: 1992 and 1996 NES; the numbers in parentheses are the total N of persons who favor and oppose the statement.

ideology scale ranging from extremely liberal to extremely conservative. Fewer than one-third of those who self-identified as extremely conservative supported policies to protect the rights of lesbians and gays in 1996. Liberals were consistently the group most likely to favor the rights of homosexuals. Interestingly, those calling themselves extremely liberal were slightly less supportive than the liberals. Otherwise, endorsement of the statements on rights declined ordinally, moving from liberal to extremely conservative. As with partisanship, the findings of the mass surveys are similar to Schroedel's conclusion that, among elites, persons who call themselves very conservative are by far the least supportive of policies to protect the civil rights of lesbians and gays.

The general patterns found in the responses to the employment question and

TABLE 7.2A.

Support of Military Service Rights for Homosexuals by Political Party and Ideology

	Percent who favor military service rights for homosexuals	
	1992	1996
All	58.5 (2127)	68.7 (1483)****
Strong Democrats	69.9 (385)	81.3 (288)***
Weak Democrats	63.6 (365)	77.3 (295)****
Independent-Leans Democratic	72.4 (312)	80.7 (197)*
Independent	61.2 (237)	68.4 (117)
Independent-Leans Republican	46.9 (262)	62.8 (156)***
Weak Republicans	53.8 (303)	61.2 (227)
Strong Republicans	31.9 (238)	39.2 (189)
Extremely Liberal	70.5 (44)	94.7 (19)**
Liberal	84.0 (187)	92.4 (129)*
Slightly Liberal	75.9 (220)	88.8 (153)***
Moderate	60.2 (497)	70.1 (354)**
Slightly Conservative	53.1 (322)	69.5 (233)****
Conservative	37.6 (271)	48.2 (251)**
Extremely Conservative	30.0 (50)	31.4 (35)

Significance levels for 2-tailed t-tests: * p .05; ** p .01; *** p .001; and **** p .0001.

Source: 1992 and 1996 NES; the numbers in parentheses are the total N of persons who favor and oppose the statement.

military service question tend to confirm patterns observed in previous studies. Support for the rights of gays and lesbians is more likely to be found among women than men and among blacks than whites. Support for the rights increases with education. The residents of the nation's largest metropolitan statistical areas (MSAs), both core city dwellers and suburbanites, endorse the rights in large majorities. Support is also strong in midsized and smaller MSAs. The highest levels of opposition are observed in the population that lives outside of metropolitan areas. The 1990 Census found that about 30 percent of the total population resided outside of metropolitan areas. Finally, younger adults are more inclined to voice support for gay and lesbian rights than are older persons. In fact, looking across all these common demographic groupings — sex, race, education, place of residence, and age — we see what appears to be solid backing for the exercise of civil rights by lesbians and gay men by 1996.

The most entrenched opposition to the exercise of rights by homosexuals appears to come from Christians. Religion can be a difficult concept to operationalize because of the diversity found within many large religions. One ap-

TABLE 7.2B.

Support of Military Service Rights for Homosexuals by Social Characteristics

	Percent who favor allowing homosexuals to serve in the armed forces	
	1992	1996
Males	47.6 (997)	60.7 (669)****
Females	68.2 (1135)	75.3 (814)***
Whites	58.6 (1784)	68.3 (1279)****
Blacks	60.5 (271)	74.4 (160)**
High School or Less Education	54.3 (1029)	64.4 (651)****
Some College	60.2 (495)	72.6 (405)****
College Graduates	64.8 (477)	71.5 (425)*
R in Core City where MSA > 2,000,000	71.2 (236)	76.8 (168)***
R in Suburb where MSA > 2,000,000	62.7 (490)	73.5 (328)*
R in Core City where MSA < 2,000,000	60.9 (289)	70.7 (215)**
R in Suburb where MSA < 2,000,000	57.2 (568)	66.7 (378)
R not in Metropolitan Area	49.7 (549)	53.6 (394)
18–29 Years of Age	60.6 (416)	72.5 (182)**
30–44 Years of Age	64.9 (766)	72.8 (525)**
45–64 Years of Age	52.8 (566)	67.5 (437)****
Over 65 Years of Age	52.3 (384)	59.7 (315)
Born again Christians	43.7 (648)	56.7 (476)****
Charismatic/Spirit Filled Christians	48.6 (315)	69.3 (228)****
Evangelical Christians	38.8 (227)	59.1 (230)****
Fundamentalist Christians	46.1 (191)	56.3 (151)
Moderate to Liberal Christians	65.4 (665)	73.4(533)**

Significance levels for 2-tailed t-tests: * p .05; ** p .01; *** p .001; and **** p .0001.

Source: 1992 and 1996 NES; the numbers in parentheses are the total N of persons who favor and oppose the propositions.

proach is to pursue an organizational analysis where indicators are constructed from organizational affiliations. In general, it is reasonable to expect to see differences of opinion on some political matters based on denominational membership. Presbyterians, for example, hold views different from Jehovah's Witnesses. While general patterns of difference may occur, not all members of any organization will share the predominant view. Therefore, a second approach to the analysis, one that seeks to understand how people define the nature of their own religious beliefs, may be preferable. Christianity is not the only religious source of opposition to the rights of homosexuals. However, in the context of American politics it is an especially potent force that dwarfs other religious communities. Moreover, the U.S. has a strand of fundamentalist Christianity unrivaled in size by those of any other modern nation. Christian fundamentalism, with its dual emphasis on evangelism and congregational autonomy, is uniquely well positioned to incubate organized opposition to gay and lesbian activism (Button, Rienzo, and Wald 1997). The zeal with which fundamentalist or evangelical convictions are held transcends many denominational lines. In 1992 and 1996 the NES asked Christians two questions about the nature of their beliefs:

1. Would you call yourself a born-again Christian, that is, have you personally had a conversion experience related to Jesus Christ? [Asked of all Christians]
2. Which one of these words best describes your kind of Christianity, fundamentalist, evangelical, charismatic, or spirit filled, moderate to liberal? [Asked of all non-Orthodox Christians]

Evangelicals were the most firmly opposed to sanctioning the rights of gay men and lesbians. In 1992 only 38.8 percent of evangelicals questioned believed that homosexuals should be *allowed* (emphasis added) to serve in the military. Opposition was also expressed by fundamentalist and born-again Christians. Conversely, majorities of those who self-describe as charismatic or moderate to liberal endorsed ending the military ban and supported the antidiscrimination law.

The hypothesis of opinion change from 1992 to 1996 holds that public debate stimulated people to think about the issues. Of the four gay-relevant controversies in Clinton's first term — gays in the military, DOMA, executive appointments, and ENDA — the military question appeared by far to draw the most press attention and by extension seemed to have the greatest potential to induce public reflection on the policy questions. Between 1992 and 1996 public opinion became more supportive of ensuring the rights of lesbians and gays, but, on the military item, support for allowing homosexuals to serve, grew from 58.5 percent to 68.7 percent. That is a jump of 10.2 percentage points. In comparison, the positive shift in support for the employment discrimination law was only 3.4 percentage points. Furthermore, the changes in opinion on military service were the greatest among those groups who were the staunchest opponents in 1992. While the net shift of opinion on the question was 10.2 percentage points for all respondents, independent partisans who lean toward the Republican Party shifted 15.9 percentage points, people who self-describe as slightly conservative conservatives 16.4 percentage points, males 13.1 percentage points, born-again Christians 13.0 percentage points, and evangelical Christians an astounding 20.3 percentage points.

By 1996 majorities in every one of the social groups observed supported the rights of homosexuals to be in the military. Majority support was lacking only among strong Republicans and people who identified as conservative or extremely conservative. This large shift in opinion suggests that public airing of the issues surrounding the ban on military service induced at least some to reevaluate their reasons for condoning the ban in the first place. The public debate seems to have had a positive educational impact, making the mass public more accepting of gays and lesbians in the armed forces. By 1996 only 31.3 percent of respondents opposed allowing homosexuals to serve in the military. If the public debate explanation is accurate, the shift in opinion could have been accomplished by two lines of causality. First, gay and lesbian activism and visibility may have changed attitudes toward homosexuals so that when respondents were asked in 1996 whether they thought homosexuals should be allowed in the military, their answers were shaped less by prejudice. Second, the same activism could have affected beliefs about the consequences of allowing lesbians and gays to serve.

The change in opinion on the employment item displayed a pattern similar to that on military service in most political, social, and religious groups, but the positive shift was much smaller in magnitude, only 3.4 percentage points. Both strong Democrats and those who lean toward the Democratic Party increased their support for the antidiscrimination law by more than 7 percentage points. Strong Republicans remained overwhelmingly opposed, and people who lean toward the Republican Party decreased their support by 2.4 percentage points to position themselves closer to the strong Republicans. Thus division of opinion on the issue became more partisan. Among the ideological categories only conservatives and extreme conservatives failed to increase their levels of support for employment rights.

Statistically significant change between 1992 and 1996 in support for the antidiscrimination law appeared in few groups. Persons with some college education moved their opinions closer to those of college graduates. The middle aged became more like younger persons and distanced their opinions from those of the elderly. Whites became more sympathetic to an antidiscrimination law. Finally, persons living in the suburbs of the smaller MSAs and the nonmetropolitan residents, those least likely to have had prior direct exposure to gay and lesbian politics, also became more supportive of the employment discrimination ban. In contrast, few of the observed groups did not alter their opinions significantly on the military service question. Interestingly, persons living in the suburbs of the smaller MSAs and the nonmetropolitan residents, who did register a big change on the employment policy question, failed to make a significant shift on military service. Otherwise, only the elderly and fundamentalist Christians were not significantly more supportive in 1996 than they had been in 1992. The widespread social, political, and religious diffusion of the shift in opinion on military service indicates that in most sectors of society some people were reevaluating their position on the issue during Clinton's first term.

Many of these political and social variables are, of course, closely related. Discriminant analyses performed on the four dichotomous policy questions, em-

TABLE 7.3.

Discriminant Analysis of Public Opinion on Issues of Gay and Lesbian Rights
Standardized Canonical Discriminant Function Coefficients

	Employment Law 1992	Military 1992	Employment Law 1996	Military 1996
Race (Black = 1)	−.10		−.16	
Sex (Male = 1)	.35	.57	.20	.40
Years of Education			−.29	−.24
Age		.16		.18
R in Core City where MSA . 2,000,000	−.11	−.11		
R in Suburbs where MSA 2,000,000			−.17	
R in Suburbs where MSA 2,000,000	.12			
R not in Metropolitan Area	.25			
Conservative/Extremely Con.			.33	
Liberal/Extremely Liberal	−.45	−.31	−.23	−.32
Republican (strong and weak)	.27	.25	.27	.45
Democrat (strong and weak)	−.12	−.12		
Born again Christian	.32	.35	.40	.32
Fundamentalist Christian		.14		
Charismatic Christian		.21	−.12	
Evangelical Christian	.24	.27	.20	
Moderate to Liberal Christian	−.14			−.12
Canonical Correlation	.32	.40	.37	.38
Percent of Cases Correctly Predicted	65.0	68.1	69.5	73.3
Percent Favoring Correctly Predicted	81.7	78.7	85.7	89.8
Percent Opposed Correctly Predicted	40.1	53.3	40.7	37.1
Test of Function	.90	.84	.86	.85
Wilks^2 (df)	214(17)***	344(17)***	209(17)***	233(17)***
N	2011	2006	1436	1481

*** indicates p .001 (Coefficients , .10 and . 2.10 are suppressed)

ployment rights and military service in 1992 and 1996, sorted out the relative contributions of each variable. The results of the four analyses are shown in table 7.3, which contains the standardized canonical discriminant function coefficients. Their interpretation is similar to standardized regression coefficients produced by OLS, but with two major exceptions. First, discriminant analysis assumes the presence of all variables in the model when the coefficients are calculated, making it impossible to estimate the statistical significance of any one indicator. However, the standardized coefficients do state the relative influence of each independent variable. For example, the coefficients in column one show the effect of Democratic Party identification as −.12 and the impact of being an evangelical Christian as .24. The former has half the effect of the latter. The equation as a whole is statistically significant, and the largest coefficients have the greatest substantive effect. As coefficients approach zero they lose any substantively significant value. Second, discriminant analysis assigns direction to the coefficients arbitrarily for each equation, but within equations all coefficients with the same sign are working in the same direction.

The observed differences of opinion on the rights of lesbians and gay men stem most fully from a mixture of what sounds like the ingredients of a tabloid front page — sex, religion, and politics. First, the opposing opinions offered by males and females clearly account for much of the overall difference in the samples. The gender differences are greater on the military service question than on the employment rights item, but the divergence of views lessened some between 1992 and 1996. The observed reluctance of males to allow homosexuals to serve in the armed forces remained a powerful source of opposition in 1996. Second, and almost as important as gender, the question of whether Christians considered themselves "born again" proved to be one of the most substantively significant predictors. Born-again Christians share the same opinion as males on all four policy questions. Among the more specific labels applied to non-Orthodox Christians, "evangelical" is associated with significant differences of opinion. Evangelicals share the same issue positions as males and born-again Christians. Fundamentalist, charismatic, and moderate to liberal Christianity have only a slight influence on opinion regarding the rights of gays and lesbians. Notably, when moderate to liberal Christianity does show an effect, it is in the direction opposite of evangelical. Third, the effects of the political variables indicate the issues show a semi-ideological, semipartisan division of opinion. The impact of ideology on the questions about the rights of homosexuals found self-identified liberals as strongly supportive in all four equations. Liberal ideology displayed a more moderate effect on the employment issue in 1996. Its substantive importance declined as the significance of conservative ideology and education increased, with this one exception: conservative ideology lacked a substantively significant relationship to both questions in 1992 and to military service in 1996. Similarly, the partisan division placed Republicans in opposition to rights across the board, but Democrats were generally no more or less likely to be supportive. That opinion on the rights of lesbians and gay men is so sharply a function of liberal but not conservative ideology and of Republican but not Democratic partisanship suggests that attitudes about the roles of gay men and lesbians in U.S. society are continuing to develop, as was suggested by the opinion shifts observed between 1992 and 1996. The future may bring either sharper ideological and partisan distinctions or a progressive shift of opinion dissolving major politically defined differences.

In addition, slight to moderate effects accrued from three other variables. First, blacks and nonblacks differed on the question of employment rights. The experience of black Americans with job discrimination could easily explain why African Americans would be more sensitive to understanding the personal vulnerability caused by a lack of legal protection in employment. Nonblacks and blacks showed no significant differences on the military service issue. Second, the years of education the respondent had received was related to willingness to protect gays and lesbians against job discrimination and allow homosexuals to serve in the armed forces. A substantively significant effect of education on issue positions appeared in 1996 but not in 1992. Education has a unique relationship to discrimination based on sexual orientation. Ordinarily, education expands an individual's knowledge and understanding of different people, leading at least to more tolerance, if not to acceptance. However, psychiatrists classified homosexuality as an illness until 1973. The better educated people who attended college before that date learned that homosexuality was a pathology. Thus, respondents, who are today middle aged or older, acquired false scientific information that would have to be discarded in order to be supportive of the rights of lesbians and gays. The "education equals knowledge produces tolerance" developmental sequence would not have a straightforward application in this age cohort. In the future it may be useful to explore whether an age-education interaction effect exists.

Third, where one lives has had some impact on opinion about the rights of gay men and lesbians. Big city residents differed significantly from people in the suburbs of smaller metropolitan areas and in nonmetropolitan areas in their support for the rights of lesbians and gays. This effect surfaced in employment but not military service, and the effect of place of residence diminished greatly between 1992 and 1996. The gay rights movement initially gained its greatest visibility in big city politics. This may explain why the effect of the type of community where one resides declined with the passage of time. In more recent years the movement has become active in an ever increasing number of localities, and the media and national politics have made the gay and lesbian presence more evident. The discriminant analyses offer insight not only into the relative effects of the various social and political forces at work but also explain the dynamics of how the interrelationships among these variables shift over time.

Overall, the discriminant analyses do a good job of predicting opinion on employment rights and military service from the independent variables. The canonical correlations range from .32 to .40. The proportion of cases correctly classified by the equations ranges from a minimum of 65.0 percent for employment rights in 1992 to a maximum of 73.3 percent for military service in 1996. Furthermore, on both policy questions the share of accurate predictions increased from 1992 to 1996. The models do especially well predicting the percentage of respondents who will favor the rights (78.7 to 89.8 percent). In contrast, none of the equations achieves the same level of accuracy in predicting opposition. In three of four models the proportion of opponents correctly predicted fell below 50 percent. The independent variables tested in the analyses are well grounded in their theoretical linkage to public opinion about homosexuals. Furthermore, previous research has demonstrated an impact of each of the variables on opinion. Nonetheless, the failure to do better predicting opponents of employment rights and military service for homosexuals indicates that a piece of the puzzle is missing. Future research should direct attention toward exploring other factors that may influence opinion about the rights of lesbians and gays. Additional variables that likely have an impact on support for civil rights include personal contact with lesbians and gay men and individual attitudes toward both groups.

OPINION AND VOTING BEHAVIOR

If elected officials are to mediate decisions on behalf of the public, voters must hold issue positions, correctly perceive the positions of candidates and parties, and cast their ballots to voice a preference for the candidates who share their views. The issues of homosexual rights were far down on the list of factors that may have affected the outcomes of the elections in 1992 (Abramson, Aldrich, and Rohde 1995; Pomper 1993; Quirk and Dalager 1993; Stokes and DiIulio 1993) and 1996 (Burnham 1997; DiIulio 1997; Keeter 1997; Pomper 1997). Nonetheless, voter behavior in the two elections shows that rank-and-file opinion on questions about the rights of gays and lesbians is becoming more consistent with partisan differences. Table 7.4 contains the distribution of opinion on the employment discrimination law and military service issues with presidential vote in 1992 and 1996. If, in fact, the public airing of gay-relevant policy debates, especially the military controversy, stimulated thinking about the questions, it should be expected that voters in 1996 casted ballots in such a way that

TABLE 7.4.

Opinion on Gay and Lesbian Rights and Voting Behavior 1992 and 1996

1992				
Opinion on Discrimination in Employment and Military Service	1992 Vote for President			
	Clinton	Bush	Perot	Total
Percent who favor a law to protect homosexuals from job discrimination	58.9 (571)	23.9 (232)	17.1 (166)	100 (969)
Percent who oppose a law to protect homosexuals from job discrimination	30.6 (188)	50.2 (309)	19.2 (118)	100 (615)
Percent who favor allowing homosexuals to serve in the armed forces	59.7 (559)	21.8 (204)	18.6 (174)	100 (937)
Percent who oppose allowing homosexuals to serve in the armed forces	31.3 (200)	50.9 (325)	17.8 (114)	100 (639)

For the relationship between employment and vote, chi^2 = 140; df = 6, p < .0001; for the relationship between military service and vote, chi^2 = 159; df = 6, p < .0001.

1996				
Opinion on Discrimination in Employment and Military Service	1996 Vote for President			
	Clinton	Dole	Perot	Total
Percent who favor a law to protect homosexuals from job discrimination	66.0 (444)	27.2 (183)	6.8 (46)	100 (673)
Percent who oppose a law to protect homosexuals from job discrimination	33.8 (131)	58.4 (226)	7.8 (30)	100 (387)
Percent who favor allowing homosexuals to serve in the armed forces	64.6 (479)	27.6 (205)	7.8 (58)	100 (742)
Percent who oppose allowing homosexuals to serve in the armed forces	30.0 (101)	63.1 (212)	6.8 (23)	100 (336)

For the relationship between employment and vote, chi^2 = 109; df = 6, p < .0001; for the relationship between military service and vote, chi^2 = 126; df = 6, p < .0001.

Source: 1992 and 1996 NES; the numbers in parentheses are the number of cases.

their opinions on questions of policy with regard to homosexuals aligned better with perceived candidate or party positions on those items than what was observed in 1992.

Although Clinton sent plenty of mixed messages about his commitment to the rights of gays and lesbians, all things considered, by 1996 he was perceived to be the more supportive of the two major party candidates. Little was known about third-party candidate Ross Perot's position on gay and lesbian issues in either election. In 1992 Clinton received the votes of clear majorities among those favoring the employment antidiscrimination law and among those who believed homosexuals should be allowed to serve in the military. Bush garnered the votes of majorities taking the opposite positions, but they were bare majorities, 50.2 percent of those opposing the employment discrimination law and 50.9 percent of those wanting to bar homosexuals from military service. Proponents and opponents of lesbian and gay rights were equally likely to vote for Perot in 1992. In 1996 voting behavior more closely mirrored the public opinion split on gay and lesbian rights. In 1992 59.7 percent of voters who favored allowing homosexuals to serve in the military cast votes for Clinton. That increased to 64.6 percent in 1996. Similarly, in 1992 58.9 percent of voters favoring a law to ban discrimination in employment voted for Clinton, but in 1996 66.0 percent of voters holding that position did so. Conversely, opponents of the rights of lesbians and gays became more likely to vote Republican in 1996. The percentage of persons voting Republican who opposed allowing military service increased from 50.9 percent to 63.1 percent. Comparable figures for opponents of the employment discrimination law were 50.2 percent and 58.4 percent, respectively. Supporters of gay and lesbian rights had drifted toward the Democratic Party and opponents toward the Republican Party.

Further tests of the connection between issue positions on gay and lesbian concerns and candidate preferences can be gained by looking at the voters who switched their vote from one party to another between 1992 and 1996. Table 7.5 presents the voters' 1996 vote and their recall of whom they voted for in 1992. Few 1992 voters defected away from Clinton to vote for another candidate in 1996 although some 1992 voters refrained from participating in 1996. The 1996 data show that over two-thirds of Perot's 1992 voters chose another major party candidate in 1996, as did 20 percent of Bush voters. Voters who had supported Perot in 1992 but who opposed sanctioning the rights of lesbians and gays in 1996 were much more likely to vote for Dole. He received the votes of 54.9 percent of those who opposed allowing homosexuals to serve in the military and 46.4 percent of those opposed to the employment discrimination law. Those favoring the rights were about equally likely to vote either for Clinton or again for

TABLE 7.5.

Opinion of Gay and Lesbian Rights and Partisan Change in Vote 1992 to 1996

	Aggregate Change (percent) 1996 Vote			
1992 Vote	Clinton	Dole	Perot	Total
Clinton	92.7	4.9	2.4	100
	(419)	(22)	(11)	(452)
Bush	17.2	80.0	2.8	100
	(69)	(320)	(11)	(400)
Perot	31.0	37.4	31.6	100
	(48)	(58)	(49)	(155)

1992 Bush Voter's 1996 Vote

Opinion on discrimination in employment and military service	1996 Vote for President			
	Clinton	Dole	Perot	Total
Percent who favor a law to protect homosexuals from job discrimination	24.3 (43)	72.9 (129)	2.8 (5)	100 (177)
Percent who oppose a law to protect homosexuals from job discrimination	10.6 (21)	87.4 (173)	2.0 (4)	100 (198)
Percent who favor allowing homosexuals to serve in the armed forces	26.0 (53)	71.1 (145)	2.9 (6)	100 (204)
Percent who oppose allowing homosexuals to serve in the armed forces	7.7 (14)	89.5 (162)	2.7 (5)	100 (181)

1992 Perot Voter's 1996 Vote

Opinion on discrimination in employment and military service	1996 Vote for President			
	Clinton	Dole	Perot	Total
Percent who favor a law to protect homosexuals from job discrimination	34.1 (31)	31.8 (29)	34.1 (31)	100 (91)
Percent who oppose a law to protect homosexuals from job discrimination	26.8 (15)	46.4 (26)	26.8 (15)	100 (56)
Percent who favor allowing homosexuals to serve in the armed forces	34.7 (35)	28.7 (29)	36.6 (37)	100 (101)
Percent who oppose allowing homosexuals to serve in the armed forces	23.5 (12)	54.9 (28)	21.6 (11)	100 (51)

Perot in 1996. Among the voters who preferred Bush in 1992 and favored rights of homosexuals, nearly 30 percent defected to another candidate in 1996. Most went for Clinton. Less than 3 percent voted for Perot. Few Bush supporters who opposed lesbian and gay rights defected from Dole in 1996. The large majority of Bush voters who supported gay and lesbian rights voted for Dole in 1996, but it was not likely an issue on which many of them held strong opinions. In short, the 1992 voting patterns showed a partisan split on support for civil rights for gays and lesbians, and that division became stronger in 1996. Moreover, the large majority of 1992 voters who switched to the candidate of a different party in 1996 did so in a way consistent with the existing partisan division on lesbian and gay rights issues.

Policy debates of the 1992 and 1996 presidential elections and President Clinton's first term in office focused an unprecedented level of national attention on the rights of lesbians and gay men in U.S. society. Between 1992 and 1996 Americans became more willing to support a law that would ban discrimination in employment based on sexual orientation and to favor allowing gays and lesbians to serve in the armed forces. Notably, the opinion shift on military service was much greater than that observed on the employment discrimination question. This likely occurred because the media gave the "gays in the military" issue far more publicity than ENDA and the problems of employment discrimination. The staunchest opponents of the rights of gay men and lesbians are males, evangelical and born-again Christians, and Republican party identifiers. Supporters of the rights include ideological liberals and females. Support is increasing among the better educated and Democratic identifiers. The voting patterns of the 1992 and 1996 presidential elections indicate that public opinion on the question of civil rights for gays and lesbians is becoming a more partisan issue. The 1996 election had larger majorities of rights supporters voting Democratic and opponents voting Republican than did the 1992 election. This probably resulted both from party identifiers adjusting their opinions to accommodate fellow partisans and from some voters defecting to cast a vote that was more consistent with their policy views. It would be premature to conclude that election outcomes hinge on questions of civil rights for lesbians and gays. However, it is clear that the parties are becoming more, not less, divergent on the issue, and those differences will likely continue to appear for many years to come.

These findings tell us who changed their minds about endorsement of the rights of gays and lesbians between 1992 and 1996, but they leave open the larger question of why opinion shifted. The hypothesis that media attention to the gays in the military debate stimulated people to think about the issue and that in turn triggered a change in opinion is one possible explanation. It deserves more thorough testing. During this time period more people have been coming out. This includes both public figures as well as ordinary citizens. It may be that exposure to lesbians and gays who are out causes people to reevaluate their opinions about employment and military service rights. Alternatively, it may not be exposure alone but rather dialogue with people who are out that stimulates opinion change. In addition, it must be remembered that not all opinion change is positive. The effects of opinion leadership may be influencing some Republicans and conservatives to become more strongly opposed to enforcement of civil rights protection for gays and lesbians. Further exploration of these questions will improve not only our understanding of gay and lesbian politics but also our knowledge about the general process of group legitimation in a pluralistic society.

REFERENCES

Abramson, Paul R., John H. Aldrich, and David W. Rohde. 1995. *Change and Continuity in the 1992 Elections*, rev. ed. Washington, DC: Congressional Quarterly Press.

Adam, Barry D. 1987. *The Rise of a Gay and Lesbian Movement*. Boston: Twayne.

Bailey, Robert W. 1999. *Gay Politics/Urban Politics: Economics and Identity in the Urban Setting*. New York: Columbia University Press.

Berke, Richard L. 1992. "Unhumbled, Buchanan Backs Bush." *New York Times*, August 18, p. A8.

—— 1993. "Time Bomb in the White House." *New York Times Magazine*, June 6, p. 28.

Bérubé, Allan. 1990. *Coming Out Under Fire: The History of Gay Men and Women in World War Two*. New York: Free Press.

Burnham, Walter Dean. 1997. "Bill Clinton: Riding the Tiger." In Gerald M. Pomper, ed., *The Election of 1996: Reports and Interpretations*. Chatham, NJ: Chatham House.

Button, James W., Barbara A. Rienzo, and Kenneth D. Wald. 1997. *Private Lives, Public Conflicts: Battles Over Gay Rights in American Communities*. Washington, DC: Congressional Quarterly Press.

Cooper, Davina. 1994. *Sexing the City: Lesbian and Gay Politics Within the Activist State*. London: Rivers Oram.

DeLeon, Richard E. 1992. *Left Coast City: Progressive Politics in San Francisco, 1975– 1991*. Lawrence: University of Kansas Press.

D'Emilio, John. 1983. *Sexual Politics, Sexual Communities*. Chicago: University of Chicago Press.

—— 1992. *Making Trouble: Essays on Gay History, Politics, and the University*. New York: Routledge.

Dewar, Helen. 1993. "Senate Votes to Confirm Achtenberg." *Washington Post*, May 25, p. A7.

DiIulio, John J. 1997. "Conclusion: Valence Voters, Valence Victors." In Michael Nelson, ed., *The Elections of 1996*. Washington, DC: Congressional Quarterly Press.

Gibson, James L. 1987. "Homosexuals and the Ku Klux Klan: A Contextual Analysis of Political Tolerance." *Western Political Quarterly* 40:427–448.

Gibson, James L. and Kent T. Tedin. 1988. "The Etiology of Intolerance of Homosexual Politics." *Social Science Quarterly* 69:587–604.

Graber, Doris A. 1997. *Mass Media and American Politics*, 5th ed. Washington, DC: Congressional Quarterly Press.

Haeberle, Steven H. 1991. "The Role of Religious Organizations in the Gay and Lesbian Rights Movement." In Barbara M. Yarnold, ed., *The Role of Religious Organizations in Social Movements*. New York: Praeger.

—— 1996. "Gay Men and Lesbians at City Hall." *Social Science Quarterly* 77:190–197.

Haider-Markel, Donald P. and Kenneth J. Meier. 1996. "The Politics of Gay and Lesbian Rights: Expanding the Scope of the Conflict." *Journal of Politics* 58:332–349.

Hartman, Keith. 1996. *Congregations in Conflict*. New Brunswick, NJ: Rutgers University Press.

Keeter, Scott. 1997. "Public Opinion and the Election." In Gerald M. Pomper, ed., *The Election of 1996: Reports and Interpretations*. Chatham, NJ: Chatham House.

Keith, Bruce E., David B. Magleby, Candice J. Nelson, Elizabeth Orr, Mark Westlye, and Raymond E. Wolfinger. 1992. *The Myth of the Independent Voter*. Berkeley: University of California Press.

Kuklinski, James H., Ellen D. B. Riggle, Victor Ottati, Norman Schwarz, and Robert S. Wyer, Jr. 1991. "The Cognitive and Affective Bases of Political Tolerance Judgments." *American Journal of Political Science* 35:1–27.

Lewis, Gregory B. and Marc A. Rogers. 1999. "Does the Public Support Equal Employment Rights for Gays?" Chapter 6, this volume.

Logan, Colleen R. 1996. "Homophobia? No, Homoprejudice." *Journal of Homosexuality* 31:31–53.

McWilliams, Wilson Carey. 1997. "Conclusion—The Meaning of the Election." In Gerald M. Pomper, ed., *The Election of 1996: Reports and Interpretations*. Chatham, NJ: Chatham House.

Marcus, Eric. 1992. *Making History: The Struggle for Gay and Lesbian Equal Rights, 1945–1990*. New York: HarperPerennial.

Page, Benjamin I. and Robert Y. Shapiro. 1992. *The Rational Public: Fifty Years of Trends in Americans' Policy Preferences*. Chicago: University of Chicago Press.

Pear, Robert. 1992. "As Bush Defends AIDS Policy, Its Critics See Flaws." *New York Times*, October 18, p. A27.

Pomper, Gerald M. 1993. "The Presidential Election." In Gerald M. Pomper, ed., *The Election of 1992: Reports and Interpretations*. Chatham, NJ: Chatham House.

—— 1997. "The Presidential Election." In Gerald M. Pomper, ed., *The Election of 1996: Reports and Interpretations*. Chatham, NJ: Chatham House.

Quirk, Paul J. and Jon K. Dalager. 1993. "The Election: A 'New Democrat' and a New

Kind of Presidential Election." In Michael Nelson, ed., *The Elections of 1992*. Washington, DC: Congressional Quarterly Press.

Riggle, Ellen D. and Alan L. Ellis. 1994. "Political Tolerance of Homosexuals: The Role of Group Attitudes and Legal Principles." *Journal of Homosexuality* 26:135–147.

Riordan, Teresa. 1993. " Patents." *New York Times*, May 3, p. D2.

Schroedel, Jean Reith. 1999. "Elite Attitudes Toward Homosexuals." Chapter 5, this volume.

Seltzer, Richard. 1993. "AIDS, Homosexuality, Public Opinion, and Changing Correlates Over Time." *Journal of Homosexuality* 26:85–97.

Sinclair, Molly. 1992. "'Die-In' Decries U.S. AIDS Policy." *Washington Post*, October 13, p. B8.

Stokes, Donald E., and John J. DiIulio, Jr. 1993. "The Setting: Valence Politics in Modern Elections." In Michael Nelson, ed., *The Elections of 1992*. Washington, DC: Congressional Quarterly Press.

Vaid, Urvashi. 1995. *Virtual Equality*. New York: Anchor.

VanderStoep, Scott W. and Charles W. Green. 1988. "Religiosity and Homonegativism: A Path-Analytic Study." *Basic and Applied Social Psychology* 9:135–147.

Wald, Kenneth D., James W. Button, and Barbara A. Rienzo. 1996. "The Politics of Gay Rights in American Communities: Explaining Antidiscrimination Ordinances and Policies." *American Journal of Political Science* 40:1152–1178.

CHAPTER EIGHT

The Effects of Sexual Orientation on Citizen Perceptions of Candidate Viability

Rebekah Herrick and Sue Thomas

On November 7, 1989, Keith St. John, an openly gay candidate, won a seat on the Albany, New York, City Council. His campaign highlighted issues important to the Ward 2 constituents, such as affordable housing, homelessness, job training, curtailing drug use, and child care. St. John's sexual orientation was publicly known; he had served as a gay representative on the police department's community relations panel. Last minute attempts were made in both the primary and the general elections to make an issue of his homosexuality (inflammatory flyers were posted throughout the ward). Still, St. John won the race with the vote of 75 percent of the electorate ("Gay Community News" 1989).

How often can the story of Keith St. John's victory on the Albany City Council be replicated in other U.S. cities? Will many candidates who work hard in their districts, tap into voters' concerns, and find acceptable solutions to problems be supported on election day regardless of their sexual orientation, race, or sex? How potent today are personal circumstances that were once thought to have disqualified candidates or doomed them to failure five, ten, or twenty-five years ago?

Certainly, we no longer think of religion as being a major barrier to candidacies, although that was a heavily debated issue in the presidential race of John F. Kennedy. We no longer worry about whether or not a candidate has been divorced to consider her or him viable. Former President Ronald Reagan was divorced and twice married before he assumed the presidency, and Bob Dole, 1996 Republican presidential nominee for president, was similarly situated. Women candidates are now equally likely as men to raise funds and win races, indicating an increased acceptance of their place in elective political office (Burrell 1994; Thomas and Wilcox 1998).

However, not all personal characteristics of candidates and potential candidates have ceased preventing office seekers from gaining their goal. Certainly, race is one. Although there are many more minority officeholders than ever before, they tend to be from majority minority districts rather than from districts that are predominantly white. What about sexual orientation of candidates? This is one of the few areas that remains underexplored.

Based on the paucity of social science evidence on public perceptions of openly gay candidates and the importance of this subject at this point in history, we offer research to detect voter perceptions of how sexual orientation of candidates for elective office affects candidate viability.

QUESTIONS OF REPRESENTATION

Questions of elite level political representation could be considered premature to some reading this chapter. Some may wonder why we are concerned with the proportion of openly gay and lesbian candidates and officeholders in the political system when, in most situations, gays and lesbians do not even have the most basic civil rights protection against job or housing discrimination, are often the targets of physical violence and verbal abuse, and cannot avail themselves of ceremonies and legal rights such as marriage, insurance coverage for their significant others, legal rights related to being the "next of kin," or even, in some cases, continued custody of their children (Button, Rienzo, Wald 1997; Sherrill 1996; Sullivan 1996; Haider-Markel 1997a, 1997b). There are several responses to this question.

First, although some sentiment exists for the argument that civil rights for lesbians and gays needs to be pursued according to a hierarchy of issues, a more widely shared perspective suggests that all avenues through which progress toward equal status can be made should be pursued. Second, the increase in gay and lesbian officeholders can help alleviate some of the policy disadvantages currently experienced by the gay population. Changing laws that either discriminate against lesbians and gays or simply ignore them would be easier with more gays in office. While we would not suggest that gay officeholders hold monolithic opinions about public policy, it is fair to assume that, like other underrepresented populations in office, the larger the gay population in office, the more interest there would be in sponsoring, cosponsoring, and voting for legislation to benefit lesbians and gays (see Thomas 1994). It is also probable that an increase in the openly gay population among officeholders would help sensitize other legislators to the needs of the gay community. Third, gays, openly or otherwise, are already in office. Of the roughly 500,000 elected officials in the United

States, approximately 120 are openly gay or lesbian (National Museum and Archive of Lesbian and Gay History 1996). It is also safe to assume that many other gays and lesbians who are not publicly open about their sexual orientation are in office. Hence, it is important to explore the extent to which citizens support growing diversity in political representation.

Broad questions of representation are also critical to this analysis. In a democratic society legitimacy of the governmental system is based, in part, on the opportunity for all citizens to serve their communities and nation. Relatedly, if all citizens are seen to have an equal opportunity to participate in the policy decisions affecting their lives, there is a greater likelihood of system stability. If openly lesbian and gay citizens are excluded from the opportunities afforded others, the legitimacy and stability of the system is at issue.

The gay and lesbian population of the United States is roughly 10 percent — approximately the same as the African American or Latino populations in the United States. This means that the representation of gays and lesbians may be among the worst in the nation (.02 percent of elected officials compared to 10 percent of the population). Although the true percentage of gay or lesbian officeholders is higher than the figure given, since many are not open about their sexual orientation, the fact that many feel they must hide underscores this discussion of representation and access to public positions.

It is also important that openly lesbian and gay candidates have access to public offices so that citizens have the opportunity to see them in the full range of public positions. As contact theory maintains, exposure to those who are different may lessen any trepidation about motives, actions, or attitudes of lesbians and gays (Herek and Glunt 1993; Button, Rienzo, and Wald 1997).

Finally, we do not know how many gay and lesbian candidates run for and win office. What we do know is how many candidates run openly. Unlike race or sex, it is possible for gay and lesbian candidates to run without voters knowing their status. Thus, information about public perceptions of tolerance or intolerance, viability or nonviability may help gay candidates decide how best to pursue their political ambitions (see also Golebiowska and Thomsen, chapter 9, this volume).

In this chapter we present original experimental research designed to test whether or not subtle or unconscious bias affects citizen attitudes toward lesbian or gay candidates for office.

RESEARCH PREMISES

How do we expect voters to perceive gay and lesbian candidates? To start, it is imperative to ask how citizens perceive gays and lesbians generally. According to

Yang (1997), nearly three quarters of Americans believe homosexual relationships to always be wrong, approximately half believe that these relationships should not be legal, and slightly less than half believe that homosexuals should not be allowed to teach in schools nor welcomed into the clergy.

However, public opinion is more tolerant about certain aspects of treatment of homosexuals. Depending on question wording, roughly half and sometimes up to three-quarters of Americans believe that lesbians and gays should be included in fair housing and employment laws. These public opinion results suggest that some degree of opposition to and perhaps intolerance of lesbians and gays governs Americans' views of fair treatment. These conclusions lead to the following hypotheses.

HYPOTHESES

Research findings from related fields provide guidance about candidate acceptance, perceptions of candidate viability, and issue preferences of underrepresented populations. For example, the experimental literature on women candidates reports that respondents expect them to be more interested than men in women's issues — all else being equal (Leeper 1991; Sapiro 1981–1982). Similarly, African American candidates are seen as more interested in civil rights than white candidates (Sigelman et al. 1995). Elsewhere, Herrick and Thomas (1997) found that lesbian and gay candidates were seen as more supportive than straight or closeted candidates of gay rights issues. Thus, it follows (and we expect) that gays and lesbians will be perceived as more concerned than straight candidates with gay rights. Since being portrayed as a single issue candidate is of concern to many gay and lesbian candidates running for office (see DeBold 1994), this is an important hypothesis to test.

Stereotypical assumptions that lesbians are more masculine than straight women and gay men more feminine than straight men abound. For example, inversion theory, which predates Freud, and has dominated psychological thinking about homosexuality, suggests that gays and lesbians are similar to the opposite sex (Miller 1995: chapter 2; Kite and Deaux 1987; Gross et al. 1980). Kite and Deaux, in a study conducted at a midwestern university, found students' stereotypes indeed coincided with the inversion theory. Based on these widespread expectations and research findings, we hypothesize that gay male candidates will be perceived as more concerned with compassion issues than straight male candidates and that lesbian candidates will be seen as less concerned with compassion issues than straight women.

Our third hypothesis concerns viability of candidates. Public sentiment about homosexuality, discussed above, and the literature on women candidates (Leeper 1991; Sapiro 1981–1982), African American candidates (Sigelman et al. 1995) and lesbian and gay candidates (Herrick and Thomas 1997) suggests that voters perceive lesbians and gays as less able than straight candidates in electoral contests. As an outgroup and one whose immutability is sometimes questioned, lesbian and gay candidates may have trouble being seen as strong contenders.

In addition to perceiving gay and lesbian candidates as less viable than straight candidates, we expect voters to be less likely to vote for them. This could result from not wanting to cast a vote for a candidate one doesn't think has a chance of winning or it could result from prejudice on the part of the respondent. Of course, an interaction of the two is also likely.

Our fifth hypothesis concerns correlates of support for or opposition to lesbian and gay candidates. In brief, we expect that stereotypical views will be stronger within certain subgroups of voters than others. Studies of prejudicial beliefs about homosexuals suggest that men, conservatives, and fundamentalist Christians have more negative emotions, more stereotypical views of gays and lesbians, and are less supportive of gay and lesbian rights than those in opposite categories (Gurwitz and Marcus 1978; Fisher et al. 1994; Herek 1988; Haddock, Zanna, and Esses 1993; Hugick 1992; Moore 1993; Gibson and Tedin 1988; Herrick and Thomas 1997). Schroedel (chapter 5, this volume) shows similar findings for elites. Thus, we expect the difference between perceptions of gay and lesbian candidates and straight candidates to be larger for men, conservatives, and conservative Christians.

RESEARCH DESIGN

To test viability of gay and lesbian candidates, and to discover any stereotypical views related to their issue preferences, we have undertaken experimental research. The experiment proceeded as follows. Participants were told they were evaluating hypothetical candidates. Each was given one of four instruments. Each instrument had a short biography of a candidate, a speech (said to be given by the candidate), and a series of questions concerning the candidate, the speech, and the respondent. The only difference among the instruments was the sex and sexual orientation of candidate. There were four types of candidates: a straight woman, a lesbian, a straight man, and a gay man.

The biography told participants that Ms. (or Mr.) Parker was running for a nonpartisan city council seat in their town. We wanted to make the race local because most openly lesbians and gays who run, run in local races (National Museum and Archive of Lesbian and Gay History 1996). We also wanted to make the race nonpartisan so as not to confound party effects with the effect of sexual orientation and sex. To do so would have required many more experimental groupings than the four already necessary. Finally, we wanted to be able to determine and report results as clearly as possible.

The biography was constructed to illustrate someone who was very mainstream, politically experienced, and noncontroversial. If participants were to respond to possible biases against lesbian and gay candidates, we wanted to make sure the response was not due to anything else readily identifiable about the candidate's background.

The speech was a variation of one originally given by former Republican governor Kay Orr of Nebraska. The original speech was also used by Leeper (1991) in his examination of stereotypes of women candidates. As with the biography, it would be difficult to find anything to disagree with or anything objectionable in the speech.

The experiment was conducted in introduction to American government classes at five public universities throughout the country: California State University, Fullerton, University of Georgia, Oklahoma State University, Temple University, and the University of Nebraska. These schools were chosen with an eye toward geographical diversity. Introductory classes were chosen since students from a variety of disciplines, not just political science majors, take these courses. Also, these classes tend to be large and, because our instrument had four variations, we needed large number of cases in each class to ensure reasonably large numbers of respondents for each variation of the survey.

RATIONALE AND DESIGN CHALLENGES

There are a number of reasons why we chose this type of design. First, experimental research allows scholars to control, through randomization, for extraneous influences on decision making (for an excellent discussion of the benefits of experimental research in this type of study, see Matland 1994). It is very difficult to imagine a situation in which scholars could study a real race or series of races in which the effects of sexual orientation of candidates could be isolated — even if enough of such races existed in a somewhat compressed time frame.

Additionally, much of the research on candidate viability of female and minority candidates provides models for well-executed studies. The work of Sapiro (1981–1982), Ekstrand and Eckert (1981), Alexander and Andersen (1993), Rosenwasser and Seale (1988), Boles (1989), Rosenwasser et al. (1987), Leeper (1991), Kahn (1992), Huddy and Terkildsen (1993a, 1993b), Sigelman et al. (1995), Riggle et al. (1997), Herrick and Thomas (1997), and Golebiowska and Thomsen (chapter 9, this volume) all use and refine experimental research to test questions of unconscious bias.

Designing an experiment to test the viability of gay and lesbian candidates presents a different set of challenges than testing unconscious bias based on sex. When studying the latter categories, the researcher need only construct a biography or candidate speech and then alter the names at the top. Subjects get a sheet with the name Roberta Parker or Robert Parker and will not be aware that everyone's sheet will not reflect the same. There will be no other indication that the variable of interest is sex. Therefore, socially desirable answers can be avoided (see Kuklinski and Cobb 1997 for an excellent discussion of measures of politically sensitive attitudes). However, when dealing with lesbian and gay candidates, one cannot signify sexual orientation without tipping subjects off as to the nature of the research. Given heterosexual assumptions about candidates, one need not say that Robert Parker is a straight male, but one does, on some portion of the biographies, need to say that Robert Parker is an openly gay candidate. Those subjects who receive biographies of gay candidates will immediately have a clue about the nature of the research design.

The most troublesome issue dealing with this problem was how to say that the candidate is gay or lesbian and where in the biography to state it. Before conducting our research we pretested two ways of handling this issue. First, we put information about sexual orientation in a long string of candidate traits. In a later test we put in a line at the end of one of the biography's paragraphs that the candidate was openly homosexual. We debated about placement because, in the first example, if participants didn't read carefully they might miss the information about sexual orientation and render the experiment useless. However, leaving it at the end of a paragraph might be so obvious that it could trigger the socially desirable response. Ultimately, analysis of the pretests showed no meaningful difference in response patterns between the two groups. We decided, based on the notion that if we were going to test candidate viability of gays and lesbians we had to make sure participants saw the reference to sexual orientation, placing the information at the end of a paragraph would be best. After all, when openly gay candidates run, their sexual orientation is a very high profile and much discussed issue.

RESULTS

The data are analyzed using a difference of means test. Given that we used four variations of the survey instrument, we found this to be the easiest way to present the patterns of most interest. Readers should know, however, that we also analyzed all the data using regression equations and obtained similar results. We present the data from all the schools combined.

Table 8.1 shows the results of a difference of means analysis in respondents' answers to questions following the biography and the speech. The means for answers in each category (lesbian candidate, straight woman candidate, gay male candidate, and straight male candidate) are displayed.

Our first hypothesis is that gay and lesbian candidates are perceived as more interested than straight candidates in gay rights issues. To test this hypothesis we asked respondents how important ensuring gay rights is for the candidate. The scale ranged from 1–7, with 1 indicating that gay rights was very important to the candidate and 7 that it was unimportant (see appendix 1 for the complete survey).

Although the speech said nothing about gay rights, students who received the biography and speech for the gay and lesbian candidate were more apt to see the candidate as interested in gay rights. Hence, our expectations are confirmed.

TABLE 8.1.

Respondent's Views of Candidate Issues and Viability: A Difference of Means Test

Interest in	Lesbians	Women*	Gay men	Men*
Gay rights	4.78WGM	5.73LG	3.99MWL	5.71lLG
Arts	4.94	5.13	4.85	4.86
Education	2.26	2.28	2.02M	2.38G
Health care	4.29	4.23	4.05	4.11
Welfare	3.84	3.87	3.90	3.99
Women's rights	4.31	4.41	4.28	4.64
Winability	2.34WM	1.90LG	2.44MW	1.83LG
Vote for	2.05	1.94	2.12W	1.99
Agree with Speech	1.95wM	2.131	1.99m	2.18Lg
Gap	−.10WM	.18LG	−.13WM	.19LG
N	136	143	142	143

W = significantly different from straight women at the .05 level.

w = significantly different from straight women at the .10 level.

M = significantly different from straight men at the .05 level.

m = significantly different from straight men at the .10 level.

L = significantly different from lesbians at the .05 level.

l = significantly different from lesbians at the .10 level.

G = significantly different from gay men at the .05 level.

g = significantly different from gay men at the .10 level.

*The sexual orientation of these candidates was not specified. However, they were likely to have been assumed to be straight.

To test our second hypothesis, that lesbians are seen as less interested in compassion issues than straight women and that gay candidates are seen as more interested in compassion issues than straight men, we asked respondents about their perceptions of how important education, health care, welfare, the economy, and women's rights were to the candidates. The scale is the same as that for gay rights, discussed above.

Table 8.1 provides no support for our second hypothesis. Only one significant relationship between sexual orientation and sex of a candidate and the importance of compassion issues to the candidate was found. Gay men were seen as more interested in education than straight men. We can offer no plausible, theoretically relevant explanation for this finding.

What is particularly interesting about the issue results is that even straight men and women candidates were not seen to differ significantly on the issues. This flies in the face of the generally accepted conclusion that women candidates are perceived to be more competent than men on compassion issues. One possible explanation for this anomalous finding is that although education, welfare, and health care reform have historically been liberal causes, today those supporting reform want to shrink the services to help balance the budget. Thus these issues may be associated with fiscal restraint more than with care of the needy.

Our third and fourth hypotheses concern electability of lesbian and gay candidates. To test these hypotheses we asked respondents three questions. The first was, "What is the likelihood that this candidate will win the election?" The options ranged from 1 (very likely) to 4 (not at all likely). To tap willingness to vote for the candidates, respondents were asked, "What is the likelihood that you would vote for Parker?" Again, the options ranged from 1 (very likely) to 4 (not at all likely). We also tested for what we call the "gap" variable. The gap measures the difference in levels of agreement with the speech and the willingness to vote for the candidate. It is not unreasonable to assume that a strong relationship exists between liking what a candidate supports and voting for that candidate. To measure the gap variable, we asked respondents if they agreed with the speech (using a four-point scale) and subtracted from that the willingness of the respondent to vote for the candidate. A large positive number indicates that respondents were more likely to vote for the candidate when they agreed with the speech, and a large negative number means that respondents were more likely to agree with the speech than to vote for the candidate.

The data largely, although not completely, confirm our expectations for hypotheses three and four. First, respondents were less likely to see lesbian and gay candidates as electable than straight candidates. Not only is this finding consonant with our expectations, it alleviates some of the concern that participants, suspecting that we were interested in perceptions of gay and lesbian candidates, would provide only socially appropriate answers.

Relatedly, although gay and lesbian candidates were not seen to be as electable as straight candidates, the evidence is mixed as to how likely respondents would be to vote for them. Only gay male candidates were less likely than straight candidates to get respondents' votes. There was no significant effect with respect to lesbians. The results for the gap variable reveal a pattern in which respondents who agree with the speech are more likely to vote for the candidate if she or he is straight than if the candidate is lesbian or gay.

Our final hypothesis, which concerned correlates of support for or opposition to lesbian and gay candidates, was measured by questions about respondents' sex, religion (individuals who identified themselves as Baptists, born again, Christians [nondenominational], Pentecostal, Eastern Orthodox, charismatic, and Latter Day Saints were considered conservative Christians), and ideology. These hypotheses, that conservatives, fundamentalist Christians, and men would be less supportive of lesbians and gays than straights, received only partial support. Although there are no clear patterns of difference in perceptions of candidates based on their sexual orientation (see table 8.2), male respondents were less likely to vote for gay men (this is true for the gap variable and the vote variable) and slightly more likely to see gay men as interested in education.

As table 8.3 indicates, religious denomination separates respondents' willingness to vote for the candidate. Those holding conservative religious beliefs are less likely to vote for gay and lesbian candidates than are others. Similarly, the gap between agreement with the speech and voting for the candidate is much stronger and negative for conservative Christians' evaluations of gay and lesbian candidates than for others. This is a finding that affects the political bottom line.

Table 8.4 presents the results of the difference of means analysis controlling for ideology. As shown, conservatives are less likely than others to vote for gay and lesbian candidates than straight candidates. This is particularly true when we control for agreement with the speech (the gap variable). Conversely, liberals are more likely than others to vote for gay and lesbian candidates than straight candidates. If one accepts the sincerity of the liberals' responses, it is conceivable that running as an openly gay or lesbian candidate could work to one's advantage in some more liberal communities in addition to those with a high lesbian and gay population.

Table 8.4 also reveals several differences in the direction as well as strength of the stereotypes that conservatives and liberals tend to hold. There is a slight tendency for liberals to see gays and lesbians as more interested in compassion is-

TABLE 8.2.

Difference of Means Test: Interaction Terms for Gender

Women Respondents

Interest in	Lesbians	Women*	Gay men	Men*
Gay rights	4.88WGM	5.60LMG	3.53WML	5.63LWG
Arts	4.99	5.03	4.67	4.82
Education	2.10	1.98	1.95	2.17
Health care	4.26g	4.07	3.74l	3.98
Welfare	3.94	3.91	3.61	3.79
Women's rights	4.40	4.31	4.19	4.50
Winability	2.37WM	1.90LG	2.40MW	1.87LG
Vote for	2.01	1.92	2.00	1.86
Gap	−.12WM	.15Lg	−.07wM	.19LG
N	78	83	76	70

Men Respondents

Interest in	Lesbians	Women*	Gay men	Men*
Gay rights	4.65WM	5.91LG	4.49MW	5.77LG
Arts	4.89	5.27m	5.07	4.91w
Education	2.47	2.72	2.11m	2.59g
Health care	4.33	4.44g	4.40w	4.23
Welfare	3.74	3.84	4.25	4.18
Women's rights	4.20	4.56	4.37	4.76
Winability	2.29WM	1.80LG	2.50W	1.79L
Vote for	2.10	1.98G	2.26W	2.10
Gap	−.09Wm	.24LG	−.20WM	.19lG
N	58	59	66	73

W = significantly different from straight women at the .05 level.

w = significantly different from straight women at the .10 level.

M = significantly different from straight men at the .05 level.

m = significantly different from straight men at the .10 level.

L = significantly different from lesbians at the .05 level.

l = significantly different from lesbians at the .10 level.

G = significantly different from gay men at the .05 level.

g = significantly different from gay men at the .10 level.

*The sexual orientation of these candidates was not specified. However, they were likely to have been assumed to be straight.

TABLE 8.3.
Difference of Means Test: Interaction Terms for Religion

		Conservative Religion Respondents		
Interest in	Lesbians	Women*	Gay men	Men*
Gay rights	5.07wM	5.72lG	4.32WM	5.88LG
Arts	4.98	5.05	4.84	4.75
Education	2.17	2.20	1.92	2.29
Health care	4.38	4.05	4.06	3.91
Welfare	3.55	3.63	4.00	4.03
Women's rights	4.30	4.17	4.35	4.40
Winability	2.28WM	1.95LG	2.40MW	1.87LG
Vote for	2.17W	1.73LG	2.27WM	1.90G
Gap	−.32WM	.22LG	−.34WM	.21LG
N	47	41	41	38

		Other Religions Respondents		
Interest in	Lesbians	Women*	Gay men	Men*
Gay rights	4.49WgM	5.71LG	3.88lWM	5.67LG
Arts	4.92	5.10	4.86	4.90
Education	2.33	2.30	2.10	2.37
Health care	4.25	4.31	4.05	4.19
Welfare	3.99	4.07	3.90	3.98
Women's rights	4.36	4.47	4.23	4.66
Winability	2.40WM	1.85LG	2.52WM	1.82LG
Vote for	2.05	2.02	2.06	2.00
Gap	−.01M	.17G	−.06WM	.23LG
N	81	88	95	87

W = significantly different from straight women at the .05 level.

w = significantly different from straight women at the .10 level.

M = significantly different from straight men at the .05 level.

m = significantly different from straight men at the .10 level.

L = significantly different from lesbians at the .05 level.

l = significantly different from lesbians at the .10 level.

G = significantly different from gay men at the .05 level.

g = significantly different from gay men at the .10 level.

*The sexual orientation of these candidates was not specified. However, they were likely to have been assumed to be straight.

TABLE 8.4.
Difference of Means Test: Interaction Terms for Ideology

Conservative Respondents				
Interest in	Lesbians	Women*	Gay men	Men*
Gay rights	4.90WgM	5.91LG	3.97lW	5.94L
Arts	5.10	4.91	5.11	4.69
Education	2.47	2.11	2.20	2.24
Health care	4.36	4.07	4.44	4.00
Welfare	3.95	3.85	4.18	3.91
Women's rights	4.56	4.46	4.61	4.51
Winability	2.33WM	1.81LG	2.50LWM	1.68LG
Vote for	2.48WM	1.84LG	2.55LWM	1.90LG
Gap	−.53WM	.03LG	−.62WM	.00LG
N	45	37	42	39

Moderate Respondents				
Interest in	Lesbians	Women*	Gay men	Men*
Gay rights	4.65W	5.69LG	4.47M	5.32
Arts	4.64	4.94	4.84	4.74
Education	2.21	2.32	2.08	2.48
Health care	4.45	4.15	4.19	4.02
Welfare	3.55	3.92	3.94	4.07
Women's rights	4.10	4.20	4.18	4.29
Winability	2.32M	2.11Gm	2.57WM	1.86LwG
Vote for	1.91	2.05	2.16	1.91
Gap	.07	.21	−.00	.09
N	43	38	49	44

Liberal Respondents				
Interest in	Lesbians	Women*	Gay men	Men*
Gay rights	4.77WGM	5.65LG	3.59LWM	5.91LG
Arts	5.20	5.31g	4.60wm	5.28g
Education	2.16	2.39g	1.80w	2.30
Health care	4.15	4.33	3.70	4.11
Welfare	4.05	3.86	3.58	4.07
Women's rights	4.33	4.46	4.10m	4.98g
Winability	2.33WM	1.85LG	2.30WM	1.92LG
Vote for	1.79M	1.95	1.74M	2.12LG

continued

TABLE 8.4.
Continued

	Conservative Respondents			
Interest in	Lesbians	Women*	Gay men	Men*
Gap	.19M	.28	.13M	.47LG
N	43	60	46	51

W = significantly different from straight women at the .05 level.

w = significantly different from straight women at the .10 level.
M = significantly different from straight men at the .05 level.
m = significantly different from straight men at the .10 level.
L = significantly different from lesbians at the .05 level.
l = significantly different from lesbians at the .10 level.
G = significantly different from gay men at the .05 level.
g = significantly different from gay men at the .10 level.
*The sexual orientation of these candidates was not specified. However, they were likely to have been assumed to be straight.

sues than straight candidates. Conversely, conservatives tend to perceive straight candidates as more interested than gay and lesbian candidates in compassion issues. This may be due to a focus on different types of stereotypes. Conservatives may see gays and lesbians as uninterested in issues such as education, presumably because they are less likely than straights to have children, whereas liberals may perceive gays and lesbians as compassionate as a result of being an outgroup in society. Unfortunately, however, we lack data to test these possibilities.

DISCUSSION

The findings from this study provide mixed support for our expectations. Gay and lesbian candidates are seen as more interested in gay rights than straight candidates (although no other issue differences were perceived between straights and gays) and less electable. Also, respondents are slightly less willing to vote for gay and lesbian candidates than straight candidates. Certain types of respondents are more likely than others to think stereotypically about gays and lesbians and are less likely to be willing to vote for them. Most notably, ideological conservatives and conservative Christians make up this group.

Although we hypothesized that this would be the case, respondents did not perceive gay candidates as similar to women on compassion issues or perceive lesbians as similar to straight men. There are two possible explanations for this finding. First, the outgroup status of gays and lesbians may suggest, at least to liberals, that gays and lesbians, regardless of sex, are more interested than straights in compassion issues. A second possible explanation is that the meaning of the compassion issues has changed. For example, "reforming welfare" used to mean expanding services, whereas now reform is more likely to refer to cutting services and controlling spending. That no gender differences in answers to questions about candidates' likelihood to consider this issue important were found provides some support for this view.

We also expected to find that respondents would see female and male candidates differently from each other, but we did not. The women and politics literature is replete with references to such findings. Although it is certainly possible that college students have changed over time, it would be irresponsible to rely on such conclusions without further testing. Given this need and the fact that there are problems with testing for bias against lesbian and gay candidates without eliciting socially appropriate answers, it is worth considering other methods of conducting this sort of research.

The results of this research suggest that citizens still harbor bias against lesbian and gay candidates, and while they were not seen as different from straights on many issues, the message of lesser levels of acceptance is fairly clear (see also the work of Golebiowska and Thomsen, chapter 9, this volume). While openly gay and lesbian candidates like Keith St. John do win election to political office (see also Hertzog 1996), full acceptance is not yet manifest in our citizenry. Future research will, undoubtedly, help us understand more about the predictors of such bias and the reasons behind it. For example, research that would be especially useful would reflect real-world situations. One such opportunity is the congressional election cycle of 1998 in which four openly lesbian candidates and three openly gay candidates are running for the U.S. House of Representatives — Retired Army Col. Margarethe Cammermeyer is running in Washington's 2nd District, Councilwoman Christine Kehoe is running in California's 49th District, State Representative Tammy Baldwin is running in Wisconsin's 2nd District, State Representative Susan Tracy is running in Massachusetts's 8th District, and Paul Barby, member of the Board of Regents for Oklahoma's Colleges is running in Oklahoma's 6th District, plus the two openly gay incumbent representatives, Barney Frank (D-MA) and James Kolbe (R-AZ). Because there is little history of openly lesbian or gay nonincumbent candidates running for the U.S. Congress, the 1998 races promise to add new levels of information and analysis to what we or others have offered to date. Barriers to citizens' ability to participate in their government is too important an issue to leave unexplored.

Appendix I

Please read the following information about the candidate and then fill out the survey about the candidate's views and your assessment of the candidate. The information you will give is completely anonymous.

Candidate Biography

Ms. Roberta Parker recently announced her plans to run for city council in your town. Ms. Parker is a college graduate, started a successful small business in town, is a well-known name who has long been an active member of civic, charity, and religious organizations, and has been in city politics for over fifteen years. Ms. Parker is considered ideologically moderate and is being supported by a wide range of local organizations including the Chamber of Commerce, the Civic Association, various professional groups, and a long list of current local officeholders including the mayor. Ms. Parker is also a homosexual.

Candidate Speech

King Solomon, who is said to have been "the wisest of all men," wrote in the Book of Proverbs, "Where there is no vision, the people perish." I believe that statement is as true today as when it was written.

I have a clear vision of a better city. I want to tell you about my dream . . . and ask you to help me make it a reality.

My vision is of a city with strong, healthy people living up to their responsibilities as well as reaping their rights.

My vision is a vision of a city with strong traditions of decency, fair play, individualism, and independence.

My vision is a vision of a city where the gates of opportunity have been opened wide, allowing all who want it to have better lives.

It is a vision of a city with a superior system of education from elementary school on up.

It is a vision of a city with jobs for all who want them.

My vision is a vision of a city with strong moral values and strong families.

My vision is a vision of a city that has eradicated crime and rid the streets of the scourge of drugs.

How can we achieve this vision?

My solution to the many problems that plague our city and cities all over our great nation contains three parts.

The first part requires the work of each individual in this city. We cannot be successful unless everyone does his or her part and we cannot expect to be taken care of or rewarded if we don't contribute. Individual responsibility is key. But, individual effort alone won't do the complete job.

That's why the second part of the solution lies in community groups — groups that will contribute time and effort to helping those who will help themselves and who will work with the government to spur economic opportunity for all.

The third part of my solution requires that government be used not to dominate our lives, but to fuel that economic opportunity I just spoke of.

Is this all feasible? You bet it is. If individuals, community groups, and the government work toward economic development and public and private partnerships; if city policies allow small business to flourish, if law enforcement is stripped free of bureaucracy and allowed to go about its job of making our streets safe; if plea bargains are not given out like Halloween candy and strict sentences guidelines are followed; if budgets are balanced and priorities chosen, if taxes stop being raised and are, in fact, lowered; if each parent is dedicated to traditional strong families and sets strict standards for children; if our school system is reformed and allowed to concentrate on the basics, then all this can be achieved.

This is not a pipedream; it is a vision for the immediate future. The vision takes honesty and courage and a willingness to stand up for what is right. The vision takes putting people in office who will stand up for what they believe in — whatever the consequences for their own political futures. The vision takes putting people in office who will ignore the naysayers and those who are not shackled to the entrenched politicians. The vision takes putting people in office who are willing to throw aside the practices of the past, the practices that didn't work, and to go with confidence into the future.

I am one of the people who has the courage and the background and the ability to move us into the future. I have experience in the private sector and in government making budgets balance and cutting overhead. I have experience working with civic and community groups that inspire people to help those who help themselves. I have the enthusiasm, energy, and dedication to give 100 percent every single day to this great city. But, I need the help of all the people of this city, working with diligence and commitment and with unity to make it even greater.

Thank you.

This survey is completely confidential. In no way can you be identified and the only use of the data will be to report aggregate findings.

Please answer the first set of questions by circling the number corresponding to the option that BEST reflect your views.

1. The speech given by Parker was very effective.
    (1) strongly agree
    (2) somewhat agree
    (3) neutral
    (4) somewhat disagree
    (5) strongly disagree

2. How much do you agree or disagree with Parker?
    (1) strongly agree
    (2) somewhat agree
    (3) neutral
    (4) somewhat disagree
    (5) strongly disagree

3. What is the likelihood that you would vote for Parker?
    (1) Very likely
    (2) Somewhat likely
    (3) Not very likely
    (4) Not at all likely

4. What is the likelihood that Parker will win the election?
    (1) Very likely
    (2) Somewhat likely
    (3) Not very likely
    (4) Not at all likely

Based on the impression you drew from the speech, please provide your best guess as to how important the following issues are to the candidate. Circle the number that is closest to your estimate of Parker's views.

1 = very important/7 = not important

1.	Strengthening the economy	1 2 3 4 5 6 7 DK
2.	Encouraging the arts	1 2 3 4 5 6 7 DK
3.	Reforming welfare	1 2 3 4 5 6 7 DK
4.	Encourage a strong business climate	1 2 3 4 5 6 7 DK
5.	Improving the educational system	1 2 3 4 5 6 7 DK
6.	Protecting women's rights	1 2 3 4 5 6 7 DK
7.	Maintaining honesty and integrity in govt.	1 2 3 4 5 6 7 DK
8.	Protecting consumer interests	1 2 3 4 5 6 7 DK
9.	Reforming Health Care	1 2 3 4 5 6 7 DK
10.	Curbing Crime	1 2 3 4 5 6 7 DK
11.	Improving family values	1 2 3 4 5 6 7 DK

12. Ensuring gay rights   1 2 3 4 5 6 7 DK

13. What are the key issues of this candidate:

_____

_____

In this last section, please circle or fill in the correct answer.

1. What is your sex?   (1) Male   (2) Female

2. What is your race?

    (1) White

    (2) African American

    (3) Hispanic

    (4) Asian-American

    (5) Other (pls note) _____

3. What is your party affiliation?

    (1) Republican

    (2) Democrat

    (3) Independent

4. Generally, do you consider yourself

    (1) Liberal

    (2) Moderate liberal

    (3) Moderate

    (4) Moderate conservative

    (5) Conservative

5. What is your religion _____

6. How often do you attend church?

    (1) more than once a week

    (2) once a week

    (3) less than once a week, but at least monthly

    (4) less than monthly, but at least yearly

    (5) less than once a year

7. What is the highest level of education achieved by your parents?

    Mother _____

    Father _____

8. What are the occupations of your parents?

    Mother _____

    Father _____

9. In what range is your family income?

    (1) $20,000–30,000

    (2) $30,000–40,000

    (3) $40,000–50,000

(4) $50,000–60,000
(5) $60,000–75,000
(6) $75,000–100,000
(7) $100,000–150,000
(8) $150,000 and above

THANK YOU FOR FILLING OUT THIS SURVEY

REFERENCES

Alexander, Deborah and Kristi Andersen. 1993. "Gender as a Factor in the Attribution of Leadership Traits." *Political Research Quarterly* 46:527–545.

Associated Press. 1997. "Rights Bill Would Protect Gays' Jobs, Ban Preferences." *Washington Post*, October 14.

Boles, Janet K. 1989. "Images of Female and Male Elected Officials: The Effect of Gender and Other Respondent Characteristics." *Journal of Political Science* 17:19–32.

Button, James W., Barbara A. Rienzo, and Kenneth D. Wald. 1997. *Private Lives, Public Conflicts: Battles Over Gay Rights in American Communities*. Washington, DC: Congressional Quarterly Press.

Burrell, Barbara. 1994. *A Woman's Place Is in the House: Campaigning for Congress in the Feminist Era*. Ann Arbor: University of Michigan Press.

DeBold, Kathleen, ed. 1994. *Out for Office: Campaigning in the Gay Nineties*. Washington DC: Gay and Lesbian Victory Fund.

Ekstrand, Laurie E. and William A. Eckert. 1981. "The Impact of Candidate's Sex on Voter Choice." *Western Political Quarterly* 34:78–87.

Erickson, Robert S. and Kent L. Tedin. 1995. *American Public Opinion*, 5th ed. Needham Heights, MA: Allyn and Bacon.

Fisher, Randy D., Donna Derison, Chester F. Polley III, Jennifer Cadman, and Dana Johnston. 1994. "Religiousness, Religious Orientation, and Attitudes Towards Gays and Lesbians." *Journal of Applied Social Psychology* 24:614–630.

"Gay Community News." 1989. *Social Policy* 20:49–51.

Gibson, James L. and Kent L. Tedin. 1988. "The Etiology of Intolerance of Homosexual Politics." *Social Science Quarterly* 69:587–604.

Gross, Alan E., Susan K. Green, Jerome T. Storck, and John M. Vanyur. 1980. "Disclosure of Sexual Orientation and Impressions of Male and Female Homosexuals." *Personality and Social Psychology Bulletin* 6:307–314.

Gurwitz, Sharon B. and Melinda Marcus. 1978. "Effects of Anticipated Interaction, Sex, and Homosexual Stereotypes on First Impressions." *Journal of Applied Social Psychology* 8:47–56.

Haddock, Geoffrey, Mark P. Zanna and Victoria M. Esses. 1993. "Assessing the Structure of Prejudicial Attitudes: The Case of Attitudes Toward Homosexuals." *Journal of Personality and Social Psychology* 65:1105–1118.

Haider-Markel, Donald P. 1997a. "Government Response to a Movement: A Time Series Analysis of Agenda Setting." Paper presented at the annual meeting of the American Political Science Association, San Francisco, California.

—— 1997b. "DOMA—Not the First and Certainly Not the Last: The Evolution of Lesbian and Gay Issues in the U.S. Congress." Paper presented at the annual meeting of the Midwest Political Science Association, Chicago, Illinois.

Herek, Gregory M. 1988. "Heterosexuals' Attitudes Toward Lesbians and Gay Men: Correlates and Gender Differences." *Journal of Sex Research* 25:451–477.

Herek, Gregory M. and Eric K. Glunt. 1993. "Interpersonal Contact and Heterosexuals' Attitudes Toward Gay Men: Results from a National Survey." *Journal of Sex Research* 19:239–244.

Herrick, Rebekah and Sue Thomas. 1997. "Gays and Lesbians on City Councils: A Study of Electoral Viability." Paper presented at the annual meeting of the Midwest Political Science Association, Chicago, Illinois.

Hertzog, Mark. 1996. *The Lavendar Vote: Lesbians, Gay Men, and Bisexuals in American Electoral Politics.* New York: New York University Press.

Horowitz, Carl F. 1991. "Homosexuality's Legal Revolution." *Freeman* 41:173–181.

Huddy, Leonie and Nayda Terkildsen. 1993a. "The Consequences of Gender Stereotypes for Women Candidates at Different Levels and Types of Office." *Political Research Quarterly* 46:503–525.

—— 1993b. "Gender Stereotypes and Perception of Male and Female Candidates. *American Journal of Political Science* 37:119–147.

Hugick, Larry. 1992. "Public Opinion Divided on Gay Rights." *Gallup Poll Monthly* (June), pp. 2–6.

Kahn, Kim Fridkin. 1992. "Does Being Male Help? An Investigation of the Effects of Candidate Gender and Campaign Coverage on Evaluations of U.S. Senate Candidates." *Journal of Politics* 54:497–517.

Kite, Mary and Kay Deaux. 1987. "Gender Belief Systems: Homosexuality and the Implicit Inversion Theory." *Psychology of Women Quarterly* 11:83–96.

Kuklinski, James H. and Michael D. Cobb. 1997. "Toward Unobtrusive Survey Measures of Sensitive Political Attitudes." Paper presented at the annual meeting of the Midwest Political Science Association, Chicago, Illinois.

Leeper, Mark Stephen. 1991. "The Impact of Prejudice on Female Candidates: An Experimental Look at Voter Inference." *American Politics Quarterly* 19:248–261.

Locksley, Anne, Eugene Borgida, Nancy Brekke, and Christine Hepburn. 1980. "Sex Stereotypes and Social Judgment." *Journal of Personality and Social Psychology* 39:821–831.

Marcus, George, John Sullivan, Elizabeth Theiss-Morse, and Sandra L. Wood. 1994. *With Malice Toward Some: How People Make Civil Liberties Judgements.* New York: Cambridge University Press.

Matland, Richard E. 1994. "Putting Scandinavian Equality to the Test: An Experimental Evaluation of Gender Stereotyping of Political Candidates in a Sample of Norwegian Voters." *British Journal of Political Science* 24:273–292.

Miller, Neil. 1995. *Out of the Past: Gay and Lesbian History from 1869 to the Present*. New York: Vintage.

Moore, David W. 1993. "Public Polarized on Gay Issue." *Gallup Poll Monthly* (April), pp. 30–34.

National Museum and Archive of Lesbian and Gay History. 1996. *The Lesbian Almanac*. New York: Berkley.

Riggle, Ellen D., Victor C. Ottati, Robert S. Wyer, James Kuklinski, and Norbert Schwarz. 1992. "Bases of Political Judgement: The Role of Stereotypic and Non-Stereotypic Information." *Political Behavior* 14:67–87.

Riggle, Ellen D. B., Penny M. Miller, Todd G. Shields, and Mitzi M. S. Johnson. 1997. "Gender Stereotypes and Decision Context in the Evaluation of Political Candidates." *Women and Politics* 17:69–87.

Rosenwasser, Shirley M., Robyn R. Rogers, Sheila Fling, Kayla Silvers-Pickens, and John Butemyer. 1987. "Attitudes Toward Women and Men in Politics: Perceived Male and Female Candidate Competencies and Participant Personality Characteristics." *Political Psychology* 8:191–200.

Rossenwasser, Shirley M. and Jana Seale. 1988. "Attitudes Toward a Hypothetical Male or Female Presidential Candidate — A Research Note." *Political Psychology* 9:591–598.

Rundquist, Barry, Gerald S. Strom and John G. Peters. 1977. "Corrupt Politicians and Their Electoral Support: Some Experimental Observations." *American Political Science Review* 71:954–963.

Sapiro, Virgina. 1981–1982. "If U.S. Senator Baker Were a Woman: An Experimental Study of Candidate Image." *Political Psychology* 3:61–83.

Sherrill, Kenneth. 1996. "The Political Power of Lesbians, Gays, and Bisexuals." *PS: Political Science and Politics*, 24:469–473.

Sigelman, Carol K., Lee Sigelman, Barbara Walkosz, and Michael Nitz. 1995. "Black Candidates, White Voters: Understanding Racial Bias in Political Perceptions." *American Journal of Political Science* 39:243–265.

Sullivan, Andrew. 1996. *Virtually Normal: An Argument About Homosexuality*. New York: Vintage.

Thomas, Sue. 1994. *How Women Legislate*. New York: Oxford University Press.

Thomas, Sue and Clyde Wilcox, eds. 1998. *Women And Elective Office: Past, Present, and Future*. New York: Oxford University Press.

Vaid, Urvashi. 1995. *Virtual Equality: The Mainstreaming of Gay and Lesbian Liberation*. New York: Anchor.

Yang, Alan S. 1997. "The Polls — Trends: Attitudes Toward Homosexuality." *Public Opinion Quarterly* 61:477–507.

CHAPTER NINE

Group Stereotypes and Evaluations of Individuals: The Case of Gay and Lesbian Political Candidates

Ewa A. Golebiowska and Cynthia J. Thomsen

Despite many advances in their social, political, and legal status, gay men and lesbians in the United States have a long way to go before achieving full equality. Toward that goal recent years have witnessed increased mobilization by gay and lesbian activists and their heterosexual supporters in a wide array of efforts at social change. Approaches to achieving this goal cover a broad spectrum: some have worked within the traditional legislative and judicial systems, for example, by proposing ballot initiatives or raising legal challenges to discriminatory statutes; others have focused their energies on educating the public, either within formal educational structures or through community-based media campaigns; still others have pursued more unconventional tactics such as direct action, demonstrations, and the like.

One promising avenue for elevating the status of gays and lesbians involves increasing the political clout of lesbians and gay men by electing them to political office. There are several reasons to expect the electoral success of lesbian and gay candidates to have salutary consequences for the welfare of the broader lesbian and gay community. First, merely increasing the public's exposure to gay men and lesbians through the high-profile visibility of openly lesbian and gay candidates and officials should contribute to the breakdown of negative stereotypes and prejudices, thereby reducing their pernicious consequences in the form of discrimination, hate crimes, and political and social intolerance of gays and lesbians. That is, through exposure to individual lesbians and gay men, members of the public are likely to recognize the heterogeneity of these groups and, therefore, to decrease their reliance on group stereotypes when forming impressions of individual lesbians and gay men or when reasoning about policies relevant to gay and lesbian rights (Herek and Capitanio 1996). In addition, to the extent that gay and lesbian officials are likely to champion legislation protecting the rights of lesbians and gays, increasing electoral success of lesbian and gay candidates is likely to translate into stronger legal protections of lesbian and gay rights and, ultimately, into greater tolerance of gays and lesbians in areas beyond the political sphere. Finally, openly gay and lesbian public officials may provide role models for lesbian and gay youth, a population that appears to be particularly vulnerable to the consequences of membership in this stigmatized group.

Our goal in this chapter is to illuminate some of the factors that might influence electoral experiences of gay men and lesbians who run for political office. While the recipe for anyone's electoral success, gay or straight, is composed of a wide variety of ingredients, lesbian and gay candidates may face special obstacles and challenges in navigating the waters of electoral politics. Gays' and lesbians' membership in an unpopular minority can be expected to affect their electoral health. In a related vein, stereotypic beliefs about lesbians and gay men may provide a lens through which the candidate's characteristics and behaviors are perceived and interpreted. To the extent that knowledge of a candidate's sexual orientation colors perceptions of him or her, impressions of the candidate may vary substantially depending on the level of perceived correspondence between the candidate's appearance, behavior, and the group stereotype.

Of course, the processes described above are not uniquely applicable to gay men and lesbians who run for political office; many racial, ethnic, and religious groups have also been traditional victims of intolerance and are likely to encounter similar obstacles when waging campaigns for office. However, the effects of membership in a stigmatized group may depend on the specific content of stereotypes about that group. In the present context this implies that the factors influencing gay men's and lesbians' electoral outcomes may vary, despite many similarities in attitudes toward these two groups, because the descriptive content of their group's stereotypes differs greatly.

Relative to other stigmatized groups, lesbians and gays are also unique in that their group membership is not immediately apparent. Lesbians and gay men thus have a choice, when running for political office, about whether, how, and when to disclose information about their sexual orientation/identification during the course of their campaigns and/or terms in office. The timing of such disclosures constitutes an important variable in predicting the impact of candidate sexual orientation on voters' responses to her or him, whether at the attitudinal (e.g., evaluations of his or her leadership potential) or behavioral levels (e.g., vote choice). It is likely, for example, that stereotypic conceptions of lesbians and gay men will influence candidate impressions more strongly when sexual orientation information is learned early in the campaign, since this circumstance affords the greatest possibility of biasing effects on perceptions of the candidate's individual characteristics.

In the present chapter we address these issues from a multimethodological perspective. We draw on a wide range of survey and experimental data to assess the effects of sexual orientation on candidate evaluations and electoral outcomes and to delineate some of the major factors that condition the impact of a candidate's sexual orientation on her or his electoral outcomes. Following a brief examination of historical trends in the numerical representation of gays and lesbians in elected political office, and evidence shedding light on the pervasiveness of antigay and lesbian prejudice, we develop a theoretical model of the factors likely to influence the electoral outcomes of gay men and lesbians. Finally, we evaluate our predictions about the impact of stereotypes on evaluations of individual lesbian and gay politicians, drawing on evidence from laboratory experiments as well as a survey of openly gay candidates and public officials.

Electoral Fortunes of Openly Gay and Lesbian Candidates

Despite marked changes in the descriptive representation of women, blacks, and other political minorities, this nation's popularly elected bodies are predominantly (and have traditionally been) populated by white males. Using the notion of descriptive representation as a point of reference, lesbians and gays have fared poorly. The first openly lesbian candidate was elected to public office only in 1974 (Elaine Noble, elected to the Massachusetts House of Representatives) and the first openly gay man did not succeed in winning elective office until 1977 (Harvey Milk, elected San Francisco city supervisor; DeBold 1994). The visibility and electoral success of openly gay and lesbian candidates has since increased. While comprehensive statistics concerning the numbers of openly gay and lesbian candidacies are difficult to find, a conservative estimate is based on the numbers of lesbians and gays actually elected over time. Following the election of only two lesbians during the 1970s, five lesbians were elected during the 1980s and thirty between 1990 and 1996 alone (DeBold 1994; Gay and Lesbian Victory Fund's Press Release 1994, 1996). Although only three openly gay men were elected during the 1970s, twenty-six were elected during the 1980s, and thirty-eight were elected between 1990 and 1996 (DeBold 1994; Gay and Lesbian Victory Fund's Press Release 1994, 1996).

As important as sheer increases in the number of elected gay and lesbian officials, recently gays and lesbians can boast about electoral successes "beyond the traditionally liberal pockets of California and Massachusetts and have become more competitive 'in the heartland'" and outside of the "geographically concentrated gay electorates" (Rayside 1993). An openly gay man, for example, was elected the mayor of Bunceton in rural Missouri in 1980 and has been reelected every election cycle since. In 1989 an openly gay black man became the first such person elected in the country by winning a seat on the Common Council in the socially conservative town of Albany, New York (Affleck 1993). In 1996 openly gay men won seats in the Illinois and Nevada state legislatures and the Dane County Board of Supervisors in Wisconsin. In the same year a lesbian won a seat in the Montana State House (Gay and Lesbian Victory Fund's Press Release 1994, 1996).

Although the increasing prominence of lesbian and gay elected officials is encouraging, it is important to note that lesbian and gay public officials are still relatively rare. Among those currently holding elective office, only about 120 are openly gay or lesbian, and these tend to be concentrated in lower-level offices; of the 100 members of the U.S. Senate, none is openly lesbian or gay; of the 425 members of the U.S. House of Representatives, a mere 2 (Barney Frank and Jim Kolbe) are openly gay and 1 is openly lesbian (Tammy Baldwin); among the 7,461 members of this nation's state legislatures, only 20 lesbians and gays are open about their sexual orientation; only 1 openly gay man (no lesbians) is serving in a statewide office (Ed Flanagan, Vermont state auditor; DeBold 1994; Gay and Lesbian Victory Fund's Press Release 1994, 1996).[1]

Pervasiveness of Antigay and Antilesbian Prejudice

Perhaps the most obvious reason for the relative paucity of open lesbians and gays in elected political office resides in the prejudices held by a large majority of the electorate. Research employing national probability samples, as well as that employing convenience samples of college students, has consistently revealed that the American public holds overwhelmingly negative attitudes toward lesbians and gay men (e.g., Sherrill 1993; Yang 1997). While acceptance of civil rights for gays and lesbians tends to be higher than might be expected on the basis of the relatively negative attitudes toward homosexual behavior and homosexual persons, significant minorities of Americans harbor intolerant attitudes toward gays and lesbians (with a clear majority of 70 percent unwilling to allow gays and lesbians to adopt children legally) (Freedom and Tolerance in the United States Survey 1987; Lewis and Rogers, chapter 6, this volume; National Election Study 1993).[2] Most relevant to our investigation, a whopping 70 percent of those who mention lesbians and gays as one of their most disliked groups agree that lesbians and gays should be banned from running for office (see also Herrick and Thomas, chapter 8, this volume). Table 9.1 below presents illustrative evidence.

Stereotypes and Political Responses to Lesbians and Gays

To the extent that attitudes toward individual lesbian and gay political candidates are a reflection of attitudes toward gays and lesbians as groups, the research reviewed above suggests rather pessimistic predictions about the electoral possibilities of gays and lesbians. In addition, albeit based on rather sparse empirical foundations, there is some reason to expect that gay males might face particular difficulty in the political arena, largely as a function of the negative attitudes held by their male constituents (Kite and Whitley 1996). The effects of the public's negative attitudes on their evaluations of gay and lesbian candidates, moreover, are likely to be exacerbated by the prevalence of antigay and antilesbian political rhetoric that is permeated with stereotypic generalizations. Our evidence comes from several sources: the antigay rhetoric of the religious right,

TABLE 9.1.

A. Unwillingness to allow gays and lesbians, and other groups to exercise their democratic rights and freedoms, 1994 General Social survey

| Group | Activity (% unwillingly to allow) | | |
	speak	teach in college	book in the library
gays and lesbians	18.7%	27.0%	29.1%
atheists	26.4	45.7	28.7
communists	31.7	41.7	31.8
milirarists	34.8	52.6	34.2
racists	37.4	55.9	32.1

B. Unwillingness to allow gays and lesbians to exercise their democratic rights and freedoms among respondents who identified gays and lesbians as one of their top four most disliked groups, 1987 Freedom and Tolerance in the United States Survey

Activity	% unwilling
ban from running for office	69.7%
outlaw	56.3%
not allow to make a speech	46.4%
not allow to hold rallies	72.4%
not allow to teach	78.3%
tap their phones	14.6%

the arguments advanced in opposition to allowing gays in the military, and re-view of experiences of a sample of openly gay candidates and public officials.

Leitmotifs in the antigay rhetoric and propaganda of the religious right, not simply academic theories, suggest that stereotypic beliefs ought to play a signifi-cant role in electoral experiences of lesbian and gay candidates for office. The denunciation of homosexuality and civil rights for lesbians and gays by forces on the religious right seems strongly related to a conviction that the gay and lesbian stereotypes have universal applicability to all gay men and lesbians re-spectively. The beliefs espoused by those on the religious right are captured well in a couple of documentarylike videos ("The Gay Agenda" and "Gay Rights, Special Rights"). In both videos the marginal elements in the gay community are featured, with numerous references to gays' alleged sexual promiscuity and propensity to molest children permeating both movies. Neither video contains a single image of a gay man who does not fit the gay stereotype (e.g., one who is dressed in a business suit and involved in a long-term monogamous relation-ship). Interestingly, lesbians are virtually absent from both videos, suggesting that when Americans think about "homosexuals" they think about gay men rather than both gay men and lesbians.

Close attention to the arguments put forward by opponents of allowing gays in the military, an issue of recent prominence on this nation's political agenda, also shows the saturation of the antigay rhetoric with stereotypic beliefs. One of the principal arguments against gays in the military has been that their presence would reduce the military's effectiveness and lead to widespread demoraliza-tion. The logic behind such objections seems to be rooted in stereotypic beliefs that gay men are so obsessed with sex that, once given permission to be open about their sexual orientation, they would seduce heterosexual members of the military (there is a similar, though mostly unstated, presumption that lesbians will seduce straight women). In sum, both the religious right and opponents of allowing gays in the military invoke stereotypes, more or less explicitly, to jus-tify their calls for intolerance directed at gays. By activating stereotypic con-ceptions of gays and lesbians, this rhetoric should increase the public's reliance on stereotypes in evaluating gay and lesbian political candidates.

Perhaps the most direct means of examining the extent to which stereotypes and prejudices based on sexual orientation come into play in the context of po-litical campaigns is to survey those who have participated in such campaigns firsthand. Of course, self-report data are not without limitations, particularly when they require inferences about the reasons for others' behavior. It is also very likely that such reports will underestimate the true extent to which respondents have been victims of prejudice and discrimination, since individuals are generally reluctant to perceive themselves as victims of intergroup hostilities, even if they freely acknowledge that pervasive prejudice against their social group exists (Taylor, Wright, and Porter 1994). Nonetheless, lesbian and gay political candidates and public officials are uniquely positioned to speak to the manner in which their sexual orientation, and stereotypic beliefs accompanying it, has influenced their political experiences, and such anecdotal evidence complements the results of experimental research we describe below.

In a survey of openly gay candidates and public officials Golebiowska (1995b) discovered that many openly gay candidates were quite explicit in their awareness of the importance of forestalling the impact of stereotypic beliefs on voters' assessments of their candidacies and reported taking deliberate action toward this end. A candidate running in 1993 for a seat in the California State Assembly, for example, decided that he "needed to buy television time with advertisements showing [he] was versed on all issues and [that he] did not fit the stereotype that Monterey County voters — where [he] was not well-known — might have had about an openly gay candidate." Another candidate, running for the West Hollywood City Council, similarly "emphasized [his] legal background and community service in an attempt to foreclose any stereotyping" (Golebiowska 1995b).

Golebiowska also uncovered several examples of the manner in which stereotypic beliefs influenced evaluations of and responses to the gay candidates and officials who participated in her survey. Some openly gay candidates have encountered political opponents who engaged in veiled attempts to exploit information about their sexual orientation by playing on the gay stereotype. President of the Minnesota State Senate Allen Spear, in his first campaign as an openly gay candidate for his senatorial seat (1976), had to contend with a political opponent who sent out literature headed, "Would you want this man to kiss your baby?" An openly gay man running for a seat in the Washington State Assembly (Cal Anderson) was faced with similar code words. His opponent in the Democratic primary ran a newspaper ad depicting her with her two children. The caption under the picture asked a rhetorical question: "Should your State Representative be someone your young children could look up to as a role model?" In both Spear's and Anderson's cases the child molester stereotype was, arguably, being activated in voters' minds.

Not only their political opponents but organized opposition as well took pains to undermine the openly gay candidates' campaigns for office by playing on the gay stereotype. In one case the opposition was responsible for spreading rumors that the openly gay candidate, if elected, had "plans to infiltrate the schools with homosexuals and change the curricula." On a similar theme, one religiously fundamentalist constituent circulated a letter in her neighborhood alleging that the gay candidate in question had "motives to hurt children."

Attitudes Toward Groups Versus Individuals: Conceptual Framework and Expectations

Research in political science and social psychology offers a variety of insights relevant to understanding attitudes toward unpopular groups. A great deal of research in political psychology has examined the factors that promote intergroup prejudice and discrimination, and sizable scholarly output on political tolerance has illuminated the general determinants of attitudes toward a wide range of outgroups (e.g., Sullivan, Piereson, and Marcus 1982; Gibson and Tedin 1986; Golebiowska 1995a; Marcus et al. 1995). However, while describing many general factors that influence tolerance and intergroup attitudes, the research does not yield specific information about the factors that promote tolerance of lesbians and gays.

This is unfortunate in light of the fact that more recent research has uncovered important differences in the determinants of attitudes toward different social groups. What is more, because researchers have often lumped attitudes toward gays and lesbians into the study of attitudes toward "homosexuals" (see, for an exception, Herrick and Thomas, chapter 8, this volume), we know little about possible differences in public reactions to gays and lesbians. These limitations are redressed by recent studies in political psychology (e.g., Gibson and Tedin 1986; Riggle and Ellis 1994) and social psychology (e.g., Esses, Haddock, and Zanna 1993; Haddock, Zanna, and Esses 1993; Herek 1984a, 1984b, 1988) that have specifically examined the determinants of attitudes toward gay men and/or lesbians as social groups but not as individuals within these groups. Although intuition might suggest that group attitudes would influence impressions of individual group members in a rather straightforward fashion, a great deal of previous research in both social and political psychology documents that individual members of stereotyped social groups will not always be evaluated in terms of group stereotypes (e.g., Golebiowska 1995b, 1996, 1997c; Locksley et al. 1980; Peffley, Hurwitz, and Sniderman 1997; Riggle et al. 1992; Sniderman and Piazza 1993).

According to Fiske et al.'s (1987) influential continuum-based model of impression formation, the extent to which a perceiver will rely on stereotypes when forming an impression of a member of a stigmatized social group depends on a number of factors including the perceiver's motivations, the availability of information about the target's social category membership, and the degree of fit between the target's attributes and those specified by the stereotype (see also Brewer 1988). Thus previous research has demonstrated that responses to members of stereotyped groups will be influenced by group stereotypes and evaluations more strongly to the extent that these individuals fit their group's stereotype. In contrast, when the individuals to be evaluated exhibit characteristics that do not match their category or group stereotype, the impact of information about category membership (including concomitant group stereotypes and evaluations) may be attenuated or even eliminated altogether (e.g., Locksley et al. 1980). Responses to atypical group members may thus be unaffected by group evaluations. By extension, this research suggests that group-targeted tolerance might not be highly predictive of tolerance directed at individuals when those individuals deviate substantially from the group prototype (Erber and Fiske 1984; Fein and Hilton 1992; Fiske 1986; Fiske and Neuberg 1989; Fiske et al. 1987; Fiske et al. 1988).

In a direct test of this hypothesis Golebiowska examined the linkage between fit to the gay stereotype and readiness to allow a gay individual to exercise his democratic rights and freedoms (Golebiowska 1995b, 1996, 1997c). Consistent with psychological work on the subject, she found that the gay target was afforded less tolerance when exhibiting stereotype-consistent than stereotype-inconsistent characteristics.

RESEARCH QUESTIONS AND PREDICTIONS

Overall Support of Gay and Lesbian Candidates

Our first question regards general levels of support for lesbian and gay candidates. Based on the pervasiveness of prejudice toward lesbians and gay men, as well as extant research demonstrating effects of sexual orientation on candidate evaluation (e.g., Herrick and Thomas, chapter 8, this volume), we expected support for the lesbian and gay candidates to be generally low. In addition, we wished to examine whether lesbian and gay candidates elicited different levels of support. However, because prior research has largely not examined this issue (see Herrick and Thomas, chapter 8, this volume), and because arguments can be mustered to support a prediction in either direction, we did not venture a directional prediction about this anticipated difference. On the one hand, some evidence suggests that attitudes toward gay men are more negative than those toward lesbians, at least among male respondents (e.g., Kite and Whitley 1996). To the extent that attitudes toward their social groups influence voters' reactions to individual candidates, this suggests that lesbian candidates, relative to their gay counterparts, might enjoy some advantage in electoral support. Alternatively, given the traditional hegemony of men within the political domain as well as lingering voter sexism, gender might exert the prepotent influence, with the lesbian candidate, by virtue of her sex, receiving less support than the gay candidate (e.g., Welch and Sigelman 1982; Clark 1991).

Stereotype Fit More central to our research is the role of stereotypes and prejudice in the evaluation of gay and lesbian candidates. Previous theory and research suggest that global attitudes toward gay men and lesbians as social groups should influence evaluations of individual gay and lesbian candidates primarily when the candidate is perceived as a "good" exemplar of the category. Thus, lesbian and gay candidates who are perceived as fitting the group stereotype should garner less support than those who are perceived as anomalous, or stereotype-inconsistent, group members. Finally, evaluations of candidates who are portrayed in stereotype-neutral terms should be intermediate.

The impact of information about a candidate's stereotype fit might also be conditioned by her or his group membership. This might be the case because of differences in the descriptive content of lesbian and gay stereotypes and in the degree of overlap between these stereotypes and the prototype of a good politician (e.g., Kinder 1986; Huddy and Terkildsen 1993). More specifically, because the lesbian target described in a stereotype-consistent manner fits the prototype of a typical politician better than the lesbian target described in a stereotype-inconsistent or neutral manner, we expected that the lesbian stereotype-consistent target might receive more electoral support than the remaining two lesbian targets. In contrast, because the gay stereotype-inconsistent target provides a better fit to the politician prototype, we expected that he would be supported more than the other two gay targets.

Timing of Sexual Orientation Information

While we expected to find an overall effect of stereotypic fit on readiness to endorse a lesbian or gay candidacy, we also anticipated that the strength of this effect would be moderated by whether information about candidate sexual orientation was acquired relatively early or late in the "campaign." As we discussed above, sexual orientation diverges from many other stigmatizing group memberships in that it can be concealed. As a result, unlike members of many other marginalized social groups, lesbians and gay men who contemplate campaigning for elective office have a potentially important decision to make: whether, and when, to disclose their sexual orientation to their constituency. In fact, among those gay men and lesbians who have won elective office in the United States over the past couple of decades, there has been substantial variability in the timing of their revelation about their sexual orientation. Some have run for office as openly gay or lesbian from the beginning. Others have become open about their sexual orientations only after they were elected (some willingly, some not). And it is likely that still others have never divulged their sexual orientations to the electorate, nor do they intend to (DeBold 1994; Golebiowska 1995b).

A candidate's decision about when to disclose her or his sexual orientation may be a very weighty one. To the extent that even a minority of the electorate harbors prejudices toward lesbians and gay men, early disclosure that one is a member of one of these groups might produce relatively severe consequences. In a sense one may be providing at least a subset of the voting public with ammunition that can be used to shoot down the candidacy without necessitating a further consideration of the candidate's qualifications and issue positions. Moreover, if the public does consider the fine points of the candidate's platform, experience, and so on, it is likely that prior knowledge of the candidate's sexual orientation will influence the manner in which other information about the candidate is perceived.

Theory and research in social and political cognition suggests that the biasing effect of group stereotypes and prejudices on impressions of individuals should be greatest when information about the individual is viewed through the prism of prior beliefs (e.g., Brewer 1996). In other words, if the candidate's sexual orientation is known from the beginning, it may color the perceiver's interpretation of all individuating information that is subsequently learned about the candidate. Although delaying the disclosure of sexual orientation until after one is known to the electorate does not obviate the possibility of electoral bias, it should diminish the impact of such bias on candidate evaluations. In the present experiment, therefore, we predicted that the impact of information about a candidate's sexual orientation on respondents' impressions of him or her would be greater when learned at the beginning rather than at the end of his or her candidacy. To the extent that the electorate harbors antilesbian and antigay prejudices, this suggests that candidates should generally enjoy more public support when their sexual orientation is learned later, rather than earlier, in their campaigns.

Toward a Model of Gay and Lesbian Candidate Appraisal

Building on Golebiowska's earlier work on individual-targeted tolerance, as well as on previous theory and research about the determinants of candidate evaluation and impression formation, we conducted a series of experiments designed to systematically examine several factors likely to influence the electoral fortunes of gay and lesbian political candidates. In addition to examining whether information about sexual orientation has similar consequences for lesbians and gay men, we consider several additional factors that are likely — based on both theoretical and practical grounds — to condition the relationship between a candidate's sexual orientation and voter support. These include attributes of the candidate (such as the degree to which her or his attributes are congruent with those specified by the group stereotype), aspects of the context within which the electoral contest takes place (e.g., the level and type of office sought), and features of the campaign itself (for example, the timing and manner of sexual orientation disclosure).

In one of the first studies in this program of research we examined the influence on support of individual gay and lesbian candidates of two of these factors: stereotypicality of candidate attributes and whether respondents learned the candidate's sexual orientation before or after learning about his or her other attributes and qualifications. Male and female undergraduates enrolled in introductory psychology courses at Tufts University (N = 120) received information about a hypothetical lesbian or gay candidate running for an unspecified political office and provided their impressions of him or her.[3] The dependent variable of primary interest, overall support of the candidate, was indexed by aggregating five items that assessed willingness to vote for the candidate, to give money and time to the candidate's campaign, to persuade others to vote for the candidate, and to attend a rally for the candidate (Cronbach's alpha = .90). Participants also rated the candidate on a variety of specific, leadership-related traits. Based on a factor analysis of these data, we constructed several additional scales assessing attributes thought to be important in candidate evaluation (e.g., Kinder 1986): leadership (4 items, alpha = .72), competence (4 items, alpha = .85), integrity (5 items, alpha = .77), compassion (4 items, alpha = .78), and stability (3 items, alpha = .55). Finally, respondents provided an overall evaluation of the target candidate (on a 0 to 100 feeling thermometer scale) as well as a variety of information about their relevant predispositions and background characteristics (see appendix 9.B for the wording of principal measures).

Each candidate description contained a brief statement of the candidate's political agenda, which was constant across conditions. To avoid possible confounding effects of the candidate's political identity, care was taken to select issues that were nondiagnostic of the candidate's partisan affiliation or ideological leanings; pilot testing confirmed that this was the case. Candidate descriptions also included information about a broad range of candidate attributes such as employment status, relationship status, physical appearance, and interests and hobbies. Six different versions of the candidate description were developed, based in part on the descriptions used by Golebiowska (1996, 1997c), by crossing group membership (gay or lesbian) and information condition (stereotype-consistent, stereotype-inconsistent, stereotype-neutral). The stereotype-consistent gay man, for example, was described as artistic, thin, and unathletic; his stereotype-inconsistent counterpart, in contrast, was described as liking to fix cars, having a college degree in engineering, and being masculine and athletic. The lesbian candidate, similarly, was described in both stereotypical (short hair, plays baseball, works at a woman's bookstore) and counterstereotypical (well-coiffed, does aerobics, likes to cook) terms. Finally, we constructed descriptions in which the gay and lesbian candidates were described in neutral terms unrelated to the stereotype (works at a local business, average height and weight, has one brother and one sister, etc.). Pilot testing confirmed that the descriptions were perceived in the intended manner and verified that they were similar in plausibility and overall valence. The complete descriptions are provided in appendix 9.A.

Finally, in addition to the group membership and information condition manipulations conveyed in the candidate descriptions, we also manipulated the timing of sexual orientation information. This was done by revealing the candidate's sexual orientation either at the beginning of the candidate description (before respondents read anything else about him or her) or at the end of the description (after respondents had already learned a variety of other information about the candidate).

Experimental Results   Consistent with our expectations, overall levels of reported candidate support were low. The mean support score of 3.23 was significantly lower than the scale midpoint of 4, $t(108) = -5.93, p < .001$. Moreover, over 90 percent of respondents indicated a support level of 5 or lower, while not a single respondent indicated extremely strong support (i.e., there were no support scores greater than 6 on a seven-point scale). This is consistent with Golebiowska's finding of lower support for a gay than a straight target ostensibly running for office (1995b).

We first examined whether lesbians and gay men differed in the level of support they elicited. The relevant data are graphed in figure 9.1 below.

Despite evidence suggesting that gay men are subject to somewhat more extreme prejudices than are lesbians, our respondents indicated somewhat higher support for the gay male ($M = 3.46$) than for the lesbian candidate ($M = 3.04$), $F(1,103) = 5.98, p < .05$.

Average responses to gay and lesbian candidates are broken down by their stereotypic fit in figure 9.2 below.

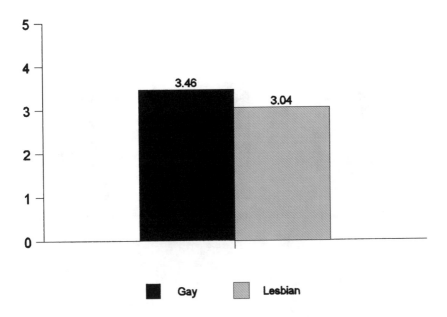

FIGURE 9.1. Candidate's Sexual Orientation and Levels of Political Support

The advantage of gay men over lesbians was maintained for candidates described in terms consistent with their group stereotypes (Ms = 3.60 and 3.00 for gay men and lesbians, respectively), as well as for those described in stereotype-neutral terms (Ms = 3.52 and 2.81 for lesbians and gay men, respectively). For lesbians and gay men who displayed counterstereotypic characteristics, however, levels of expressed support for gay men (M = 3.27) and lesbians (M = 3.28) were virtually identical. The disjunction between the pattern of results for overall differences in prejudice toward gays and lesbians as social groups and the pattern of differences in support of individual gay men and lesbians highlights once again the importance of distinguishing general group tolerance or prejudice from the tolerance or prejudice directed at a specific individual group member.

We also found gender differences in support of gay men and lesbians. Although both male and female respondents preferred gay male to lesbian candidates, females indicated higher levels of support for both groups (Ms = 3.59 and 3.25 for gay men and lesbians, respectively) than did males (Ms = 3.13 and 2.76 gay men and lesbians, respectively). However, respondent gender did not moderate any of the other effects, indicating that the responses of male and female participants to the information and timing manipulations did not differ.

More central to the present research, and of equal practical importance, is the question of whether support for gay and lesbian political candidates varies

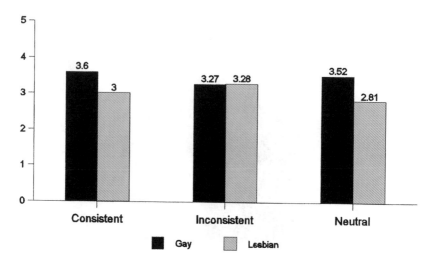

FIGURE 9.2. Stereotypic Consistency and Political Support for Gay and Lesbian Candidates

as a function of whether they are depicted as having characteristics consistent, inconsistent, or neutral with respect to the category stereotype. For the lesbian candidate, the predicted pattern emerged; respondents indicated more support of the lesbian candidate when she was described as having characteristics inconsistent, rather than consistent, with the stereotype. For the gay male candidate, however, the opposite pattern was obtained; counter to our expectations, support was actually greater for the stereotypical than for the counter-stereotypical candidate. If these results are examined in light of the content of lesbian and gay group stereotypes, they suggest that respondents were more supportive of both lesbian and gay candidates who were described in relatively feminine terms than of those described in more masculine terms. This seems paradoxical, given that many of the central attributes thought to be important in candidate evaluation (e.g., leadership, competence) are stereotypically masculine.

Our next set of predictions concerned the impact on candidate support of whether sexual orientation information was learned early or late in the campaign. The relevant means are presented in figure 9.3 below.

As predicted, our results strongly suggest that timing of disclosure influences responses to lesbian and gay candidates (three-way interaction $F [2, 90] = 4.70$, $p < .05$). Candidate support was minimally affected by the nature of the information provided about her or him (i.e., whether it was consistent, inconsistent, or neutral with respect to the stereotype) when sexual orientation was learned

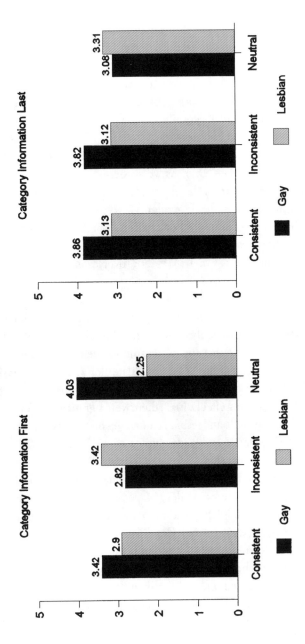

FIGURE 9.3. Stereotypic Consistency, Timing of Information About Sexual Orientation, and Political Support for Gay and Lesbian Candidates

after the individuating information (Information Condition F [2, 90] = 1.29; Group x Information Condition F = 0.69, p > .25). When candidate sexual orientation was known from the outset, however, the nature of the information provided about the candidates did affect participants' responses to them (Group x Information F [2, 90] = 4.97, p < .01). For the lesbian candidate these results were in the predicted direction: the counterstereotypical lesbian (M = 3.42) was preferred to her stereotypical counterpart (M = 2.90). In the case of the gay male, however, the stereotypical candidate (M = 3.42) was preferred to the counterstereotypical one (M = 2.82). As we suggested previously, this could reflect a preference on the part of the electorate for candidates with feminine characteristics, regardless of candidate gender. This is somewhat puzzling, however, in light of the fact that our respondents generally preferred male to female candidates. This pattern was most apparent in the neutral information condition, in which preferences for gay men (M = 4.03) over lesbians (M = 2.25) were particularly pronounced.

We also examined whether attributions about the candidate's characteristics might account for differences in candidate support as a function of group membership, information stereotypicality, and timing of disclosure about the candidate's sexual orientation. To this end, we examined the effects of these three manipulated factors on perceptions of the candidate along several dimensions: leadership, competence, integrity, compassion, stability, and liking. Our analyses revealed several interesting effects. First, there were significant differences in overall perceptions of gay male and lesbian candidates on two of the trait dimensions we assessed: competence and leadership. In general, gay men (M = 5.10) were perceived as more competent than were lesbians (M = 4.62; F [1, 97] = 6.80, p < .05). In contrast, lesbians were viewed as having stronger leadership abilities (M = 5.44) than were gay males (M = 5.02). Second, the perceived emotional stability of the candidate was affected by the timing of sexual orientation disclosure (F [1, 97] = 5.49, p < .05). Candidates were perceived as more stable when respondents learned other individuating information about the candidate before learning his or her sexual orientation (M = 5.16), compared to when sexual orientation was learned relatively early in the "campaign" (M = 4.82). However, a significant interaction of Group x Order (F [1, 97] = 8.12, p < .01) shows that the timing of disclosure significantly influenced the perceived stability of gay men (t [48] = −3.58, p < .001) but not that of lesbians (t [57] = 0.28, p > .7). That is, disclosure of one's sexual orientation early in a political campaign does not appear to affect adversely attributions about the stability of lesbian candidates (Ms = 5.03 and 4.98 for early and late disclosure, respectively); gay male candidates, in contrast, are perceived as much less stable if they disclose their sexual orientation early ($M = 4.57$) rather than later ($M = 5.38$) in their campaigns.

We conducted a series of mediational analyses to examine whether the observed differences in candidate support as a function of the candidate's gender, the stereotypicality of information provided about him or her, and the timing of sexual orientation disclosure might be mediated by perceptions of the candidate along any of the trait dimensions we assessed. To this end, we examined whether statistically controlling for each of the trait dimensions (both individually and jointly, using analysis of covariance) would eliminate or attenuate the effects of our independent variables on candidate support. However, even statistically controlling for all of the dimensions of candidate evaluation (i.e., liking, competence, leadership, integrity, compassion, and stability) produced only a slight reduction in the strength of our effects (for Group the percentage of variance accounted for, calculated using partial eta-squared, was reduced from .06 to .05; for the Group x Information x Order interaction, the reduction was from .09 to .06). Although the set of character attributions we assessed is not exhaustive, it does include the characteristics most commonly thought to influence candidate evaluations. We therefore believe that the differences in support of lesbians and gay men as a function of their attributes' stereotypic consistency and the timing of their disclosure must occur through some other mechanism than trait-based attributions (e.g., through influencing emotional reactions to the different candidates).

DISCUSSION

We set out in our research to gain insight into the dynamics of attitudes toward openly lesbian and gay candidates for office. We were particularly interested in the linkages between gay and lesbian stereotypes and timing of disclosure about candidate's sexual orientation on the one hand and political support for openly lesbian and gay candidates on the other. The picture of these linkages that emerged from our multifaceted investigation is quite complex.

The extensive nonexperimental evidence we canvass to scrutinize public attitudes toward gays and lesbians generally, and the role of stereotypic beliefs in those attitudes in particular, suggests that levels of support for individual gay men and lesbians running for elective office should be relatively low. What is more, public enthusiasm about gay and lesbian candidacies should be particularly low when lesbian and gay candidates are perceived through the lens of their respective group stereotypes (or when they exhibit attributes consistent with those stereotypes). Our experimental evidence confirms these expecta-tions in part but also results in some interesting patterns we did not anticipate.

This experimental evidence demonstrates that the gay candidate, all else be-ing equal, is supported somewhat more enthusiastically than the lesbian candi-date. This finding runs counter to the literature showing that lesbians are evalu-ated more favorably than gay men (e.g., Herek and Capitanio 1996) as well as to Herrick and Thomas's findings (chapter 8, this volume). Nonetheless, it makes sense in light of our expectation that gay men might benefit from their "maleness" when attempting to secure positions of power in a male-dominated realm. This finding is particularly interesting because it might be interpreted as a serendipitous way of demonstrating that candidate gender, in and of itself, and contrary to other research on the subject, continues to be an important dimension of candidate evaluation. Recent experimental research examining the influence of gender on political support shows that female candidates no longer appear to be disadvantaged by their gender per se (e.g., Huddy and Terk-ildsen 1993). However, there are good reasons to believe that this research might underestimate the vestiges of gender-based prejudice; questions tapping sup-port for a female target are highly reactive, tipping respondents off to politically correct answers. The advantage of our approach is that respondents might have an "out," or justification, for their less enthusiastic responses to a female candi-date if she also happens to be a lesbian; that is, they can attribute their negative feelings about the candidate to her sexual orientation rather than her gender, because discrimination is less strongly proscribed on the former than the latter basis. Unfortunately, our conclusions in this regard are suggestive rather than definitive; in ongoing research we are continuing to examine this issue, for ex-ample, by including additional scenarios (equivalent "straight" conditions).

The story of the candidates' gender and their political appeal, however, is not as straightforward as it appears from this scrutiny of the gay and lesbian candi-date's political support. While the preference for the gay candidate holds true when the lesbian and gay targets are described either in stereotype-consistent or neutral terms, the gay candidate's edge disappears when the two candidates are described in terms inconsistent with their group stereotypes (gay masculine, les-bian feminine). The elimination of the male advantage in this condition might be a consequence of the rising prominence of female candidates running for and winning elective office. In a related vein, the ground rules for competing within the electoral arena appear to have changed. Traditionally, female candidates for office felt compelled to emphasize their masculine qualities in order to maxi-mize their political support (e.g., Witt, Paget, and Matthews 1996). Women wag-ing electoral campaigns in recent years have been able to "run as women," capitalizing on their stereotypically female strengths and areas of policy expertise without being penalized for it. In a dramatic reversal of men's and women's campaign styles, what is more, even male candidates running for office in recent years have found it advantageous to emphasize their "femininity." For example, one of Barbara Boxer's opponents declared breast cancer a national emergency. Similarly, Clayton Williams, Ann Richards's political nemesis in her gubernatorial campaign, took pains to emphasize his kinder, gentler qualities by appearing surrounded by children (though he generally did a much better job of playing into the macho stereotype instead; Tolleson-Rinehart and Stanley 1994). In short, the lesbian candidate might be benefiting from a boost in voter support when she is described in feminine terms, because of the greater value attached to feminine attributes in recent political campaigns.

This interaction between a candidate's sexual orientation and her or his stereotypic fit also suggests that the linkage between group stereotypes and candidate evaluation might be conditioned by the political context. It suggests, to elaborate, that failure to fit one's group stereotype might not always spell electoral profit for an individual running for office and, conversely, that exhibiting stereotypic consistency need not inevitably spell electoral doom. Candidates exhibiting stereotypically feminine traits (stereotype-consistent gay candidates and stereotype-inconsistent lesbian candidates) are likely to get more political mileage in electoral contexts in which stereotypically female issues are emphasized (as in, for example, the 1992 election cycle); those exhibiting stereotypically masculine traits (stereotype-inconsistent gay candidates and stereotype-consistent lesbian candidates), on the other hand, should benefit more in electoral contexts in which stereotypically male issues are more dominant (as in, e.g., the 1994 election cycle; see Kahn 1996 for a similar argument). Our sample — predominantly female, better educated than the public at large, more liberal, and embedded in an environment promoting acceptance of all forms of diversity — might have been particularly sensitized to value feminine qualities, despite the fact that feminine issues and attributes did not loom as prominently in the 1994 and 1996 campaigns.

The linkage between stereotypic consistency and candidate support varies with the candidate's group membership. Only in the case of the lesbian candidate is our expectation of higher support for a stereotype-inconsistent candidate confirmed. A reversal of this pattern occurs for the gay candidate, with the stereotype-inconsistent gay candidate actually receiving *less* support than his stereotype-consistent equivalent. The latter finding is partially inconsistent with our expectation of higher political support for stereotype-inconsistent candidates but is entirely consistent with the argument developed above. That the feminine candidates, both gay and lesbian, are favored over their masculine counterparts might be reflective of contemporary appreciation of contributions that female candidates bring into politics. Alternatively, and we cannot rule out this possibility conclusively on the basis of available evidence, it is possible that penalties for sex-role reversal are stronger in the case of the gay than the lesbian target (e.g., Costrich et al. 1975). The gay candidate whose traits are inconsistent with the gay stereotype, to put it differently, might be evaluated less favorably than the gay stereotype-consistent candidate because his unpredictability is more threatening than that of a stereotype-inconsistent lesbian.

As we expected, the effect of stereotype-inconsistency on political support is conditioned not only by the candidates' gender but also by the timing of disclosure about their sexual orientation. We did not find evidence of overall differences in support of lesbian and gay candidates as a function of when respondents became aware of their sexual orientations. However, information about the candidate was apparently processed quite differently when sexual orientation information was known from the beginning than when it was learned only after respondents had been exposed to other individuating information about the candidate. When information about the candidate's sexual orientation is revealed prior to other information about him or her, feminine candidates (stereotype-consistent gay man and stereotype-inconsistent lesbian) are preferred. When information about the target candidate's traits comes before information about her or his sexual orientation, on the other hand, no difference in responses to the feminine and masculine candidates emerges. This finding is consistent with our prediction of the biasing influence of the candidate's group membership revealed prior to other information about him or her. In terms of its political implications this finding suggests that the extent to which lesbian and gay candidates are perceived to fit their group's stereotypes factors into voters' decisions only when such candidates campaign as openly lesbian or gay from the start. The importance of group stereotypes in the gay and lesbian candidates' political campaigns diminishes, on the other hand, when the candidates in question are not initially open about their sexual orientation.

The findings of our initial foray into the etiology of support for openly gay and lesbian candidates for office have important political implications. On one hand, they suggest that, all else being equal, a lesbian candidate might have to work twice as hard as a gay candidate to get elected because responses to her candidacy will be channeled through two prisms: that of sexual orientation as well as gender. On the other hand, these results also suggest that the double bind in which a lesbian candidate might find herself is not automatic. In some electoral contexts being lesbian rather than gay might actually be an advantage, particularly when exhibiting characteristics inconsistent with the lesbian stereotype.

Appendix 9A: Experimental Target Descriptions

Gay, Stereotype-Consistent

Gary D. is an extremely busy person. In addition to working full time, he serves as the president of the Gay and Lesbian Rights Fund. While living a busy life, Gary has a few hobbies. One of the things he likes to do best in his spare time is to paint nature and human portraits. Gary is unlike many other men in that he is rather feminine, thin, and unathletic. He has numerous friends, especially female, with whom he maintains good relationships. While Gary has many friends, he continues to be "unattached." Although he has been involved in a great number of relationships, most of them were very brief, and he has thus far not found a partner for life.

Gay, Stereotype-Inconsistent

Gary D. is an extremely busy person. In addition to working full time, he serves as the president of the Gay and Lesbian Rights Fund. While living a busy life, Gary has a few hobbies. One of the things that he likes to do best in his spare time is to fix up old cars. He has a college degree in engineering and likes doing mechanical things. Like many men, Gary is rather masculine, big, and athletic. Although he does not have too many friends, Gary has had more luck on the personal front, as he has been involved in a long-term relationship for over a decade now. Thus it appears that Gary has found a partner for life.

Gay, Stereotype-Neutral

Gary D. is an extremely busy person. In addition to working full time, he serves as the president of the Gay and Lesbian Rights Fund. While living a busy life, Gary has a few hobbies. Some of the things he likes to do best in his spare time include reading, exercising, watching television, and listening to the radio. He is of average height and has brown hair and blue eyes. He has a college degree in international relations from a medium-sized public university. He works as a customer service representative at a local bank. He lives in a two-bedroom apartment outside of the city and commutes to his job by car.

Lesbian, Stereotype-Consistent

Jane M. is an active member of the Gay and Lesbian Rights Fund. She also works at a local woman's bookstore, and takes college courses at night. In her spare time Jane enjoys woodworking and plays in a community baseball league. Jane has short brown hair and brown eyes. She is somewhat overweight and doesn't pay much attention to her physical appearance; she typically wears casual clothing (e.g., jeans and sweatshirts) and seldom wears makeup. Jane has been living with the same romantic partner for the past three years. Their social life revolves around a small and close-knit group of mutual friends who share many of the same values and interests.

Lesbian, Stereotype-Inconsistent

Jane M. is an active member of the Gay and Lesbian Rights Fund. At various times she has worked as a secretary and a cocktail waitress; she also takes college courses at night. In her spare time Jane enjoys cooking, and she is a member of a health club where she regularly does aerobics. Jane has long brown hair and brown eyes. She is thin and attractive, usually dresses nicely, and rarely leaves the house without styling her hair and applying makeup. Jane has dated several different people over the past several years but has not been involved in a committed long-term relationship. However, she has many good friends with whom she socializes regularly.

Lesbian, Stereotype-Neutral

Jane M. is an active member of the Gay and Lesbian Rights Fund. For the past several years she has worked at a local business. She lives on the outskirts of the city and commutes to work by car. Jane also takes classes at night and enjoys going to movies and taking walks in the outdoors. Jane has brown hair and brown eyes and is of average height and weight. She dresses casually or formally depending on the situation. Jane has one brother and one sister, both of whom she rarely sees since they live in another state. In the local area Jane has several good friends, some of whom she works with, and she goes out with them frequently.

Appendix 9.B

First, please indicate your overall evaluation of the candidate using the feeling thermometer. You may use any number between 0 and 100 for this rating. A rating of 100 means that your overall evaluation of the candidate is extremely favorable, while a rating of 0 means that your overall evaluation of the candidate is extremely unfavorable.

Select any number between 0 (extremely unfavorable) and 100 (extremely favorable) that best represents your overall evaluation of the candidate and write it in the space below.

My overall evaluation of the candidate: _____ degrees on the feeling thermometer.

Next, we'd like you to give us some more specific information about your impression of this candidate. Below are several scales that ask about your impression of this candidate's characteristics. We realize that you have limited information upon which to base your impression of the candidate, but it would be very helpful if you would give us your "gut impression" of this candidate.

Please circle the number on each scale that best represents your impression of the candidate.

Leader	1	2	3	4	5	6	7	Follower
Honest	1	2	3	4	5	6	7	Dishonest
Untrustworthy	1	2	3	4	5	6	7	Trustworthy
Weak	1	2	3	4	5	6	7	Strong
Kind	1	2	3	4	5	6	7	Unkind
Qualified	1	2	3	4	5	6	7	Unqualified
Unintelligent	1	2	3	4	5	6	7	Intelligent
Compassionate	1	2	3	4	5	6	7	Uncaring
Masculine	1	2	3	4	5	6	7	Feminine
Incompetent	1	2	3	4	5	6	7	Competent

How much do you think that you would like this candidate as a person?

Like Very Much	1	2	3	4	5	6	7	Dislike Very Much

The next several questions ask you to indicate how likely you would be to engage in a variety of political activities relevant to this candidate's campaign. When answering these questions, please assume that you did intend to vote in the election for which the candidate was running.

Please answer each question by writing a number from the scale below in the blank next to each item.

Not at All Likely	1	2	3	4	5	6	7	Extremely Likely

If you were voting in this election, how likely is it that you would . . .
_____ 1. vote for this candidate?

_____ 2. contribute money to this candidate's campaign?

_____ 3. volunteer time to help with this candidate's campaign?

_____ 4. attempt to persuade others to vote for this candidate?

_____ 5. attend a campaign rally for this candidate?

NOTES

1. Flanagan, elected in the 1996 election cycle, is also the first openly gay person *ever* elected to a statewide office.

2. One drawback of extant research is that it has failed to assess attitudes toward lesbians and gay men separately, instead tapping responses to *homosexuals*. Although this term may be intended to encompass both groups, there is evidence that respondents typically interpret it as referring to gay men (Haddock, Zanna, and Esses 1993). As a result, available data may be informative primarily with regard to attitudes toward gay men, shedding little light on current attitudes toward lesbians. In a recent meta-analysis of gender differences in attitudes toward gay men and lesbians, Kite and Whitley (1996) further note that although a few studies have examined affective reactions toward lesbians, virtually none have examined other components of attitudes toward them (e.g., attitudes toward sexual behavior or political tolerance).

3. Experimental participants were recruited for participation in partial fulfillment of course requirements. Women constituted a majority of participants (63.6 percent). While whites accounted for a majority of respondents (67.7 percent), a sizable proportion of racial minorities participated in the study (3.8 percent African Americans, 18.5 percent Asian Americans, 2.3 percent Hispanic Americans). Ideological liberals and moderates were overrepresented in the sample (46.2 percent and 38.5 percent respectively) and conservatives underrepresented (9.3 percent). Individuals from families with high incomes accounted for a plurality of participants (46.9 percent from families with incomes of $90,000 or more), with those from families with low incomes constituting a minority (13.4 percent from families with incomes of $34,999 or less).

REFERENCES

Affleck. 1993. "Keith St. John Settles In." *Bay Windows*, February 18.

Brewer, Marilynn B. 1988. "A Dual-Process Model of Impression Formation." In T. K. Srull and R. S. Wyer, Jr., eds., *Advances in Social Cognition*, vol. 1. Hillsdale, NJ: Erlbaum.

—— 1996. "When Stereotypes Lead to Stereotyping: The Use of Stereotypes in Person Perception." In C. N. Macrae, C. Stangor, and M. Hewstone, eds., *Stereotypes and Stereotyping*. New York, London: Guilford.

Clark, Janet. 1991. "Getting There: Women in Political Office." *Annals of the American Academy of Political and Social Science* 515:63–76.

Costrich, Norma, Joan Feinstein, Louise Kidder, Jeanne Marecek, and Linda Pascale.

1975. "When Stereotypes Hurt: Three Studies of Penalties for Sex-Role Reversal." *Journal of Experimental Social Psychology* 11:520–530.

DeBold, Kathleen, ed. 1994. *Out for Office: Campaigning in the Gay Nineties.* Washington, DC: Gay and Lesbian Victory Fund.

Erber, Ralph and Susan Fiske. 1984. "Outcome Dependency and Attention to Inconsistent Information." *Journal of Personality and Social Psychology* 47:709–726.

Esses, Victoria, Geoffrey Haddock, and Mark Zanna. 1993. "Values, Stereotypes, and Emotions as Determinants of Intergroup Attitudes." In D. M. Mackie and D. L. Hamilton, eds., *Affect, Cognition, and Stereotyping: Interactive Processes in Group Perception.* New York: Academic.

Fein, Steven and James L. Hilton. 1992. "Attitudes Toward Groups and Behavioral Intentions Toward Individual Group Members: The Impact of Nondiagnostic Information." *Journal of Experimental Social Psychology* 28:101–124.

Fiske, Susan T. 1986. "Schema-Based Versus Piecemeal Politics: A Patchwork Quilt, But Not a Blanket of Evidence." In R. R. Lau and D. O. Sears, eds., *Political Cognition.* Hillsdale, NJ: Erlbaum.

Fiske, Susan T. and Steven L. Neuberg. 1989. "Category-Based and Individuating Processes as a Function of Information and Motivation: Evidence from Our Laboratory." In D. Bar-Tal, C. F. Graumann, A. W. Kruglanski, and W. Stroebe, eds., *Stereotypes and Prejudice: Changing Conceptions.* New York: Springer-Verlag.

Fiske, Susan T., Steven L. Neuberg, Ann E. Beattie, and Sandra J. Milberg. 1987. "Category-Based and Attribute-Based Reactions to Others: Some Informational Conditions of Stereotyping and Individuating Processes." *Journal of Experimental Social Psychology* 23:399–427.

Fiske, Susan T., Steven L. Neuberg, Felicia Pratto, and C. Allman. 1988. "Stereotyping and Individuation: Degree of Attribute-Oriented Processing as a Function of the Number and Stereotypic Inconsistency of Potentially Individuating Attributes." Unpublished paper, University of Massachusetts, Amherst.

Freedom and Tolerance in the United States Survey. 1987. Computer File. Chicago, IL: University of Chicago. National Opinion Research Center, producer. Ann Arbor, MI: Inter-university Consortium for Political and Social Research, distributor.

Gay and Lesbian Victory Fund's Press Release. 1994. "Record Number of Openly Gay Officials Elected: Seventy-Five Percent of Victory Fund Candidates Win Nationwide." http://qrd.rdrop.com/qrd/orgs/GLVF/1994/election.results-11.10.94

—— 1996. "Winning Slate Topped by the First Openly Gay Candidate Ever Elected to Statewide Office." http://plato.divanet.com /mansco/qnn/1996/nov/QNN-96–11–06%20Some%2OUS%20elections%20results.txt

General Social Surveys. 1994. Chicago, IL: University of Chicago. National Opinion Research Center, producer. Ann Arbor, MI: Inter-university Consortium for Political and Social Research, distributor.

Gibson, James L. and Kent L. Tedin. 1986. "Etiology of Intolerance of Homosexual Politics." *Social Science Quarterly* 69:587–604.

Golebiowska, Ewa A. 1995a. "Individual Value Priorities, Education, and Political Tolerance." *Political Behavior* 17:23–48.

—— 1995b. "Cognitive Underpinnings of Political Intolerance." Ph.D. diss, Ohio State University, Columbus.

—— 1996. "The 'Pictures in Our Heads' and Individual-Targeted Tolerance." *Journal of Politics* 58:1010–1034.

—— 1997a. "Gender and Attitudes Toward Political Unorthodoxy: Why Are Women Less Tolerant?" Unpublished paper.

—— 1997b. "The Contours of Feminist and Racist Stereotypes." Unpublished paper.

—— 1997c. "The Etiology of Individual-Targeted Tolerance." Unpublished paper.

Haddock, Geoffrey, Mark Zanna, and Victoria Esses. 1993. "Assessing the Structure of Prejudicial Attitudes: The Case of Attitudes toward Homosexuals." *Journal of Personality and Social Psychology* 65:1105–1118.

Herek, Gregory M. 1984a. "Beyond Homophobia: A Social Psychological Perspective on Attitudes Toward Lesbians and Gay Men." *Journal of Homosexuality* 10:1–21.

—— 1984b. "Attitudes Toward Lesbians and Gay Men: A Factor Analytic Study." *Journal of Homosexuality* 10:39–51.

—— 1988. "Heterosexuals' Attitudes Toward Lesbians and Gay Men: Correlates and Gender Differences." *Journal of Sex Research* 25:451–477.

Herek, Gregory M. and John P. Capitanio. 1996. "'Some of My Best Friends': Intergroup Contact, Concealable Stigma, and Heterosexuals' Attitudes Toward Gay Men and Lesbians." *Personality and Social Psychology Bulletin* 22:412–424.

Herrick, Rebekah and Sue Thomas. 1999. "The Effects of Sexual Orientation on Citizen Perceptions of Candidate Viability." Chapter 8, this volume.

Huddy, Leonie and Nayda Terkildsen. 1993. "The Consequences of Gender Stereotypes for Women Candidates at Different Levels and Types of Office." *Political Research Quarterly* 46:503–525.

Kahn, Kim. 1996. *The Political Consequences of Being a Woman: How Stereotypes Influence the Conduct and Consequences of Political Campaigns.* New York: Columbia University Press.

Kinder, Donald R. 1986. "Presidential Character Revisited." In R. R. Lau and O. Sears, eds., *Political Cognition.* Hillsdale, NJ: Erlbaum.

Kite, Mary E. and Bernard E. Whitley, Jr. 1996. "Sex Differences in Attitudes Toward Homosexual Persons, Behaviors, and Civil Rights: A Meta-analysis." *Personality and Social Psychology Bulletin* 22:336–353.

Locksley, Anne B., Eugene Borgida, Nancy Brekke, and Catherine Hepburn. 1980. "Sex Stereotypes and Social Judgment." *Journal of Personality and Social Psychology* 39:821–831.

Marcus, George E., John L. Sullivan, Elizabeth Theiss-Morse, and Sandra Wood. 1995. *With Malice Toward Some: How People Make Civil Liberties Judgments.* New York: Cambridge University Press.

National Election Studies. 1992, 1993, 1994. Conducted by University of Michigan, Center of Political Studies. ICPSR, ed. Ann Arbor, MI: University of Michigan, Center for Political Studies and Inter-university Consortium for Political and Social Research.

Peffley, Mark, Jon Hurwitz, and Paul M. Sniderman. 1997. "Racial Stereotypes and Whites' Political Views of Blacks in the Context of Welfare and Crime." *American Journal of Political Science* 41:30–60.

Rayside, David. 1993. "Openly Gay and a Member of Congress: The Role and Impact of Representative Barney Frank." Paper presented at the 1993 Annual Meeting of the American Political Science Association, Washington, DC

Riggle, Ellen D. and Alan L. Ellis. 1994. "Political Tolerance of Homosexuals: The Role of Group Attitudes and Legal Principles." *Journal of Homosexuality* 26:135–147.

Riggle, Ellen D., Victor C. Ottati, Robert S. Wyer, James Kuklinski, and Norbert Schwarz. 1992. "Bases of Political Judgments: The Role of Stereotypic and Nonstereotypic Information." *Political Behavior* 14:67–87.

Sherrill, Kenneth. 1993. "On Gay People as a Politically Powerless Group." In M. Wolinsky and K. Sherrill, eds., *Gays and the Military: Joseph Steffan Versus the United States*. Princeton: Princeton University Press.

Sniderman, Paul M. and Thomas Piazza. 1993. *The Scar of Race*. Cambridge: Belknap Press of Harvard University Press.

Sullivan, John L., James Piereson, and George E. Marcus. 1982. *Political Tolerance and American Democracy*. Chicago: University of Chicago Press.

Taylor, Donald M., Stephen Wright, and Lana E. Porter. 1994. "Dimensions of Perceived Discrimination: The Personal/Group Discrimination Discrepancy." In M. P. Zanna and J. M. Olson, eds., *The Psychology of Prejudice: The Ontario Symposium*, vol. 7. Hillsdale, NJ: Erlbaum.

Tolleson-Rinehart, Sue and Jeanie R. Stanley. 1994. *Claytie and the Lady: Ann Richards, Gender, and Politics in Texas*. Austin: University of Texas Press.

Witt, Linda, Karen M. Paget, and Glenna Matthews. 1996. *Running as a Woman: Gender and Power in American Politics*. New York: Free Press.

Welch, Susan and Lee Sigelman. 1982. "Changes in Public Attitudes Toward Women in Politics." *Social Science Quarterly* 63:312–322.

Yang, Alan S. 1997. "The Polls — Trends: Attitudes Toward Homosexuality." *Public Opinion Quarterly* 61:477–507.

CHAPTER TEN

Institutions Matter:
Local Electoral Laws, Gay and Lesbian Representation, and Coalition Building Across Minority Communities

Gary M. Segura

The literature on local representation suggests that while districts tend to benefit racial and ethnic minorities, at-large systems in general, and those that employ some alternative form of vote aggregation especially, may better serve interests diffused throughout the jurisdiction.[1] Breaking at-large plurality systems into single-member districts, then, has been the principal method used to redress evidence of historic vote dilution problems for racial and ethnic minorities. Some very modest evidence suggests that women, a group dispersed throughout the society, are disadvantaged by such a change. If we extend this logic to the electoral prospects of gays and lesbians, these findings would appear to suggest that the interests of homosexuals and women on the one hand are directly at odds with the interests of racial and ethnic minorities on the other.

In this effort I will challenge the logic underpinning this apparent conflict of interests. I will be closely examining both the literature on local representation and the case of a 1996 charter change in the City and County of San Francisco, California. San Francisco is a jurisdiction with significant minority and gay and lesbian populations that has undergone a number of changes in the local elec-toral system, making the case particularly useful in addressing these questions.[2] I want, specifically, to demonstrate four propositions. First, I will show that the advantages of district-based systems to geographically concentrated minorities are overstated and contextually dependent. That is, under specific circum-stances even ethnic minorities will do better in an at-large electoral arena. Sec-ond, a district-based system is likely to be helpful to gays and lesbians only under very specific — and unlikely — circumstances. The more likely scenario is that districting hurts lesbian and gay candidates and interests. Third, I will argue that the potential advantages of at-large elections are not, as has been suggested (Rosenblum 1996), dependent upon the presence of alternative voting schemes such as preference or cumulative voting, though such measures clearly augment the advantages and mitigate the remaining disadvantages. Finally, if these arguments are correct, the possibility of coalitional politics between lesbians and gays on the one hand and ethnic minorities on the other is greater than conclusions based on the literature would envision.

Though there has been surprisingly little behavioral research of gay and lesbian political participation, much of the discussion concerning gay and lesbian interaction with the political system has, naturally, focused on the national level.[3] I say "naturally" because this is the locus of action on such great debates as the so-called Defense of Marriage Act, the ban on homosexuals in the military, funding for the fight against AIDS, etc. Three important factors have been largely overlooked in this focus and together they suggest an alternative area of inquiry. First, many — indeed most — of the governmental policy decisions affecting the daily lives of Americans, gay and nongay alike, are made at the local level (see Gossett, chapter 4, this volume). Police treatment of gays and lesbians and attention to crimes committed against them, domestic partner benefits, adoption policies, sodomy laws, and, in fact, the regulation of marriage are all state and local decisions. Second, though homosexuals, by their very nature, emerge in every corner of society, substantial concentrations of gays and lesbians occur, as a product of internal migration, principally in either sizable cities or gay-identified hamlets. Finally, much of the success achieved by openly lesbian and gay candidates for public office has occurred at or below the state level. Indeed, of the twenty-seven new gay officeholders elected in the 1996 general election with the support of the Gay and Lesbian Victory Fund only one (Sabrina Sojourner [D-DC], house delegate from the District of Columbia) was elected to a federal office — and a shadow office, at that (Gay and Lesbian Victory Fund 1996). The remaining candidates were elected to state legislatures, school boards, city and county councils, and judgeships. These factors would appear to suggest that the time is ripe for a study of gay and lesbian representation at the state and local level.

UNDERSTANDING AND FOSTERING REPRESENTATION IN LOCALITIES

What factors shape representation at the local level? Many local contests are ostensibly nonpartisan (MacManus and Bullock 1992:171), though this varies across regions and city size. And while such a designation does not mean that voters are unaware of a candidate's ideological or partisan predilections, it does complicate the usual methods of assessing the representativeness of electoral outcomes, namely, partisan vote share compared with partisan seat share. The alternative has been, almost invariably, to look at the sociodemographics of the winners vis-à-vis the underlying distributions in the community represented (Bullock and MacManus 1987, 1990, 1991; Cole 1974; Engstrom and McDonald 1981; Heilig and Mundt 1983; Karnig 1976; Karnig and Welch 1979, 1980, 1982; Latimer 1979; Robinson and Dye 1978). More specifically, we can assess the representativeness of local bodies by assuming that similar voters have similar interests.[4] We then look to see whether these groups, usually defined by gender, ethnicity, race, or socioeconomic class, find a voice in the decision-making chamber.

Here the literature on local representation is rich and well-developed. Scholars have demonstrated that the replacement of at-large elections (at least those that do not use alternative aggregation methods such as cumulative or preference voting) with single-member district systems have generally improved the level of representation (or, more likely, diminished the underrepresentation) of African American and Latino citizens alike. Many of the abolished at-large systems were structured in such a manner that white majorities could, as a bloc, out-vote ethnic minorities and elect an all-white city council or, if the minorities all pooled their votes behind a single candidate and cast no extra ballots for majority candidates, a council with all but one member from the white majority.[5]

The move to single member districts, on the other hand, may improve matters since ethnic and racial minorities tend to concentrate, either by choice or as a by-product of discriminatory housing practices, in segregated neighborhoods and are often, then, a substantial portion or even a majority of one or more districts. In such an instance no amount of white bloc voting can deprive the minority of a reasonable chance of electing one of their number into office if that minority is a significant majority in the district. In addition, these district-based schemes are likely to better reflect the underlying population distribution.

DISTRICT-BASED SOLUTIONS AND THEIR PROBLEMS

This change to district-based elections is not a panacea for the minority representation problem. Any number of possible abuses and unintended outcomes reduce the efficacy and desirability of such a scheme. There are six particular issues that come to mind: the willingness of existing authorities to draw such districts, the potentially negative effect on turnout among the minority in question, the loss of attention to minority concerns by majority legislators, the static nature of such a solution, the possibility that overall policy representation is diminished by such a redistricting, and the constitutional questions surrounding the practice of racial gerrymandering.

First, the benefit of majority-minority districts presupposes that such a district will be created. An equally likely alternative is that district lines are used to divide the minority into small segments of majority-dominated districts, thus ensuring the continued unrepresentativeness of the assembly. This practice, commonly called "cracking" (Blacksher and Menefee 1984; Derfner 1984), has been found to constitute intentional "vote dilution" and be an unconstitutional violation of the equal protection clause of the Fourteenth Amendment. Proving that underrepresentation in districts constitutes minority vote dilution is a challenging undertaking. Though both the 1982 amendments to the Voting Rights Act and *Thornburg v Gingles* (1986) clearly establish a set of judging criteria broader than "intent" alone, as established in *Mobile v Bolden* (1980), applying these standards to district arrangements is not judicially established. And the U.S. Supreme Court and Congress, both suspicious of proportional representation, have clearly *not* mandated that the number of minority districts be maximized (Grofman, Handley, and Neimi 1992). Geography is an additional complicating factor in that minority populations not sufficiently concentrated or separated by some physical feature such as a river or freeway can be cracked, attracting little or no judicial skepticism.

Guinier (1994) and others have suggested another potential pitfall, that majority-minority districts serve to lower rates of registration and turnout among minorities, particularly when minority incumbents face no challenge from others in that social group—a common occurrence. "Black registration and turnout increase in response to first-time election opportunities, but after an initial surge, black voter participation declines in many single-member jurisdictions" (Guinier 1994:85). The mechanism is not entirely clear. For example, she suggests that this effect might be driven by frustration with the lack of policy change in the wake of electoral success. Nevertheless, the result is that minority votes have a declining impact on races further up levels of aggregation, namely, state legislatures, Congress, and statewide elections for constitutional officers and senator, further exacerbating seats/votes disparities.

A third problem is the discounting of minority concerns by majority representatives (even sympathetic ones) whose districts now include only the tiniest fraction of minority group voters. For example, a minority constituent may go to see a white legislator representing her or his district only to be redirected to another member of the body — a minority — despite the fact that this other member was not this citizen's elected representative.

Fourth, districts redrawn on a decennial basis are not responsive in environments where demographics are changing rapidly. In environments where populations grow quickly or change in demographic composition, those changes are extremely unlikely to be reflected in the composition of representative bodies until after the next redistricting process. That is, the unchanged district lines serve to preserve the status quo until they are redrawn. For example, a number of municipalities in Southern California (e.g., Santa Ana) experienced rapid Latino immigration in the 1980s with little or no concurrent change in the demographics of their elected bodies until after the 1990 census.

A fifth concern is the effect that the creation of majority-minority districts has on the neighboring districts. Several scholars have suggested (Brace, Grofman, and Handley 1987; Cameron, Epstein, and O'Halloran 1996; Hill 1995; McDonald 1992) that the creation of majority-minority districts, almost invariably Democratic, has the perverse effect of increasing the representation of the other party in the legislative body in question. Neighboring districts that were previously solidly Democratic, by virtue of sacrificing some share of their minority electorates to the new districts, become competitive, while previously competitive districts become Republican. As a result, while the descriptive representation of the minority group has improved, the policy representation, i.e., the number of legislators voting on policy as the minority would prefer, has actually declined.[6]

And, finally, lest we forget, the United States Supreme Court has cast considerable doubt upon whether any racially or ethnically gerrymandered electoral district can pass constitutional muster, thus threatening the viability of the entire approach. In *Shaw v Reno* (1993) and subsequent opinions (*Miller v Johnson* 1995; *Shaw v Hunt* 1996) the Court has consistently struck down districts that were drawn with demographic characteristics, in this case race or ethnicity, as the principal factor. This is particularly the case for districts that violate the "compactness" criterion.

In short, single-member districts have been relied upon as the principal method of redressing unrepresentativeness at the local level. This approach, however, is fraught with difficulties and is potentially counterproductive to the long-term interests of the group at issue.

NOT SO BAD: THE POSSIBLE ADVANTAGES OF AT-LARGE SYSTEMS

The literature on local electoral systems and their effect on women is more equivocal in its findings but, perhaps, more suggestive about the strategic placement of lesbians and gays in the representational system (Rosenblum 1996). While there is some dispute regarding the generalizability of these findings, there is evidence to suggest that women running for public office are disadvantaged in single-member district systems since some portion of the electorate is less comfortable with a woman as their sole representative (Bullock and MacManus 1991). This line of work suggests that this same portion of the electorate is more comfortable voting for women in multimember or at-large representational environments. A victory by a female candidate, under such an arrangement, would not imply that the uncertain voter would be exclusively represented by a woman. Rather, this citizen could call upon any number of representatives elected at-large and, by natural extension, interested in his or her vote. Further, since women are evenly distributed throughout the society, at-large or multimember district systems, even those without alternative voting schemes, at least allow for the possibility of pooling votes to ensure representation.

HOMOSEXUALS AND THE LOCAL REPRESENTATION SYSTEM

The relevance of electoral structure to gay representation should be apparent on its face. First, like women, homosexuals are widely distributed throughout the population, and this is particularly true outside of the purely urban setting. Second, though many of these self-identified gays and lesbians may live in a recognizable "gay ghetto" like the Castro district (San Francisco), Montrose (Houston), Wrigleyville or Halstead (Chicago), or the French Quarter (New Orleans), seldom are their numbers sufficient to assure representation in a district system. This is particularly true in cities and counties where districts are few and large. Third, even were local authorities motivated to secure lesbian and gay representation it is not clear in a district system (or any other for that matter) how this is done, given that the homosexual population is largely invisible, intentionally hard to find, and generally of inestimable size. Finally, even more so than in the case of women politicians, it is not hard to imagine that many in the electorate would be less comfortable with a homosexual as their sole representative (Herrick and Thomas, chapter 8, this volume). This suggests that some percentage of the voters would be more likely to cast their vote for a gay candidate in an at-large race than in a district race.

At this stage it might appear that homosexuals should be more likely to succeed electorally in at-large systems where gay voters both within gay ghettos and dispersed throughout the population can pool votes for a single candidate.

Rosenblum (1996) has argued persuasively that at-large systems with alternative voting and vote counting schemes, e.g., preference voting or cumulative voting, are most likely to facilitate lesbian and gay interests. If an electoral system must employ one of these alternatives to work for homosexual interests, some could argue that the pursuit of such a system puts the interests of lesbians and gays at odds with the racial and ethnic minorities who have pursued district-based solutions. Let us turn our attention now to a natural experiment underway in the City and County of San Francisco, California to see if such a conclusion is warranted.

San Francisco — A Fortuitous Experiment

In November 1996 the voters in the City and County of San Francisco voted 57 percent to 43 percent for Proposition G, a measure to return the city's eleven-member Board of Supervisors to a district-based electoral system requiring the winning candidate to gain a majority of the district's vote, including runoffs if needed. The change, which takes effect in the 2000 election, was opposed by the Alice B. Toklas Lesbian and Gay Democratic Club, anticipating that the new system would elect only one supervisor from the gay and lesbian community, based on the data used by the academicians retained to draw the lines. But the initiative was actually supported by the Harvey Milk Lesbian/Gay/Bisexual Democratic Club, whose take on the initiative's effects was more positive.[7] This division stands in stark contrast to the more general support district elections received from homosexual voters in times past.

At-Large to Districts, 1976   This change from an at-large plurality system where voters cast multiple but unpoolable votes to a district system is a replay of a similar change some twenty years before in the election of 1976. In that election San Franciscans replaced an identical at-large board with district representatives, and did so with overwhelming gay support. The districts, as it turned out, would last only until 1980. The difference between that change and the one in progress now is one of context and is informative when seeking to understand how electoral systems shape outcomes, which system best serves the interests of gay and lesbian voters, and how that determination might be contextually dependent.

In 1977 Harvey Milk was elected to the San Francisco Board of Supervisors and became the country's first openly gay elected official. Milk was not the first gay candidate to run for the board, nor was the 1977 election his first try. In fact, in 1975, running in an at-large election with six seats available, Milk placed seventh and lost. He also ran for State Assembly one year later and narrowly lost to

Art Agnos, who later became mayor of San Francisco. In both the 1975 and 1976 elections Milk, as one would expect, did extremely well in the predominantly gay precincts in the Castro District. On the day of his assembly defeat, however, district elections passed with extensive gay support, and Milk saw an opportunity. After an aborted attempt to repeal the change, San Francisco held a municipal election in November 1977, and Milk defeated sixteen other challengers and was elected supervisor of the fifth district with about 30 percent of the vote.[8]

The gay population of San Francisco was sufficiently small at the time that winning in an at-large contest, particularly one where multiple ballots could not be preference ordered, transferred, or accumulated, would have been very difficult. In short, Harvey Milk, and gays and lesbians living in the Castro, needed district elections to have a reasonable chance of winning an election. Even though Milk's celebrity and popularity had begun to extend to progressive nongay elements of the city's population, it is not clear whether he would have won a runoff election had 50 percent + 1 been required.

Runoff requirements were added by the 1979 election. Harvey Milk, sadly, would not live to contest that election, having been assassinated along with Mayor George Moscone by fellow supervisor Dan White. His appointed successor, Harry Britt, who was also openly gay, did succeed in holding the seat.

At-Large in 1980 to District Elections in 1996 — Again   By 1980, after a special election pushed by the city's more conservative forces restored the at-large electoral process in place before 1977, Britt again won reelection in an at-large contest and was among the highest vote getters. Gay population growth and the increasing comfort and coalitional associations between the gay community and the nongay population made this success possible where it had been impossible just five years before.

Gay candidates have continued to enjoy electoral success despite the lack of districts or, ironically perhaps, because of it, and by the election of 1996 the Board of Supervisors had three gay members.[9] The Alice B. Toklas Club opposed district elections because they suspected that the result would be the reduction of lesbian and gay representation to a single seat, despite the estimates that homosexuals represent about 20 percent of the city's electorate.[10]

There is evidence in support of the Toklas club's conclusion. The reason for this reduction is based on the empirical evidence as well as legal cases brought under the 1982 amendments to the Voting Rights Act and is illustrated in figure 10.1. In district-based systems a minority group is likely to capture and hold a seat when their numbers reach 60 percent of the district's voters, allowing for variable turnout rates and median ages of African American and Latino citizens (Grof-

FIGURE 10.1. Illustrated Variations in District Drawing Within and Across Identifiable Subpopulations

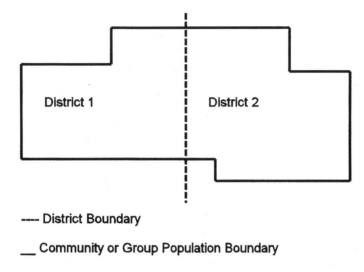

FIGURE 10.1a. Population Evenly Divided and Concentrated in Two Districts (If Population Is Sufficient, Group Will Win Both Districts)

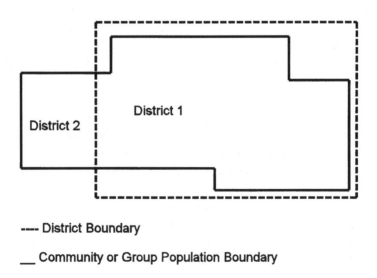

FIGURE 10.1b. Population Concentrated in a Single District (with Remainder Comprising a Minority in the Second District)

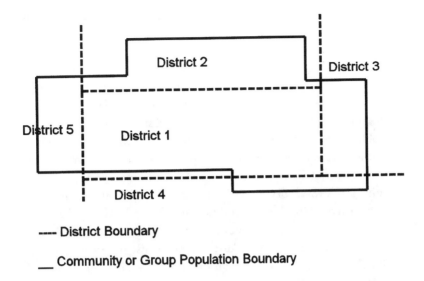

---- **District Boundary**

__ **Community or Group Population Boundary**

FIGURE 10.1c. District Carved from the Core of the Community (Remaining Members Splintered Among Several Districts)

man and Handley 1992). Of course, the group must be geographically compact enough to be in a single district. Ostensibly, that minority group could be "over-represented" until its population reaches the size of a single district. When a minority population grows above the percent represented by a single seat, in the case of San Francisco 1/11 (or 9.1 percent of the population), each additional voter provides no marginal return until the population reaches at least 60 percent of two districts (or 10.9 percent of the population) — and then only if the entire group is contained within, and evenly distributed across, two electoral districts, as in figure 10.1a. If a district is comprised nearly in its entirety by a particular group, then no other district is likely to feel the group's influence until it, too, is at least half-comprised of the group in question (13.6 percent of the total population in San Francisco, still assuming perfect geographic concentration, illustrated in figure 10.1b). If, however, the district is carved from the heart of the minority community, the remainder is likely divided between a number of other districts (figure 10.1c). And, if the minority becomes widely dispersed, that group's population could double or triple without capturing a single additional seat.[11]

The central problem is creating a system of representative government based on geography and evaluating its performance based on demography. The district system, by changing the level of aggregation, creates a fundamental disjuncture between the relative size of subpopulations and their representation in legislative bodies. This is the logic of the seats/votes disparity, just applied to group politics rather than political parties.

The district-based system adopted by the voters in 1996 is displayed in figure 10.2. District 8 includes the heavily gay neighborhoods of the Castro, Upper Market, Noe/Eureka Valley, and the Duboce Triangle. In fact, it is the only district with a gay population of sufficient estimated size to elect a supervisor.[12] This problem of broadly distributed populations affects other minorities in San Francisco as well, and this observation is suggestive regarding the conflict or co-incidence of interests between homosexuals and other minorities.

In July 1995 the State of California's Department of Finance estimated the following breakdown by racial and ethnic category for the City and County of San Francisco: white non-Hispanics 43 percent, Asians and Pacific Islanders 32 percent, Latinos 15 percent, African Americans 10 percent, all others including Native Americans less than 1 percent.[13] With an eleven-member Board of Supervisors, the opportunity for diverse composition would appear to be high.

The composition of the current board (in the wake of the 1996 at-large elections) includes three gays and lesbians (two white, one Latina), three Asians, a nongay Latino, and one African American, with Anglos comprising the balance. But the transition to districts, which the literature suggests would augment minority representation, is very likely to result in a substantial reduction by virtue of the distributions of these minorities throughout the city. The ethnic and racial composition of the newly created districts is presented in table 10.1.

The electoral commission charged with drawing the districts was able to create only one majority Asian district (55.23 percent in District 3) and one majority Hispanic district (50.06 percent in District 9), neither sufficiently tilted to ensure minority electability, if previous experience is a guide. African Americans are a plurality of 39.6 percent in only one district.[14] In short, despite the census data and best reasonable estimates of the gay population suggesting that San Francisco is among America's most diverse cities, the best-case scenario for minority representation is a Board of Supervisors with only one homosexual (District 8) and, at most, three nonwhites (Districts 3, 9, and, though unlikely, 10), with the remaining seven seats (63.6 percent) being composed of heterosexual whites. Given that no minority group in any district achieves the 60 percent threshold, it is possible that, after the 2000 election, not a single nonwhite member will be elected to the San Francisco Board of Supervisors in a city that is only 43 percent white (many of whom are gay), and all but one of these members will be a heterosexual.[15]

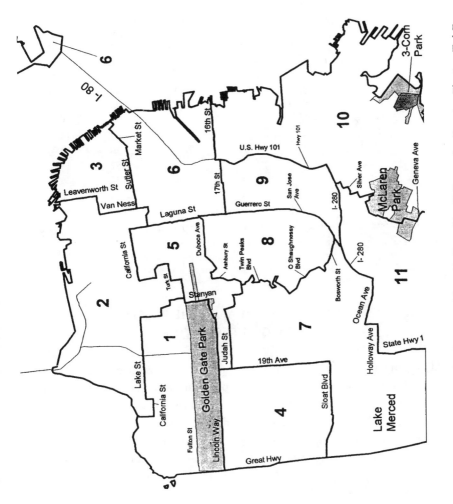

FIGURE 10.2. Single-Member Districts as Adopted in Proposition G. Source: San Francisco Elections Task Force.

TABLE 10.1.

Summary Demographics by New Districts, City and County of San Francisco, California

District	% White	% Black	% Asian/PI	% Nat Am	% Other	% Hispanic
1	47.88	2.62	47.69	.31	1.50	4.82
2	81.63	3.40	13.20	.30	1.47	4.67
3	41.30	2.16	55.23	.25	1.06	3.57
4	50.53	1.85	45.71	.32	1.60	5.75
5	57.04	26.87	12.93	.59	2.56	6.55
6	51.47	12.68	27.79	1.00	7.06	16.68
7	66.31	4.82	26.06	.37	2.45	8.12
8	80.70	4.13	9.16	.59	5.42	14.79
9	51.39	6.08	16.51	.71	25.30	50.06
10	25.16	39.56	29.27	.44	5.57	13.12
11	36.41	15.11	36.00	.41	12.07	26.84

Source: U.S. Census data collected by the San Francisco Elections Task Force.

Columns 2–6 add to 100. Hispanic/non-Hispanic is a separate coding category from race. For practical purposes, Hispanic percentages are a subset of the white and other numbers.

THE AT-LARGE SYSTEM AND THE PREFERENCE VOTING ALTERNATIVE

At the same time voters in San Francisco were able to decide on districts, they were also presented with Measure H, a proposal for implementing a preference voting scheme to replace the plurality system within their existing at-large framework.[16] Rules governing the referendum process in San Francisco provided that, should both propositions pass, the one garnering the most votes would be implemented. No such adjudication was necessary, however, as Measure H, the preference voting option, failed at the polls, 44 percent to 56 percent.

The Harvey Milk club, disenchanted with the current system, supported Measure H, and their president, in fact, was the consultant to the "Yes on H" campaign. The Toklas club took no official position (though its cochair did send a letter of personal endorsement to all the membership as well as the Board of Supervisors).

Rosenblum (1996) has argued that cumulative voting is the best electoral form for ensuring representation for gays and lesbians.[17] Other advocates of reform have suggested that preference voting is superior to cumulative voting in helping minorities since cumulative voting still faces the possibility of "wasted" votes, that is, additional votes for candidates already past the threshold for election.[18] Objections to either system usually focus on the complexity, suggesting that the confusion resulting from the novelty of the system to the voters would essentially disenfranchise a substantial segment of the population by raising the costs of voting. But those objections have not held up empirically, as Engstrom, Taebel, and Cole's (1989) examination of Alamogordo, New Mexico demonstrated. In that instance cumulative voting was implemented as a response to a vote dilution finding. Engstrom and his colleagues found that the electorate clearly understood the system, used it for electoral effect, and clearly understood the implications.[19]

The argument that alternative vote schemes are superior to at-large plurality systems and districts for ensuring minority representation is not questioned here, but, unfortunately, San Franciscans did not provide us an opportunity to test this finding.[20] The case of San Francisco, however, does provide evidence that the superiority of districts to at-large plurality systems is not a given but is dependent upon context.

Lessons from the San Francisco Example

The political interests of lesbians and gays in San Francisco were likely not well served by the adoption of districts. The number of homosexuals on the Board of Supervisors is likely to decline by at least one and, more likely, two. But if district-based elections served the purposes of minority voters, this would suggest that gay and lesbian interests were at odds with the best interests of minorities. This assumes that majority-minority districts do serve the interests of minorities, an assumption questioned both here and elsewhere. Being at cross-purposes would, of course, severely limit opportunities for coalitional politics between homosexuals and other groups, particularly on issues of equity in representation. And such coalitional politics is of greater importance to lesbian and gay interests in cities where the population is smaller and has relatively less political power than in San Francisco.

The evidence from the census data used to draw the new districts suggests otherwise. Minorities do not gain as a result of the gay and lesbian loss. The dispersion of ethnic groups in the city makes the creation of districts with a supermajority of minority voters essentially impossible, despite the relatively large number of districts for the population size. In this instance even a well-intentioned effort to ensure minority representation will result in the minority being cracked into several districts by virtue of disaggregating groups across districts. Their vote, in short, will be diluted.

Careful consideration would seem to suggest that the identified advantages of districts are conditioned upon a set of assumptions that may not be true. For starters, the group in question must be geographically concentrated. Widely dispersed groups — like virtually every group in San Francisco — are difficult to collect in a single district. And it is important to note that as minority populations grow vis-à-vis non-Hispanic whites, or as the socioeconomic status of minority group members acquires greater variance, geographic dispersion of minority populations will almost certainly increase, making their objective political circumstances more like those of women and homosexuals.

Second, a minority group must have sufficient political strength (unlikely by definition), enjoy federal "suspect class" protection, or live in a geographic area subject to the preclearance provisions of the 1982 Voting Rights Act to avoid cracking across a number of districts. While women and racial or ethnic minorities enjoy such protection, homosexuals do not. In the absence of either gay-friendly majorities, or sufficient political power in advance of any change, lesbians and gays are not likely to see districts drawn in any jurisdiction to suit their interests.

Third, the minority is more likely to benefit from districts if it is small when compared to the population at large. Larger groups, whose share of the population exceeds one divided by the number of seats at stake, are likely underrepresented in a district system that caps their share of the seats at one.

Finally, not all district systems are alike. The research is unequivocal that district elections requiring runoffs, that is those with officeholding thresholds at 50 percent +1, are less likely to benefit very small groups than those with plurality winners and no runoffs (Bullock and MacManus 1990, 1991; Guinier 1994).

It should be clear now that district based elections need not be automatically superior to at-large systems and represent an improvement only under specific, and somewhat restrictive, circumstances. Nevertheless, the existence of those circumstances is common enough, and the empirical record of minority descriptive representation clear enough, that simple at-large systems are a tough political sell and not always a Pareto optimal outcome vis-à-vis districts, as I have suggested the San Francisco at-large system was.

Another important caveat is worth noting here. In jurisdictions covered by the Voting Rights Act and its attendant restrictions, statutory and case law serve to severely circumscribe the options available to address minority vote dilution problems. Much of the "preclearance" provisions enacted in the 1982 extension were specifically designed to thwart electoral engineering schemes that would serve to undercut minority representation. Since in most instances a shift to districts has been perceived as an effective strategy for redressing previous vote dilution problems, well-intentioned attempts to move away from districts, however flawed those districts are, will almost certainly be viewed with judicial skepticism and, hence, a tough sell.

An at-large system with an alternative voting scheme dominates all other strategies of electoral engineering in securing the interests of geographically clustered racial and ethnic minorities on the one hand and geographically diffuse groups such as homosexuals and women on the other. Although the preference voting mechanism was defeated in San Francisco, other cities may adopt such measures and act as a strong facilitator of coalition-based politics.

The case of San Francisco's charter amendment has provided some insight into both the assumptions that underly the work demonstrating the advantages of districts for minorities and how the nature of local electoral laws affects the likelihood of gay and lesbian descriptive representation and cooperation with other minority groups. For sure, San Francisco is a unique place, and on more dimensions than just the political. Few major cities in America have such variety of minority populations and a gay and lesbian community of this magnitude. In addition, since San Francisco is outside the area covered by the Voting Rights Act, it is easier for that city to experiment with its electoral system, which, as the history suggests, is an opportunity it has frequently taken.

But my purpose in using this case was to focus on the problem of lesbian and gay representation under a set of specific contextual conditions that occur in other environments with some frequency, namely, the presence of multiple minority groups in the community and the dispersed residential patterns of one or more of those groups. In addition, since the Board of Supervisors is relatively large for the population — making minority representation through districts *more* likely — to show that districts may not be useful even in this environment helps to make a more compelling case for challenging conventional wisdom.

My arguments, then, are not San Francisco-specific, but rather they are relevant to these contextual conditions (San Francisco is, without doubt, a unique environment in many ways). Specifically, my arguments suggest the following:

1) Geographically dispersed minorities are helped less by a district-based electoral system. That is, the benefit of districts to minorities is negatively related to the level of minority dispersion throughout the population and positively related to the number of districts.
2) Unless a city includes both a gay ghetto with population sufficient to comprise a voting majority of a single district *and* an existing power base through friendly legislators to ensure the drawing of district lines to en-

compass rather than divide the ghetto, districts do not serve the interests of gays and lesbians.

3) Even if the gay population meets these criteria, it might still be disadvantaged by a district system should its size become sufficiently large that districts serve to cap gay representation at one.

4) If ethnic and racial minorities are small and highly concentrated, their interests in terms of electoral systems may be at odds with those of homosexuals. As a group becomes larger and/or more geographically spread out the representational interests of the group, on the one hand, and lesbians and gays, on the other, become coincident, and successful coalition building becomes more likely.

At some level these conclusions are testable hypotheses that, through additional work of both a formal and empirical nature, should be borne out.

In broad terms what this work suggests about gay political activism in America's cities is of more pressing interest. For lesbians and gay men intent upon improving their level of electoral success or securing more favorable policy outcomes, the clear message is that there are at least three games going on: maximizing electoral clout, changing the institutions to facilitate that clout, and building coalitions with other similarly disadvantaged groups for the collective benefit of all.

The value of coalition building is clearly not lost on the gay and lesbian leadership, who have worked for years to build partnerships with racial and ethnic groups, friendly religious groups such as Jews, organized labor, and other organized interests.[21] Similarly, the face value of securing more elective offices for lesbian and gay candidates is hard to dispute, although it raises a number of questions about the "authenticity" of representation, as suggested by Guinier. But, to secure this outcome, politically astute homosexuals should also examine whether the electoral institutions are structured in a manner that facilitates or impedes gay electability. And efforts to change these structures will require changing some long and firmly held beliefs about the advantages of single-member districts to minorities, else we risk any chance of coalition building.

NOTES

The author wishes to acknowledge the effective research assistance of Elizabeth Bergman, Bethany Barratt, and Nathan Woods, without whom this work would have been impossible. The manuscript was greatly improved through the comments of the editors of this volume and the anonymous reviewers. My sincere gratitude to Kevin Francis Piediscalzi, the cochair of the Alice B. Toklas Lesbian and Gay Democratic Club of San Francisco, whose patience, insight, and information were critical to the effort.

1. In this effort the "interests" are conceived as being representational alone, and it is on this dimension that electoral systems are judged rather than, say, efficiency. I am indebted to my colleague, Aldo Flores, for this observation.

2. San Francisco is, admittedly, among the nation's more unique environments, and, indeed, every city is potentially a unique case study (see Gossett, chapter 4, this volume). My focus here, however, is on the contextual conditions that are relevant to my argument, conditions replicated elsewhere.

3. For an exception, see Hertzog (1996).

4. This assumption, though an analytic convenience, is a potential oversimplification, and a potentially offensive one at that, as Justice O'Conner suggested in her opinion in *Shaw v Reno*. While it is empirically true that high percentages of Latinos, African Americans, and self-identified gays and lesbians vote similarly, the level of unity varies across these groups, does *not* apply at all to other groups such as women, and is certainly not an immutable characteristic of these specific groups.

5. This is not to assume any particular motive on the part of white voters. I am agnostic as to whether the cause of white bloc voting at the local level is racism, economic interests, campaign spending, or the like.

6. This argument admittedly makes some assumptions about the policy preferences and voting behavior of the nonminority Democratic officeholders in question as well as the Democratic preference of the preponderance of the minority group. While not automatically true by definition, these assumptions are generally perceived to be empirically valid (Robinson and Dye 1978).

7. The Milk club's support was premised on three contentions: the belief that districts would impede machine-based and money-driven politics, the belief that three supervisors was unsustainably high under any electoral arrangement, and the conclusion that two, and not one, of the resulting districts would elect lesbian or gay supervisors (Handler 1996).

8. Runoffs to secure simple majorities were not required under the system adopted in November 1976.

9. It is worth noting that mayoral appointments played a role in reaching this level of gay representation. A number of gay supervisors received their seats the first time by appointment rather than by election as a challenger. Nevertheless, they have been successful at defending these seats under the current (pre-1996) electoral arrangements.

10. This estimate is from the Harvey Milk Gay and Lesbian Democratic Club and is difficult to verify for reasons too numerous to recount. Careful attention needs to be paid to the difference between the population and the electorate, which is reduced by age distribution and citizenship status, each varying dramatically across ethnic and social groups.

11. Strictly speaking, if the minority outside the majority-minority district is perfectly evenly distributed, that minority can grow to be a majority and still hold only one seat. In the San Francisco example gays and lesbians could comprise 100 percent of one district and 49.9 percent of all ten others, or 54.45 percent of the vote, and win only one

seat. Although this is an unlikely scenario at this extreme, it is illustrative of the problem of imposing geographic representation over demographic categories.

12. District 5 has a large gay and lesbian minority, but not a majority, as a Milk Club newsletter suggested. In the absence of diagnostic census data, estimating the gay population of any area requires considerable inference. In this instance the San Francisco Elections Task Force (Craig et al. 1995) relied upon a "Gay Voting Index" compiled by Lisel Blash and Richard DeLeon of the Public Research Institute of San Francisco State University. The index was based on factor scores resulting from a principle components factor analysis of precinct vote for three gay supervisorial candidates in the 1994 election (Blash and DeLeon 1995).

13. That the numbers do not add to 100 percent is a product of rounding error.

14. It is hard to predict what outcome would emerge from District 10. The sizable Asian and white populations (together over 54 percent) suggest that African Americans would be unsuccessful in electing an African American to the supervisor's seat. Some portion of "white" and "other" are, in fact, Hispanic, which, when added to the black population, together comprise 52.7 percent of the population. Black electoral success, however, would still be entirely dependent upon successful coalition building and extremely high turnout among the two demographic groups with the lowest historical propensity to go to the polls. Among the possible results in this extremely diverse district, an African American supervisor represents one of the lowest probability outcomes.

15. It is worth noting that an eleven-member body in a city of only 750,000 actually improves the chances for representation of diverse groups. That is, when compared to other jurisdictions of comparable or larger size with smaller boards (Los Angeles County has only five supervisors for 9.5 million people), the San Francisco district arrangement is actually more conducive to minority representation than most. A more common arrangement in San Francisco would have resulted in even less representative results.

16. Preference voting, sometimes called the single transferable vote system, allows citizens to cast their ballot by ordering candidates from their most preferred to their least preferred. In this manner, should the voter's most preferred alternative be eliminated by receiving too few first-place votes, the voter's vote is then switched to the next preferred alternative. In addition, once the candidate at the top of the list receives enough votes to cross the threshold to election, remaining ballots for that candidate are also transferred to the next preference, so that votes are not wasted on already elected candidates. The result should be an elected body whose composition closely reflects the collective preference ordering of the electorate.

17. Cumulative voting systems allocate a number of votes to each voter equal to the number of seats at stake. The voter may distribute or concentrate those votes across candidates as they please. This allows the voter to express multiple preferences, or act on multiple identities, simultaneously. For example, an African American female voter might cast some of her votes for a white female candidate and some for an African

American male candidate, thereby expressing both identities (or preferences) in her political choice.

18. At least two groups weighed in on the San Francisco case, the Electoral Reform Coalition — an ad hoc organization created for these specific fights — and Northern California Citizens for Proportional Representation — an ongoing group interested in electoral reform.

19. Not surprisingly, they find that many whites dislike this new system while, among the Latinos it was implemented to help, the cumulative voting scheme was more popular.

20. Strictly speaking, however, preference voting need not be superior to districts. In the case of a geographically concentrated ethnic or racial minority of so small a size that it comprises only 60 percent of one electoral district and no more, the group will likely *not* reach the threshold for electing one of their own in a preference system, but *would* succeed should a district be drawn around them. This exception is dependent upon very restrictive circumstances and is an unlikely occurrence; nevertheless, it suggests the contextual dependence of this comparison as well.

21. The value of coalition building to nongay constituencies is also becoming clearer, as many lesbians and gays share identificatory interests with these other groups. See Walston (1997) for an excellent example.

REFERENCES

Blacksher, James and Larry Menefee. 1984. "At Large Elections and One Person, One Vote: The Search for the Meaning of Racial Dilution." In Chandler Davidson, ed., *Minority Vote Dilution*, pp. 203–248. Washington, DC: Joint Center for Political Studies.

Blash, Lisel and Richard DeLeon. 1995. "Appendix of Additional Maps." In Gwenn Craig, Carmen White, Ramon Arias, Christopher Bowman, Dale Butler, Nancy Lanvin, Eric Mar, Dale Shimasaki, Samson Wong, and Germaine Q. Wong, *A Report of the Elections Task Force to the Board of Supervisor.* City and County of San Francisco.

Brace, Kimball, Bernard Grofman, and Lisa Handley. 1987. "Does Redistricting Aimed to Help Blacks Necessarily Help Republicans?" *Journal of Politics* 49:167–185.

Bullock, Charles S. III and Susan A. MacManus. 1987. "The Impact of Staggered Terms on Minority Representation." *Journal of Politics* 49:543–552.

—— 1990. "Structural Features of Municipalities and the Incidence of Hispanic Councilmembers." *Social Science Quarterly* 71:664–681.

—— 1991. "Municipal Electoral Structure and the Election of Councilwomen." *Journal of Politics* 53:75–89.

Cameron, Charles, David Epstein, and Sharyn O'Halloran. 1996. "Do Majority-Minority Districts Maximize Substantive Black Representation in Congress?" *American Political Science Review* 90:794–812.

Cole, Leonard A. 1974. "Electing Blacks to Municipal Office: Structural and Social Determinants." *Urban Affairs Quarterly* 10:17–39.

Craig, Gwenn, Carmen White, Ramon Arias, Christopher Bowman, Dale Butler, Nancy Lanvin, Eric Mar, Dale Shimasaki, Samson Wong, and Germaine Q. Wong. 1995. *A Report of the Elections Task Force to the Board of Supervisor.* City and County of San Francisco.

Derfner, Armand. 1984. "Vote Dilution and the Voting Rights Act Amendments of 1982." In Chandler Davidson, ed., *Minority Vote Dilution.* Washington, DC: Joint Center for Political Studies.

Engstrom, Richard L. and Michael C. McDonald. 1981. "The Election of Blacks to City Councils: Clarifying the Impact of Electoral Arrangements on the Seats/Population Relationship." *American Political Science Review* 75:344–354.

Engstrom, Richard L., Delbert A. Taebel, and Richard L. Cole. 1989. "Cumulative Voting as a Remedy for Minority Vote Dilution: The Case of Alamogordo, New Mexico." *Journal of Law and Politics* 5:469–497.

Gay and Lesbian Victory Fund. 1996. "Record Number of Victory Fund Candidates Triumph." Gay and Lesbian Victory Fund Press Release, November 7.

Gossett, Charles W. 1999. "Dillon's Rule and Gay Rights: State Control Over Local Efforts to Protect the Rights of Lesbians and Gay Men." Chapter 4, this volume.

Grofman, Bernard, and Lisa Handley. 1992. "Preconditions for Black and Hispanic Congressional Success." In Wilma Rule and Joseph F. Zimmerman, eds., *United States Electoral Systems: Their Impact on Women and Minorities.* New York: Praeger.

Grofman, Bernard, Lisa Handley, and Richard Neimi. 1992. *Minority Representation and the Quest for Voting Equality.* Cambridge: Cambridge University Press.

Guinier, Lani. 1994. *The Tyranny of the Majority: Fundamental Fairness in Representative Democracy.* New York: Free Press.

Handler, Jim. 1996. "District Elections." *Milk Club Newsletter*, March.

Heilig, Peggy, and Robert J. Mundt. 1983. "Changes in Representational Equity: The Effect of Adopting Districts." *Social Science Quarterly* 64:393–397.

Herrick, Rebekah and Sue Thomas. 1999. "The Effects of Sexual Orientation on Citizen Perceptions of Candidate Viability." Chapter 8, this volume.

Hertzog, Mark. 1996. *The Lavender Vote.* New York: New York University Press.

Hill, Kevin. 1995. "Does the Creation of Majority Black Districts Aid Republicans?" *Journal of Politics* 57:384–401.

Karnig, Albert K. 1976. "Black Representation on City Councils: The Impact of District Elections and Socioeconomic Factors." *Urban Affairs Quarterly* 12:223–242.

Karnig, Albert K. and Susan Welch. 1979. "Sex and Ethnic Differences in Municipal Representation." *Social Science Quarterly* 60:465–481.

——— 1980. *Black Representation and Urban Policy.* Chicago: University of Chicago Press.

——— 1982. "Electoral Structure and Black Representation on City Councils." *Social Science Quarterly* 63:99–114.

Latimer, Margaret K. 1979. "Black Political Representation in Southern Cities: Election Systems and Other Causal Variables." *Urban Affairs Quarterly* 15:65–86.

McDonald, Laughlin. 1992. "The 1982 Amendments of Section 2 and Minority Representation." In Bernard Grofman and Chandler Davidson, eds., *Controversies in Minority Voting.* Washington, DC: Brookings Institution.

MacManus, Susan A. and Charles S. Bullock III. 1992. "Electing Women to City Council: A Focus on Small Cities in Florida." In Wilma Rule and Joseph F. Zimmerman, eds., *United States Electoral Systems: Their Impact on Women and Minorities.* New York: Praeger.

Miller v Johnson. 1995. 132 L. Ed. 2d 762.

Mobile v Bolden. 1980. 446 US 55.

Robinson, Theodore P. and Thomas R. Dye. 1978. "Reformism and Black Representation on City Councils." *Social Science Quarterly* 59:133–141.

Romer v Evans. 1996. 116 S. Ct. 1620.

Rosenblum, Darren. 1996. "Geographically Sexual? Advancing Lesbian and Gay Interests Through Proportional Representation." *Harvard Civil Rights–Civil Liberties Law Review* 31:119–154.

Shaw v Hunt. 1996. 135 L. Ed. 2d 207.

Shaw v Reno. 1993. 113 S. Ct. 2816.

Thornburg v Gingles. 1986. 478 U.S. 30.

Walston, Charles. 1997. "Black Atlantans Split as Mayoral Candidates Appeal to Northside." *Atlanta Journal-Constitution,* November 9.

Welch, Susan and Albert K. Karnig. 1979. "Correlates of Female Office Holding in City Politics." *Journal of Politics* 41:478–491.

CHAPTER ELEVEN

Creating Change — Holding the Line: Agenda Setting on Lesbian and Gay Issues at the National Level

Donald P. Haider-Markel

Since the 1950s a series of citizen-based movements have created profound cultural and political change in the United States. The black civil rights movement, the women's movement, the antiwar movement, the student movement, the environmental movement, and the American Indian movement are the most prominent examples. Researchers have written a great deal about these movements, but little of the work is empirical (notable exceptions include Costain and Majstorovic 1994; Hardin 1982; McAdam 1982; and Chong 1991). Further, most social movement research overlooks a movement that has probably made its greatest strides in the 1980s and 1990s.

The lesbian and gay movement has received the attention of a select group of authors (for example, see Adam 1995; Altman 1974; Blasius 1994; Cruikshank 1992; D'Emilio 1983, 1992; Vaid 1995) and is sometimes mentioned in recent editions of textbooks on American politics. Disappointingly little research on the lesbian and gay social movement, however, has been empirical in nature (but see Button, Rienzo, and Wald 1997; Haider-Markel 1997a, 1997b; Haider-Markel and Meier 1996; Harry and DeVall 1978). While much has been conjectured about the impact of the lesbian and gay social movement, few researchers have attempted to demonstrate systematically the influence of the movement on government activity or, for that matter, American society and culture.

This chapter is an exploratory effort to investigate the response of the national government to the gay and lesbian social movement from 1960 to 1996. First, I construct a theoretical framework concerning the birth of social movements and governmental response. Second, I present a brief history of the gay and lesbian movement to establish the growth of the movement over time and examples of government response. Third, based on the theoretical framework and my discussion of the lesbian and gay movement, I specify important factors for a time series analysis of the movement along with the strategy of analysis. Finally, the results of my analysis are presented along with their implications.

SOCIAL MOVEMENTS AND GOVERNMENT RESPONSE

While social movements strive to transform their participants and change the society around them, it is not clear how movements influence government institutions and policy. The two main schools of thought on how social movements exert influence are resource mobilization theory and political process theory.[1] Both theories argue that a number of factors need to be present for movements to form, survive, and influence policy. These include a communications network, a series of crises or general social change, the attention of the media, political opportunity, movement resources, movement activity, and supportive public opinion (Arnowitz 1992; Costain 1992a, 1992b; Costain and Majstorovic 1994; Freeman 1975:62; Gamson 1968, 1975; Huberts 1989; McAdam 1982; Mac-Dougall 1991; Salisbury 1969; Tarrow 1994). All these factors must be consolidated within a movement and brought to bear on important institutions.

A movement's communications network must be able to disseminate ideas to persons throughout the country and be composed of like-minded persons (Freeman 1975:48). Networks include newsletters, periodicals, friendship networks, books, government institutions and commissions, and even existing communications networks used by movements concerned with other issues (Costain 1992a, 1992b).

Crisis and general social change give movements a reason to organize and may assist in the articulation of demands. A movement already organized can also be reinvigorated by new threats. Freeman (1975:69) argues, "Nothing makes desire for change more acute than a crisis. If the strain is great enough, such a crisis need not be a major one; it need only symbolically embody collective discontent" (see also Tarrow 1994:25).

General social change also helps make movements possible. For the lesbian and gay movement, social changes included increasing levels of urbanization and education and the move away from an agricultural economy at the beginning of the twentieth century. Such changes made it easier for gays and lesbians to create communities in urban centers where economic survival was not based in the traditional family unit (D'Emilio 1992; Posner 1992:126–128, 215). Harry and De Vall (1978:147–150) argue that political mobilization stems from the creation of gay institutions within an urban center that benefit gay entrepreneurs. Entrepreneurs protect their economic interests by pressuring local authorities to stop their crackdowns on bookstores, bars, and the sex industry. These "pockets" of nonrepressive political climates provide space in which a movement can be nurtured and a pool of potential movement leaders that are familiar with pressuring government (see also Adam 1995; Altman 1974; D'Emilio 1983; Posner 1992:215; Shilts 1988).

The media are also important for social movements. Without regular coverage the movement will find it difficult to hold the attention of the public or politicians, thereby making policy change difficult (Costain and Majstorovic 1994; Davis 1991:106, 117–118; Freeman 1975:148; Tarrow 1994:127). For example, the media's increasing coverage of the women's movement in 1969 led to growing membership in women's groups and increasing participation in political demonstrations (see Davis 1991:117–118; Freeman 1975;148), while media coverage of the "gays in the military" debate may have led to a decline in public opposition to gays openly serving (see Haeberle, chapter 7, this volume). At minimum, however, press coverage informs potential participants that groups, and a movement, exist.

Political opportunities for movements are created within the context of general social change, but opportunities are also structured by government response and changing electoral coalitions (Costain 1992a, 1992b; Freeman 1975:231; Gamson 1968, 1975; Schattschneider 1960; Tarrow 1994). For example, Costain (1992a) argues that the women's movement was energized by the inclusion of gender in the 1964 Civil Rights Act—a policy change that the movement itself did not bring about. Rosenthal (1995) notes that political opportunities for lesbians and gays in Albany, New York only arose after the local Democratic Party organization was divided into two camps—a situation that gays and lesbian did not create. Freeman (1975:233) argues, however, that "the correlation between movement strength and the development of policy in accord with its aims is at best a rough one. Sympathetic policy can destroy a movement by preempting it; and non-sympathetic policy can strengthen a movement by creating a crisis which mobilizes its adherents" (see also Chong 1991; Costain 1992a; Tarrow 1994).

Government response is also strongly related to movement resources and activity. Without strong leaders, organizations, and public activism, the demands of movements will not be heard (Freeman 1975:232–233; see also Costain and Majstorovic 1994). Policy change does not occur overnight. For movements to be successful they must sustain the mobilization of participants; mobilization is more likely to be sustained when formal organizations and strong leaders are present, a notion that Sherrill's chapter (chapter 12, this volume) supports.

Another factor, public opinion, complicates the relationship between the factors listed above and government response. Public opinion can be influenced by the movement and, in turn, influence policy. Changes in public policy, however, may also influence public opinion and subsequently shape the movement (see Costain and Majstorovic 1994; Freeman 1975:231; Tarrow 1994). Harry and De Vall (1978) specifically argue that reductions in police raids on gay bars leads to a decrease in negative public opinion toward homosexuals, thereby giving the movement more space in which to grow. Rosenthal (1995) implies that the passage of an ordinance in Syracuse, New York created more favorable public opinion toward gays and encouraged greater mobilization and "organization building" by the lesbian and gay community in that city.

Finally, a large part of the work movements engage in, both to reach the government's agenda and mobilize constituents, is creating issue "frames." Snow (1992:137) argues that movements attempt to construct the meaning of events and objects for participants and observers through an "interpretive schemata that simplifies and condenses the 'world out there' by selectively punctuating and encoding objects, situations, events, experiences, and sequences of actions within one's present or past environment." Successfully constructed frames usually appeal to widely held values and are, therefore, more likely to invoke government response and mobilize potential participants (Tarrow 1994:123).

Movements, however, do not have free rein in their attempts to frame issues — they must compete with politicians, opposition groups, the media, and citizens as they contend for a place on the political agenda. How an issue is framed will determine whether or not an issue reaches the political agenda, what venues are suitable for a discussion of the issue, what actors will be mobilized and/or allowed to participate in the policy process, and the focus of policy that actors are demanding (Baumgartner and Jones 1993:23–25, 30; also see Sherrill, chapter 12, and Haeberle, chapter 7, this volume, for a similar argument). The struggle over how an issue is framed, moreover, will often determine who wins and who loses within political institutions (Baumgartner and Jones 1993:16, 29).

A BRIEF HISTORY OF THE GAY MOVEMENT AND FEDERAL GOVERNMENT RESPONSE

This section briefly outlines the history of the lesbian and gay movement and the response of the federal government. For ease of discussion and because the literature on the movement tends to divide the development of the movement into at least three parts, this section will discuss the rise of the movement and federal activity from 1920 to 1968, from 1969 to 1976, and from 1977 to the present. I argue that homosexuality reached the political agenda of Congress because of concerns raised by the defense community over national security, Evangelical Christians over traditional values, lesbian and gay activists over equality and civil rights, and because of concerns raised by many political actors over AIDS.

Each of these groups defined homosexual issues differently, but, most important, each tried to tie homosexual issues to strong and positive symbols (or frames) in American politics. During the 1950s members of the defense community linked homosexuality with the threat posed by communism (D'Emilio 1992:68), while Evangelicals framed their opposition to homosexuality in terms of declining moral standards and the rise of secular humanism in the 1960s (Vaid 1995:320–321). Throughout the 1960s and 1970s lesbian and gay activists argued that homosexuals were an oppressed group facing discrimination and the denial of their civil rights (Vaid 1995:106). In the 1980s the AIDS epidemic was linked to homosexuality, thereby expanding the scope of homosexual issues. AIDS also brought new political actors into the debate over homosexuality, and these actors each brought their own values, judgments, and issue frames to the debate (see Shilts 1988).

1920 to 1968: Homophile Groups and the Beginnings of Political Activity

Early congressional action on homosexuality focused on homosexuals as an internal security threat. Framing homosexuality in terms of national defense not only gave Congress jurisdiction to address the issue of homosexuality, it also limited what actors could participate and what specific issues could be addressed. Congress first addressed homosexuality during a 1920 Senate investigation of "'immoral conditions' of a homosexual nature at the naval training station in Newport, Rhode Island" (D'Emilio 1992:64). In the 1950s members of Congress expanded the debate on homosexuality by linking homosexuality to communism, thereby placing homosexuals on the wrong side of cold war politics. The Senate released a report on the security threat homosexuals posed to the federal government in December 1950. The security threat posed by homosexuals was also raised within the context of communist infiltration of the government during the 1953 McCarthy hearings (Adam 1995:60–65; D'Emilio 1992:59).[2] During the McCarthy hearings witnesses suggested that homosexual government employees could be blackmailed by communist spies. The underlying logic was that homosexuality is immoral and, therefore, inherently corrupting. At minimum, however, the enemy's knowledge of such immoral behavior could be used as an espionage tool against individuals in cold war politics (D'Emilio

1992:60). Members of Congress also attacked homosexual activist groups; in 1954 Senator Wiley (R-WI) sent a letter to the U.S. postmaster that demanded a gay magazine (*ONE*) be blocked from using the U.S. mail because of its devotion to the "advancement of sexual perversion" (Streitmatter 1995:32). The postmaster complied with the request until the decision was overruled by the Supreme Court in 1958 (Streitmatter 1995:343).

Although they were under heavy attack, gay men and lesbians began to build community institutions and create a collective identity of what it meant to be homosexual. Three of the first national lesbian/gay organizations were formed in the early 1950s, the Daughters of Bilitis, the ONE Institute, and the Mattachine Society. These organizations called themselves homophile groups, and while their stated purpose was to influence public perception of homosexuals and change public policy toward gays and lesbians, they mainly focused on cultural change through education. In fact, the first homophile organizations did little but begin to establish communications networks between communities of homosexuals (D'Emilio 1983).

In the early 1960s the attempts to frame homosexuality as security threat and immoral created a natural alliance between cold warriors and Evangelical Christians; the narrow scope of the debate also limited the ability of homosexual activists to participate. The conservative alliance reflected broader trends in American society and the Republican Party. At the time, Evangelical Christians were increasing their political involvement (especially within the Republican Party) because of the threat to traditional values posed by a Supreme Court ruling on school prayer and the increasing demands of the black civil rights movement (see Diamond 1995:104–106). The alliance between cold warriors and Evangelicals was further reinforced by the cold warriors' conceptualization of the black civil rights movement as subversive (see Diamond 1995:109–111; Horne 1996). Republican presidential candidate Barry Goldwater used political rhetoric that reflected the alliance between cold warriors and Evangelicals; Goldwater ran on a platform of staunch anticommunism, but also advocated a Constitutional amendment to allow school prayer (Diamond 1995:105).

This political debate set the stage for the first known congressional vote on a gay-related issue. The early lobbying efforts of a homosexual group, the Mattachine Society, so enraged Representative John Dowdy that in May of 1963 he initiated hearings on the issue and introduced a bill to revoke Mattachine's permit to raise funds in Washington, DC. During congressional hearings Mattachine representatives tried to frame homosexuality as a civil rights issue by discussing employment discrimination, but committee members used the venue to speak against the immorality of homosexuality and to question witnesses on deviant sexual behavior. The bill, HR 5990, overwhelmingly passed the House on August 11, 1964. Most important, gays and lesbians had gained limited political access during the consideration of HR 5990. Although gays found little support in the House, the bill was watered down to the point of being largely symbolic and never reached a vote in the Senate (D'Emilio 1983:156–157). Homosexuality had reached the congressional agenda, but cold warriors and Evangelicals were still firmly in control of how the issue was framed.

By 1965 some local groups began to call for more radical tactics in their efforts to create change. Such calls resulted in the first known gay political protests at the White House, the Pentagon, and Independence Hall in Philadelphia during 1965. These protests, however, did not appear to elicit a direct response from the federal government (see D'Emilio 1983; Thompson 1994).

1969 to 1976: Stonewall and Lesbian and Gay Liberation

By most accounts, 1969 was the birth year of the modern gay and lesbian social movement. The three days of riots following a police raid of the Stonewall Inn of New York City sent shock waves throughout gay communities and provided an incentive for many gays to become involved with the burgeoning movement (Sherrill, chapter 12, this volume; Thompson 1994; Vaid 1995). Stonewall became the rallying point of the movement, with lesbians and gays demanding political attention for their concerns in ways similar to the black civil rights movement, antiwar movement, and women's movement.

In the early 1970s gay activists increasingly attempted to frame homosexuality in positive terms, stressing discrimination and civil rights as the issues that should be under consideration. The advent of a new gay activism was soon followed by government response, reactions to the growing movement came from the Congress and the bureaucracy. On their face each of these government actions appeared to be a response to an increasingly vocal movement. In 1973 the U.S. Civil Service Commission proposed that a ban on hiring or retaining homosexuals should be removed, and in 1975 the ban was dropped (Thompson 1994). Gay activists achieved limited success when a bill was introduced to extend civil rights protections to lesbians and gays by two New York Democrats, Representatives Bella Abzug and Edward Koch, in May 1974 (Thompson 1994). The bill failed in committee but was reintroduced by Abzug as HR 166 again in 1975 (Vaid 1995:62). Both bills would have made an incremental change in civil rights policy by revising the 1964 Civil Rights Act to include sexual orientation, a clear effort by Democrats to define the main issue as civil rights and to frame the policy change as incremental in nature. Framing the issue as one of civil rights allowed gays to expand the definition of homosexual issues and thereby mobilize nonparticipants, such as ethnic minorities and other traditional Democrats. The expansion of the debate also coincided with the Immigration and Naturalization Service's 1976 move to limit its ban on homosexuals only to those that had been convicted of sex crimes (see Thompson 1994).

The effort to expand the scope of conflict and mobilize nonparticipants continued as bills to protect gays from discrimination were introduced in Congress every year following 1974. House committee hearings were first held on the issue in October of 1980 (Thompson 1994); six witnesses provided testimony in support of the proposed law (HR 2074) and two witnesses opposed the measure (Congressional Information Service 1981, H341–25). A Senate version of the bill was first introduced in 1979 by Senator Paul Tsongas (D-MA). After two decades without a floor vote, legislation concerning antigay discrimination was narrowed to cover discrimination in employment in 1994 (Vaid 1995: 7). Even this limited legislation, however, did not reach the floor of either chamber until the Senate voted against it (50–49) in September of 1996.

1977 to 1996: Anita Bryant, AIDS, and an Evolving Movement

By 1977 pro- and antigay forces were heavily mobilizing throughout the country. The impetus for this mobilization was the Dade County, Florida antigay referenda spearheaded by Anita Bryant and her organization, the Save Our Children Network. Bryant's efforts were focused on overturning a Dade County law passed early in 1977 that protected gays and lesbians from discrimination. The battle captured the attention of national media, which responded by publishing a wave of stories on the movement (Harry and De Vall 1978; Thompson 1994). It also appears to have provided the impetus for federal government activity on gay and lesbian issues and the birth of new gay groups throughout the country (see Thompson 1994).

The Federal government became more involved on the issues concerning lesbians and gays after the Dade County fight. A policy barring gays from employment in the Foreign Service was lifted in 1977, the same year that gay and lesbian activists were invited to the White House for the first time. The Internal Revenue Service canceled a policy that had forced homosexual education and charity groups to publicly state that homosexuality is a "sickness, disturbance, or diseased pathology" before being given tax-exempt (501) status. At the same time, the federal Department of Housing and Urban Development gave in to congressional pressure and repealed a regulation that had allowed same-sex couples to apply for public housing (see Adam 1995; Thompson 1994).

Gay-related issues increasingly reached the congressional agenda as the 1970s progressed (see figure 11.1). The Congressional Information Service (CIS) lists the participation of gay activists at several congressional hearings dealing

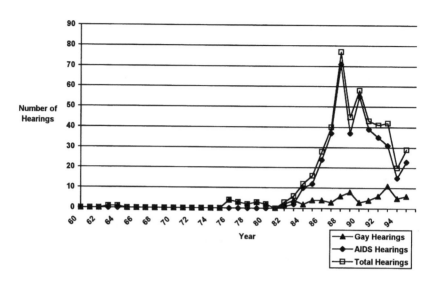

FIGURE 11.1. Number of Congressional Hearings on Gay, Lesbian, and AIDS Issues, 1960–1995

with diverse issues, among them cutting Washington, DC funding of homosexual venereal disease clinics (1976, H181–77.29, S181–55.4), television portrayal of homosexuals (1977, H501–16.4), alcoholism among lesbians (1977, S541–9), welfare reform (1978, H161–32.3), revisions of Washington, DC's sodomy law (1978, H301–3.8), homosexuality in prisons (1978, H701–45.10), the access of special interest groups to telecommunications (1979, H501–95.7), including questions in the census to identify homosexuals (1979, H621–37.2), and the repeal of federal welfare benefits to homosexuals under HR 4122, the Family Protection Act (1979, H782–45). Because some of the hearings were biased toward a pro-gay position, congressional attention to these diverse issues suggests that gay groups were able to expand the scope of conflict over homosexuality — a tactic often used by groups losing a political battle (see Schattschneider 1960). Furthermore, gay groups were able to change the institutional venues where homosexuality was addressed. Specifically, homosexuality was increasingly discussed in nondefense-related congressional committees, demonstrating that cold warriors and Evangelicals no longer had complete control over framing the issue.

In the late 1970s and early 1980s representatives opposed to gays used the House floor to expand the scope of conflict over homosexuality. Amendments were introduced to prevent the Legal Services Corporation from using any of its funds to deal with homosexual issues or promote gay rights and to prevent the District of Columbia from repealing its laws against homosexual sodomy.

In 1981 urban areas around the country saw the first appearances of what was called "gay cancer" (later known as AIDS). AIDS came to redefine both homosexuality and the gay movement — it gave antigay forces fodder to attack gay rights laws but also created new organizing opportunities for gay activists. The number of gay, lesbian, and bisexual groups grew steadily throughout the 1980s, and some of these groups reintroduced the early radical protest tactics of the movement in their calls for AIDS funding and ending the cultural stigma attached to gays and lesbians (see Vaid 1995).

The media attention on gay issues that had exploded in 1977 was also reinvigorated. With the advent of AIDS, reporters and editors now seemed determined to chronicle every victory and loss of the lesbian and gay movement (Thompson 1994). The increased media attention may have played a part in increasing congressional response to gay and lesbian issues.

The AIDS epidemic brought renewed visibility to gay and lesbian issues, with each congressional chamber increasingly considering floor votes on AIDS and homosexuality. In fact, with the first congressional hearing on AIDS in 1982, AIDS became the focal point of most congressional activity regarding homosexuals (see figure 11.1).[3] In Schattschneider's (1960) terms, the expansion of homosexual issues by AIDS constituted an expansion of the scope of conflict. When gay issues were expanded to include AIDS, new actors were brought into the debate, including broad civil liberties groups, medical professionals, and members of Congress who had previously been uninterested in gay-related issues. While some new actors focused on the medical or technical aspects of AIDS, many of the existing actors defined AIDS in terms of the immorality of homosexuality. Gay lobbyists were successful in convincing Congress to spend money on AIDS by 1985, but nearly all legislation increasing AIDS funding in later years contained amendments prohibiting any of the funds from being used to promote homosexuality (Vaid 1995:139–140). Furthermore, not all AIDS legislation was directed at research and education — some legislation, such as S 1352 (1987), would have required mandatory HIV/AIDS testing under certain conditions. Antigay legislators, such as Senator Jesse Helms (R-NC), introduced legislation throughout the 1980s and early 1990s that cut funds to gay causes, banned any federal program that condoned homosexuality as a valid lifestyle, and attempted to block any pro-gay legislation introduced.

Evangelicals expanded the conflict again in the late 1980s by prodding conservative members of Congress to repeal funding for the National Endowment for the Arts (NEA) after controversy erupted over the homoerotic photography of Robert Mapplethorpe (Bull and Gallagher 1996:164; Streitmatter 1995:289). While Congress did cut $45,000 from the NEA's budget in 1989, the expansion of conflict also helped to rally liberal members of Congress who hoped to save the NEA from extinction (Bull and Gallagher 1996:164). As had occurred in the past, each time homosexual issues were expanded, new actors became involved and existing actors became more divided along ideological lines.

During the early 1990s gay lobbyists achieved some of their greatest gains in Congress — the Ryan White CARE Act was passed to provide emergency funding for AIDS, sexual orientation was included in the Hate Crimes Statistics Act, and the Americans with Disabilities Act prevented discrimination against persons with HIV/AIDS. In 1992 gays saw their political stature increase as they were credited with assisting in the election of Bill Clinton, openly gay members of Congress retained their seats, and gay political action committees contributed more than $760,000 to congressional candidates (see Bull and Gallagher 1996:95; Haeberle, chapter 7, this volume).

As the 1990s progressed, however, gay lobbyists faced a number of devastating losses. In 1993 an increasingly conservative Congress defeated the attempt to lift the ban on gays in the military, replacing existing administrative rules with the now infamous "Don't ask, don't tell" policy. In part, the battle over gays in the military was along the old issue cleavage created by cold warriors who argued that homosexuals posed a threat to national security. Funding for AIDS programs, such as project Aries (a $1.2 million study on whether phone counseling can persuade men to practice safe sex), faced increasing opposition in the House. Congress continued to prevent Washington, DC from using federal funds in providing insurance benefits to the domestic partners of city employees. Finally, both houses passed HR 3396 in 1996, a bill that prevents federal recognition of same-gender marriages.

To summarize, at least three advocacy coalitions have tried to frame the debate over homosexuality in their own terms. Before the 1960s the dominant actors in the congressional venue were able to set the agenda and define homosexuality in terms of national security, the immorality of homosexuality, and along the ideological divisions of cold war politics. The notion of homosexuality as immoral allowed for an alliance between cold warriors and Evangelicals, especially within the Republican Party. These groups were able to frame the debate in their terms until the 1970s, when gay activists gained limited access to Congress and the congressional agenda. As gay activists gained access, they began a process of expanding the debate over homosexuality to include the notion of homosexual civil rights. The advent of AIDS in the 1980s allowed gay activists and Evangelicals to expand the debate over homosexuality — gays gained increasing access to the congressional agenda and were able to enlist the support of medical professionals. Evangelicals, meanwhile, tried to make a negative connection between AIDS and homosexuality by arguing that AIDS was God's retribution on homosexuals for their immoral behavior.

From the anecdotal evidence it seems clear the opposing advocacy coalitions, Evangelicals (with some cold warriors) and gay activists (with their supporters), have reached a virtual stalemate in the 1990s — each coalition has access and influence, but neither coalition can fully dominate the debate. The anecdotal evidence, however, may lend itself to multiple interpretations. The next section constructs a quantitative model of government response to the gay movement and specifies variable operationalization and measurement.

VARIABLES AND MEASUREMENT

Dependent Variable Measurement

As illustrated above, government activity can be measured many different ways, this section, however, limits itself to examining the responsiveness of Congress. Congressional activity in an issue area consists of hearings, legislation introduced, and legislation that reaches a vote in the full chamber. I use two different measures of congressional response — committee hearings and floor votes. Both measures are used because each captures slightly different aspects of the congressional agenda. First, most legislation must be subjected to subcommittee or committee hearings before going to the floor. Committee hearings are also used as a venue to evaluate existing policy. Issues and legislation raised in committee, however, may never reach the floor of either chamber for a vote — committees may refuse to act on legislation or they may vote against it (Smith 1989). Second, while all bills must pass first through committee, floor activity constitutes a related measure of congressional activity. On the floor of either chamber lesbian and gay legislation could be amended and/or blocked with motions. Furthermore, legislators may introduce lesbian and gay related amendments on legislation that is itself only remotely related to the amendment. This final maneuver, what Smith (1989:130) calls "doing it on the floor," has increased in both the House and the Senate over the past fifteen years.

The first dependent variable is measured as the number of House and Senate hearings held each year on gay, lesbian, and AIDS issues. I constructed this measure by using keywords in the index of Congress's publication, the *Congressional Information Service Annual* (see figure 11.1 above).[4] I also estimate a separate model for hearings solely on gay and lesbian issues. Both models include all years from 1960 to 1995.

254 DONALD P. HAIDER-MARKEL

The second dependent variable is measured simply as a count of the number of House and Senate (voice and roll call) votes taken each year on issues concerning gays, lesbians, and AIDS.[5] To distinguish between negative and positive congressional response on gay issues, I also separate this measure into the number of votes on pro-gay legislation and the number of votes on antigay legislation. This separation allows me to determine whether the independent variables have similar influences on negative and positive congressional response — an important distinction considering that many congressional votes on lesbian and gay issues are "antigay" (see Haider-Markel 1997a).

To construct the measure I used the *Congressional Quarterly Almanac* and tracked all legislation concerning lesbians and gays for each year from 1960 to 1996. To determine which legislation specifically concerned lesbians and gays, I consulted the roll call votes that the National Gay and Lesbian Task Force Policy Institute found to be important for the 100th, 101st, and 102d Congresses. Based on the votes they considered important, I counted similar votes for all years on legislation and amendments that specifically mentioned homosexuals.

A vote in the House was counted as a separate vote from one in the Senate, and while legislation and amendments usually were only voted on once, some pieces were voted on several times and had to be counted as such.[6] Each piece of legislation was tracked through the entire legislative process until it was either killed or reached the president. The topics covered by legislation voted on range from the appropriateness of discussing homosexuality in schools to allowing gays and lesbians to serve in the military. Finally, to determine which votes were on pro-gay legislation and which votes were on antigay legislation, I consulted congressional report cards from the National Gay and Lesbian Task Force and the Human Rights Campaign. Based on these groups, positions, I was able to nearly always determine what legislation could be considered pro-gay and what legislation could be considered antigay (see figure 11.2).

Independent Variables

Because social movements are made up of a diverse number of components and their activities are wide-ranging, measuring their activities and growth is never easy. In general, however, movements are composed of many interconnected groups that are located within a broad communications network and usually tracked by the media (Freeman 1975; McAdam 1982). Moreover, contemporary movements struggle to influence public opinion (Lewis and Rogers, chapter 6, Haeberle, chapter 7, this volume); they do this in order to both create cultural change (Sherrill, chapter 12, this volume) and, sometimes, to influence

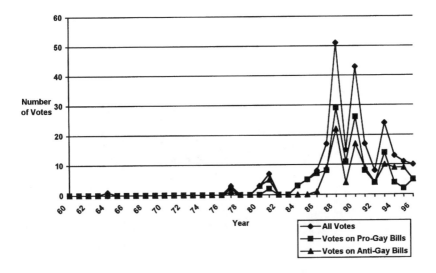

FIGURE 11.2. Number of Congressional Votes on Gay, Lesbian, and AIDS Issues, 1960–1996

public policy indirectly (Klawitter and Hammer, chapter 2, this volume). The earlier discussion on social movement theory suggested that analysis of social movements should take into account the size of the movement, the size of the opposition, the activities of the movement, and public opinion toward those that might identify with the movement.

Size of the Movement: Interest Groups.   Because movements manifest themselves in a variety of ways, I used several measures of movement size. I attempted to measure the size of the movement by counting the number of gay, lesbian, and bisexual groups existing at the national level for each year from 1960 to 1996. Using the subject index of the *Encyclopedia of Associations* (various years), I created a list of groups that were listed under bisexual, gay, homosexual, and lesbian for each year. Creating my own list prevented double counting and allowed me to verify that a group formed the same year that it was listed in the *Encyclopedia*.[7] From that point I was able to simply count the number of gay, lesbian, and bisexual groups. The number of groups in each year is expected to be positively related to congressional response (see figure 11.3).

Size of the Opposition.   Individuals, groups, and coalitions opposed to the goals of a social movement are likely to try and influence how government responds to the movement. In the case of lesbians and gays the opposition is likely to try and block pro-gay government responses and push for antigay government responses. Because many Christian groups are opposed to what they call the

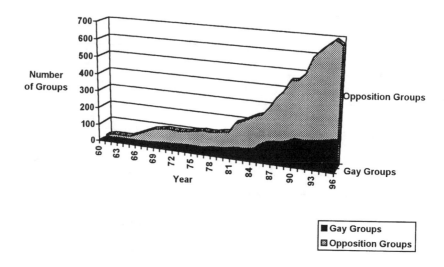

FIGURE 11.3. Number of Gay and Lesbian Groups and Number of Opposition Groups, 1960–1996

"homosexual agenda," I measure the size of the opposition movement by counting the number of Christian groups existing at the national level for each year from 1960 to 1996. Using the *Encyclopedia of Associations* (various years), I created a list of groups that were listed in each year under the subject word *Christian* (see figure 11.3 above). The number of Christian groups in each year is expected to be negatively related to congressional response.[8]

Size of the Movement: Communications Network.   For my second measure of the size of the gay movement, I attempted to measure the lesbian and gay social movement communications network. This was accomplished by counting the number of books published in each year concerning bisexuals, gays, homosexuality, and lesbians as listed in the subject guide to *Books in Print* (various years). I attempted to count only nonfiction books, but titles do not always reveal a book's status. While *Books in Print* does include independent publishers, there is no guarantee that all publishers are included. Independent lesbian and gay publishers that proliferated in the 1970s, however, published mostly fiction (see Streitmatter 1995). Furthermore, while books are not the most rapid means of communicating ideas and information, few gay and lesbian publications have existed at the national level for the period under study. For example, the most suitable periodical would have been the *Advocate* and a count of its subscribers for each year. The *Advocate* began in 1967 but did not become a national publication until the early 1970s. In my preliminary analysis I made use of the incomplete figures on subscribers, but the variable did not perform any better than my books variable. Even with the problems associated with my measure the number of books published in each year from 1960 to 1996 should be a rough measure of the movement's communication network (see figure 11.4 below).[9] The publication of books is expected to be positively related to congressional response.

Size of the Movement: Movement Activity. The number of groups, the size of their membership rolls, and the movement's communications network means little unless the groups are active and have the attention of the media. Following Costain and Majstorovic (1994) and McAdam (1982), I created a measure of movement activity by counting the number of *New York Times* stories concerning bisexuals, gays, homosexuality, and lesbians that appeared in each year from 1960 to 1996 (see figure 11.4).[10] While this measure of activity is crude, it should measure the relative amount of lesbian and gay social movement activity in a given year. As with the communications network measure, this measure should not only capture the size of the movement but also the efforts by the movement to convey ideas and pressure publishers and editors to cover the movement. Movement activity is expected to be positively related to congressional response.

Public Opinion. Measuring changing public opinion toward homosexuals over time was problematic. The General Social Survey (GSS) did not begin asking questions about homosexuals until 1973, and the Gallup Poll began in 1977; such short time frames create problems for any time series. Furthermore, pollsters did not ask questions of respondents that directly tapped feelings toward ho-

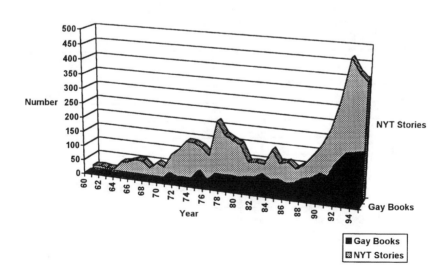

FIGURE 11.4. Number of News Stories and Number of Books, 1960–1995

mosexuals until after 1977. Instead, the GSS asked respondents, "What about sexual relations between two adults of the same sex — do you think it is always wrong, almost always wrong, wrong only sometimes, or not wrong at all?" (Smith 1994:70).

Using this question, I measured public opinion as the percent of respondents answering "not wrong at all" in each year; this positive response suggests some acceptance of homosexuals (see figure 11.5). To capture time points before 1973 I averaged the results of national surveys from 1965, 1966, and 1969 that asked various questions about homosexuality and homosexuals.[11] Favorable public opinion toward homosexuals from 1965 to 1996 is expected to be positively related to pro-gay congressional response.

METHODS AND RESULTS

Each model was estimated using ARIMA time series. To control for any independent variables that I may not have included in the model, the dependent variable in each model was lagged one year and used as an independent variable. Lagging the dependent variable, however, is a tougher empirical test; the lag will often eat most of the variation in the dependent variable, leaving little for the independent variables to explain. In cases where the lagged dependent variable was not significant in the model, therefore, the measure was removed for parsimony.[12] Finally,

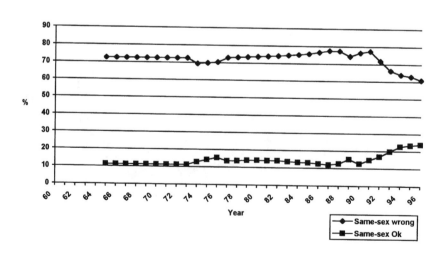

FIGURE 11.5. Attitudes Toward Homosexuality, 1965–1996

because some degree of collinearity exists between the independent variables, insignificant variables were eliminated and reduced models estimated.

Congressional Hearings

The results of the full and reduced models explaining congressional hearings on gay and lesbian issues and congressional hearings on gay, lesbian, and AIDS issues are presented in table 11.1. In the full and reduced models of hearings on gay and lesbian issues only, the important factors are the number of gay groups, the number of opposition groups, and favorable public opinion. Each of these variables perform as expected and are significantly related to congressional hearings. The slope coefficients can be interpreted as follows, the introduction of one new gay and lesbian group is associated with .098 more congressional hearings on gay issues. The variables measuring movement activity and communications network were not significant in the full model.[13] While their lack of significance may be because of poor measurement, it does not appear to be because of collinearity within the model.[14] At a minimum the results suggest that movement activity and communications may not have a systematic influence of government response. It is quite likely, however, that movement activity indirectly influences government response by providing the foundation for the formal organizations of the movement.

The results for the full and reduced model of hearings on all gay issues, including AIDS, are slightly different from the models estimating hearings on gay and lesbian issues only. While significant, favorable public opinion performs in a manner contrary to expectations. The negative sign on this variable appears to be the result of collinearity.[15] The results suggest that the influence of public opinion on the number of hearings may have been considerably weakened by the advent of the AIDS crisis or that AIDS evoked more congressional attention than changes in public opinion toward homosexual relations warranted.

My measures of movement activity and the movement's communications network again perform poorly in the model, suggesting that these variables do not significantly influence congressional hearings. The most consistent overall predictors of congressional hearings on gay-related issues are the number of movement groups and the number of opposition groups.

Congressional Votes

As Baumgartner and Jones (1993) suggest, an important predictor of congressional votes on an issue is the number of congressional hearings on an issue.

TABLE 11.1.

Determinants of Congressional Hearings on Gay, Lesbian, and AIDS Issues

Independent Variables	1) Hearings on Gay and Lesbian Issues		2) Hearings on Gay, Lesbian, and AIDS Issues	
	Full Model (b) Slope	Reduced Model (b) Slope	Full Model (b) Slope	Reduced Model (b) Slope
Gay Movement				
Groups	.098**	.081	.300#	.438**
	(.023)	(.019)	(.168)	(.117)
Opposition				
Groups	−.015*	−.015*	−.008	−.091**
	(.006)	(.006)	(.061)	(.025)
Gay Movement				
Events	.003	—	−.019	—
	(.005)		(.042)	
Gay Movement				
Communications	−.025	—	.082	—
	(.021)		(.194)	
Positive Public				
Opinion	.683**	.484**	−3.166*	—
	(.193)	(.124)	(1.468)	
Lagged Congress				
Response	−.204	—	.300#	.679**
	(.189)		(.171)	(.141)
Constant	−7.934**	−5.544**	32.66#	−.94
	(2.107)	(1.4)	(16.21)	(1.74)
Schwartz Bayesian				
Criterion	1.24	1.04	4.81	4.61
Standard Error	1.37	1.382	8.52	8.39
R-Square	.82	.79	.87	.86
Adjusted R-Square	.76	.76	.84	.84
F Statistic	13.6	22.55	26.92	42.75
Sig. of F	.0000	.0000	.0000	.0000
Lagrange Multiplier				
Test (5df)	1.01	1.43	1.09	1.17
Prob. LM Test	.45	.30	.41	.36
Number of Cases	29	33	29	33

Note: slope coefficient for number committee hearings in House and Senate; standard errors are in parentheses; significance levels ** < .01; * < .05; # < .10. Model 1 error term: AR2; model 2: AR1.

Hearings indicate that an issue has reached the congressional agenda and hearings are often the precursors to the introduction of legislation. My models of congressional voting on gay issues should, therefore, control for the number of hearings on gay issues. The results of table 11.1, however, suggest that congressional hearings are significantly correlated with some of my independent variables. To control for the influence of hearings and my independent variables in a model predicting congressional votes on gay issues, therefore, I combined the number of hearings with my independent variables by creating interaction terms for each. For example, the number of movement groups was multiplied by the number of congressional hearings and included as a variable in the model.

Table 11.2 presents the results of my models estimating the determinants of the number of congressional votes on pro-gay legislation, antigay legislation,

TABLE 11.2.

Determinants of Congressional Response: Number of Votes on Pro- and Antigay Bills and all Gay, Lesbian, and AIDS Issues

Independent Variables	Pro-Gay Bills	Anti-Gay Bills	All Bills
Interaction 1: Gay Movement Groups and Hearings	.007* (.003)	—	.182** (.005)
Interaction 2: Opposition Groups and Hearings	−.0006 (.0007)	−.0009** (.0001)	−.003# (.002)
Constant	−.198 (.254)	.169 (.307)	−.378 (.539)
Schwartz Bayesian Criterion	2.14	2.45	3.41
Standard Error	2.52	3.04	4.75
R Squared	.88	.69	.86
Adj. R Squared	.87	.67	.84
Lagrange Multiplier Test (5df)	.34	.62	.80
Prob. of LM Test	.56	.55	.54
F Statistic	72.69	33.29	57.89
Sig. of F	.0000	.0000	.0000
Number of Cases	32	32	32

Note: slope coefficient for number of votes in House and Senate; standard errors are in parentheses; significance levels: ** < .01; * < .05; # < .10. Each model was estimated with an AR2 error term.

262 DONALD P. HAIDER-MARKEL

and all legislation on gay, lesbian, and AIDS issues. The only interaction terms significant in any of the models were the interaction terms for hearings and movement groups and hearings and opposition groups. Table 11.2, therefore, shows only the results for these models.

In the model estimating the number of votes on pro-gay legislation, only the interaction term for hearings and movement groups is significant, suggesting that opposition groups are unable to block all pro-gay legislation from reaching the House or Senate floor. Interestingly, the opposite phenomenon occurs for the number of votes on antigay legislation: movement groups do not have a significant negative influence on the number of votes on antigay legislation, while opposition groups have a positive influence. The model predicting the number of votes on all legislation shows a similar pattern: movement groups significantly increase the number of votes while opposition groups decrease the number of votes. These results are consistent with the continuing struggle between pro-gay and antigay forces in national politics — each side has influence, but its influence is weakened by the strength of the opposition.

This chapter examined the response of the national government to the gay and lesbian movement. For my study I used social movement theory to develop hypotheses concerning the role of movement groups, opposition groups, public opinion, and movement activities. I provided anecdotal evidence to illustrate government response to the movement, but I also tested my hypotheses using a time series analysis of congressional response to the movement. The findings of my analyses indicate that social movements can indeed invoke government response. Congressional response in this case, however, appears to be driven largely by organized groups representing gays and lesbians, opposition groups, and, at least to some extent, changes in public opinion rather than by the grassroots activity of the movement or the movement's communications infrastructure.

These findings conflict with studies of the women's movement, which found that grassroots activity and communications infrastructure had a significant influence on congressional activity (see Costain 1992a; 1992b; Costain and Majstorovic 1994). The conflicting findings may be the result of measurement differences. Costain failed to measure the possible influence of formal movement organizations or opposition groups, making it more likely grassroots activity would perform well in her model. But the results may also indicate that there are important differences between the women's movement and the gay and lesbian movement and their influence on government activity. At a minimum, the results and indicate a significant shortcoming in the political process theory of social movement influence.

The significant influence of the gay movement's organized groups on congressional response suggests that the movement has its greatest impact on legislative activity when movement resources are focused through formal organizations. This conclusion, however, may be premature for several reasons. First, my results do not prove that movement activity at the grassroots has no impact, simply that the direct influence of such activity is likely to be small when compared to the influence of interest groups. Second, grassroots activity may indirectly influence congressional response though changes in public opinion (Lewis and Rogers, chapter 6, this volume) or the opinions of political elites (Schroedel, chapter 5, this volume). Grassroots activity also often provides the impetus to create formal groups in the first place (see Chong 1991). Any government response those groups evoke is the indirect result of the original grassroots activity. Third, while grassroots activity does not appear to have a systematic influence on congressional response, elsewhere I have shown that grassroots organization by gays has influenced the individual voting behavior of legislators (Haider-Markel 1999).

Fourth, as I argue elsewhere, the findings presented here suggest a discontinuity between national groups and the activities of local activists (Haider-Markel 1997a, 1997b) — a position supported by movement leaders (Vaid 1995) and journalists (Bull 1998). Recent evidence of a disconnect between national groups and grassroots activists surfaced in 1996, as most states considered banning same-sex marriages (see Haider-Markel 1997a), and in 1998, when many in the movement were split over the wisdom of proposing a millennium march on Washington — an action that might take resources away from local grassroots activity (see Bull 1998). At a minimum, the partial answers and new questions raised by this research will hopefully attract the attention of future researchers.

NOTES

Portions of this chapter were presented at the 1997 meeting of the American Political Science Association, Washington, DC. I would like to thank Kenneth J. Meier, Kenneth Sherrill, and the editors for their comments on earlier drafts of this chapter. This research was funded, in part, by a University of Kansas Post-Doctoral Fellowship, a University of Wisconsin-Milwaukee Graduate School Dissertation Fellowship, and a Southwestern Political Science Association Ted Robinson Memorial Award for 1995.

1. Costain (1992a) and McAdam (1982) both argue for the use of Political Process Theory, but, overall, the factors identified as being important are virtually the same as resource mobilization theory. As such, I choose to focus on factors here and not argue which school of thought offers the best framework. New social movement theory bor-

rows heavily from the two theories outlined here and will not be discussed as a separate framework.

2. The report is cited as U.S. Senate, 81st Congress, 2d session, Committee on Expenditures in Executive Departments, *Employment of Homosexuals and Other Sex Perverts in Government* (Washington, DC: 1950).

3. The hearing was held regarding Kaposi's sarcoma among gay men (CIS 1982, H361-84). Kaposi's sarcoma is a rare form of skin cancer that appears among many persons in the advanced stages of AIDS.

4. I used a variety of keywords in my search; these included *bisexual, civil rights, Department of Defense, federal employees, gay, hate crimes, homosexual, military branches, lesbian, pornography*, and *sexual behavior*. To make sure I located all relevant hearings, I attempted to verify my list with hearings discussed in Adam (1995), Bull and Gallagher (1996), D'Emilio (1983; 1992), Marotta (1981), Rueda (1982), Shilts (1988), Thompson (1994), and Vaid (1995). These methods were also used to track floor votes.

5. This variable is measured virtually the same way that Costain (1992a, 1992b) and Costain and Majstorovic (1994) measured congressional response to the women's movement, but they computed the number of votes as a percentage of the total number of votes taken by the Congress in each year. Costain argued that the two different measures were highly correlated, thus researchers could use either. Since I have no reason to believe that years with higher levels of overall voting will have any influence on the number of votes taken on gay and lesbian issues, I use the simple count.

6. For example, an amendment may have been introduced and the first vote was an attempt to table the motion; the second vote was actually a vote on the amendment. In some cases I counted votes on legislation that returned to each chamber from conference committee. This was only done if there was a debate in conference committee over the content of the bill that specifically mentioned gays and lesbians. If I could not determine whether the legislation was pro- or antigay, the vote(s) were not included in the measure. These "missing cases" account for less than 1 percent of all possible votes on lesbian and gay issues. For a complete list of all possible votes see Haider-Markel (1997a:appendix B).

7. Verification of formation dates was conducted using a wide variety of sources including Altman (1974), Blasius (1994), D'Emilio (1983), Rueda (1982), Shilts (1988), Thompson (1994), Vaid (1995) and by contacting groups that had formed more recently. While this was no small task, the effort paid off; even some of the larger groups were not listed in the *Encyclopedia* until two years after they had formed. Furthermore, some groups became defunct in the period under study but continued to be listed by the *Encyclopedia*. I also attempted to measure the membership of several large gay and lesbian groups over time. However, of the groups that still exist, none existed before 1970. This created a problem in using time series analysis since a minimum of thirty data points are necessary.

8. I attempted to measure the membership of several large Christian groups over time,

but I was unable to obtain reliable figures for a significant number of years. I also counted groups listed under the subject words *Evangelical* and *conservative*. Neither of these measures performed as well as Christian groups in the models, but both appear to have a significant negative influence on congressional response.

9. Given the publication delay of books, we might expect their influence to be delayed. However, since books are often the accumulation of ideas that have been floating around for some time, their publication may actually come after there is some government response to the events, ideas, or processes they describe. The variable will be lagged at different years to look for a range of relationships.

10. This variable was constructed using the annual index of the *New York Times*. While Costain and Majstorovic (1994) code events in the women's movement into categories, I chose to use a simple count of all stories. I did this for three reasons; first, Costain and Majstorovic found little reason in their analysis to separate events when they used them as a variable in their analysis. They created distinct categories only to combine them using factor analysis. Second, as part of an ongoing project I plan to code the events data in the manner first outlined by McAdam (1982) and also used by Costain and Majstorovic (1994) on a monthly basis. Third, while stories about the movement may be positive or negative, the point here is to measure movement activity, not favorable media coverage.

11. The surveys are from Weinberg and Williams (1974:19–20). They cite a Harris poll from 1965 that asked respondents what group was most harmful to the country. Homosexuals were placed third by 82 percent of males and 58 percent of females. A CBS poll from 1966 found that only one in five respondents would support legalizing homosexual behavior between consenting adults. Last, a 1969 Harris poll found that 63 percent of respondents considered homosexuals harmful to American life.

12. Each model was estimated as an (2,1,0) ARIMA model, except the model for total hearings, which was estimated as an (1,1,0) ARIMA model. Once differenced, each of the dependent variables is stationary. The Dickey-Fuller unit root test with a single lag and a trend variable allows for a rejection of the unit root hypothesis, indicating the series is stationary. Lagging also often creates a moving average problem, but this did not occur in the models used here. To reduce the need for a lagged dependent variable, I attempted to measure other possible influences including a time counter variable, a dummy variable for the 1977 Dade County, Florida events, and public opinion that did not look positively upon homosexual relations. None of these significantly improved the model.

13. These results conflict with Baumgartner and Jones (1993:275), who found a significant relationship between articles on drug abuse and congressional hearings on drug abuse. Baumgartner and Jones, however, control for few other factors and do not control for the influence of interest groups or public opinion.

14. In bivariate models neither movement activity nor movement communications network were significantly related to hearings on lesbian and gay issues. Because the effects of these variables may not be immediate, I also estimated models where these

variables were lagged from one to four years. Lagging did not improve the performance of these variables. I also purged the collinear variables by regressing them on one another. The residuals from these purges were then used as independent variables. In each case the results varied little from those shown in table 11.1. Because each of the variables, except public opinion, could be argued to measure the size of the gay and lesbian movement in some aspect, I also combined the variables to create one or two measures. This does not significantly improve the results. In another attempt to measure the communications network of the movement, I constructed a variable measuring the estimated number of subscribers to gay and lesbian publications for each year from material in Streitmatter (1995). This measure was not significant in any of the models.

15. In a bivariate model favorable public opinion was not significantly related to hearings on gay, lesbian, and AIDS issues.

REFERENCES

Adam, Barry. 1995. *The Rise of a Gay and Lesbian Movement.* Boston: Twayne.

Altman, Dennis. 1974. *Homosexual Oppression and Liberation.* London: Allen Lane.

Arnowitz, Stanley. 1992. *The Politics of Identity: Class, Culture, Social Movements.* New York: Routledge.

Baumgartner, Frank R. and Bryan D. Jones. 1993. *Agendas and Instability in American Politics.* Chicago: University of Chicago Press.

Blasius, Mark. 1994. *Gay and Lesbian Politics.* Philadelphia: Temple University Press.

Books in Print. 1960–1995. New Providence, NJ: Bowker.

Bull, Chris. 1998. "The Power Brokers." *Advocate,* June 23, pp. 66–70.

Bull, Chris and John Gallagher. 1996. *Perfect Enemies: The Religious Right, the Gay Movement, and the Politics of the 1990s.* New York: Crown.

Button, James W., Barbara A. Rienzo, and Kenneth D. Wald. 1997. *Private Lives, Public Conflicts: Battles Over Gay Rights in American Communities.* Washington, DC: Congressional Quarterly Press.

Chong, Dennis. 1991. *Collective Action and the Civil Rights Movement.* Chicago: University of Chicago Press.

Congressional Information Service. 1960–1995. *Congressional Information Service Annual.* Washington, DC: Congressional Information Service.

Congressional Quarterly Press. 1960–1995. *Congressional Quarterly Almanac.* Washington, DC: Congressional Quarterly Press.

Costain, Anne N. 1992a. *Inviting Women's Rebellion: A Political Process Interpretation of the Women's Movement.* Baltimore: John Hopkins University Press.

Costain, Anne N. 1992b. "Social Movements as Interest Groups: The Case of the Women's Movement." In Mark P. Petracca, ed., *The Politics of Interests: Interest Groups Transformed.* Boulder: Westview.

Costain, Anne N. and Steven Majstorovic. 1994. "Congress, Social Movements, and

Public Opinion: Multiple Origins of Women's Rights Legislation." *Political Research Quarterly* 47:111–135.

Cruikshank, Margaret. 1992. *The Gay and Lesbian Liberation Movement.* New York: Routledge.

Davis, Flora. 1991. *Moving the Mountain: The Women's Movement in America Since 1960.* New York: Simon and Schuster.

D'Emilio, John. 1983. *Sexual Politics, Sexual Communities.* Chicago: University of Chicago Press.

———— 1992. *Making Trouble: Essays on Gay History, Politics, and the University.* New York: Routledge.

Diamond, Sara. 1995. *Roads to Dominion: Right-Wing Movements and Political Power in the United States.* New York: Guilford.

Encyclopedia of Associations. 1960–1995. Detroit: Gale Research.

Freeman, Jo. 1975. *The Politics of Women's Liberation.* New York: McKay.

Gamson, William. 1968. *Power and Discontent.* Homewood, IL: Dorsey.

———— 1975. *The Strategy of Social Protest.* Homewood, IL: Dorsey.

Haeberle, Steven H. 1999. "Gay and Lesbian Rights: Emerging Trends in Public Opinion and Voting Behavior." Chapter 7, this volume.

Haider-Markel, Donald P. 1997a. "From Bullhorns to PACs: Lesbian and Gay Politics, Interest Groups, and Policy." Ph.D. diss., University of Wisconsin-Milwaukee.

———— 1997b. "Interest Group Survival: Shared Interests Versus Competition for Resources." *Journal of Politics* 59(3):903–912.

———— 1999. "Redistributing Values in Congress: Interest Group Influence Under Sub-Optimal Conditions." *Political Research Quarterly* 52: 1–32.

Haider-Markel, Donald P. and Kenneth J. Meier. 1996. "The Politics of Gay and Lesbian Rights: Expanding the Scope of the Conflict." *Journal of Politics* 58:352–369.

Hardin, Russell. 1982. *Collective Action.* Baltimore: John Hopkins University Press.

Harry, Joseph and William B. De Vall. 1978. *The Social Organization of Gay Males.* New York: Praeger.

Horne, Gerald. 1996. "Marshall — FBI News Reminder of Movement's Compromises." *Detroit News,* December 15, 1996, sec. C.

Huberts, Leo W. 1989. "The Influence of Social Movements on Government Policy." *International Social Movement Research* 2:395–426.

Klawitter, Marieka and Brian Hammer. 1999. "Spatial and Temporal Diffusion of Local Antidiscrimination Policies for Sexual Orientation." Chapter 2, this volume.

Lewis, Gregory B. and Marc A. Rogers. 1999. "Does the Public Support Equal Employment Rights for Gays and Lesbians?" Chapter 6, this volume.

McAdam, Doug. 1982. *Political Process and the Development of Black Insurgency, 1930–1970.* Chicago: University of Chicago Press.

MacDougall, John. 1991. "The Freeze Movement, Congress, and the M-X Missile: Processes of Citizen Influence." *International Social Movement Research* 3:263–282.

Marotta, Toby. 1981. *The Politics of Homosexuality.* Boston: Houghton-Mifflin.

Posner, Richard A. 1992. *Sex and Reason*. Cambridge: Harvard University Press.

Rosenthal, Donald B. 1995. "Gay and Lesbian Participation in Urban Politics: Community Mobilization and the Structure of Regime Opportunities in Four New York Cities." Presented at the annual meeting of the American Political Science Association, Chicago.

Rueda, Enrique. 1982. *The Homosexual Network*. Greenwich, CT: Devin Adair.

Salisbury, Robert H. 1969. "An Exchange Theory of Interest Groups." *Midwest Journal of Political Science* 13:1–32.

Schattschneider, E. E. 1960. *The Semi-Sovereign People*. New York: Holt, Rinehart and Winston.

Schroedel, Jean Reith. 1999. "Elite Attitudes Toward Homosexuals." Chapter 5, this volume.

Sherrill, Kenneth. 1999. "The Youth of the Movement: Gay Activists in 1972–1973." Chapter 12, this volume.

Shilts, Randy. 1988. *And the Band Played On*. New York: Penguin.

Smith, Steven S. 1989. *Call to Order: Floor Politics in the House and Senate*. Washington, DC: Brookings Institution.

Smith, Tom W. 1994. "Attitudes Toward Sexual Permissiveness: Trends, Correlates, and Behavioral Connections." In Alice S. Rossi, ed., *Sexuality Across the Life Course*. Chicago: University of Chicago Press.

Snow, David A. 1992. "Master Frames and Cycles of Protest." In Aldon Marris and Carol McClurg Mueller, eds., *Frontiers in Social Movement Theory*. New Haven: Yale University Press.

Streitmatter, Rodger. 1995. *Unspeakable: The Rise of the Gay and Lesbian Press in America*. Boston: Faber and Faber.

Tarrow, Sidney. 1994. *Power in Movement: Social Movements, Collective Action, and Politics*. New York: Cambridge University Press.

Thompson, Mark, ed. 1994. *The Long Road to Freedom*. New York: St. Martin's.

Vaid, Urvashi. 1995. *Virtual Equality: The Mainstreaming of Gay and Lesbian Liberation*. New York: Anchor.

Weinberg, Martin S. and Colin J. Williams. 1974. *Male Homosexuals*. New York: Oxford University Press.

CHAPTER TWELVE

The Youth of the Movement: Gay Activists in 1972–1973

Kenneth Sherrill

This chapter is an abridged version of my 1973 paper, "Leaders in the Gay Activist Movement: The Problem of Finding the Followers." In 1973 the paper was the first empirical research on the gay rights movement to be presented at a meeting of the American Political Science Association. Perhaps because of its length and sprawling structure (or perhaps because of its subject matter and its not terribly "professional" style), the paper has taken a quarter-century to be published. I am extremely grateful to the editors of this volume for including it and for their assistance in cutting it down, by more than 50 percent, to a manageable length.

Coming back to an ancient research project fills me with mixed emotions. Too many of the activists that I interviewed in 1972–73 are dead; men and women who were not born at the time of the original research now are taking on positions of responsibility in the movement. As you will see, the movement's political demands have not changed dramatically over the past twenty-five years. We still are denied protection against discrimination in most jurisdictions. Back then, as today, we wanted the right to get married, to serve in the military, and to be guaranteed equal protection of the laws. Back then, as today, we and those who support our rights were vilified by the right wing and by religious zealots. Back then, as today, average people supported our rights more than many elected officials realized.

There also are dramatic changes. Most notably, majorities of Americans now support most specific applications of our rights, and support for our rights has increased in virtually every demographic group in the nation, while, at the same time, partisan and ideological division regarding our rights has intensified.

(That is, Democrats and independents support our rights more than they did a decade ago, and Republicans do not; liberals and moderates support our rights more, and conservatives do not.) In this sense the optimism of the early movement activists I interviewed has been rewarded with significant successes.

The most dramatic changes have been in the movement for lesbian and gay rights. Today, in major metropolitan areas and on the two coasts, the movement no longer is a radical movement driven by the energy of young activist cadres. Instead, the movement has bureaucratized and professionalized. In 1973 we had no national organizations. Some of the respondents in this study and I were in Dr. Howard Brown's living room the night he decided to organize what has become the National Gay and Lesbian Task Force (NGLTF). In the course of doing this research I met the people who went on to found Lambda Legal Defense and Education Fund (LLDEF). We all were movement activists and most of us were alumni of the civil rights movement and the antiwar movement. In those days one had to be a radical to contemplate being active in our cause. Today, one does not have to be radical to come out or to become active in the struggle for our rights. Indeed, Log Cabin Republicans organized on a national level before Stonewall Democrats did. Politically, our community is far more diverse than it was before. No doubt this move toward the center among openly gay people represents the "maturing" of the movement, just as the transformation of leadership from movement organizations such as the Gay Activists' Alliance (GAA) into more traditionally organized lobbying groups and PACs reflects the maturing of the movement. The fact that most of the original activists in the movement had political roots in the left and in other progressive political movements means that subsequent cohorts of rank-and-file lesbians and gay men moved the movement's political center of gravity to a more moderate location. I suspect that this accounts for some of the differences between my findings of virtually no differences in opinion between leaders and followers in GAA and Donald Haider-Markel's findings reported in this volume (chapter 11). Haider-Markel finds that "congressional response in this case . . . appears to be driven largely by organized groups representing gays and lesbians, opposition groups, and . . . changes in public opinion rather than by the grassroots activity of the movement." One major difference between movement activists and interest group leaders is that movement activists recruit other activists and give generously of their time and energy. Interest groups raise money and hire professional staffs to do what activists try to do. When one has to raise money, one moderates one's political views in the direction of the donors' views, and this often means moving away from the countercultural urges of the activist cadres. It also means that those in leadership positions have had to become more sensitive to the more conservative views of those able to make more sizable financial contributions.

Nevertheless, the radical vision of movement activists persists — often to the frustration of movement leadership. It is hardly a secret, for example, that the leadership of the major movement organizations did not want same-sex marriage to be an issue because it was perceived to be a loser. This did not stop lesbians and gay men from wanting the simple justice of being treated equally and it did not stop individuals from taking action that compelled the organizations to move away from their more moderate strategy of incrementalism. Similarly, equal rights to serve in the military never was a high priority issue for movement organizations until average men and women who combined courage with patriotism attempted to assert their right to serve their country and not hide their sexual orientation.[1]

I ended the paper with speculation about electoral politicians' coming out and indicated that it would be difficult. Today — twenty-five years later — less than one-tenth of 1 percent of all people holding elected office in the United States are openly lesbian, gay, or bisexual. The four openly gay men who have served in Congress were, in one form or another, "outed" after being elected. This year an open lesbian has been elected to Congress. In the interest of historical accuracy I have not changed the analysis I presented in 1973.

Much of my point in presenting this essay today is to help us remember the roots of the movement and to enable us to have a better sense of how we have changed. I hope that we have not sacrificed too much of the illustrative narrative in the interest of preserving the paper's hard data. We should not forget our roots in the radical youth culture of the 1960s and early 1970s. We also should not sanitize it in the interest of presenting a history more in keeping with the preferences of today's readers — or today's leaders.[2]

LEADERS IN THE GAY ACTIVIST MOVEMENT: THE PROBLEM OF FINDING THE FOLLOWERS

This chapter will take a form that many political scientists will find unusual. It is a report of a survey of the attitudes of "leaders" and "followers" in the New York Gay Activists Alliance. These attitudes are also compared to a control group of college students, most of whom claimed to be heterosexual.

The essay is also a report of how I learned that survey research does not always give us the qualitative (if less systematic) understanding that participant observation and lengthy, semistructured conversations can give us. I will also report some of the information I have gathered in the time since I conducted the survey, including the fact that the problem with participant observation is that you become a participant. Finally, although the essay is not polemical, I will argue that a significant number of gay people have translated their "personal problems" into shared political grievances, that redress for these grievances is being demanded, and that it is time those of us interested in political movements should start paying serious attention to the gay movement.

Some Background

The catalytic event occurred on June 27, 1969. New York's police raided a popular Greenwich Village gay bar, the Stonewall. New York police had been in the habit of raiding gay bars for many years (particularly in mayoral election years), and gay people had accepted these oppressive tactics as a way of life. But that night's raid was different (Teal 1971).[3]

Gays fought back, throwing bottles, coins, rocks, and other makeshift weapons at the police. The Tactical Police Force was called in, and they acted with the mixture of cultural insensitivity and brutality they had demonstrated in ghetto uprisings. The following night there was another full-fledged confrontation. The *New York Mattachine Newsletter* reported that "the police were scared shitless and the massive crowds of angry protesters chased them for blocks screaming 'Catch them! Fuck them'" (Teal 1971). Sporadic violence continued for about a week.

The uprising and ensuing controversy gave gay men and women a new sense of pride, collective identity, militance, and determination to organize to attain basic civil rights. The next month New York's Gay Liberation Front (GLF) was organized. It rapidly formed alliances with the Black Panthers, the Young Lords, the Weather Bureau of SDS, and other radical groups. In December of 1969 about twelve people split off from GLF to form the Gay Activists Alliance, which was designed to be a single-issue, nonpartisan organization. The radical ties of GLF had made it difficult to negotiate with local politicians and discouraged gay people who were not radicals from joining. Many had particular difficulty with the Panthers' use of "faggot" as a pejorative. Also, GLF was characterized by ideological opposition to rules and formal organization, whereas GAA's goal of maximum efficiency and minimum loss of energy was represented by the lambda chosen as its symbol.[4] By May of 1970 membership was about 100 men and women, and in 1971 it reached 250. (GLF folded in 1971.) At the time of this study there were 236 eligible members. (Membership is determined by attending meetings with regularity, serving on committees, and attending orientation sessions. Some of the people most active in GAA cannot qualify for membership.) In 1973 an estimated 30,000 people took part in the annual march and rally commemorating the Stonewall Uprising.

Every Thursday night GAA holds business meetings at its headquarters, a former firehouse. These business meetings are comparable to faculty meetings and reform Democratic meetings in terms of length, articulateness, civility, and parliamentary virtuosity. Average attendance is about 100. This essay reports some results of a questionnaire, administered to 69 respondents at a business meeting in October 1972. For current purposes, these people are defined as "leaders."

In addition to the predictably constant committee meetings, GAA turns the firehouse into a discotheque on Saturday nights. The dances are intended to provide an alternate structure to the Mafia-controlled bars and the dangers of the streets. The dances are also intended to liberate and to recruit new members. Average attendance is about 700; it has reached 2,000. In addition to being amid flashing lights and deafening music, the dancers constantly view a collage-mural designed to heighten the senses of gay pride, liberation, and identity and to encourage the identification of these feelings with GAA. Literature is widely dispersed about the firehouse. The second floor is a coffee shop where conversations occur away from the blare of the loudspeakers. There is a meeting room on the top floor, where political (and occasional hard-core) videotapes are shown. This chapter reports some results of 206 questionnaires administered at Saturday night dances in November of 1972. These questionnaires were slightly revised versions of those used at the business meetings. Finally, questionnaires identical to those used at the dances were administered to a control group of 80 students at Hunter College.

The Insight

I was standing outside of the firehouse at three in the morning at the end of a Saturday night dance last December when I understood what I should be studying. A Trotskyite in the leadership sample (who looks like every Trot I've ever seen: brown hair and mustache, hulking, underweight and flabby at once, wearing a peaked cap) approached a young man who may be in the dance sample. The young man was compact and muscular, wearing a John Hopkins T-shirt. In his most revolutionary fashion, the Trot addressed the young man, "I don't think I've ever seen you here before."

"I don't come here very often," the young man replied. "I usually go to the bars. I make out better there."

The Trot said, "When you go to the bars you give your money to the Mafia. When you come here you give your money to the movement."

The young man looked at the Trot and before walking away said, "I don't care about the movement. I care about making out."

POLITICAL ATTITUDES: PERCEPTIONS OF
DISCRIMINATION AND OPPRESSION

Perhaps the major finding of this paper is the absence of substantial differences on almost all substantive issues between leaders and followers in GAA or between the gay samples and the student sample, which is entirely heterosexual, 61 percent female, modally Roman Catholic and working class. The differences are generally of intensity rather than of direction.

Nine items, based on a questionnaire sent by GAA to candidates for public office in 1970, were used to measure attitudes on issues of particular concern to gay people.

1. Homosexual men and women should be allowed to hold any job that is available to heterosexual men and women.
2. Homosexual men and women should not be allowed to immigrate to the United States.
3. Homosexual men and women should be allowed to serve in the armed forces if they want to.
4. The FBI has a perfect right to investigate a person's sexual preferences.
5. All housing should be open to homosexual men and women.
6. Being a homosexual shouldn't affect a person's insurance and bonding premiums and rates.
7. Two people who live together but are not legally married should be allowed to file a joint tax return.
8. There should be a law which guarantees equal protection of the laws to homosexual men and women.
9. Hotels should be required to accept male and female homosexual guests.

The respondent then chose among these alternatives: A. I agree, and this is important to me; B. I agree, but this is not important to me; C. I don't know; D. I disagree, but this is not important to me; and E. I disagree, and this is important to me.

A majority of respondents in each sample opposed discrimination of all nine cases. Students were modally found in the "but this is not important to me" categories, while the gay respondents indicated stronger feelings. The items formed an acceptable Guttman scale for all three groups (with slight variations in order). Seventy percent of the students gave at least eight pro-gay responses, and only 1.4 percent gave consistently discriminatory responses. Among the dance sample, 86.8 percent opposed discrimination on at least eight items, and only 2.5 percent gave fewer than six pro-gay responses. As would be expected, 76.8 percent of the leaders consistently opposed discrimination, and 97 percent opposed it on at least eight items. (The relevant data are presented in table 12.1.)

The only item on which a majority of students provided strong support for the pro-gay position was preventing the FBI from investigating a person's sexual preferences — an issue affecting heterosexuals as well as homosexuals. Similarly, the joint tax issue, ranked second on the student scale, is not limited to homosexuals. Significantly, the employment, housing, and insurance items — which come next for the students — anchor the scale for the leaders and are among the easiest for the dance group to support. Both the students and the dance samples find the equal protection law the second easiest item to support. This raises some question in my mind about the rationality of politicians who oppose such legislation. Perhaps the reason lies in this (and other) items being phrased in terms of generalities. The students were not asked whether homosexual couples should be able to rent the upstairs of their parents' two-family house, teach twelve year olds, or sleep with other firefighters, and we do not know how they would have responded to such items. Perhaps the questionnaire had a consciousness-raising function. In any case, I find little support for the notion that voting for equal rights legislation would be a political liability.

Discrimination and Oppression

There is a meaningful difference between discrimination and oppression. Discrimination is overt action on the part of socially dominant groups designed to subordinate others. Oppression is a state of mind in which people believe they do not legitimately have certain rights or options or in which they believe it would be imprudent to exercise these rights. Oppression may also be the social process of training people that certain rights are not theirs. In this sense discriminatory acts can be oppressive and they can reinforce oppression. Laud Humphreys has a somewhat similar definition of oppression: "Oppression obtains when those holding authority systematically impose burdens and penalties upon relatively powerless segments in a society" (Humphreys 1972).

My position is that oppression is primarily a state of mind and need not be systematic or result from an explicit threat. To confuse discrimination and oppression is to run the risk of underestimating both and to confound cause and effect.

In my semistructured discussions I asked respondents if they felt oppressed as homosexuals. Whether or not they answered "yes," almost all indicated that they had difficulty in talking about homosexuality with their parents, that they could not feel free showing physical affection toward other men in all parts of the city, that they recognized the possibility of job discrimination, and, most important, they referred to a sense that society attempted to alter (perhaps demean) their self-image.

Some of the most interesting discussions of oppression come from the men

TABLE 12.1.

Attitudes Opposing Specific Discriminatory Acts (% Opposing) by Group

	Leaders	
Item	Agree Important	Agree Not Important
Equal Jobs	88.4	10.1
Housing	91.3	5.8
Insurance	87.0	10.1
FBI Wrong	83.8	11.8
Hotels	86.8	5.9
Equal Protection	86.6	4.5
Joint Tax	65.2	19.7
Military	57.4	33.8
Immigration	84.1	11.3

N = 69

	Dance	
Item	Agree Important	Agree Not Important
Equal Jobs	80.7	14.2
Housing	81.1	15.3
Insurance	72.7	21.6
FBI Wrong	80.5	9.7
Hotels	71.3	23.1
Equal Protection	90.7	5.7
Joint Tax	48.5	30.4
Military	42.6	47.9
Immigration	56.7	14.4

N = 70

	Students	
Item	Agree Important	Agree Not Important
Equal Jobs	19.2	64.1
Housing	19.2	62.8
Insurance	15.6	67.5
FBI Wrong	64.6	26.6
Hotels	15.8	63.2
Equal Protection	23.1	64.1
Joint Tax	28.0	38.7
Military	12.2	66.2
Immigration	11.7	49.4

N = 70

who say they don't feel oppressed as homosexuals. One comes from a young man who is frequently viewed as GAA's lobbyist at City Hall:

KS: Do you feel oppressed as a homosexual?

E: No. Not really. I'll tell you, 98–99 percent are, but I'm not.

KS: Why not?

E: Well, I pretty much limit my activities. I stay in the Village, so I'm not as oppressed as others.

KS: How are they oppressed?

E: Oh, you know: fear of losing jobs; parents, relatives . . .

KS: You say you're not oppressed. Don't you think that not being able to leave the Village is a form of oppression?

E: No, I like it in the Village. I can do what I want there.

Six respondents answered positively. The most lengthy and moving response is that of a scientist who works for the federal government. He's been to the firehouse once and amuses himself by reading Supreme Court decisions.

KS: Do you feel oppressed as a homosexual?

A: Give me a kiss first.

KS: Now you *don't* feel oppressed as a homosexual?

A: No. I do.

KS: How?

A: Not being able to let my feelings on things be known. Not to be able to respond when someone makes a sexist remark. Not being able to be open about myself. I find this particularly oppressive. It annoys me when someone talks of marriage and I'm assumed not to be competent to discuss the question. I even feel a bit hesitant to talk about "my roommate," in spite of the fact that that's the way I feel. It oppresses me to have to "launder" my conversation and monitor my thoughts. Not being able to be open with my parents and family about people who are so important in my life. Not to talk about shared finances. I feel oppressed to be unable to be physically affectionate in public. I can't even hold hands with someone walking down the street without it being a big thing. Even walking arm in arm with a man is something which causes tense feelings. I feel oppressed to have to hesitate to bring the subject up at work or in the course of normal discussions of homosexuality. It would reveal knowledge on my part which would be imprudent.

An historian said he was oppressed by "all the stuff inside my head that society put there, by how society prevented me from knowing that the feelings I have toward men were sexual."

These notions of oppression are as interesting for what they don't contain as they are for their contents. These are bright and articulate respondents. All are college graduates. Two have master's degrees, four have doctorates. Six have publicly asserted their homosexuality in some manner, but the realization of possible reprisal remains. None refer to the police, blackmail, entrapment, or loss of economic credit. Yet, in other parts of the conversations fear of (or hostility to) the police is constantly introduced. There is no explicit mention of religious or educational institutions; only one mentions psychiatry, and only one mentions the stereotypes in the mass media.

Finding that people are more concerned with the problems of day-to-day survival than with the political issues emphasized in the media (even the gay media) is not unusual. Robert Lane's working-class men were more concerned with the freedoms of consumption, travel, and privacy than they were with speech and political equality (Lane 1962). Samuel Stouffer (1995) found that personal and family problems are of first concern and that a truly minuscule proportion (under 6 percent) were concerned about internal Communism at the height of the McCarthy era. But my respondents are not poorly educated, nor are they a national cross-sample. Six are somewhat active in the movement. The New York City Council had recently killed an equal protection bill for the third time in a year. The only candidate in the Democratic mayoral primary who refused to attend GAA's candidate night, and who had "reservations" about the equal protection bill, had just won the nomination. I know that my respondents were aware of discrimination and the danger of increased repression. The difference is that when asked about *oppression,* they all responded in terms of "all the stuff inside my head." That is where the marker of oppression lies. This threshold of stereotypes prevents both straights and gays from recognizing how much gay power there already is, not to mention how much there may be.

ATTITUDES TOWARD OTHER POLITICAL GROUPS

There is ample reason for being interested in the attitudes of the three samples toward other groups. First, some group theorists have argued that leaders of interest groups are more likely than the membership or the public at large to have multiple memberships and allegiances. This leads, it is argued, to overlapping groups and thus to a more consensual political system. Second, throughout its existence GAA has been involved in confrontation politics. We would expect both leaders and followers in GAA to feel closer than the students to groups outside the "normal" boundaries of political action. We would also expect GAA's members to feel closer to "new left" types of organizations.

The three samples were asked, "How close do you feel to the following organizations?": VVW (Vietnam Veterans Against the War), NOW (National Organization of Women), GAA (Gay Activist Alliance), Mattachine Society, Amorphia (Society for the Legalization of Marijuana), the Black Panthers, the Young Lords, S.D.S. (Students for a Democratic Society), the Democratic Party, and the Republican Party.[5] Possible responses were "very close," "close," "don't know," "fairly distant," and "very distant." Responses are presented in table 12.2. Once again, the intensity of the leader's feelings made it advisable to construct the scale twice: once dichotomizing at "close"/"not close," and, second, accepting only "very close" as a positive response.

There is clear support for the notion that activists are more likely to feel close to other groups. Almost a third of the students feel close to no groups, as opposed to a fifth of the dance sample and only 2.9 percent of the leaders. Over half the students are not close to more than one group, while the median for the dance is between two and three, and among the leaders it is close to five.

Analysis of the differing organization of the scale items for the three groups is also revealing. It comes as no surprise that GAA is the easiest organization for the gay respondents to feel close to, while 60.3 percent of the students say they feel very distant from it, a sense of distance exceeded only by the two gay samples' distance from the Republican Party. None of the groups array the organizations along a left-right continuum. The students' closeness to the Republican Party falls between their feeling for GAA and the Mattachine Society; similar anomalies exist in the gay data.

I would suggest that all three samples array the organizations in terms of their proximity to the samples' everyday concerns. The Republican Party exists only as the "enemy" (as one GAA leader termed it), representing the possibility of representation for all three groups. Groups opposing the war and favoring the legalization of marijuana are probably as likely to be on the Nixon White House's "enemies list" as they are to be close to the students. The proximity of working-class students — Roman Catholic, Jewish, black, and Latino — to the Democratic Party should be obvious.

Again, we do not find substantial differences between leaders and followers, nor do we find substantial differences between gays and straights. The leaders are less likely to be in the "don't know" category, with three notable exceptions: Amorphia, a California-based organization that does not exist in New York, the Panthers and Lords, and the Democratic Party. My hunch is that the uncertainty with which they are viewed is a consequence of mixed experiences in negoti-

TABLE 12.2.

Attitudes Toward Other Organizations by Closeness and Scale Positions (%)

	Very Close		
Organization	Leaders	Dance	Students
Vietnam Vets	23.2	18.7	19.0
NOW	15.9	11.2	11.5
GAA	70.6	29.6	1.3
Mattachine	17.6	7.7	1.4
Amophia	23.2	20.0	10.1
Panthers	7.2	4.6	3.8
Lords		3.6	3.8
SDS	4.5	8.2	10.1
Democrats	10.4	11.5	14.3
Republicans	0.0	3.6	1.3

	Close		
Organization	Leaders	Dance	Students
Vietnam Vets	36.2	26.4	25.3
NOW	34.8	21.9	20.5
GAA	22.1	39.8	10.3
Mattachine	42.6	30.6	2.9
Amophia	23.2	26.7	29.1
Panthers	18.8	10.8	13.9
Lords		14.6	12.7
SDS	14.9	14.9	15.2
Democrats	26.9	29.7	31.2
Republicans	4.5	5.2	8.0

	Don't Know		
Organization	Leaders	Dance	Students
Vietnam Vets	15.9	20.2	20.3
NOW	17.4	26.5	24.4
GAA	4.4	15.3	15.4
Mattachine	13.2	29.6	61.4
Amophia	24.6	19.0	16.5
Panthers	18.8	16.0	5.1
Lords		17.6	10.1
SDS	11.9	18.0	15.2
Democrats	14.9	13.5	13.0
Republicans	6.0	7.3	9.3

continued

TABLE 12.2.

(Continued)

Fairly Distant			
Organization	Leaders	Dance	Students
Vietnam Vets	13.0	16.1	17.7
NOW	18.8	15.8	14.1
GAA	2.9	10.2	12.8
Mattachine	22.1	13.8	8.6
Amophia	17.4	15.9	17.7
Panthers	21.7	23.2	19.0
Lords		18.1	16.5
SDS	20.9	20.6	13.9
Democrats	22.4	21.9	22.1
Republicans	17.9	16.7	58.7

Distant Organization			
Organization	Leaders	Dance	Students
Vietnam Vets	11.6	18.7	17.7
NOW	13.0	24.5	29.5
GAA	0.0	5.1	60.3
Mattachine	4.4	18.4	25.7
Amophia	11.6	18.5	26.6
Panthers	33.3	45.4	58.2
Lords		43.0	57.0
SDS	47.8	38.1	45.6
Democrats	25.4	23.4	19.5
Republicans	71.6	67.2	22.7

ating with these organizations. Familiarity can breed disrespect and mistrust, if not contempt.

AN EXCURSION INTO THE SOCIAL ISSUE

One of the more prevalent canards is that Richard Nixon twice won the presidency on the "social issue," summarized during the 1972 Nebraska Democratic primary by Senator Henry Jackson as "amnesty, abortion, and acid." We have seen that only 9.3 percent of the students feel close to the Republican Party, as opposed to 45.5 percent who are close to the Democrats. Those who see an emerging Republican majority tell us that one of the groups from which it will emerge is urban, upwardly mobile Roman Catholics, like most Hunter College students. We have heard that in 1972 Richard Nixon's supporters in the Committee to Re-Elect the President (CREEP) included "dirty tricksters" who tried to hire a "gay liberationist" to disrobe at the Democratic convention, and President Nixon has often spoken out against amnesty, abortion, and acid. To be sure, 28.8 percent of the students voted for Nixon (compared to 7.1 percent of the dance sample), but we have also seen general support for gay rights among the students, and the students feel closer to Vietnam Veterans Against the War, Amorphia, NOW, SDS, the Black Panthers, the Young Lords, and GAA than they do to the Republican Party. We turn now to comparing the three groups in terms of their feelings on specific "social" issues.

Social Authoritarianism

The first dimension is what I call social authoritarianism, or, more accurately, moral fascism: tolerance for violence and repression in the name of national security or law and order. This sentiment was measured by four items (table 12.3 presents these four items and the percent authoritarian for the three groups):

1. If we had used the A-bomb on China in 1951, things would be a lot better now.
2. Eichmann got what he deserved.
3. Amnesty should be granted to all men who refused to fight in Vietnam.
4. If we bring back the death penalty, there would be fewer violent crimes.

For the first time we find clear differences. The leaders are always least in favor of legalized murder or repression. This is particularly the case on the death penalty and bombing items. Of all items other than condoning Eichmann's execution (certainly an extreme case of opposing capital punishment) the gay

TABLE 12.3.

Social Authoritarianism Among Gay Leaders and Followers and College Students
(% Authoritarian)

Item	Leaders	Dance	Students
Bomb China	1.6	5.2	8.7
Eichmann	53.3	64.3	56.4
Amnesty	12.1	13.8	29.9
Death Penalty	11.9	19.4	29.6

samples are consistently to the left of the students. But on all items the three groups come down on the same side of the issue.

There is evidence that support for social authoritarianism among students is related to maintaining family ties. Kendall's tau is $-.21$ between authoritarianism and having any religious identification and $-.20$ with living at home.[6] (The dance group correlates $-.22$ with religion, but only .02 with residence. For leaders the figures are $-.10$ and .05). The chances are that the students will eventually leave their parents, if not their churches. In any case, there is little evidence that students are about to be mobilized by the right wing.

To find that political activists are more tolerant than the mass public is not new. Why should the dance sample be about half as likely as the student sample to be social authoritarians? One guess is that as gay people they have suffered discrimination and oppression and are much more wary about giving public officials license to commit mayhem. A second guess is that the Saturday night dances have raised these respondents' consciousness and that, unlike other gay people, they are more tolerant. A third guess — perhaps the one that I find most persuasive — is that there is some self-selection at work here. Gay people who have such beliefs are more likely to choose to go to a dance at the firehouse than gays with more conservative beliefs who opt for the more traditional mating rituals at a gay bar.

Permissiveness

Just as *permissiveness* is the code word of the Nixon administration for changing social values, *liberation* implies considerable sexual freedom. The items used to measure "liberated" norms were in no way directly related to homosexuality:

1. Nowadays, too much pornography is easily available.
2. The government has no right to prevent a woman from getting an abortion.
3. Getting a divorce should be no more complicated than getting married.
4. The government has no right to regulate what people do in bed.

As can be seen from table 12.4, the only issue on which the students disagreed with the gay samples was pornography. There were no substantial differences between leaders and followers.

Right Wingism

Cluster analysis of the student data revealed a dimension that I have come to call "right wingism," and which may serve to summarize differences on the social is-

TABLE 12.4.
"Permissive Attitudes"
(% Permissive)

Item	Leaders	Dance	Students
Pornography	89.6	80.7	41.1
Abortion	91.2	91.3	89.2
Divorce	80.6	81.3	75.0
Gov't Reg. of Sex	98.6	98.9	98.6

sue. Analogous scales emerged from the other data. The relevant data appear in table 12.5.

Although the three scales are not comprised of identical items, they clearly tap the same dimension that characterized Nixon in 1972: the Southern strategy and the Sun Belt, seeking an emerging Republican majority, and the White House Horrors. (The *White House Horrors* was a term coined by Nixon's attorney general, John Mitchell, referring to the illegal break-ins, the spying, the disruptions and harassment of opponents' campaigns and of opposition groups that led to the bill of impeachment of President Nixon for abuse of power.) The results below summarize this section.

First, it *is* possible to find a common dimension that underlies the social issue. It combines racism, dogmatism, authoritarianism, opposition to drugs, and support for the Republican party.

Second, while we find the standard leaders-followers differences, there is no suggestion that the leaders' positions are so out of line with the followers or with the students (and, we can infer, the mass public) as to hinder their success.

We have come this far. We know that the attitudes of the leadership of the Gay Activist Alliance on specific issues are not substantially different from their supporters or from straight students' attitudes. We must then ask why the leaders don't have more followers and why they have not been more successful at influencing local politicians.

ORIENTATIONS TOWARD THE POLITICAL SYSTEM

We know very little about why political movements get started. We don't know with certainty, for example, precisely what motivated black students in Greensboro to sit in at a lunch counter until they were served or arrested. We don't know much about why other blacks followed these examples. We can take certain guesses, however.

Peter Lupsha has suggested that the violation of the norms of justice generates a sense of outrage or righteous indignation that gives rise to protest behavior (Lupsha 1971). I made a mental note of his article one night when about 250 people left a Saturday night dance and marched on the home of the chairman of the City Council committee that had kept the equal rights bill bottled up. There were many chants that night. The most frequent, accompanied by raised fists, was "Justice!" With the possible exception of *pride*, the most frequently used words in the rhetoric of the leadership are *justice, outrage*, and *insult*. We have already seen that both leaders and followers in GAA have more humane political attitudes, and I think we can infer that a sense of justice underlies these attitudes. This sense is particularly strong among the leaders.

A second guess would be that people who start political movements expect to succeed. This may be because of high self-esteem, because of belief in the

TABLE 12.5.
Right Wingism (% Right-Wing)

Item	Leaders	Dance	Students
1. White people behave better than (or worse than) black people.*	15.3	16.7	13.6
2. Since we don't have full knowledge of the effects of marijuana, it is a good thing to keep the laws against it on the books	8.8	9.2	41.3
3. If we bring back the death penalty, there would be fewer violent crimes.	11.9	19.4	29.6
4. Even though freedom of speech is a worth-while goal, it is unfortunately necessary to restrain the opinions of certain political groups.	5.9	15.4	24.4
5. Feeling close or very close to the Republican Party.	4.5	8.8	9.3
6. The U.S. is probably guilty of war** crimes in Vietnam.		5.3	6.6
7. Civil rights groups have been moving too fast	1.5	7.6	2.7

*This item was coded racist/non-racist, with indications that one race behaved better than the other coded as racist.

**This item was left off the leadership questionnaire.

openness or responsiveness of the system, because of thinking that large numbers of reasonable people (read "target groups") will be persuaded by the legitimacy of the demands and provide support for them, or some combination of these sentiments. Political scientists have used words like *civic competence, political efficacy, ego strength, open ego, faith in people, mastery,* and *competence* to describe these sentiments. I find the literature in this field to be somewhat confused, and I fear that I am about to add to the confusion.

There is general agreement that most of these sentiments are multidimensional, referring to evaluations of the self, the generalized other, and the operation of the political system. I designed my questionnaire to measure the presence of these attitudes, and I found their presence. I also found them to be highly intercorrelated. After presenting them, I will present another dimension, which includes items on the efficacy, mastery, and competence scales. I call this dimension "wild-eyed optimism"[7].

Mastery

Three standard items were used to measure the sense of mastery. Table 12.6 presents the relevant data. Certainly, these data do not reinforce the "Boys in the Band" stereotype of gays as frightened and ineffectual people. The dance sample is at least as confident as the student sample. In the extreme, 91.5 percent of the leaders think they have pretty good luck and a majority fall in the highest scale category. Perhaps such optimism is unrealistic, but when we realize the difficulty of mobilizing homosexuals at all — not to mention getting the institutions of straight society to take the issue of equal rights for gay people seriously — we realize that it would be impossible to persist in the day-to-day work of orga-

TABLE 12.6.
Sense of Mastery (% Agreeing)

Scale Order	Leaders	Dance	Students
1. Generally, I have pretty good luck.	91.5	81.6	71.2
2. My plans usually go as expected.*	74.2	49.7	50.0
3. I usually feel sure my life will work out the way I want it to.*	69.8	46.9	44.3

*At the suggestion of GAA leadership, a "don't know" option was added to the revised questionnaire for these items. The percent "don't know" on the items was 29.2 and 14.6 for the dance group and 32.9 and 19.0 for the students. I am not sure what the impact of this option was.

TABLE 12.7.
Political Efficacy (% Agreeing)

Item	Leaders	Dance	Students
There is no real difference between the Democrats and the Republicans	47.8	43.0	44.2
If you want politicians to pay attention to you, you have to do more than vote.	98.5	96.4	96.2
Groups that demonstrate usually get what they want	50.8	29.3	20.8
In the long run, what counts in politics is money.	64.4	81.2	88.2

nizing the gay movement without a strong sense of mastery over the environment and eventual good luck.

Political Efficacy, or Something of That Sort

One thing is clear. A commitment to confrontation politics generates (or results from) the pattern found among the leaders (see table 12.7). A majority of them believe groups that demonstrate usually get what they want, and consequently they are the group least likely to believe that what counts in politics is money. Pluralism lives! Those lacking in one political resource compensate with another. Who would have thought that gay militants agree with *Who Governs?* But, if Robert Dahl's argument is right, how are we ever to develop objective measures of efficacy? The Committee to Re-Elect the President (Nixon) used some of its $55 million to hire demonstrators. People who despised demonstrators gave millions to CREEP.

The problem gets more complex. As the data in table 12.7 indicate, the followers of GAA are only 60 percent as likely as its leaders to believe that demonstrators get what they want, and they are 126 percent as likely to believe that what counts in politics is money. This is probably why much less than half the dance crowd will go on a protest march at the end of a dance, and why GAA doesn't receive vast amounts of laundered funds from rich gay people (39.7 percent of the dance crowd report that they have never taken part in gay political demonstrations). We inevitably get into questions of a vicious cycle. What alternatives to demonstrations does GAA have? Can it use demonstrations to broaden its base? Does the object of a demonstration matter as much as the fact of demonstrating?

We should note that the only meaningful differences occur on the money and demonstration items. Perhaps the items scale all three ways by chance for the other groups. But, no matter how you measure it, you can't deny the high levels of efficacy (whatever that is) to be found among all three groups.

Faith in People

We generally agree that a positive self-image is reflected in trust and respect for people in general. This sense is taken to be at the root of democratic character (Lasswell 1951; Sherrill 1968), and we would expect to find such trust particularly prevalent among leaders of a movement in search of target groups or potential allies (Lipsky 1968). Even in gay ghettos gay people are rarely, if ever, a majority. As the data in table 12.8 indicate, the leaders of GAA are about 150 percent as likely as the students to be in the most trusting category and less than half as likely to be among the most misanthropic.

Once again, there is little that is surprising here and, with the exception of the bimodal distribution for the students, there is much that is encouraging. And, once again, I wonder how realistic the extreme trust of the leaders is. Granted that this trust is essential to the willingness and ability to devote much time to the movement, I think that it occasionally results in a sort of gullibility. Politicians' statements of support and goodwill are too often taken at face value. This results in exaggerated expectations of success (and, in my judgment, ineffective tactics) and a reaction to failures that emphasizes discussion of betrayal and outrage at the cost of calculation.[8]

Wild-Eyed Optimism

All this brings me to wild-eyed optimism. The cluster analysis revealed a group of eleven items that serve to summarize (or organize) GAA's basic orientation toward the system. Table 12.9 presents the percent positive for each group, item ordering, and scale distributions.

TABLE 12.8.
Faith in People (%)

Item	Leaders	Dance	Students
1. People can generally be trusted.	80.6	72.2	58.3
2. People will usually be fair.	71.9		
3. People are usually helpful.	70.0		

TABLE 12.9.
Wild-Eyed Optimism (% Positive)

Item	Leaders	Dance	Students
Must do more than vote	98.5	96.4	96.2
Usually lucky	91.5	81.6	71.2
My plans work	74.2	49.7	50.0
Life the way I want	69.8	46.9	44.3
Demonstrators effective	50.8	29.3	20.8
Would try to stop unjust law	47.4*	79.9	70.0
Money counts (negative)	35.6	18.8	11.9
End employment discrimination	28.8(65.2)**	53.8	27.8
End housing discrimination	28.8(59.1)**	59.2	22.8
End government discrimination	27.3(59.1)**	49.4	12.9
Would succeed if tried change	11.5(39.3)**	27.7	12.4

*This is artifically low due to a typo in the leadership questionnaire.

**The figures in parentheses are the percent of leaders who responded "partially effective" and who would also have been given positive scores had the leaders been dichotomized at the same point as the followers.

The important point is that over 20 percent of each of the GAA samples fall in the three most optimistic categories, as opposed to 10.5 percent of the students. In twenty of twenty-two cases the gay respondents are more optimistic than the students. In nine of the twenty-two cases the gays are twice as optimistic as the students. Significantly, this extreme optimism is found most frequently on the items about ending discrimination. I hope that such optimism is realistic. I have argued earlier that such optimism is essential to all civil rights movements if not to all political campaigns.

Another interpretation that may be of some merit is that we are faced with a When Prophecy Fails syndrome. First, we have a group that intensely holds beliefs that are the object of some derision.[9] Second, the members of the group are frequently in communication and provide mutual support. The result is that every setback is met with a renewal of determination. For example:

New York's City Council kept Intro 475, a bill barring discrimination in public accommodations, housing and employment on the basis of sexual orientation, locked in committee for the third time this spring. A majority of members of the Council had signed a petition supporting the bill, as had a majority of the committee to which the bill had been assigned. This vote was the culmination of a 3½ year effort on GAA's part. When the vote to discharge the bill came, it failed by one vote. One signer of the petition was out of town. Another, after a lengthy conference with the Majority Leader (who opposed the bill) switched his vote. A third, after a similar conference, left City Hall and didn't vote. A fourth resisted such pressure. A number of GAA people were standing in the rain outside of City Hall expecting to be closer to equal rights. When word of the defeat came out, some of the crowd reacted by blocking the Brooklyn Bridge and were arrested. As the "traitors" emerged from City Hall, they were cursed by the crowd. That night I went down to the Firehouse where a meeting was in progress, discussing the day's events. In the couple of hours that I was there, I heard no discussion of how GAA might have assured that signatures were firm votes or how they might have lobbied more effectively for the bill. Instead, there was talk of Majority Leader Tom Cuite's perfidy, of Committee Chair Aileen Ryan's betrayal and of how revenge was to be wrought. There was talk of raising a huge campaign chest and mobilizing hordes of campaign workers to defeat those who voted against the bill. I was then coordinating the City Council campaign of New York's first openly gay candidate. Not more than 10 percent of the people at that meeting had ever done any work on the campaign. Not more than 2 percent had donated any money to the campaign. Everything I was hearing was unreal. A gay journalist who writes for the Village Voice got up and said, "Everyone has been saying something constructive. I'd like to say something destructive." After some applause, he proposed disrupting all City Council meetings until the bill was passed. More cheers. I left and went off to a bar, where I met a politician who thinks he would lose his job if it were discovered that he's gay. We talked about the day's events, the night's meeting, and got drunk. The next morning, an attorney friend (and closet case) called me to say "You people are doing us so much damage that people like me can never support you." I asked why and he complained to me about the previous night's "riots." I made some calls and found out that after the meeting at the Firehouse there had been a cathartic march through Greenwich Village. Some people apparently made crank calls to the Councilwoman who had been talked into leaving the meeting. A vigilante group manufactured a grotesque dummy, stuffed it with back copies of the GAA newsletter, and threw this dummy into her home. That night, she was on television saying that she had been singled out because she was a woman. (In fact, she was the only "traitor" who didn't have the sense to leave town that night.) and said further that she would never support the bill in the future.[10]

My perverse argument is this: only belief in the ultimate victory of a protracted struggle can keep people active in a civil rights movement. Yet the relation between optimism and righteous indignation and the capacity for moral outrage can result in tactics that delay the ultimate victory.

PROSPECTS FOR THE MOVEMENT AND PROSPECTS FOR RESEARCH

I must include some material on what affects straight attitudes toward the movement. Cluster analysis of the student data produced a nine-item cluster, which I called "straight attitudes toward gays." Obviously, much of the support is lip service. Only 10 percent of the students fall into the extremely negative category. Few have difficulty opposing equal employment or open housing. But we see the obvious threshold at feelings of success in ending discrimination and another at feelings of closeness to the movement. One sign of success would be changing the order of items, so students found it easier to identify with the movement than to think that they are likely to influence the city government.

I prepared a matrix of the values of Kendall's tau between each of the scales and between the scales and the demographic variables (see table 12.10). Tau is a very conservative measure of association (much more conservative than the more fashionable gamma), but recent research indicates that gamma does not behave well under partialling. This is probably because of its extreme sensitivity to unequal marginals. Tau, on the other hand, provides excellent results, even in the case of monotonic but nonlinear relationships (Reynolds 1971; Blalock 1972).[11]

So, as Suzannah Lassard told us, gay is good for us all. The attitudes associated with straight students feeling close to the movement are those that we value in participation and activism. The ones that are associated with a sense of distance from the movement are the ones we wish our students did not have: a need for social control, the inability to cope with everyday life, social authoritarianism, estrangement, and racism.

Prospects for the Movement

I have good reason to believe that four (perhaps five) of the top twenty people on President Nixon's "enemies list" are homosexuals.[12] None of them are active in the movement, and I don't think that anyone in the movement has tried very hard to get them involved.

TABLE 12.10.

Some Variables Associated With Positive Attitudes Toward
the Gay Movement

Variables*	TAUC
Following Politics	.20
Need for Social Control	−.17
Activist Orientation	.16
Pro-Drugs	.15
Income	−.14
Hopelessness	−.13
Social Authoritarianism	-.12
Father's Education	.12
Estrangement	.10
Racism	.20
Partisanship	.09
Atheism	.08
Leaving Home	.03
Sex: Female	.03

*All of the attitudinal measures formed minimally acceptable Gutt-
man scales.

The movement's immediate problems are to broaden its base and to encourage more high status people — particularly politically active and experienced
people — to come out. There are some signs this is occurring. One is that the
movement is less monolithic. Distinct splits between people who believe the
revolution is political and those who see it in terms of culture and life style are
apparent. Splits between the radical left and those who remain attached to the
Democratic Party are intensifying, as are those between people committed to
confrontation and people prepared to work within more conventional political
channels. I take this to be a sign of success, just as fragmentation in the black and
women's movements followed initial success.

Proliferation of organizations, separate from more fundamental fragmentation, is also an indication of success. We haven't paid enough attention to the ac-
ademic-journalistic complex. Gay caucuses have been developing within professional associations; gay liberation organizations have become an established
part of the campus scene at Big Ten, Big Eight, and other major state universities.
But, surprisingly, this is not true at the Ivy League (with the exceptions of Columbia and Cornell): the Gay Academic Union holds its first national meeting this
November. Certainly, the movement is a popular subject for New Journalists.

Politicians have a different problem. Other minorities wear a badge of identity. Blacks and women are visible: ethnics' names are readily recognized. Gay politicians pass. Worse, having passed, they have to face the problem of coming out. Fear of coming out is clearly related to expectations of a negative public reaction. Educating the public requires authority figures coming out, and authority figures will stop being afraid to come out only when they do not fear the public's reaction. (The fashionability of bisexuality among the radical chic may enable entertainers to facilitate some of this. But I'm not very optimistic on this count.) What is a politician to do when forced to choose between self-interest and *self*-interest?

In sum, my expectation is for protracted conflict, for occasional bombshells, and, necessarily, for eventual victory.

Appendix 12.1. Demographic Characteristics of the Three Samples (%)

Race	Leaders	Dance	Students
White	96.8	98.7	82.4
Black	1.6	3.21	0.8
Puerto Rican	1.6	1.1	6.8

Religion	Leaders	Dance	Students
Protestant	8.8	12.8	7.8
Catholic	17.5	16.9	50.6
Jewish	8.8	16.9	10.4
Other	8.8	11.3	5.2
None	56.1	42.1	26.0

Sex	Leaders	Dance	Students
Male	92.5	97.0	39.0
Female	7.5	3.0	61.0

Variable	Leaders	Dance	Students
Age (Median)	25	24	20
Income (Median)	$8,000	$8,000	$6,500
Father's education (Median)	12 years	12 years	12 years
Living with family (percent)	18.5	21.1	63.2

Sexual Orientation	Leaders	Dance	Students
Exclusively homosexual	71.6	55.1	0.0
Mostly homosexual	6.43	2.8	0.0
Equally homosexual & heterosexual	10.0	8.6	1.4
Mostly heterosexual	1.5	2.5	5.4
Exclusively heterosexual	0.0	1.0	93.2

NOTES

1. My guess is that it is somewhat easier to find this radical vision among the activists and volunteers in the great American heartland today. The movement has not had the same opportunities to "mature" in the heartland that it has had on the two coasts and in major metropolitan areas. I certainly have sensed that difference when speaking with student groups in Indiana, Kentucky, and Tennessee in recent years. Public opinion data show somewhat lower levels of support for equal rights for gay people in the Midwest and the South than on the two coasts. Similarly, the data reveal that support for our rights tends to be an urban phenomenon.

2. In the interest of not sanitizing the past, I also have not modified my 1973 rhetoric to reflect my current views or to reflect my current standards of academic professionalism in 1998.

3. I draw heavily here on the excellent description of the Stonewall uprising in Donn Teal's *The Gay Militants*, pp. 1–23, and the July 3, 1969 *Village Voice* articles by Lucian Truscott IV and Howard Smith that Teal cites. The *Voice* articles are particularly worth reading because they help to balance subsequent reconstructions of the events during the uprising.

4. Not many know the origin of lambda as the movement's symbol. A Columbia University physics student, frustrated by GLF's ideological dithering, proposed that GAA adopt it to reflect its commitment to not wasting time or energy and to being efficient in the quest for equality.

5. The leadership questionnaire combined the Panthers and the Lords into a single item, causing considerable difficulty, although attitudes toward one predict toward the other very highly in the dance and student samples.

6. This finding is consistent with Theodore Newcombe's finding that Bennington students who were conservative were closer to their parents than to their fellow students.

7. On two evenings in July 1973 a group of members of the Gay Academic Union met with me to discuss these data. I was talking about this scale, which I then called "mastery competence." One member of the groups said, "I think you're talking about optimism," to which another said, "I'd call it wild-eyed optimism." Some discussion followed about whether it was *wide-eyed* or *wild-eyed*. I came to the conclusion that since we use the term *wildly optimistic, wild-eyed* made more sense. I have since been informed that *wide-eyed optimism* is the term in everyday parlance. I like *wild-eyed*, and do not intend the phrase to be pejorative. I mean it to imply optimism beyond reasonable expectation. Such optimism, I believe, is essential to start a civil rights movement. We didn't really expect to be served hamburgers on U.S. 40.

8. I have been told (this may be apocryphal) that one member of the City Council voted against the equal rights bill after being overwhelmed by the sight of a transvestite at a urinal in the City Hall men's room. If this is true, I can only conclude that a legitimate concern for the rights of transvestites outweighed any consideration of politicians' tolerance for ambiguity.

9. Footnotes are a good place to vent spleen. I was talking with a colleague about this study, asking about some footnotes. He gave me some good references. Talking about one book he said something like, "You'll find this helpful. He studies all sorts of kooky movements." I responded that I was studying a civil rights movement, involving perhaps a million New Yorkers.

   In the process of trying to get foundation support for this study, I was told by the representative of one foundation that he doubted whether this was a movement at all. Another foundation official (whom I know to be gay) told me that he was sorry, but there was no program to justify a study of the gay movement. No one else in the foundation would agree to diverting funds earmarked for the study of "blacks, women and other minorities." It's very hard when you're not taken seriously.

10. I should add that there were many acts of individual outrage that night. One person told me of throwing boards into subway cars to prevent the doors from closing. Another spoke of breaking windows on his way home.

11. I have excluded all scales having items overlapping with the "straight attitudes" scale.

12. The larger list also contains attempts to link many prominent Democrats to homosexuality. Nixon's fear of homosexuality strikes me as being characteristically pathological. The television show that reportedly upset Nixon the most in 1972 was the Archie Bunker episode featuring a gay football player.

REFERENCES

Blalock, H. M. 1972. *Social Statistics*, 2d ed. New York: McGraw Hill.

Haider-Markel, Donald P. 1999. "Creating Change — Holding the Line: Agenda Setting on Lesbian and Gay Issues at the National Level." Chapter 11, this volume.

Humphreys, Laud. 1972. *Out of the Closets: The Sociology of Gay Liberation*. Englewood Cliffs, NJ: Prentice-Hall.

Lane, Robert E. 1962. *Political Ideology*. New York: Free Press.

Lasswell, Harold D. 1951. *Political Writings*. Glencoe, Ill.: Free Press.

Lipsky, Michael. 1968. "Protest as a Political Resource." *American Political Science Review* 62:1144–1158.

Lupsha, Peter. 1971. "Explaining Political Violence: Some Psychological Theories vs. Indignation." *Politics and Society* 2:89–104.

Reynolds, Henry T. 1971. *Making Causal Inferences with Ordinal Data*. Chapel Hill, NC: Institute for Research in Social Science.

Sherrill, Kenneth S. 1968. "The Attitudes of Modernity." *Comparative Politics* 1:1–20.

Stouffer, Samuel. 1955. *Communism, Conformity, and Civil Liberties*. New York: Wiley.

Teal, Donn, 1971. *The Gay Militants*. New York: Stein and Day.

LIST OF CONTRIBUTORS

John B. Dorris is a Ph.D. candidate at the University of Houston. His master's thesis was awarded the "Outstanding Thesis or Dissertation Award" from the College of Graduate Studies at Central Michigan University. He is active in community volunteer work as a member of the Citizen's Advisory Board of the Colt 45s AIDS TroubleFund and as vice president and patrol coordinator for Q-Patrol, a local Citizens on Patrol program. His research interests include feminist jurisprudence, lesbigay employment protection, and HIV entry restrictions in foreign countries.

Ewa A. Golebiowska is assistant professor of political science at Tufts University. Her research interests focus on intergroup attitudes generally speaking and those toward political outgroups in particular. In her work to date Golebiowska develops a distinction between intolerance directed at unpopular groups and intolerance directed at individual group members and examines the etiology of the latter. She has published her research findings in various journals, including the *Journal of Politics* and *Political Behavior*.

Charles W. Gossett is associate professor of political science and director of the Master of Public Administration program at Georgia Southern University. He previously held positions with both the federal government and the District of Columbia city government. Gossett has published articles on sexual orientation employment discrimination and public sector domestic partnership benefits in public administration professional journals.

Steven H. Haeberle is an associate professor in the Department of Government and Public Service at the University of Alabama at Birmingham. He is the author of *Planting the Grassroots: Stucturing Citizen Participation*. He has published on urban community participation, gays and lesbians in urban politics, and homosexuality and religion.

Donald P. Haider-Markel is director of the Survey Research Center and a postdoctoral associate at the University of Kansas. He has authored or coauthored several articles on gay and lesbian politics, abortion, hate crimes, and citizen militia groups, some of which have appeared in the *Journal of Politics, Political Research Quarterly, Social Science Quarterly,* and *Demography.* He is currently researching the implementation and enforcement of hate crime laws.

Brian Hammer is a graduate student in the Geography Department of the University of Washington. His primary research interests are in the demography of China and Vietnam.

Rebekah Herrick is associate professor at Oklahoma State University. Her main areas of research include congressional behavior and gender politics. Her work has been published in *Journal of Politics, American Politics Quarterly,* and *Legislative Studies Quarterly.*

Marieka Klawitter is an associate professor at the University of Washington's Graduate School of Public Affairs. Her research focuses on family work and income, including welfare, child support policies, and antidiscrimination policies for sexual orientation.

Gregory B. Lewis is a professor of public administration at Georgia State University and director of the joint Ph.D. program in policy studies of Georgia State University and Georgia Institute of Technology. His research, which focuses on the effects of race, sex, sexual orientation, and other personal and job characteristics on the careers of public employees, has appeared in several journals.

Ellen D. B. Riggle is associate professor of political science at the University of Kentucky. Her research on the evaluation of political candidates, political tolerance, and in the area of lesbian and gay studies has been published in a number of journals, including the *American Journal of Political Science, Political Behavior, Journal of Personality and Social Psychology, Journal of Homosexuality,* and *Women in Politics.* She is also coeditor of *Sexual Identity on the Job: Issues and Services.*

Marc A. Rogers is a Ph.D. candidate in political science at American University. His dissertation examines trends in public opinion toward gays and lesbians since 1965.

Jean Reith Schroedel is an associate professor in the Department of Politics and Policy at Claremont Graduate University. She has written two books, *Alone in a Crowd* and *Congress, the President, and Policymaking: A Historical Analysis.* Schroedel has published articles on a wide range of topics, including her most recent article, "Senate Voting and the Social Construction of Target Populations: A Study of AIDS Policymaking, 1987–1992," which was published in the *Journal of Health Politics, Policy, and Law* in 1998. She is currently working on a book analyzing the relationship between women's status in the fifty states and state laws dealing with the fetus.

Gary M. Segura is an associate professor of American politics and Latino policy at Claremont Graduate University. He received his Ph.D. from the University of Illinois. Segura's work focuses on issues of political representation, especially congressional elections, public opinion, the capabilities of citizens, and the mobilization of oppressed and/or minority groups within a society. His research has appeared in the *Journal of Politics, Legislative Studies Quarterly*, the *Journal of Conflict Resolution*, the *Journal of Hispanic Policy*, and *Rationality and Society*.

Kenneth Sherrill is a professor of political science at Hunter College and the CUNY Graduate Center specializing in the study of public opinion, political participation, and political tolerance. He has been an expert witness on the political power of lesbian, bisexual, and gay people in such cases as *Romer v Evans, Equality Foundation v Equal Rights, Not Special Rights*, and *Steffan v Cheney*. His book (with Mark Wolinsky), *Gays and the Military*, won the Gustavus Magnus Award for the distinguished book on human rights in North America. In 1977 he was elected Democratic district leader in part of Manhattan's West Side, becoming New York's first openly gay elected official. Sherrill's articles and reviews have appeared in *Comparative Politics, Public Opinion Quarterly, Gai Saber, APSR, Social Policy*, and *Christopher Street*, among other publications.

Barry L. Tadlock is senior research associate and project manager at the Institute for Local Government Administration and Rural Development and an adjunct professor of political science at Ohio University. Tadlock's research interests include the study of gays and lesbians and the democratic process and the study of congressional elections. His article on media and House elections is published in *Legislative Studies Quarterly*.

Sue Thomas is associate professor of government and director of women's studies at Georgetown University. In addition to the research she has conducted on gay and lesbian candidates for political office, she has concentrated on the study of women officeholders. Recent work includes *How Women Legislate* and *Women and Elective Office: Past, Present, and Future*. She is currently working on a project entitled "Legislative Careers: The Personal and the Political."

Cynthia J. Thomsen is currently the project director of a longitudinal study of sexual victimization at the Center for the Study of Family Violence and Sexual Assault at Northern Illinois University, also teaching part time at DePaul University. Her research interests include attitude structure and function, social cat-egorization and social identification, intergroup attitudes and relations, motiva-tional influences on social cognition, and political cognition and behavior. She has published articles in the *Journal of Personality and Social Psychology*, the *Journal of Experimental Social Psychology*, and *Social Cognition*.

Index

Power, Conflict, and Democracy: American Politics Into the
Twenty-first Century
ROBERT Y. SHAPIRO, EDITOR